A Guide to Dallas Private Schools

A Guide to Dallas Private Schools

A handbook of everything you
need to know about the
Dallas-Fort Worth Metroplex
private schools

Lynn H. Magid
assisted by Erina O'Brien
and Cristine L. Watson, M.S.

BookCrafters
140 Buchanan
Chelsea, Michigan 48118
(313) 475-9145

First printing 1991
Second printing 1993
Third printing   1996

Although the author has attempted to ensure the accuracy and completeness of the information contained in this book, she assumes no responsibility for errors, inaccuracies, omissions, or any inconsistency herein. Readers should use their own judgement and consult the individual school of their choice.

ISBN
0-9627445-1-4

Printed in the United States of America

Table of Contents

Acknowledgments

It's always exciting when I finally see this product finished and mailed to the printer! The third edition would be impossible without the wonderful support of the more than 180 participating schools. They were always available to answer phone calls and fill out endless paperwork. I am delighted to be able to present an additional 34 entries of newly participating schools. The advertisers are helpful to the community and I thank you for your professional services and for taking part in the guide. Dallas continues to grow with schools to accommodate the diversified needs of our children. We are fortunate to have numerous choices from various categories of schools. The Executive Directors of the accrediting organizations were instrumental in explaining what guidelines the schools must adhere to, and I thank them for their involvement.

The elements of actually doing this enormous project are made possible by a fantastic staff of people who helped me combine information and are deserving of an acknowledgment. Without the continuous help of Erina O'Brien with advertising sales and coordination, phone calls, endless typing, organizing my files, and sending out paperwork this project would still be delayed. The big moment has finally arrived! Cris Watson, can you believe we have now mastered three publications and a total of five children? I know you got off to a slow start on this edition, but your support, knowledge, and ability to acquire closure is deeply appreciated! You know that I could not survive this alone! Ingrid Trevino, I am glad you provided a fresh new set of eyes to proof this publication. You were a pleasure to work with and had great follow through skills.

Many thanks to Gary Klingemann for the *"new look"* of the book. Thanks for all your professional designs and focus on details! William Matter and Mary Frances Gibbons, thanks so much for editing and typesetting another wonderful manuscript. I know it really takes 16 months of commitment to compile this project. Enjoy two years off, as I gather information for *Educational Issues: A Parent's Perspective.* (See page 9 to submit your opinions and experiences.) The maps would not be complete without the assistance of Michael Wright. They are a valuable part of the book. To Helene Cohen, the legal advice and maintenance of this project is greatly appreciated. Alan Stalarow, RU Computing, thank you for your emergency on-call computer service. Thank you to Lynn Yanez and everyone else who worked on the project in some way!

Additionally, I am so thankful for my wonderful family and friends who tolerate me as I devote my time compiling this book. Also, I want to thank some special people that keep me going so I have the ability to persevere. Tammy Johnson, thanks for everything–like driving to the post office, getting copies, driving carpool, cooking, typing, and help with my motherhood role! I would be lost without your skills and flexible talents. Vacation time will be soon! Debbie, Carolyn, Lesley, Tess, and Diane thanks for always being friends even though I get wrapped up in this project. To Kid's Town and Rebecca: thanks for allowing me to use my creative talents since the conception of the facility. I enjoy seeing children benefit from the environment as it allows the opportunity for children to foster their dramatic talents naturally. Finally, I know I could not make it week to week without the support of John Hain, who questions and keeps me challenged, expecting me to grow personally and intellectually. I'm sure our educational debate will continue, but your emotional support and teachings have been very reassuring. Additional thanks to Maria, Shanaz, Charlotte, Cheryl, Shawn W. Mash, Janice, Nancy McClellan, D.C., and Elka–the moment you have been waiting for–IT'S DONE! I know you have had a lot of patience and understanding with my schedule, but have always been a great cheering team and have tried to keep my body and mind in top performance!

Now, after 1 1/2 years and all the excitement, I now return to my family who understands, most of the time, that they are not allowed to touch any "files or piles," while they tolerate a mom who becomes all absorbed in this project. I am blessed by their never-ending understanding and acceptance of me. Jeffrey, I could not be without your help in accounting, delivering, and keeping up with my paperwork. Your endless support, patience, and love are invaluable to me. To A. J., Kelsey, and Kirby, you have been tremendous advocates and have made it possible to pursue my interest in education as I really learn through your experiences. I love each of you and your laughs, hugs, and kisses and constant interruptions are always welcome as they keep me in line for my motherhood role. All the Magids have always encouraged me while I did my research, and I treasure your support.

To my parents, Nancy and Ronnie Horowitz, thanks for always supporting me in this endeavor and I am immensely grateful that you taught me I have the courage to pursue an idea. My brother Larry, thanks, I did enjoy the week vacation and our experience as it made me a better person. One day soon I may actually get to California and "party hardy." Helen, your CPA skills are always appreciated as well as being a great sister. Dad, Precious (our surprise Rhodesian Ridgeback puppy) will be a symbol of this edition!

Without the endless support of those listed above, the third edition would have been impossible!

In closing, during the past three years I have had the pleasure of assisting many students who are special and have worked hard in many skills to be successful in school. They keep me up-to-date from their perspective as to what is actually happening in school and share their thoughts about education. To each of you, I am proud of all your accomplishments and dedication to yourselves and always know that learning is the gift of life!

This edition is dedicated to :

My Special Students
&
A.J., Kelsey and Kirby
&
All parents giving the gift of education.

3

Introduction:

A Guide to Dallas Private Schools has been an idea of mine for many years. I am a native of Dallas and was educated in the local public school system. I attended college at the University of Texas in Austin where I received degrees in the fields of Child Development and Education. After returning to Dallas, I began teaching in a private school. There I found that a concern of many parents is knowing what the many Dallas private schools have to offer as well as how they differ and compare. While a good reputation and "word-of-mouth" are always excellent sources of information, I felt a factual resource book about the private schools would better help parents decide what educational facilities are available to them and their children.

The book was compiled from a questionnaire designed to cover the most typical concerns and questions parents may have about a private school. The schools were asked to voluntarily complete the four-page form and to represent themselves on an independent basis. After receiving their forms, I visited many schools. While I have attempted to verify the information provided by the schools, my personal opinion has not been included. Also, the reader should bear in mind that tuition, policies, and other issues change from time to time, so information which was accurate when this book went to press is subject to change.

These facts are all gathered for you as a parent to decide what school might best meets your needs. The accreditation information was also submitted by each individual organization. Schools have voluntarily sought out the accrediting organization of their choice.

I have made very effort over the past year to include all schools in the Dallas-Fort Worth Metroplex. As new schools are always opening, a few may have been inadvertently omitted.

How to use this book:

This handbook is designed to assist you in acquiring information about the participating private schools. Each school submitted information in identical areas to allow comparison and a detailed overview of the school. A glossary of terms has been provided to assist you in understanding the terminology commonly used by the private schools. In the front of the book there is an alphabetical listing in the Directory of Schools. Schools are listed in order after their accrediting organization's statement. School geographic sites can also be located on the maps, provided by Wright Information Systems, in the last section of this publication.

4

A Note to Parents:

This handbook was written as an informative guide for parents about the private schools in the Dallas-Fort Worth Metroplex. Any parent interested in a particular school should visit the educational facility and follow procedures designed by that school for application and admission.

Each school was responsible for providing the factual information for this publication. While the author compiled this material, no representation or guarantee is made by the author for its accuracy. All information is subject to change. Limited advertising was accepted to help finance this publication. Please contact **Private In Print** (214/739-4501) if you are interested in advertising in future editions.

Key Points to Consider
When Selecting a School:

_____ Set up an appointment to tour the school (some have pre-arranged days).

_____ Fill out the necessary paperwork for each school in which you have an interest.

_____ Set up an appointment for an assessment, if required (each school varies regarding this procedure).

_____ Grades 5 and above require scores from the ISEE test. Ask the school for forms to take the test and choose your date and location site. Your child's test results may provide necessary entrance requirement information in addition to his/ her current school records.

_____ Check on the final notification procedure (example: personal call or letter format).

_____ Schedule and attend your child's follow-up testing/ evaluation performance conference with admissions (again, this varies with different schools). Be sure to attend whether your child is accepted or declined.

A Note to Private Schools:

Every attempt was made to contact each private school within the Dallas-Fort Worth Metroplex to provide the opportunity to participate in this publication. While we made all reasonable efforts to accurately reflect the information we received, we are not liable for any errors or omissions. If your school would like to be included in future editions, please call or write:

Private In Print
5232 Forest Lane
Suite 120
Dallas, Texas 75244
(214) 739-4501

We look forward to your reply.

Preface

It is exciting to provide a third edition of a publication on private schools. It has grown to include 183 school choices, and I hope you once again find it to be an easy-to-use reference guide. It is designed to assist you in locating a school that meets your child's needs. Advertising and some new questionnaire information have been added to this edition.

While I was preparing this edition, I was also preparing for the transition to the next level of education for my own middle child. As a parent, I carefully searched for the perfect school environment for my soon-to-be six-year-old child. I began in the same manner that I recommend to parents in school consultations. First, purchase and read *A Guide to Dallas Private Schools*. Select five schools that feel right for your child, and understand the expectations and goals placed on the grade you are investigating. Next, call the schools, find out the admissions policies, and start the train of paperwork and appointments.

Since the age of three, my daughter has been in an environment that offered a developmental approach to education. We were pleased with this approach and looked forward to her natural growth process. I carefully watched her academics develop to formulate my current school choices: repeat kindergarten at her present school, repeat kindergarten at a different school, find a primer program, or go on to first grade. I became overwhelmed with choices, and the decision process became a real commitment as I searched for the best solution to her needs. At school she was learning all her letters and numbers, could write her name, and even draw a man correctly. I was delighted she had mastered all these milestones, but she was not independently reading even short vowel words and her general maturity level for being successful in first grade became questionable. Because I am the eternal optimist, believing that everything works out as it should, I thought that maybe I should leave her school place-ment up to the school. I followed all policies and was astounded at the actual amount of time I was investing once again in this process.

Schools recommend that interested parents tour the facilities and obtain the necessary forms. You leave the tour wondering, "How will my child do in this school setting?" First, you evaluate your own personal feelings about this experience. Next, you sit down and eagerly fill out the basic forms which always include a week's worth of writing and rewriting the questions, "Describe your child honestly" and "How does this facility meet your child's needs?" After the masterpiece is complete, you anxiously write the accompanying testing fee check and submit all the forms. The ball is in the school's court now. They call you to arrange a tour of the facility and to schedule one to two testing appointments, depending on the school. In addition, you may be required to have your own personal interview to share your child's characteristics with them.

Let me recount my experience selecting a school for my five-year-old. After hours of filling out applications to schools, the time came for the testing experience for my happy-go-lucky average five-year-old. At one school, she was required to visit two different days for testing: one a group test and the other an individual assessment. This experience reduced me to bribery in its finest form. That Saturday morning she decided to select an outfit that could only be unique to her. Then we made it out the door with tears and the words "I don't want to go." A Slurpee promise helped to change her mind. She cried in the middle of the first interview, and my heart sank as I knew the school would add her emotional reaction to the Magid file folder. Now on to the second school. It was set up as a parent-child united front and we happily decided to tour the school together so she could answer questions with me next to her. To my amazement she began to regress and became a lap child unable to answer any of the evaluator's questions. Luckily, " Mom" came to her rescue and gently began to shed some light on the getting to know you questions. As I walked out, I began to realize how much the admissions process was overwhelming my daughter. I only had her best interest in heart.

Next, came the school's private assessment. I picked her up from school and explained that a nice lady just wanted to ask a few questions and play some games. At first, she thought this sounded like a great idea, but upon arrival hesitated when the nice lady said, "Will you come with me?" Tears of anxiety fell as she lunged into my body grasping for dear life. I thought, "What words will ever calm her down?" My soft verbal and physical reassurance helped her separate. Now came the hard part as I began to ask myself, "What's wrong with this picture?" I had decided that we needed to see if a school would accept her. I was confident that the schools were able to recognize all the pressure that admissions places upon young children. Then, as spring break drew near, in the mail came not one, but TWO rejection letters! I was so sad for her and really didn't know what new energy and options I had left.

I waited a brief time and found a suitable half-day kindergarten and two schools that offered primer. My first stop was the primer school. This experience struck my daughter as the wrong environment for her which she openly expressed. I was embarrassed and we went home. Several calls later, one school was doing late testing for availability in first grade and primer, but the testing classes were full. I asked to be placed on the wait list and prayed someone would have to cancel. The call came that she could test the next morning at 8 a.m. I quickly re-did my morning schedule and stressed to her that she had to go to school, and again the Slurpee promise got us out the door. Timidly we trotted off and in she went, a little more aware of the process. While waiting for news from the last round of schools, I visited with the local public school, toured the facility, and talked to the principal, who reassured me that 1st grade placement would be fine.

Again exhausted by decisions, I visited another well-balanced program that offers academics and fun in the course of a three-hour day. As this book goes off to the printer, I am back filling out paperwork and waiting for word from the schools. At that point, I will decide which educational plan, assuming I have a choice, I need to select that will benefit her needs. If, as parents, we feel overwhelmed by this time consuming and emotionally draining admissions experience, we need to stop and reflect how it equally affects our children.

Educational Concerns

Educational concerns have heightened in the 1990s, and I am seeing more parents really involved in school issues. I am delighted parents are searching for the correct educational environment and are really committed to their children. More parents are touring facilities and applying to more schools. Increasingly, parents are beginning to understand the variety of philosophies and the importance of an accredited facility. What I find is all parents handle their concerns in a variety of ways. I am interested in and committed to understanding your feelings as a parent. I want to encourage you to write about the subjects listed below so I can group concerns and gather some community feelings about these various subjects. *The goal is to share experiences* and realize that other children and parents have these same thoughts and feelings. Do **not** use a child's real name or the name of the educational facility. Please send your comments in writing to:

Private in Print
5232 Forest Lane
Suite 120
Dallas, Texas 75244
214-739-4501
www.dallasprivateshools.com

I would appreciate your name and phone number on a separate sheet of paper so I can contact you if I have any questions. Your name will remain confidential.

If this idea develops and I can gather information for a valuable parent-to-parent guide on ideas about *Educational Issues,* I will attempt to provide, in the future, a separate parents' handbook to share community concerns.

Please write about any topics that interest you. You might select topics that you think are shared by other parents. I have included a story example dealing with testing issues in the preface of this guide.

Listed below are some concerns that parents mention frequently:

Educational Issue topics:

Application Process
Discuss the testing experience (for you as a parent and/or your child's reaction).
- Preschool • Elementary School • Middle School • Secondary School

Discuss your experience and reactions to school tours.

Adult Interviews with the School

Describe your experiences.

Children Assessments/ Follow-up Conferences

Describe your experiences.

Decisions Concerning Student's Age

- General policies

- Placing students with summer birthdays

Discovering Your Child's Learning Difference

- How did you feel? How did your child feel? What steps were next?

Alternative School Placements

Waiting for Notification

Receiving Acceptance/ Rejection letters

Acceptance letters

- How did you feel? How did your child feel? What steps were next?
  Did your child receive more that one acceptance letter? How did you decide which one to accept?

Rejection letters

- How did you feel? How did your child feel? What steps were next?

Filling out School Forms

Homework Policy

- Is it really necessary? Is it too easy, too hard, or just right?
  What do you think is the best time limit?
- Are homework requirements reasonable?

Reactions to First Grade

- What were the reading expectations?
- Do children get much time just to play and have fun?

Helpful Hints for Finding a Wonderful School:

How did you find a good school for your child?

Mention special tips that led to your success. Did your search involve
- transferring to Dallas from another city

- transferring from one school to another

- leveling out—developing positive feelings about the school's environment

Has your child attended only one school? How does it feel? Does your child love learning? Describe a moment of glory for your child.

What is your opinion about coed vs. single-sex schools?

Preparing your child for school
- testing experience
- adjusting to a new school

Additional Areas : (Other important topics)

School Solutions: (Any suggestions that may prove useful to schools)

If you have stories to share, please submit them to our office in a typed format. Please include your name and phone numbers so we can contact you if we have questions about your experience.

Format:

Name_____ Address_____

City_____ State_____ Zip_____Phone Number_____

Topic_____

Include your experiences, comments, and suggestions. Thank you for your interest and participation.

Send to:
Private In Print

5232 Forest Lane

Suite 120

Dallas, Texas 75244

You will be notified by mail when we finalize the details about this project! We also welcome your comments about the 3rd Edition of *A Guide to Dallas Private Schools.*

Glossary of Terms

Accreditation: A voluntary process that schools may choose to pursue. The various accrediting organizations have specific requirements, standards, and guidelines to which each school must adhere. Upon completion, the participating schools receive credentials which maintain the standards for their institution.

ACSI: Association of Christian Schools International

ACST: Association of Christian Schools of Texas

ACTABS: Accreditation Commission of the Texas Association of Baptist Schools

Additional Schools: An educational facility that is currently not licensed or accredited. Accreditation is NOT MANDATORY in Texas. It is a voluntary process.

Affiliation/Organization: A variety of educational associations which are available to schools and individuals by voluntary membership to enhance their professional development.

Alternative Schools: An educational facility that implements an individualized or alternative curriculum to meet the specific needs of its students.

AMI: American Montessori International

AMS: American Montessori Society

ASESA: Association for Specialized Elementary School Accreditation

CASE: Council for the Advancement and Support of Education

CCMS: Child Care Management Services

COPSES: Council Of Private Specialized Educational Services

Curriculum Alternatives: An educational facility that implements a specialized curriculum which is unique to that school.

DAEYC: Dallas Association for the Education of Young Children

ICAA: International Christian Accrediting Association

ISAS: Independent Schools Association of the Southwest

LSAC: Lutheran Schools Accreditation Commission

MACTE: Montessori Accreditation Council for Teachers in Education

Montessori: An educational facility that implements Maria Montessori's philosophy of early childhood education.

NAEYC: National Association for the Education of Young Children

NAIS: National Association of Independent Schools

NCACS: North Central Association of Colleges and Schools

NCSA: National Christian Schools Association of America

Non-public/private school: An institution that educates students independently according to its own curriculum. Schools operate under a profit or non-profit status.

NLSA: National Lutheran School Association

Public school: A school or educational institution supported by taxation from local or state sources.

SACS: Southern Association of Colleges and Schools

SAES: Southwestern Association of Episcopal Schools

SAILS: Schools with Alternative and Independent Learning Strategies

SECA: Southern Early Childhood Association

TAAPS: Texas Alliance of Accredited Private Schools

TACLD: Texas Association of Children with Learning Disabilities

TAEYC: Texas Association for the Education of Young Children

TANS: Texas Association of Non-Public Schools

TAPS: Texas Association of Private Schools

TCCED: Texas Catholic Conference Education Department

TDPRS: Texas Department of Protective and Regulatory Services requires child care programs to meet minimum standards and guidelines in order to be licensed.

TEA: Texas Education Agency

TEPSAC: Texas Private School Accreditation Commission

TSDA: Texas Seventh-Day Adventists School System

TEPSAC
Overview of
The Texas Private School
Accreditation Commission

ACCREDITATION INFORMATION

The Texas Private School Accreditation Commission (TEPSAC) helps ensure quality in private schools by monitoring and approving organizations that accredit the various non-public elementary and secondary educational institutions in Texas.

TEPSAC, which began operating in 1986, is NOT an accrediting organization. It is instead a confederation of accrediting associations whose primary purpose is to maintain standards of accreditation among its membership. Individual schools may seek accreditation from a TEPSAC associate member. Accrediting organizations monitor the quality of the accredited schools through on-site visits at least once every five years.

The following organizations have been recognized by TEPSAC and the Commissioner of Education:

Accreditation Commission of the Texas Association of Baptist Schools (ACTABS)
Hyde Park Baptist Schools
3901 Speedway
Austin, Texas 78751
Dr. Gene L. Johnson, President
(512) 465-8333

Association of Christian Schools International (ACSI) South-Central Region
4300 Alpha Road, Suite 205
Dallas, Texas 75244
John Schimmer, Ed.D.
(214) 991-2822

Independent Schools Association of the Southwest (ISAS)
P.O. Box 52297
Tulsa, Oklahoma 74152-0297
Richard W. Ekdahl, Executive Director
(918) 749-5927

International Christian Accrediting Association (ICAA)
7777 Lewis–LRC 310
Tulsa, OK 74171
David Hand, Director
(918) 495-7054

The Texas District, The Lutheran Church—Missouri Synod (LSA)
7900 E. Highway 290
Austin, Texas 78724-2499
(512) 926-4272
(512) 926-1006 FAX

National Christian Schools Association of America (NCSA)
P.O. Box 28295
Dallas, Texas 75228-0295
(214) 270-5495

Texas Secondary Committee
Southern Association of Colleges and Schools (SACS)
The University of Texas
P.O. Box 7307
Austin, Texas 78713-7307
(512) 471-6660

Southwestern Association of Episcopal Schools (SAES)
5952 Royal Lane, #204
Dallas, Texas 75230
William P. Scheel, Ed.D
Executive Director
1-800-752-8280

Texas Alliance of Accredited Private Schools (TAAPS)
522 North Commerce
Port Lavaca, Texas 77979
(512) 552-5757

Texas Catholic Conference Education Department (TCCED)
3725 Blackburn
P.O. Box 190507
Dallas, Texas 75219
(214) 528-2360

Texas Seventh-Day Adventists School System (TSDA)
P.O. Box 800
Alvarado, Texas 76009-0800
(817) 783-2223

Additional Recognized Organizations:

Montessori Educator International, Inc.
P.O. Box 143
Cordova, Tennessee 38018
Jane Dutcher
(Montessori schools do not currently have an accrediting organization.)

National Association for the Education of Young Children (NAEYC)
1509 16th Street N.W.
Washington, D.C. 20009
Dr. Sue Bredekamp
1(800) 424-2460
(NAEYC, a nationally recognized organization,
is **not** an accrediting body of TEPSAC.)

Directory of Schools

School Name	Phone	Accreditations	Grades	Page
Academic Achievement Associates	214/490-6399	Curriculum Alternative	K–Adult	454-456
Akiba Academy	214/239-7248	SACS/NAEYC	18 mo.–8th	197-199
The Alexander School	214/690-9210	Alternative/SACS	8th–12th	378-381
All Saints Episcopal School	817/246-2413	SAES	K–12th	243-245
Arbor Acre Preparatory School	214/224-0511	Alternative/SACS	K4–8th	382-385
Autistic Treatment Center	214/644-2076	Alternative	Varies	386-388
Bending Oaks High School	214/669-0000	Alternative/SACS	9th–12th	389-392
Bent Tree Child Development Center	214/931-0868	TDPRS	18 mo.–K	631-633
Bethany Christian School	214/596-5811	ACSI	Pre-K3–12th	33-35
Beth Torah Preschool	214/234-1549	TDPRS	18 mo.–K	634-636
Bishop Lynch High School	214/324-3607	TCCED/SACS	9th–12th	276-280
Branch Schools	214/826-5717	Montessori	Preschool	484-487
Bridgeway School	214/770-0845	Alternative/SACS	7th–12th	393-396
Callier Child Development Preschool	214/883-3094	NAEYC	Pre-K–K	562-565
Cambridge Square Private School of DeSoto	214/224-5596	TDPRS	3 yrs.–8th	637-640

18

School Name	Phone	Accreditations	Grades	Page
The Canterbury Episcopal School	214/230-8851	SAES	K–6th	246-249
The Carlisle School	214/351-1833	Curriculum Alternative	2 yrs.–K	457-460
Carrollton Christian Academy	214/242-6688	SACS	3 yrs.–12th	200-202
A Child's Garden Montessori	214/446-2663	Montessori	2 yrs.–3rd	481-483
The Children's Center of First Community Church	214/823-2119	TDPRS	Pre-K–K	641-643
The Children's Workshop	214/424-1932	NAEYC	Pre-K3–5th	566-569
Christ the King School	214/365-1234	TCCED	K–8th	281-284
Christ Our Savior Lutheran School	214/393-7074 214/393-2875	LSA/TDPRS	2 yrs.–5th	160-162
Christian Childhood Development Center	214/349-4489	TDPRS	5 mo.–4 yrs.	644-646
ChristWay Academy	214/296-6525	ACSI	1st–12th	36-39
Cistercian Preparatory School	214/438-4956	ISAS/TCCED	5th–12th	87-90
The Cornerstone School	214/387-8567	TDPRS	Pre-K–6th	647-650
Coughs & Cuddles Care for Mildly Ill Children	214/608-8585	Curriculum Alternative	6 wks–16 yrs.	461-463
Country Day School of Arlington, Inc.	817/275-0851	SACS	2 yrs.–8th	203-206
Creative Preschool Co-op	214/234-4791	NAEYC	Preschool	570-573
The Creative School	214/352-0732	NAEYC	18 mo.–K	574-576
Cross of Christ Lutheran School	214/223-9586	LSA	3 yrs.–8th	163-165

School Name	Phone	Accreditations	Grades	Page
The daVinci School	214/373-9504	TDPRS	18 mo.–Primer	651-655
Dallas Academy	214/324-1481	Alternative/SACS	7th–12th	397-399
Dallas Christian School	214/270-5495	SACS/NCSA	K3–12th	207-210
Dallas International School	214/991-6379	Curriculum Alternative (French)	Pre-K–12th	464-467
Dallas Learning Center	214/231-3723	Alternative/NCACS	9th–12th	400-403
Dallas Montessori Academy	214/388-0091	Montessori	3 yrs.–8th	488-491
Dallas North Montessori School	214/669-3322	Montessori/TDPRS	Pre-K–3rd	492-494
DeSoto Private School	214/223-6450	TDPRS	Pre-K3–6th	656-658
Discovery School at Canyon Creek	214/669-9454	TDPRS	3yrs.–3rd	659-662
Early Learning Center at First Christian Church	214/235-8233	NAEYC	6 mo.–5 yrs.	577-579
Eastlake Christian School	214/249-4547	ACSI	4 yrs.–6th	40 - 42
East Dallas Community School	214/824-8950	Montessori/NAEYC	Pre-K–3rd	495-497
East Dallas Developmental Center	214/821-7766	TDPRS	Infant–Pre-K	663-665
Epiphany Day School	214/690-0275	SAES/NAEYC	1 yr.–3rd	250-253
Episcopal School of Dallas	214/358-5827	ISAS/SAES	3yrs.–12th	91-96
Evangel Temple Christian School	214/264-1303	ACSI	PreK–12th	43 - 45
Fairhill School and Diagnostic Assessment Center	214/233-1026	Alternative/SACS	1st –12th	404-408
Fair Oaks Day School	214/340-1121	TDPRS	Pre-K–K	666-668
Faith Lutheran School	214/423-7448	LSA	Pre-K3–8th	166-168
First Baptist Academy	214/969-2488	ACTABS/ACSI/SACS	K–12th	46-49

School Name	Phone	Accreditations	Grades	Page
First United Methodist Church Day School	214/494-3096 214/272-3471	NAEYC	Pre-K–K	580-583
Fort Worth Christian School	817/281-6504	SACS/NCSA	PreK–12th	211-213
Fort Worth Country Day School	817/732-7718	ISAS	K–12th	97-100
Garland Christian Academy	214/487-0043	ACSI	K–12th	50-52
Glen Lakes Academy	214/383-2614	Alternative	K–8th	409-411
Glen Oaks School	214/231-3135	NAEYC	18 mo.–5 yrs.	584-587
Glenview Christian School	817/281-5155	ACSI	Pre-K–6th	53-55
Glenwood Day School	214/530-4460	NAEYC	18 mo.–K	588-590
Good Shepherd Catholic School	214/272-6533	TCCED	Pre-K–8th	285-287
Good Shepherd Episcopal School	214/357-1610	ISAS/ SAES	Pre-K4–8th	101-106
Good Shepherd Montessori School	972/547-4767	Montessori	18 mo.–6th	498-501
Gospel Lighthouse Christian Academy	214/339-2207	ACSI	K4–12th	56-58
Grace Academy of Dallas	214/696-5648	ACSI	K3–6th	59-61
Greenhill School	214/661-1211	ISAS	3 1/2 yrs.–12th	107-110
Happy Hill Farm Academy/ Home	817/897-4822	Alternative/SACS	K–12th	412-415
The Harrington School Private Early Childhood Academic Center	214/484-4215	TDPRS	Pre-K–K	669-672
Hearthstone Kindergarten	214/324-9020	TDPRS	K	673-675
Helen-Hardrick Christian School	214/572-9630	ACSI	Pre-K4–3rd	62-64
Highland Academy	214/238-7567	Alternative/ASESA	K–8th	416-418

School Name	Phone	Accreditations	Grades	Page
Highland Meadow Montessori Academy	817/488-2138	Montessori	2 yrs.–6th	502-504
Highland Park United Methodist CCDP	214/521-2600	NAEYC	Infants–K	591-594
Highland Park Presbyterian Day School	214/559-5353	TAAPS	Pre-K3–4th	261-263
The Highlander School	214/348-3220	Curriculum Alternative (Carden)	Pre-K–6th	468-470
The Highlands School	214/554-1980	TCCED	Pre-K3–12th	288-292
The Hillcrest Academy	214/490-1161	TDPRS/Montessori	Pre-K–8th	676-679
Hillier School of Highland Park Presbyterian Church	214/559-5363	Alternative/TAAPS	1st–7th	419-421
The Hockaday School	214/363-6311	ISAS	Pre-K–12th	111-115
Holy Cross Lutheran School	214/358-4396	LSA	Pre-K3–6th	169-172
Holy Family of Nazareth School	214/255-0205	TCCED	Pre-K–8th	293-296
Holy Trinity Catholic School	214/526-5113	TCCED	Pre-K3–8th	297-299
Immaculate Conception School	214/264-8777	TCCED	Pre-K–8th	300-303
J. Erik Jonsson Community School	214/941-9192	TAAPS	4th–8th	264-267
Jesuit College Preparatory School	214/387-8700	TCCED/SACS	9th–12th	304-307
Jewish Community Center of Dallas Preschool	214/739-0225	NAEYC	16 mo.–K	595-597
Keystone Academy	214/250-4455	Alternative/SACS	Pre-K–8th	422-424

School Name	Phone	Accreditations	Grades	Page
Lakehill Preparatory School	214/826-2931	ISAS/SACS	K–12th	116-121
Lakemont Academy	214/351-6404	SACS/Montessori	18 mo.–12th	214-217
Lakewood United Methodist Developmental Learning Center	214/824-1352	NAEYC	6 weeks–Pre-K	598-600
Lakewood Presbyterian School	214/321-2864	TDPRS	7th–12th	680-682
The Lamplighter School	214/369-9201	ISAS	Pre-K3–4th	122-126
Lexington Academy	214/620-0073	ACSI/ICAA	3 yrs.–12th	65-67
Liberty Christian School	817/565-0466	SACS	K–12th	218-221
The Little Red Schoolhouse	214/285-3962	TDPRS	Pre-K–1st	683-685
Lovers Lane UMC Weekday School	214/691-4721	NAEYC	6 mo.–K	601-603
Lutheran High School of Dallas	214/349-8912	LSA	7th–12th	173-176
Maryview Academy and Private School	214/709-7991	TDPRS	2 yrs.–5th	686-688
Meadowbrook Private School	214/369-4981	Montessori/TDPRS	Pre-K–K	505-507
Meadowview School	214/289-1831	Alternative/ASESA	1st–8th	425-427
Metropolitan Christian School	214/388-4426	ACSI	4 yrs.–9th	68-72
Montessori Children's House & School, Inc.	214/348-6276	Montessori	3 yrs.–6 yrs.	508-510
Montessori Episcopal School	214/221-3533	Montessori	2 yrs.–2nd	511-514

23

Montessori School of Las Colinas	214/717-0417	Montessori	Infants–K	515-517
Montessori School of North Dallas	214/985-8844	Montessori	Pre-K–1st	518-520
Montessori School of Park Cities	214/350-2503	Montessori	6 weeks–6 yrs.	521-523
Montessori School– (of) Pleasant Grove	214/391-2176	Montessori	K	524-526
Montessori School of Westchester	214/262-1053	Montessori	Pre-K–K	527-529
Northbrook School	214/369-8330	TDPRS	Pre-K2–4th	689-692
NorthPark Presbyterian Day School	214/361-8024	TDPRS	1 yr.–K	693-695
Northaven Co-operative Preschool	214/691-7666	NAEYC	20 mo.– K	604-607
North Dallas Day School	214/341-4366	NAEYC	6 weeks–2nd	608-611
Notre Dame of Dallas Schools, Inc.	214/720-3911	Alternative/ TCCED	3 yrs.–21 yrs.	428-430
Oak Hill Academy	214/368-0664	Alternative/ASESA	Pre-K–8th	431-433
The Oakridge School	817/654-9746	ISAS/SACS	Pre-K3–12th	127-130
Our Redeemer Lutheran School	214/368-1465	LSA	Pre-K3–8th	177-179
Palisades Day School	214/423-5557	TDPRS	Pre-K–4th	696-698
The Parish Day School of The Episcopal Church of the Transfiguration	214/239-8011	ISAS/SAES/NAEYC	3 yrs.–6th	131-135
The Peanut Gallery	214/492-2448	TDPRS	6 weeks–12 yrs.	699-702
Preston Hollow Presbyterian Week Day School	214/368-3886	Alternative/ASESA	1st–6th	434-437

School Name	Phone	Accreditations	Grades	Page
Preston-Royal Preschool	214/987-3446	NAEYC	2 yrs.–Pre-K	612-614
Prince of Peace Catholic School	214/380-5505	TCCED	Pre-K3–4th	308-311
Prince of Peace Christian School	214/245-7564	LSA/TDPRS	3 yrs.–8th	180-183
Primrose School at Chase Oaks	214/517-1173	TDPRS	Infant–4 yrs.	703-705
Providence Christian School of Texas	214/340-7768	TDPRS	1st–8th	706-709
Rainbow Connection of Central Christian Church	214/644-0283	NAEYC	Pre-K–K	615-617
Redeemer Lutheran School	817/560-0032	LSA	Pre-K3–7th	184-186
Redeemer Montessori School	214/257-3517	Montessori	2 1/2 yrs.–5th	530-532
Richardson Adventist School	214/238-1183	TSDA	1st–10th	356-359
Schreiber Methodist Preschool	214/387-8191	NAEYC	MDO–Pre-K	618-621
Scofield Christian School	214/349-6843	ACSI	K3–6th	73-76
The June Shelton School and Evaluation Center	214/352-1772	Alternative/SACS/SAIS	Pre-K–10th	438-442
Study Skills Course (SMU)	214/768-2223	Curriculum Alternative	7th–12th	471-473
Summer Accelerated Language Training (SMU)	214/768-2223	Curriculum Alternative	6th–12th	474-476
Solomon Schecter Academy of Dallas	214/248-3032	SACS	Pre-K–8th	222-226
Southwest Academy	214/349-7272	TAAPS	K–8th	268-270

School Name	Phone	Accreditations	Grades	Page
St. Alban's Episcopal School	817/460-6071	SAES	Pre-K3–6th	254-256
St. Alcuin Montessori School	214/239-1745	Montessori	18 mo.–8th	533-536
St. Andrew's Episcopal School	214/262-3817	SAES	3 yrs.–5th	257-259
St. Barnabas Pathways Preschool	214/690-4107	TDPRS	3 yrs.–4yrs.	710-712
St. Bernard of Clairvaux	214/321-2897	TCCED	K–8th	312-315
St. Elizabeth of Hungary School	214/331-5139	TCCED	K–8th	316-319
St. James Episcopal Montessori School	214/348-1349	Montessori	2 yrs.–3rd	537-539
St. John the Apostle Catholic School	817/284-2228	TCCED	K3–8th	320-322
St. John's Episcopal School	214/328-9131	ISAS	Pre-K–8th	136-139
St. Mark's School of Texas	214/363-6491 ext. 172	ISAS	1st–12th	140-144
St. Mary of Carmel School	214/748-2934	TCCED	Pre-K–8th	323-325
St. Mary's Catholic School	903/893-2127	TCCED	Pre-K3–6th	326-328
St. Monica School	214/351-5688	TCCED	K–8th	329-331
St. Patrick School	214/348-8070	TCCED	Pre-K–8th	332-335
St. Paul the Apostle School	214/235-3263	TCCED	K–8th	336-338
St. Paul Lutheran School	817/332-2281	LSA	4 yrs.–8th	187-189

School Name	Phone	Accreditations	Grades	Page
St. Philip the Apostle Catholic School	214/381-4973	TCCED	K–8th	339-342
St. Philip's School & Community Center	214/421-5221	ISAS	Pre-K3–4th	145-147
St. Rita School	214/239-3203	TCCED	K–8th	343-346
St. Therese Academy	214/252-3000	Additional	Pre-K–12th	371-373
St. Thomas Aquinas School	214/826-0566	TCCED	Pre-K3–8th	347-349
The Selwyn School	817/382-6771	ISAS	Pre-K–8th	148-150
Sycamore School, Inc.	817/292-3434	Alternative/SACS	K–12th	443-446
Temple Emanu-El Preschool	214/368-3613	NAEYC	6 mo.–K	622-624
Texas Christian Academy	817/274-5201	ACSI	Pre-K4–12th	77-80
TreeTops School International	817/283-1771	SACS	Pre-K–12th	227-231
Trinity Christian Academy	214/931-8325	SACS	K–12th	232-234
Trinity Christian School	214/291-2501	ICAA	Pre-K–12th	82-84
Trinity Episcopal Preschool	817/926-0750	TDPRS/Montessori	2 yrs.–5 yrs.	713-716
Trinity Valley School	817/292-6060	ISAS	K–12th	151-154
Tyler Street Christian Academy	214/941-9717	SACS	3 yrs.–12th	235-238
The Ursuline Academy of Dallas	214/363-6551	TCCED/SACS	9th–12th	350-354
Vanguard Preparatory School	214/404-1616	Alternative/ASESA	Pre-K–8th	447-449

School Name	Phone	Accreditations	Grades	Page
Walden Preparatory School	214/233-6883	Alternative/SACS	9th–12th	450-452
Westminster Preschool and Kindergarten	214/350-6155	NAEYC	MDO–K	625-628
West Plano Montessori School	214/618-8844	Montessori	Pre-K–1st	540-542
Westwood Montessori School	214/239-8598	Montessori	Pre-K–8th	543-546
White Rock Montessori School	214/827-3220	Montessori	Pre-K–8th	547-551
White Rock Montessori/ Satellite Location	214/827-3220	Montessori	Pre-K–8th	552-555
White Rock North School	214/348-7410	SACS	1st–6th	239-241
Windsong Montessori School	214/239-0537	Montessori	K5–4th	556-559
The Winston School	214/691-6950	ISAS/Alternative	1st–12th	155-157
Williamson School	214/946-3846	TDPRS	18 mo.–2nd	717-719
Yavneh Academy	214/363-7631	TAAPS	9th–12th	271-273
YouthCrossing Academy	214/686-0685	Additional	7th–12th	374-376
Zion Lutheran School	214/363-1630	LSA	Pre-K3–8th	190-193

ACTABS
Accreditation Commission of the Texas Association of Baptist Schools

Hyde Park Baptist Schools
3901 Speedway
Austin, TX 78751
Dr. Gene L. Johnson, President
(512) 465-8333

Constitution

Article I. Description and Membership
The Accreditation Commission of the Texas Association of Baptist Schools (ACTABS) is an approved unit of the Texas Association of Baptist Schools (TABS). It is made up of schools that voluntarily meet the following criteria:

    A. are affiliated with churches cooperating as members of local associations of churches of the Southern Baptist Conventions (or the school may be affiliated with the Baptist General Convention of Texas or a local Texas Southern Baptist Association)

    B. are members of the Texas Association of Baptist Schools

    C. are certified by ACTABS as having met (and are continuously meeting) the standards of accreditation prescribed by ACTABS

Thus, ACTABS is an association of schools sponsored by TABS and authorized to accredit Southern Baptist schools operating in Texas.

Christian schools not meeting the criteria above may become affiliate members by meeting the criteria stated in Section 1.B. of the Standards for Accreditation.

29

Article II. Purpose

ACTABS has two (2) primary purposes:

A. to promote high standards in academic, physical, and spiritual programs among Southern Baptist schools of Texas and to honor by accreditation those schools that demonstrate such standards are being maintained;

B. to maintain recognition of ACTABS as an approved accreditation commission by any Texas non-public school umbrella approved to grant such recognition by the Texas State Board of Education (e.g., the Texas Private School Accreditation Commission of the Texas Association of Non-Public Schools).

STANDARDS FOR ACCREDITATION
A SCHOOL OR SYSTEM OF SCHOOLS

I. Eligibility for Membership and Affiliate Membership

A. Any Texas preschool, elementary, middle or high school, or system of schools is eligible to seek accreditation by ACTABS. The combination of grades offered must be contiguous and reasonable for the philosophy of the school.

B. The school seeking accreditation and membership must be affiliated with a church that is a member of a local association of Southern Baptist churches. (The school may be affiliated directly with the Baptist General Convention of Texas or a local association.)

C. The school seeking accreditation must be a member of the Texas Association of Baptist Schools. If not a member, it may seek accreditation as an affiliate school.

D. The entire school, consisting of all grades currently offered (K–12 with preschool optional), must be evaluated for accreditation initially, and all grades must have been operated successfully for at least one (1) year prior to the site visit. If an accredited school adds grades, the new grades must operate successfully for a minimum of one (1) year. The new grades will remain unaccredited until a request is made for a team visit and approval by a majority vote of ACTABS.

First Baptist Academy (see ACSI)

ACSI
Association of Christian Schools International

South-Central Region
4300 Alpha Road, Suite 205
Dallas, TX 75244
(214) 991-2822
John Schimmer, Ed.D.
Director, South-Central Region

The Association of Christian Schools International is a service organization serving Protestant, evangelical Christian schools across the United States and around the world. Each member school or college retains its individual distinctions and operating independence. Member schools must annually sign a doctrinal statement and confirm their policy of non-discrimination in enrollment and hiring. Services are provided through a network of regional offices. The South-Central Region's headquarters are in Dallas, Texas.

ACSI offers a national elementary and secondary school accreditation program. ACSI accreditation is recognized in Texas through TEPSAC (Texas Private School Accreditation Commission). The association publishes its standards for accreditation in a manual entitled *Manual for School Accreditation for Christian Elementary and Secondary Schools.*

A school must be in existence for a minimum of three years before applying for candidacy status. Once candidacy is granted, a consultant is assigned to guide the school through the self-study process. The school is expected to spend a minimum of one year in the process of preparing for the accreditation visit. The final decision regarding accreditation rests with the Accreditation Commission. The commission is comprised of six members elected by member-accredited schools.

Bethany Christian School (membership only)
ChristWay Academy (accredited)
Eastlake Christian School (membership only)
Evangel Temple Christian School (accredited)
First Baptist Academy (accredited)
Garland Christian Academy (accredited)
Glenview Christian School, Elementary (accredited)
Gospel Lighthouse Christian Academy (accredited)
Grace Academy of Dallas (membership only)
Helen-Hardrick Christian School
Lexington Academy (accredited)
Metropolitan Christian School (accredited)
Scofield Christian School (accredited)
Texas Christian Academy (accredited)
Trinity Christian Academy (membership only, see SACS)

Bethany Christian School

3300 West Parker
Plano, TX 75075
(214) 596-5811

Mapsco: 657K

Fax: (214) 596-5814

Office Hours: 8:00 a.m.–4:00 p.m.
School Hours: 8:30 a.m.–3:30 p.m.
Grades: Preschool (3-year-olds)—grade 12
Enrollment: 175
Co-ed: Yes
Boy/Girl Ratio: Varies
Student/Teacher Ratio: Preschool–12:1; kindergarten–grade 12–15:1
Average Class Size: 15
Calendar School Year: August 26, 1996–May 29, 1997
Holidays: Thanksgiving, Christmas, Martin Luther King Day, Presidents' Day, spring break, Good Friday, Easter Monday
Uniform Requirements: Dress code
Founded in: 1979

Philosophy of School

Academic Curriculum

Content: Preschool-grade 6–A Beka; grades 7-12–Bob Jones
Grading System Used: Preschool–none; kindergarten–E, S, U; grades 1-12–numerical grades
Conferences per Year: Three scheduled; others as needed
Tests Administered: Stanford Achievement Test (April); entrance exam
Homework Policy: 10 minutes per grade level (i.e., grade 6–60 minutes; grade 8–80 minutes)
Method of Discipline: Christ-centered and lovingly administered

Enrichment Curriculum
A Beka is an enrichment curriculum.

Extracurricular Activities
None

Goals for Students
To excel to the best of their abilities

Faculty/Staff Requirements
Qualifications of Staff: College degree; certification (kindergarten-grade 12)
Qualifications of Administrator: College degree, experienced educator in field of administration

School Information
Brochure Available: Yes
Number of Students in Each Grade: Most grades have only one class of 15.
Parochial: No
Organization Affiliations: Association of Christian Schools International
Accreditations: None
Parental Involvement: Welcomed
Other Information:

Admittance
Whom to Contact: School office
Date to Apply: Open admissions
Testing Procedure per Age/Grade Level: Entrance exam (kindergarten–grade 12)
Fees Involved: Testing fee–$15; registration fee–$100; book/supply fee $150 (K-grade 4), $200 (grades 5-12); activity fee
Type of Student Preferred:
Forms Required: Health, permission slips, student information, transcripts
Individual/Group Appointments: Individual appointments
Notification Procedure: By phone or meeting
Waiting List Policy: Ongoing

Tuition
Approximate Tuition for 1996-97 School Year: K-grade 12–$2200; preschool rates determined by number of days

Methods of Payment Available: Monthly
Financial Assistance Offered: Some financial scholarships;
approved by Board
Cancellation Insurance Available: No
Profit/Non-profit: Non-profit

Additional Costs

Books/Bag/Uniform: Books/supplies–$150 (k-grade 4), $200 (grades 5-12)
Lunch Fee: School's lunch program lets student choose daily.
Parents Club Dues: None
Annual Fund Drive: None
Discount for Siblings: Tuition only (25%)

Facilities/Services Provided

Computer Lab: Yes
Library: Public library
Snack Procedures: Preschool and kindergarten (provided by school)
Before-school Care Program Available: None
After-school Care Program Available: Yes, 3:45–6:00 p.m.
Nurse on Staff: No–staff trained in first aid and CPR
Emergency Procedure Used:
Transportation to and from School: Provided by parents
Counseling and Evaluation Available: No

Graduation Information

Testing: The 1995 senior class was our first graduating class.
Average SAT Scores: The 1995 senior class was our first graduating class.
High School Our Students Usually Attend: N/A
Percentage of Seniors Attending College: N/A

Additional Information

ChristWay Academy

419 N. Cedar Ridge
Duncanville, TX 75116
(214) 296-6525

Mapsco: 62W

Fax: (214) 780-7273

Office Hours: 8:30 a.m.–4:00 p.m.
School Hours: 8:30 a.m.–3:30 p.m.
School Grades Offered: 1-12
Enrollment: 230
Co-ed: Yes
Boy/Girl Ratio: 1:1
Student/Teacher Ratio: 20:1
Average Class Size: 22
Calendar School Year: August–May
Holidays: Labor Day, Fair Day, Thanksgiving, Christmas,
spring break, Easter Friday and Monday
Uniform Requirements: Yes
Founded in: 1976

Philosophy of School

Christway Academy's philosophy is rooted in the conviction that true wisdom comes in revering God as we know Him in Jesus Christ. Our primary responsibility to our community is to provide an education established in Christ and His example and to require a standard of academic excellence–to know truth and He that is!

Academic Curriculum

Content: College preparatory; all basic subjects, fine arts, and advanced courses (physics, calculus, etc.)
Grading System Used: Numerical (90–100=A; 80–89=B; 70–79=C; below 70=F)
Conferences per Year: No set number; as often as needed
Tests Administered: Iowa Test of Basic Skills, P.L.A.N., P.S.A.T., S.A.T., A.C.T

Homework Policy: Elementary students–45 minutes; junior high students–1 hour, 15 minutes; high school students–1 1/2 to 2 hours
Method of Discipline: Corporeal (rarely); detentions; suspensions; expulsion

Enrichment Curriculum

Journalism, speech and drama, keyboarding, computers, community service, calculus, physics, honors physics, biology, Spanish I, II, and III

Extracurricular Activities

Beta Club (honor society); Fellowship of Christian Athletes
High school: six-man football, girls' volleyball, boys' and girls' basketball, track, tennis, golf; junior high: girls' volleyball, boys' and girls' basketball, track, varsity and junior high cheerleaders

Goals for Students

- To maximize their abilities–academically, athletically, and socially
- To be credible ambassadors for Christ
- To be exceptional citizens

Faculty/Staff Requirements

Qualifications of Staff: College degrees; teacher certification desired; Association of Christian Schools International (ACSI) certification
Qualifications of Administrator: Master's degree; professional certification in administration from ACSI.

School Information

Brochure Available: Yes
Number of Students in Each Grade: 20 students (grades 1 and 2); 25 students (grades 3–12)
Parochial: Independent Christian school
Organization Affiliations: Association of Christian Schools International; Texas Association of Private Schools
Accreditations: ACSI under TEPSAC; state accreditation
Parental Involvement: Parent-Teacher Fellowship (PTF)
Other Information:

Admittance

Whom to Contact: Administrators or secretary/registrar

Date to Apply: After March 15 for next school year
Testing Procedure for Age/Grade Level:
Fees Involved: $50 registration fee
Type of Student Preferred: On or above grade level; high moral character
Forms Required: Application, medical, previous school transcript
Individual/Group Appointments: Individual
Notification Procedure: Notification after interview
Waiting List Policy: After June 1, the first applicants get the available positions

Tuition

Approximate Tuition for 1996-97 School Year: Elementary–$2600; junior high–$2750; high school–$3050
Methods of Payment Available: 10- or 12-month pay schedule
Financial Assistance Offered: No
Cancellation Insurance Available: No
Profit/Non-profit: Non-profit

Additional Costs

Books/Bag/Uniform: No costs except for uniform ($145–$200)
Lunch Fee: Optional
Parents Club Dues: No
Annual Fund Drive: No
Discount for Siblings: 20% for second child; 20% for third child; 75% for fourth child and additional children

Facilities/Services Provided

Computer Lab: Yes
Library: Yes
Snack Procedures: Available for purchase
Before-school Care Program Available: Yes
After-school Care Program Available: Yes
Nurse on Staff: Yes
Emergency Procedure Used: Medical forms on file with emergency numbers, names of physicians, and permission to seek treatment
Transportation to and from School: No
Counseling and Evaluation Available: Yes

Graduation Information

Testing: Not required for graduation
Average SAT Scores: 1120

High School Our Students Usually Attend: ChristWay
Percentage of Seniors Attending College: 80

Additional Information

Eastlake Christian School

721 Easton Road
Dallas, TX 75228
(214) 249-4547

Mapsco: 38A

Fax: (214) 341-6238

Office Hours: 8:00 a.m.–4:00 p.m.
School Hours: 8:20 a.m.–3:30 p.m.
School Grades Offered: 4-year-olds–grade 6
Enrollment: 145
Co-ed: Yes
Boy/Girl Ratio: 1:1
Student/Teacher Ratio: 15/1
Average Class Size: 16
Calendar School Year: August–May
Holidays: Thanksgiving, Christmas, New Year's Day, Good
Friday, Labor Day, Martin Luther King Day, President's Day
Uniform Requirements: Yes
Founded in: 1979

Philosophy of School
Conservative Evangelical Christian

Academic Curriculum
Content: A Beka
Grading System Used: A (90-100), B (80-89), C (75-79), D (70-74), F (69 and below)
Conferences per Year: Two
Tests Administered: Stanford Achievement Test
Homework Policy: 30 minutes 3 nights/week
Method of Discipline: Age-appropriate

Enrichment Curriculum
Spanish, gymnastics, music, computer, library, private lessons: piano, violin, art, tap, ballet, tumbling

Extracurricular Activities
ECS Singer; Bible Quiz Team

Goals for Students
See philosophy and mission.

Faculty/Staff Requirements
Qualifications of Staff: College degrees; certification
Qualifications of Administrator: Graduate degree

School Information
Brochure Available: Yes
Number of Students in Each Grade: 18–30
Parochial: Yes
Organization Affiliations: Assembly of God
Accreditations: None
Parental Involvement: Required
Other Information:

Admittance
Whom to Contact: Larry W. Wilson
Date to Apply: Early enrollment begins in February
Testing Procedure for Age/Grade Level: Entrance exam required
Fees Involved: $15
Type of Student Preferred: Open
Forms Required: Application
Individual/Group Appointments: Both
Notification Procedure: Phone call
Waiting List Policy: Ongoing

Tuition
Approximate Tuition for 1996-97 School Year: $1750 (1/2-day kindergarten); $2650 (grades 1-6)
Methods of Payment Available: 10 equal payments; Visa, MasterCard; 10%

discounts for pre-payment
Financial Assistance Offered: Yes
Cancellation Insurance Available: N/A
Profit/Non-profit: Non-profit

Additional Costs

Books/Bag/Uniform: Registration fee–$200; curriculum fee–$50 (k4 and k5), $1130 (grades 1-6)
Lunch Fee: $20 for 10 meals
Parents Club Dues: $6.00
Annual Fund Drive: Open
Discount for Siblings: 10%

Facilities/Services Provided

Computer Lab: Yes, 20 IBM computers in lab, one per class
Library: Yes
Snack Procedures:
Before-school Care Program Available: Yes; 6:30 a.m., breakfast served until 7:30 a.m.
After-school Care Program Available: Yes, 3:30 p.m.–6:00 p.m.; afternoon snack
Nurse on Staff: One day per week
Emergency Procedure Used: Posted
Transportation to and from School: No
Counseling and Evaluation Available: Yes

Graduation Information

Testing: N/A
Average SAT Scores: N/A
High School Our Students Usually Attend: N/A
Percentage of Seniors Attending College: N/A

Additional Information

Evangel Temple Christian School

302 West Highway 303
Grand Prairie, TX 75051
(214) 264-1303

Mapsco: 51V

Fax: 237-0772

Office Hours: 7:30 a.m.–4:30 p.m.
School Hours: 8:10 a.m.–3:15 p.m.
School Grades Offered: Preschool–grade 12
Enrollment: 320
Co-ed: Yes
Boy/Girl Ratio: 1:1
Student/Teacher Ratio: 10:1
Average Class Size: 16
Calendar School Year: August 21–May 31
Holidays: Federal holidays, Christmas, spring break,
Good Friday
Uniform Requirements: Standardized dress
Founded in: 1966

Philosophy of School

To complement the church and home, the school seeks to develop the student's aptitude and talents according to Biblical principles and to provide the student a God-centered, Bible-based approach to academic, physical, spiritual, and social development.

Academic Curriculum

Content: College-preparatory with a Christian world view
Grading System Used: A = 90-100; B = 80-89; C = 75-79; D = 70-74; F = 69 and below
Conferences per Year: Two
Tests Administered: Stanford Achievement Test annually
Homework Policy: Practical assignments; increases as student advances
Method of Discipline: Scriptural approach encouraging parental involvement

43

Enrichment Curriculum

Elementary Spanish, computer, foreign language, drama, choral, band, yearbook, Bible, life management

Extracurricular Activities

Soccer, volleyball, basketball, baseball, softball, track and field, cheerleading, academic and fine-arts competitions

Goals for Students

To qualify students academically, morally, spiritually, and socially to represent God's revelation to their generation

Faculty/Staff Requirements

Qualifications of Staff: College degree; ACSI certification
Qualifications of Administrator: Master's degree; ACSI certification; background in Christian School Administration

School Information

Brochure Available: Upon request
Number of Students in Each Grade: 20
Parochial: Church-sponsored; interdenominational
Organization Affiliations: ACSI, ORUEF, TAPPS
Accreditations: ACSI
Parental Involvement: Parent-Teacher Fellowship
Other Information: Licensed extended care for ETCS preschool and elementary students; office open year round for information and registration

Admittance

Whom to Contact: School office
Date to Apply: Applications accepted year round
Testing Procedure per Age/Grade Level: Short-form diagnostic test (grades 1-12)
Fees Involved: Registration, book use, activity
Type of Student Preferred: One from Christian family open to receiving Godly instruction on or near grade level
Forms required: Comprehensive registration packet
Individual/Group Appointments: Family interviews
Notification Procedure: Following testing and interview; notification in writing
Waiting List Policy: Ongoing

44

Tuition

Approximate Tuition for 1996-97 School Year: One-half day preschool, $1660; elementary $2300; secondary $2400–$2700
Methods of Payment Available: Yearly with discount; 9- or 10-month schedule
Financial Assistance Offered: National School Lunch Program available
Cancellation Insurance Available:
Profit/Non-profit: Non-profit

Additional Costs

Books/Bag/Uniform: Standardized dress from school uniform company; school supplies
Lunch Fee: K-5–$1.75; elementary–$2.25; secondary–$2.50
Parents Club Dues: Optional
Annual Fund Drive: QSP magazine sale; fall festival
Discount for Siblings: Second child–20%; third child–40%; fourth child–80%; fifth child–100%

Facilities/Services Provided

Computer Lab: Yes, 10 IBM compatible computer stations
Library: Yes, comfortable environment with over 10,000 volumes servicing K-3–12th graders
Snack Procedures: Available for preschool and extended-care students
Before-school Care Program Available: Yes, state licensed opening 6:30 a.m.
After-school Care Program Available: Yes, closing at 6:00 p.m.
Nurse on Staff: No
Emergency Procedure Used: Parent notified
Transportation to and from School: Provided by parents
Counseling and Evaluation Available:

Graduation Information

Testing: Arrange for PSAT, SAT, ACT
Average SAT Scores: Unavailable
High School Our Students Usually Attend: N/A
Percentage of Seniors Attending College: 80

Additional Information

Summer day care available, N2–6th graders: $75–$80 weekly with family discounts offered

First Baptist Academy

1704 Patterson
Dallas, TX 75201
(214) 969-2488
Mailing address:
Box 868
Dallas, TX 75221

Mapsco: 45K

Fax: (214) 969-7797

Office Hours: 8:00 a.m.–4:30 p.m.
School Hours: 8:00 a.m.–3:30 p.m.
School Grades Offered: Kindergarten–grade 12
Enrollment: 920
Co-ed: Yes
Boy/Girl Ratio: 49:51
Student/Teacher Ratio: 17:1
Average Class Size: 15–24 students; varies by grade
Calendar School Year: August–May
Holidays: Usual holidays, two weeks at Christmas, one week in March
Uniform Requirements: Yes
Founded in: 1972

Philosophy of School

FBA emphasizes the historic, theistic Christian view of life as presented in the Bible, along with academic excellence and extracurricular activities to develop the student's spiritual, academic, social, and physical growth.

Through the academy's rigorous, college-preparatory curriculum and emphasis on developing Christian character, students are prepared for success in college and to serve as responsible, God-honoring citizens in their community.

Academic Curriculum

Content: College-preparatory; advanced placement courses; foreign languages; computer

Grading System Used: Letter grades in elementary; numerical grades in secondary; report cards every six weeks

Conferences per Year: At least two in elementary; as needed in secondary

Tests Administered: Stanford Achievement; Otis-Lennon; PSAT, SAT, ACT, AP testing

Homework Policy: Varies by grade

Method of Discipline: Biblically consistent, graduated discipline plan based on natural consequences leading to self-discipline

Enrichment Curriculum

Academic contests, spring musical, newspaper, yearbook, community service, field trips, library and reading programs

Extracurricular Activities

Drill team, cheerleaders, 16 sports in secondary grades, band, student council, honor society, Spanish and French clubs, lecture series, other various activities

Goals for Students

That they will know Christ, develop Christian character, be prepared for college, and then be responsible, God-honoring citizens in their communities

Faculty/Staff Requirements

Qualifications of Staff: Degree from accredited college (advanced degree preferred); state and ACSI certification; Christian lifestyle

Qualifications of Administrator: Advanced degree and experience in administration; Christian lifestyle

School Information

Brochure Available: Yes

Number of Students in Each Grade: 65–90

Parochial: Yes; all denominations accepted

Organization Affiliations: First Baptist Church

Accreditations: ACSI, ACTABS, SACS

Parental Involvement: Parent-Teacher Fellowship; booster club; volunteers

Other Information: FBA has two campuses: K–12 located in downtown Dallas and k–6 in Casa View-White Rock Lake area. Its student body of more than 900 students makes FBA one of the largest Christian schools in Texas.

Admittance

Whom to Contact: Sonya Darr, Director of Admissions
Date to Apply: January–April
Testing Procedure per Age/Grade Level: Developmental readiness for kindergarten; entrance testing grades 1–12
Fees Involved: Application fee is $20.
Type of Student Preferred: Score of 50% or above on Stanford Achievement Test; committed Christian family and student
Forms Required: Yes
Individual/Group Appointments: Family interview for all grades; campus visits are encouraged.
Notification Procedure: In writing at end of application process
Waiting List Policy: Parents are notified if grade is full.

Tuition

Approximate Tuition for 1996-97 School Year: $2965–$4595
Methods of Payment Available: 11 monthly payments or one annual payment
Financial Assistance Offered: Need-based only
Cancellation Insurance Available: No
Deposit Required: Yes
Profit/Non-profit: Non-profit

Additional Costs

Books/Bag/Uniform: Books–none; lab fees vary from $15-$55; bag–none; uniforms cost $85-$100
Lunch Fee: $2.75; optional in elementary; students may bring lunch.
Parents Club Dues: N/A
Annual Fund Drive: Yes
Discount for Siblings: Yes

Facilities/Services Provided

Computer Lab: Elementary and secondary labs
Library: Two separate libraries connected by computer
Snack Procedures: Students may purchase or bring snacks from home.
Before-school Care Program Available: Yes
After-school Care Program Available: Yes
Nurse on Staff: Yes; also a speech therapist

Emergency Procedure Used: School policies are followed.
Transportation to and from School: Car pools, DART
Counseling and Evaluation Available: Yes

Graduation Information

Testing: SAT, ACT, AP testing
Average SAT Scores: 1063 for class of 1995; 30% of 1994 and 1995 seniors were named National Merit Scholars
High School Our Students Usually Attend: FBA
Percentage of Seniors Attending College: 98+

Additional Information

Garland Christian Academy

1522 Lavon Drive
Garland, TX 75040
(214) 487-0043

Mapsco: 19A-N

Fax: (214) 487-1813

Office Hours: 7:30 a.m.–3:30 p.m.
School Hours: 8:00 a.m.–2:45 p.m.
School Grades Offered: Kindergarten (5-year-olds)–grade 12
Enrollment: 676
Co-ed: Yes
Boy/Girl Ratio: 333:343
Student/Teacher Ratio: 17:1
Average Class Size: 25–30
Calendar School Year: Late August through May
Holidays: Christmas, two weeks; spring break, one week; summer, three months
Uniform Requirements: Yes; 4th–12th
Founded in: 1972

Philosophy of School

To support the historical Christian view of life as presented in the Bible and to integrate biblical truth and principle in the academic, social, and character-development programs of the school

Academic Curriculum

Content: College-preparatory using a combination of curriculum materials
Grading System Used: A = Excellent, 93–100; B = Good, 85–92; C = Average, 78–84; D = Below Average, 70–77; F = Poor, 0–69; I = Incomplete (70 is the lowest passing grade); grades are sent home every six weeks
Conferences: May be arranged at any time; formal conference dates scheduled on school calendar
Tests Administered: ITBS

50

Homework Policy: Daily when needed
Method of Discipline: Demerits for behavior; detentions for academic reasons

Enrichment Curriculum
Art, choir, band, computers, Spanish, German

Extracurricular Activities
Grades 6-12: football, volleyball, basketball, baseball, softball, and track

Goals for Students
To achieve academic excellence, spiritual growth, and social responsibility

Faculty/Staff Requirements
Qualifications of Staff: Bachelor's degree
Qualifications of Administrator: Master's degree

School Information
Brochure Available: Yes
Number of Students in Each Grade: Varies (35–66)
Parochial: Yes, a ministry of Lavon Drive Baptist Church
Organization Affiliations: Association of Christian Schools International (ACSI), Texas Organization of Christian Schools (TOCS), Texas Association of Private and Parochial Schools (TAPPS)
Accreditations: Association of Christian Schools International (state-recognized)
Parental Involvement: Yes
Other Information:

Admittance
Whom to Contact: Dr. John McCartt
Date to Apply: March 1
Testing Procedure per Age/Grade Level: N/A
Fees Involved: $20
Type of Student Preferred: From Christian families
Forms Required: Yes
Individual/Group Appointments: Both
Notification Procedure: Letter within a week of testing
Waiting List Policy: Ongoing

Tuition

Approximate Tuition for 1996-97 School Year: K–5, $1450 (mornings only), $2250 (all day); grades 1–5, $2350; grades 6–8, $2500; grades 9–12, $2700
Methods of Payment Available: Full amount August 1, or one-tenth each month from August 1 through May 1
Financial Assistance Offered: Limited
Cancellation Insurance Available: No
Profit/Non-profit: Non-profit

Additional Costs

Books/Bag/Uniform: Fees for materials: k5 morning class ($40), k5 all-day class ($60), grades 1–5 ($75), grades 6–12 ($95); bag–no requirement; uniform–$200
Lunch Fee:
Parents Club Dues: No
Annual Fund Drive: No
Discount for Siblings: Yes (from $100 to $400 annually)

Facilities/Services Provided

Computer Lab: 30 networked IBM compatible computers
Library: Over 16,000 volumes
Snack Procedures: N/A
Before-school Care Program Available: No
After-school Care Program Available: Yes
Nurse on Staff: Yes, part-time
Emergency Procedure Used: Contact parents; take to local hospital emergency room if necessary
Transportation to and from School: No, but many families car pool.
Counseling and Evaluation Available: Yes

Graduation Information

Testing: Yes
Average SAT Scores: Available upon request
High School Our Students Usually Attend: N/A
Percentage of Seniors Attending College: 90

Additional Information

Glenview Christian School

4805 N.E. Loop 820
Fort Worth, TX 76137
(817) 281-5155

Mapsco: 659P

Fax: (817) 281-7413

Office Hours: 8:00 a.m.–4:15 p.m.
School Hours: 8:30 a.m.–3:30 p.m.
School Grades Offered: Pre-k–grade 6
Enrollment: 300
Co-ed: Yes
Boy/Girl Ratio: Approximately 1:1
Student/Teacher Ratio: 20:1
Average Class Size: 20
Calendar School Year: August-May
Holidays: Fall break, Thanksgiving, Christmas, winter break, Easter, spring break
Uniform Requirements: None
Founded in: 1971

Philosophy of School

The educational philosophy of Glenview Christian School is based on a God-centered world view. Our instructional program encompasses the spiritual, intellectual, physical, social, and emotional areas. Our philosophy compels us to promote high academic standards which enable students to advance to secondary school successfully. Our school exists to assist and to serve parents in their divine directive to instruct and discipline their children.

Academic Curriculum

Content: Full academic curriculum, including music, physical education, computer
Grading System Used: Numerical
Conferences per Year: Six (minimum); as many as needed
Tests Administered: Stanford Achievement

Homework Policy: Homework is a purposeful extension of the day's activities and provides the opportunity for further development
Method of Discipline: Assertive discipline

Enrichment Curriculum

Voyage of the Mimi-interdisciplinary computer/video, teacher-directed curriculum

Extracurricular Activities

Basketball, student council, math olympics, speech meet, science fair

Goals for Students

1) To enable students to see things as God sees them, resulting in a life conformed to His will
2) Successful advancement to secondary school

Faculty/Staff Requirements

Qualifications of Staff: B.S. degrees; state certification
Qualifications of Administrator: B.S. degree

School Information

Brochure Available: Yes
Number of Students in Each Grade: 40
Parochial: No
Organization Affiliations: Association of Christian Schools International
Accreditations: Association of Christian Schools International (TEPSAC approved)
Parental Involvement: Parents are very involved.
Other Information:

Admittance

Whom to Contact: Judy Dodson
Date to Apply: March 1
Testing Procedure for Age/Grade Level: Placement testing when school records do not give clear picture
Fees Involved: Annual tuition paid monthly; registration/supply fee
Type of Student Preferred: Students of families seeking Christian education
Forms Required: Applicaton, immunization record, previous cumulative records
Individual/Group Appointments: Individual

Notification Procedure: Upon application
Waiting List Policy: Annually

Tuition

Approximate Tuition for 1996-97 School Year: $2500
Methods of Payment Available: 10 monthly payments (August-May)
Financial Assistance Offered: Yes
Cancellation Insurance Available: No cancellation penalty
Profit/Non-profit: Non-profit

Additional Costs

Books/Bag/Uniform: Minimal field trip costs
Lunch Fee: Lunches–$2.50 per day
Parents Club Dues: $10 per year
Annual Fund Drive: Optional participation
Discount for Siblings: 10%

Facilities/Services Provided

Computer Lab: 20-unit, matched, network lab
Library: Fully automated 8000-volume elementary research library
Snack Procedures: None
Before-school Care Program Available: Yes, 7:30 a.m.–8:15 a.m.
After-school Care Program Available: No
Nurse on Staff: No
Emergency Procedure Used: Call 911; call parent; faculty-staff trained in first aid and CPR
Transportation to and from School: No
Counseling and Evaluation Available: Upon referral

Graduation Information

Testing: N/A
Average SAT Scores: N/A
High School Our Students Usually Attend: N/A
Percentage of Seniors Attending College: N/A

Additional Information

Gospel Lighthouse Christian Academy

5525 W. Illinois
Dallas, TX 75211
(214) 339-2207

Mapsco: 52T

Fax: (214) 331-6695

Office Hours: 8:00 a.m.–4:00 p.m.
School Hours: 8:25 a.m.–3:25 p.m.
School Grades Offered: Kindergarten(4)–grade 12
Enrollment: 350
Co-ed: Yes
Boy/Girl Ratio: 157:161 (in July 1995)
Student/Teacher Ratio: 8:1–25:1
Average Class Size: 20
Calendar School Year: August–May
Holidays: Christmas, spring break
Uniform Requirements: Yes
Founded in: 1984

Philosophy of School

GLCA bases its philosophy on the Christian world view. We use the word of God as our foundation, and it is central to all subjects.

Academic Curriculum

Content: A Beka and Bob Jones curricula in elementary school; A Beka, Bob Jones, Saxon, and Houghton Mifflin in secondary school
Grading system used: A = 100–92; B = 91–83; C = 82–75; D = 74–70; F = 69 or below
Conferences per Year: One required, more if needed
Tests Administered: Stanford Achievement Test
Homework Policy: None on Wednesdays or Fridays; amount of time spent varies by grade
Method of Discipline: Assertive discipline

Enrichment Curriculum
Computer class (K–12); library class (K4–6); music (K4–6); art (K4–12); physical education

Extracurricular Activities
Secondary: track, soccer, baseball, basketball, volleyball, cheerleading

Goals for Students
To receive a quality education in all subject areas with Christian principles and the Bible as central focus

Faculty/Staff Requirements
Qualifications of Staff: College degrees; most are certified by Association of Christian Schools International (ACSI)
Qualifications of Administrator: Master's degree; ACSI certification

School Information
Brochure Available: Yes
Number of Students in Each Grade: K–4 (half day), 12; K–4 (all day), 8; (K–5), 20; 1st, 19; 2nd, 17; 3rd, 25; 4th, 19; 5th, 20; 6th, 24; 7th (2 classes), 32; 8th, 25; 9th (2 classes), 39; 10th, 29; 11th, 26; 12th, 23
Parochial: Yes
Organization Affiliations: Sponsored by Gospel Lighthouse Church; member of ACSI
Accreditations: Association of Christian Schools International
Parental Involvement: Yearbook; fundraisers; class parties; Booster Club
Other Information:

Admittance
Whom to Contact: Cindy Heidecker (elementary); David Pruett (secondary)
Date to Apply: Any time
Testing Procedure per Age/Grade Level: Testing (achievement); occasionally school-ability testing
Fees Involved: Yes
Type of Student Preferred: From Christian home
Forms Required: Yes–application, health, birth certificate, school records
Individual/Group Appointments: Individual
Notification Procedure: After testing and interview
Waiting List Policy: Ongoing

Tuition

Approximate Tuition for 1996-97 School Year: $1000–$2575; K4 (1/2day)–$1000; K4 (full day)–$2000; K5–$2200; grades 1-6–$2350; grades 7-12–$2575
Methods of Payment Available: Yearly, monthly, weekly
Financial Assistance Offered: On a limited basis
Cancellation Insurance Available: N/A
Profit/Non-profit: Non-profit

Additional Costs:

Books/Bag/Uniform: Book fees: K4–$60; k5–$100; grades 1-6–$125; grades 7-12–$150; registration fee–$150 per child; one-time application fee $25
Lunch Fee: $2.50 per lunch
Parents Club Dues: N/A
Annual Fund Drive: N/A
Discount for Siblings: Second child–$200; third child–$400; fourth child–$800; fifth child–free

Facilities/Services Provided

Computer Lab: Yes
Library: Yes
Snack Procedures: Mid-morning snack for elementary students; parents provide snacks
Before-school Care Program Available: 7:45 a.m.–8:25 a.m. free
After-school Care Program Available: Until 4:30 p.m.–$15 per week
Nurse on Staff: No, staff members are trained in first aid.
Emergency Procedure Used: Outlined in parental release form
Transportation to and from School: Van from Christ for the Nations, if needed
Counseling and Evaluation Available: Yes

Graduation Information

Testing: SAT, ACT, PSAT, PLAN, Stanford Achievement Test, OLMAT
Average SAT Scores: 950+
High School Our Students Usually Attend: N/A
Percentage of Seniors Attending College: 90

Additional Information

Grace Academy of Dallas

11306 Inwood Road
Dallas, TX 75229
(214) 696-5648

Mapsco: 24D

Fax: (214) 696-8713

Office Hours: 7:45 a.m.–4:30 p.m.
School Hours: 8:30 a.m.–3:00 p.m.
School Grades Offered: K3–grade 6
Enrollment: 200
Co-ed: Yes
Boy/Girl Ratio: 94:91
Student/Teacher Ratio: 18:1 (kindergarten–grade 6)
Average Class Size: 18
Calendar School Year: Late August–May
Holidays: Labor Day, Thanksgiving, Christmas, Easter, Memorial Day
Uniform Requirements: Kindergarten (k5)–grade 6
Founded in: 1974

Philosophy of School

The mission of Christian education at Grace Academy of Dallas is to prepare students to live successful godly lives in an ungodly world. It is our objective to assist parents to fulfill their God-given commission by teaching the children entrusted to us that:
1. Each person is made in God's own image, unique in personality.
2. Each person is endowed with special gifts of genius which he/she can discover.
3. Each person can achieve with excellence God's purpose in his/her life.

Academic Curriculum

Content: Pre-college prep.
Grading System Used: ✓ system (age 3–grade 1); number/letter (grades 2–6)
Conferences per Year: Two (fall and spring); others as requested by teacher or parent
Tests Administered: Stanford Achievement Testing in spring

59

Homework Policy: Yes; 30-45 minutes per assignment
Method of Discipline: Procedure stated in *Parents' Handbook*

Enrichment Curriculum

Computer, Spanish, physical education, music, art, science lab

Extracurricular Activities

Sports program in conjunction with Town North YMCA

Goals for Students

At Grace Academy of Dallas, children are influenced to become learners for life, striving for excellence in every undertaking; to achieve mastery learning and not mere memorization; to embrace the processes of learning–organization, research, reading and writing, communication, and independent study skills. Central to our philosophy of education is the conviction that God's Word, our only infallible source of Truth, must be integrated into all school learning and into every aspect of life.

Faculty/Staff Requirements

Qualifications of Staff: Degrees and certification by state of Texas and ACSI
Qualifications of Administrator: Degree and experience in teaching and administration

School Information

Brochure Available: Yes
Number of Students in Each Grade: 15 (K3); 16 (K4); 18 (K5–grade 6)
Parochial: Non-denominational
Organization Affiliations: ACSI
Accreditations: ACSI (Association of Christian Schools International)–pending
Parental Involvement: Encouraged
Other Information:

Admittance

Whom to Contact: Charlene Sadley, school secretary
Date to Apply: January
Testing Procedure per Age/Grade Level: Spring and summer
Fees Involved: Annual $200 registration fee; one-time new student enrollment fee $250 per family
Type of Student Preferred: Average to gifted

Forms Required: Enrollment form and parent interview form
Individual/Group Appointments: Individual
Notification Procedure: In person or by phone
Waiting List Policy: Reapply annually

Tuition

Approximate Tuition for 1996-97 School Year: $3510
Methods of Payment Available: Annually, semi-annually, monthly
Financial Assistance Offered: Yes
Cancellation Insurance Available: No
Profit/Non-profit: Non-profit

Additional Costs

Books/Bag/Uniform: Books and bag–N/A; uniform–approximately $100 (girls) and $75 (boys)
Lunch Fee: N/A
Parents Club Dues: $20
Annual Fund Drive: Auction
Discount for Siblings: No

Facilities/Services Provided

Computer Lab: Eighteen 386 computers, some with CD ROM (class size, 18)
Library: Computerized 5000 volume facility
Snack Procedures: From home for preschool through grade 2
Before-school Care Program Available: Yes
After-school Care Program Available: No
Nurse on Staff: Yes
Emergency Procedure Used: 911; parents notified
Transportation to and from School: Family vehicles
Counseling and Evaluation Available:

Graduation Information

Testing: N/A
Average SAT Scores: N/A
High School Our Students Usually Attend: N/A
Percentage of Seniors Attending College: N/A

Additional Information

The Helen-Hardrick Christian School

1200 Southpointe
DeSoto, TX 75115
(214) 572-9630

Mapsco: 74U

Fax: (214) 572-9126

Office Hours: 8:00 a.m.–5:00 p.m.
School Hours: 6:30 a.m.–6:00 p.m. (Monday-Thursday);
6:30 a.m.–3:30 p.m. (Friday); class time: 8:00 a.m.–3:00 p.m.
School Grades Offered: Pre-K (age 4)–grade 3 (adding one grade per year)
Enrollment: 45 (first-year goal)
Co-ed: No (girls only)
Boy/Girl Ratio: N/A
Student/Teacher Ratio: 12:1
Average Class Size: 18
Calendar School Year: August-June
Holidays: Labor Day, Thanksgiving, Christmas, Martin Luther King Day, Good Friday, spring break
Uniform Requirements: Yes
Founded in: 1990

Philosophy of School

The Helen-Hardrick School's (HHCS) philosophy is to provide a biblical-based, academic-advanced education (college preparatory) for girls of above-average potential who may assume a position of responsibility and/or leadership in later years.

Academic Curriculum

Content: A Beka
Grading System Used: A-F
Conferences per Year: Three
Tests Administered: Stanford Achievement Test; Otis-Lennon Ability Test

Homework Policy: Yes
Method of Discipline: Discipline policy administered by the parents

Enrichment Curriculum
Dance, drama, music, gymnastics, Business Econimics (Class III only), French

Extracurricular Activities
Thanksgiving play, Christmas play, Resurrection play, girl scouts, commencement exercise

Goals for Students
To strengthen leadership and academic skills and provide each student with a firm foundation in our Lord and Savior Jesus Christ

Faculty/Staff Requirements
Qualifications of Staff: College degree
Qualifications of Administrator: College degree, certification

School Information
Brochure Available: Yes
Number of Students in Each Grade: 14
Parochial: Yes, Christianity
Organization Affiliations: Association of Christian Schools International
Accreditations: ACSI (membership only)
Parental Involvement: Parents' Association
Other Information:

Admittance
Whom to Contact: Wendy A. Gonzalez
Date to Apply: March 1-June 1
Testing Procedure for Age/Grade Level: Entrance examination
Fees Involved: Yes
Type of Student Preferred: Christian; strong study skills; stable home environment; strong moral values; good social skills
Forms Required: Yes
Individual/Group Appointments: Yes
Notification Procedure: Yes (admission acceptance/denial)
Waiting List Policy: Ongoing

Tuition

Approximate Tuition for 1996-97 School Year: $3,000
Methods of Payment Available: Annually; by semester; quarterly; monthly
Financial Assistance Offered: Yes
Cancellation Insurance Available: No
Profit/Non-profit: Profit

Additional Costs

Books/Bag/Uniform: Yes–books, folder, uniform
Lunch Fee: $40 monthly
Parents Club Dues: Yes
Annual Fund Drive: Pending organization
Discount for Siblings: Yes, $1000 annual discount

Facilities/Services Provided

Computer Lab: Yes
Library: Yes (pending)
Snack Procedures: No
Before-school Care Program Available: Yes, 6:30 a.m.–7:30 a.m.
After-school Care Program Available: Yes, 3:30–6:00 p.m. (Monday–Thursday)
Nurse on Staff: N/A
Emergency Procedure Used: Yes
Transportation to and from School: No
Counseling and Evaluation Available: Yes

Graduation Information

Testing: Yes
Average SAT Scores: Our students score 1-4 levels above grade level.
High School Our Students Usually Attend: N/A
Percentage of Seniors Attending College: N/A

Additional Information

Lexington Academy

2427 Carrick Street
Farmers Branch, TX 75234
(214) 620-0073

Mapsco: 12V

Fax: (214) 888-3458

Office Hours: 8:00 a.m.–5:00 p.m.
School Hours: 8:15 a.m.–3:45 p.m.
School Grades Offered: Three-year-olds–grade 12
Enrollment: 350
Co-ed: Yes
Boy/Girl Ratio: 1:1
Student/Teacher Ratio: 12:1
Average Class Size: 15
Calendar School Year: Mid-August through May
Holidays: Labor Day, Thanksgiving, Christmas (2 weeks),
Martin Luther King Day, Presidents' Day; spring break
(one week)
Uniform Requirements: Yes
Founded in: 1978

Philosophy of School

The primary mission of Lexington Academy is to educate and produce responsible patriotic citizens who will be strong ambassadors for Christ. The school seeks to help each child, from pre-kindergarten through grade 12, develop his or her God-given talents.

Academic Curriculum

Content: College-preparatory; accredited
Grading System Used: Number grades and letter grades
Conferences per Year: Ongoing
Tests Administered: Stanford Achievement
Homework Policy: Homework expected
Method of Discipline: Logical consequences

Enrichment Curriculum
Computer science, foreign language, band, journalism, choral, speech/drama, and honors

Extracurricular Activities
Texas Association of Private and Parochial Schools (TAPPS) full schedule of varsity and junior high athletics for boys and girls; championship caliber program

Goals for Students
Preparation for college in a Christian environment

Faculty/Staff Requirements
Qualifications of Staff: College degree; certified; competent
Qualifications of Administrator: College degree; certified; competent

School Information
Brochure Available: Yes
Number of Students in Each Grade: Average of 30 students per grade; two sections in high school
Parochial: Independent, evangelical, interdenominational
Organization Affiliations: None; independent
Accreditations: Association of Christian Schools International (ACSI); International Christian Accrediting Association (ICAA); TEA (Texas Education Agency); TEPSAC
Parental Involvement: Homeroom mothers; booster club
Other Information:

Admittance
Whom to Contact: School office
Date to Apply: Throughout year; transfers accepted upon qualification
Testing Procedure per Age/Grade Level: Stanford Achievement
Fees Involved: $100 admissions fee; $400 registration fee
Type of Student Preferred: Christian; willing to excel and learn; college-preparatory
Forms Required: Yes
Individual/Group Appointments: Individual
Notification Procedure: Yes
Waiting List Policy: Re-apply annually

Tuition

Approximate Tuition for 1996-97 School Year: $4200-$5000
Methods of Payment Available: One payment; two payments; ten payments
Financial Assistance Offered: No
Cancellation Insurance Available: No
Profit/Non-profit: Non-profit

Additional Costs

Books/Bag/Uniform: Books–included in tuition; bag–n/a; uniform–$200
Lunch Fee: $2.50 for k3–12
Parents Club Dues: Yes
Annual Fund Drive: N/A
Discount for Siblings: Yes

Facilities/Services Provided

Computer Lab:
Library:
Snack Procedures: Kitchen/school
Before-school Care Program Available: No
After-school Care Program Available: No
Nurse on Staff: Yes
Emergency Procedure Used: Yes
Transportation to and from School: No
Counseling and Evaluation Available: No

Graduation Information

Testing: Yes
Average SAT Scores: 1183 (Upper 50% of seniors)
High School Our Students Usually Attend: N/A
Percentage of Seniors Attending College: 95% over past 4 years

Additional Information

Metropolitan Christian School

8501 Bruton Rd.
Dallas, TX 75217-1947
(214) 388-4426

Mapsco: 58A

Fax: (214) 388-7934

Office Hours: 8:00 a.m.–5:00 p.m.
School Hours: 8:15 a.m.–3:30 p.m.
School Grades Offered: Age 4–grade 9
Enrollment: 290
Co-ed: Yes
Boy/Girl Ratio:
Student/Teacher Ratio: 40:60
Average Class Size: 20
Calendar School Year: August–May
Holidays: Labor Day, Fair Day, Thanksgiving, Christmas, Martin Luther King Day, Presidents' Day, spring break, Easter
Uniform Requirements: Dress code
Founded in: 1966

Philosophy of School

Metropolitan Christian School bases its educational philosophy on the Christian world view of truth and man as found in the infallible, inerrant, and inspired Word of God. The Bible is authoritative, reliable, and the ultimate source of truth.

We believe the universe and all life are dynamically related to God and have the purpose of glorifying Him, since God created, sustains, and will consummate all things through His Son, the Lord Jesus Christ.

Man is created in God's image with the ability and capacity to know and respond to God personally. Since man is a sinner by nature and by choice, he cannot in this condition know nor honor God in his life. Man can only be reconciled to God by receiving Jesus Christ as Savior and Lord by faith and by being born again to do God's will, which is the ultimate purpose of his life.

68

The total process of education must seek to guide this reconciliation in Christ and help each student to develop as a whole person–spiritually, mentally, socially, and physically. We believe each student needs to learn to see all truth as God's truth and integrate it into every aspect of his/her life. He/She must learn to live and work with others in a secular world and needs to become discerning about the world's attitudes and philosophies, understanding and evaluating them with a biblically based world view.

Biblically, the parents are given the responsibility for their children's education and discipline. The family, the school, and the church are to be partners in educating the student for a life of service to God and man. The school is an extension–not a substitute– for the home. It is one means through which parents fulfill the responsibility the Lord has given them.

Academic Curriculum

Content: Language arts, math, science, social studies, music, art, physical education
Grading System Used: Numerical
Conferences per Year: One required; others scheduled at request of parent or teacher
Tests Administered: Stanford Achievement
Homework Policy: From 1st grade, the homework progressively increases
Method of Discipline: Time out; removal of privileges; older students– detention

Enrichment Curriculum

Music, field trips, band, choir, art; grades 7, 8, 9–drama, speech, debate

Extracurricular Activities

Soccer, volleyball, track (boys and girls), basketball (boys and girls)

Goals for Students

For the student's spiritual and moral growth, the school seeks to
1. teach the Bible as God's inspired Word and to develop attitudes of love and respect toward it
2. teach the basic doctrines of the Bible
3. lead the student to a decision of receiving Christ as Savior and Lord
4. develop a desire to know and obey the will of God as revealed in the Scriptures
5. impart an understanding of each Christian's place in the church and its worldwide task of witness, evangelism, and discipleship, and to stimulate the student's involvement in this task

6. teach the application of Biblical ethics and standards of morality to every part of life
7. encourage the development of self-discipline and responsibility in the student, based on respect for and submission to God and all other authority

For the student's personal and social development, the school aims to
1. help the student develop his/her full potential and accept himself/herself as a unique individual created in the image of God
2. teach the students to manifest fairness, courtesy, kindness, love, and respect to others, realizing that others, too, are made in God's image
3. teach the student to work independently and cooperatively
4. promote physical fitness, good health habits, and wise use of the body as the temple of God

For the student's academic development, the school endeavors to
1. promote high academic standards within the potential of the individual
2. help each student gain a thorough comprehension and command of the fundamental processes used in communicating and dealing with others, such as reading, writing, speaking, listening, and mathematics
3. teach and encourage the use of good study habits
4. teach the student how to do independent research, reason logically, and pursue independent study in areas of personal interest
5. develop creative and critical thinking, and proper use of biblical criteria for evaluation
6. promote good citizenship through developing the understanding and appreciation of our Christian and American heritage of responsible freedom, human dignity, and acceptance of authority
7. discuss current affairs in all fields and relate them to God's plan for man
8. produce an understanding and appreciation for God's world, an awareness of man's role in his environment and his God-given responsibilities to use and preserve it properly
9. engender an appreciation of the fine arts through the development of the student's understanding and personal expression

Working with the homes from which the students come, the school desires to
1. cooperate closely with the parents in every phase of the student's development, especially as it relates to the school's program
2. help parents understand the school's purpose and program
3. aid families in Christian growth and to help them develop Christ-centered homes
4. encourage attendance and involvement in their church

Faculty/Staff Requirements
Qualifications of Staff: ACSI certification
Qualifications of Administrator: ACSI certification

School Information

Brochure Available: Yes
Number of Students in Each Grade: K–preschool (15); K–2 (20); 3–9 (25)
Parochial: Church sponsored
Organization Affiliations: ACSI
Accreditations: ACSI
Parental Involvement: Parent-Teacher Christian Association
Other Information:

Admittance

Whom to Contact: Mrs. Dorothy Howe
Date to Apply: April 1
Testing Procedure for Age/Grade Level: All classes are tested.
Fees Involved: Testing–$20; registration–$100
Type of Student Preferred: Students working at or above grade level
Forms Required: Admission, medical, report card from the last school attended
Individual/Group Appointments: Individual
Notification Procedure: Personal interview
Waiting List Policy: Ongoing

Tuition

Approximate Tuition for 1996-97 School Year: $2500
Methods of Payment Available: Yearly, by semester, monthly
Financial Assistance Offered: None
Cancellation Insurance Available: None
Profit/Non-profit: Non-profit

Additional costs:

Books/Bag/Uniform: None
Lunch Fee: $2.50; fifth grade and up, a la carte
Parents Club Dues: $5
Annual Fund Drive: None
Discount for Siblings: 15%

Facilities/Services Provided

Computer Lab: Yes, 18 IBM compatible computers
Library: Yes
Snack Procedures: After school
Before-school Care Program Available: Yes, 6:30–8:30 a.m.

After-school Care Program Available: Yes, 3:30 p.m.–6:00 p.m.
Nurse on Staff: No
Emergency Procedure Used: Parents contacted; emergencies–call 911
Transportation to and from School: No
Counseling and Evaluation Available: No

Graduation Information

Testing: N/A
Average SAT Scores: N/A
High School Our Students Usually Attend: 1995-96 was our first year to offer 9th grade. An additional grade will be added each year until all 12 grades are available.
Percentage of Seniors Attending College: N/A

Additional Information

Scofield Christian School

7730 Abrams Road
Dallas, TX 75231
(214) 349-6843

Mapsco: 27J

Fax: (214) 342-2061

Office Hours: 8:00 a.m.–4:00 p.m.
School Hours: 8:15 a.m.–3:30 p.m.
School Grades Offered: 3K–T and Th
4K–M, W, F (morning and afternoon); 5K–M-F (morning and afternoon); morning session: 8:15 a.m.-11:30 a.m.; afternoon session: 12:15 p.m.-3:30 p.m.; grades 1-6–8:15 a.m.-3:30 p.m.
Enrollment: 380
Co-ed: Yes
Boy/Girl Ratio: 1:1
Student/Teacher Ratio: 20:1 (approximately)
Average Class Size: 17
Calendar School Year: Middle of August–end of May
Holidays: Fair Day (October), Thanksgiving break (November), Christmas break (end of December–first week of January), spring break (second week of March), Easter holiday (April)
Uniform Requirements: Uniforms
Founded in: 1961

Philosophy of School

The mission of Scofield Christian School is to provide children with an education based on Biblical precepts incorporated into the curriculum that will prepare each child academically, spiritually, and morally to lead a life that honors God.

We believe it is desirable for the student body to contain a cross-section of society racially, socially, and economically, and that it be limited in size so that a sense of community can be established and maintained. We further believe the school can be of special service to the children of parents who share our concern for each person's relationship to God.

We believe our curriculum should be governed largely by the word "excellence." Consequently, we have chosen to be accreditied by the Association of Christian Schools International and comply with its standards for curriculum, student assessment, and promotion. ASCI is recognized by the Texas Education Agency.

Academic Curriculum

Content: Bible, language, math, social studies, science

Grading System Used: Grades 1-3–A-F; grades 4-6–A (93-100), B (85-92), C (76-84), D (70-75), F (below 70); preschool and kindergarten receive check plus or check minus

Conferences per Year: Two and at parental request

Tests Administered: Stanford Achievement and Otis-Lennon tests

Homework Policy: Students are required to turn in homework on time, with a two-day grace period to turn in late assignments; work turned in after the two-day grace period receives a grade of zero. Homework is assigned three days a week.

Method of Discipline: Students are expected to show respect for the school facilities, property, and equipment through proper care and use. Students are expected to show respect for the administration, faculty, and staff of both the school and Scofield Memorial Church. A student's behavior should never jeopardize another student's welfare or opportunities to learn in any way.

Rather than emphasize the negative, SCS chooses to encourage the development of postive character qualities, such as obedience, truthfulness, self-control, diligence, patience, fairness, goodness, compassion, initiative, and responsibility.

Behavior requiring discipline is addressed by the teacher in charge. Should efforts to correct the problem prove unsuccessful, the teacher will request the involvement of the parents. If the problem is not resolved, the administration will become involved.

Enrichment Curriculum

Art, music, physical education, library, computer, Spanish, Latin, study skills, character qualities

Extracurricular Activities

ACSI student activities: speech meet, spelling bee, science fair, choir festival, art festival

Goals for Students
Our goal is for each student to receive a well-rounded academic education.

Faculty/Staff Requirements
Qualifications of Staff: Christian; bachelor's degree; certification
Qualifications of Administrator: Christian; master's degree

School Information
Brochure Available: Upon request
Number of Students in Each Grade: (Maximum enrollment) 3K–14; 4K–17; 5K–18; grade 1–18; grades 2-6–20
Parochial:
Organization Affiliations: Scofield Memorial Church
Accreditations: Association of Christian Schools International
Parental Involvement: Parent-Teacher Fellowship (PTF)
Other Information:

Admittance
Whom to Contact: Gloria Brinkman, Administrative Assistant
Date to Apply: January 1
Testing Procedure for Age/Grade Level: None for preschool; readiness for kindergarten; achievement tests for grades 1-6
Fees Involved: $35 (entrance testing); $175 (portion of the registration fee)
Type of Student Preferred: Average to above average academically
Forms Required: Application, immunization records, proof of medical insurance, copy of birth certificate, signed doctrinal statement, signed philosophy statement
Individual/Group Appointments:
Notification Procedure: Letter sent if the child is accepted or rejected; notifiction sent if the child is on the waiting list
Waiting List Policy: Ongoing; everyone applies each year.

Tuition
Approximate Tuition for 1996-97 School Year: $1660 (3K), $2070 (4K), $2700 (5K), $3300 (grades 1-6); additional charge for extended-day program
Methods of Payment Available: 10 monthly payments (August–May); cash, check, or money order
Financial Assistance Offered: Yes
Cancellation Insurance Available: N/A
Profit/Non-profit: Non-profit

75

Additional Costs

Books/Bag/Uniform: Study-skills fee–$35 (grades 3-6); field-trip fee–$28; uniform–approximately $150-$220 annually
Lunch Fee: $2.50 per day (optional)
Parents Club Dues: None
Annual Fund Drive: Fund raiser in the fall
Discount for Siblings: 10% for second child; 15% for third child; 20% for fourth child; all students pay $250 annual registration fee.

Facilities/Services Provided

Computer Lab: Yes, weekly on site
Library: Yes, weekly on site
Snack Procedures: Preschool and extended-day students
Before-school Care Program Available: No
After-school Care Program Available: No
Nurse on Staff: On call
Emergency Procedure Used: Depends on problem
Transportation to and from School: Provided by parents and local daycare
Counseling and Evaluation Available: In house and contracted locally

Graduation Information

Testing: N/A
Average SAT Scores: N/A
High School Our Students Usually Attend: Most local private and public high schools
Percentage of Seniors Attending College: N/A

Additional Information

Texas Christian Academy

915 WEB
Arlington, TX 76011
(817) 274-5201

Mapsco: 83B

Fax: (817) 265-5329

Office Hours: 8:00 a.m.–4:30 p.m.
School Hours: 8:10 a.m.–3:00 p.m.
School Grades Offered: Pre-K (age 4)–grade 12
Enrollment: 419
Co-ed: Yes
Boy/Girl Ratio: Varies
Student/Teacher Ratio: 23:1
Average Class Size: 23
Calendar School Year: August–May
Holidays: All traditional holidays
Uniform Requirements: St. Agnes of Fort Worth
Founded in: 1972

Philosophy of School

Our philosophy is based upon a Christian world view holding that God is the Creator and Sustainer of the universe, the ultimate reality, and the source and essence of all goodness and truth. We believe the Bible is the inerrant Word of God and the final authority. Effective education can best be accomplished in an environment which recognizes that all truth is God's Truth. The Bible clearly teaches that parents are responsible for the education and discipline of their children. Teacher and administrators assist the parents, helping them fulfill their God-given responsibilities. Together the home, the school, and the church should prepare the student for a life of fellowship with God and service to man.

Academic Curriculum

Content: College-prepatory
Grading System Used: 4.0
Conferences per Year: Ask school for schedule

Tests Administered: Stanford Achievement; OLSAT; PSAT; PLAN
Homework Policy: Late work receives points off or may not be accepted.
Method of Discipline: Parental conferences; detention; disciplinary board

Enrichment Curriculum

We offer a band and choral program. The Fine Arts Department produces a musical each year. We offer a Junior Statesman program for juniors and seniors. This year we are adding a Junior Achievement program to the junior high.

Extracurricular Activities

Volleyball, basketball, football, spring play; sophomores and juniors go on a retreat to Pine Cove Encampment each year; seniors go on a retreat to Mo Ranch in south Texas; seniors also take a trip to Washington, D.C.

Goals for Students

To challenge men and women to know the Lord Jesus Christ and, through knowing Him, fulfill their intellectual, emotional, and spiritual potential, thus gaining the understanding and skill necessary for living lives of integrity and influence. We are committed to ministering to the family, the individual, and the community in a spirit of compassion and cooperation.

Faculty/Staff Requirements

Qualifications of Staff: College degree
Qualifications of Administrator: College degree and at least three years classroom experience

School Information

Brochure Available: Yes
Number of Students in Each Grade: Up to 46
Parochial: No
Organization Affiliations: Texas Association of Private and Parochial Schools
Accreditations: Certified by the Association of Christian Schools International
Parental Involvement: Parents' Day at School; Grandparents' Day at School; two conferences per year; school welcomes volunteer work.
Other Information:

Admittance

Whom to Contact: School office; Angela Arthur–elementary principal, Tim

Vanderveer–secondary principal
Date to Apply: April 1 for 1996-97 school year
Testing Procedure for Age/Grade Level: Students in all grades are tested before they are admitted. There is a $25 testing fee.
Fees Involved: Registration, entrance test, tuition, sports, character and responsibility activities fee
Type of Student Preferred: All students are reviewed and accepted on their own merit regardless of academic achievement or religious background.
Forms Required: School records, any testing, immunization records, medical background
Individual/Group Appointments: Individual interviews
Notification Procedure: By phone within 5 days
Waiting List Policy: Ongoing

Tuition

Approximate Tuition for 1996-97 School Year: Half-day kindergarten–$1830 per year; elementary (grades 1-6)–$2800 per year; secondary (grades 7-12)–$3080 per year
Methods of Payment Available: Single payment–5% discount if paid before the first day of school; 10 installments (July1-April 1); 12 installments (July1-June 1)
Financial Assistance Offered: See Administration.
Cancellation Insurance Available: No
Profit/Non-profit: Non-profit

Additional Costs

Books/Bag/Uniform: Uniforms can be purchased from St. Agnes Uniforms in Fort Worth.
Lunch Fee: $2.25 per day for full lunch
Parents Club Dues: Parent-Teacher Fellowship $5.00
Annual Fund Drive: Magazine sales drive in August
Discount for Siblings: 20% for second child; 30% for third child

Facilities/Services Provided

Computer Lab: IBM Compatibles
Library: Yes
Snack Procedures: We have a snack counter for the secondary students. Kindergarten students bring their snacks.
Before-school Care Program Available: No
After-school Care Program Available: Extended care for grades K4–6, 12–3 and/or 3–6 p.m.
Nurse on Staff: No, we are less than one mile from the local hospital. Several

teachers are schooled in first aid and CPR.

Emergency Procedure Used: 911

Transportation to and from School: None provided

Counseling and Evaluation Available: A certified teacher tests for learning disabilities.

Graduation Information

Testing: SAT/ACT

Average SAT Scores:

High School Our Students Usually Attend: N/A

Percentage of Seniors Attending College: 80+

ICAA
The International Christian
Accrediting Association

The International Christian Accrediting Association, an affiliate of Oral Roberts University Educational Fellowship, is an accrediting agency dedicated to the recognition and support of excellence in Christian education.

With an ever-growing number of schools participating in its accreditation process nationwide and overseas, ICAA is meeting the needs of Christian schools and post secondary institutions by establishing a credible and reliable witness to their performance, integrity, and quality.

Lexington Academy (see ACSI)
Trinity Christian School

Trinity Christian School

1313 E. Pleasant Run Rd.   Mapsco: 72X
Cedar Hill, TX 75104
(214) 291-2501   Fax: (214) 291-4739

Office Hours: 8:00 a.m.–4:30 p.m.
School Hours: 8:00 a.m.–3:00 p.m.
School Grades Offered: Pre-kindergarten–grade 12
Enrollment: 600
Co-ed: Yes
Boy/Girl Ratio: 50:40
Student/Teacher Ratio: 18:1
Average Class Size: 18
Calendar School Year: August 15–May 24
Holidays: Labor Day, Thanksgiving, Christmas, Martin Luther King Day, spring break, Good Friday
Uniform Requirements: Yes, Parker Uniform Co.
Founded in: 1981

Philosophy of School

It is the mission of Trinity Christian School to help each student become as much like Jesus Christ as possible. This means each student is trained spiritually, academically, and physically in an excellent manner. Furthermore, it is the mission of TCS to create Christian leadership that is part of the five-fold ministry–for other professionals in various fields that help carry out the "Great Commission" as stated in Matthew 28: 19-20.

Academic Curriculum

Content: A Beka, Bob Jones, Merrill, Secular
Grading System Used: Percentage grades given in all subjects for grades 1-12
Conferences per Year: Two
Tests Administered: Stanford Achievement Test
Homework Policy: Teachers give homework to help students advance.

Method of Discipline: Instruction correction, exhortation, rebuke and rod of correction

Enrichment Curriculum
AP English; AP biology; pre-calculus; honors classes in English, history, and science

Extracurricular Activities
Football, volleyball, soccer, basketball, track, tennis, golf, softball, baseball, clubs, student government, Spiritual Life Council, field trips

Goals for Students
Spiritual: 100% of TCS students will have a personal relationship with Jesus Christ
Academic: 100% of TCS students will score at the 75% level as measured by Stanford Achievement
Physical: 100% of TCS students will score at the 75% level on the Prudential Health Test

Faculty/Staff Requirements
Qualifications of Staff: College degree; certified
Qualifications of Administrator: College degree; certified

School Information
Brochure Available: Yes
Number of Students in Each Grade: K3–22; K4–34; K5–46; 1st–33; 2nd–32; 3rd–32; 4th–38; 5th–33; 6th–35; 7th–50; 8th–51; 9th–50; 10th–50; 11th–50; 12th–50
Parochial: Yes
Organization Affiliations: Assembly of God
Accreditations: International Christian Accrediting Association
Parental Involvement: Parent-teacher conferences, Parent Intercessory Prayer, Band Booster, Athletic Booster
Other Information: We welcome involvement of our parents in the activities of the school. We welcome parents who wish to visit.

Admittance
Whom to Contact: Laqueta Whitfield, Registrar
Date to Apply: Mid-January for the next school year
Testing Procedure per Age/Grade Level: After enrollment; WRAT test (K-12)
Fees Involved: Registration fee includes testing fee

Type of Student Preferred: Christian lifestyle
Forms Required: Transcript, birth certificate, immunization records
Individual/Group Appointments: Individual
Notification Procedure: Letter
Waiting List Policy: Re-apply

Tuition

Approximate Tuition for 1996-97 School Year: K3, half day–$1985, full day–$2429; K4, half day–$1985, full day–$2429; K5–$2580; 1-6–$2731; 7-8–$2977; 9-11–$3279; 12–$3800
Methods of Payment Available: Nine and twelve monthly payments
Financial Assistance Offered: Yes
Cancellation Insurance Available: Yes
Profit/Non-profit: Non-profit

Additional Costs

Books/Bag/Uniform: Books, uniforms, activity fee, facility fee
Lunch Fee: Elementary–$2.25 per meal; secondary–$3.00 per meal
Parents Club Dues: N/A
Annual Fund Drive: Magazine sales, spring auction
Discount for Siblings: Second child–$270; third child–$630; fourth child–$945; fifth child–free

Facilities/Services Provided

Computer Lab: Elementary and secondary
Library: Two libraries
Snack Procedures: Students bring their snacks; snack bar open to secondary students during lunch
Before-school Care Program Available: Begins at 7:30 a.m.
After-school Care Program Available: 3:00 p.m.–6:00 p.m.
Nurse on Staff: Yes, full time
Emergency Procedure Used: Nurse
Transportation to and from School: Car pool list available; bus to/from CFNI
Counseling and Evaluation Available: Yes

Graduation Information

Testing: No exit test
Average SAT Scores: 950
High School Our Students Usually Attend: N/A
Percentage of Seniors Attending College: 95

ISAS
Independent Schools
Association
of the Southwest

P.O. Box 52297
Tulsa, Oklahoma 74152-0297
(918) 749-5927

Richard W. Ekdahl
Executive Director

The Independent Schools Association of the Southwest, a non-profit, tax-exempt, voluntary accreditation organization, serves 63 independent elementary and secondary schools in Texas, Arizona, New Mexico, Louisiana, Oklahoma, and Kansas.

ISAS welcomes variety and diversity in its membership. Schools range in size from 100 to over 1200 students. They include boarding schools and day schools; single-sex and coeducational schools; elementary schools, secondary schools, and various combinations of the two; nonsectarian schools, church schools, and church-related schools; schools which serve students with clearly defined college ambitions, as well as students with learning differences.

The Association was a leader in the creation of the Texas Private School Accreditation Commission, an approach to private school accreditation conceptualized by its Executive Director, who has served as Chairman of the Commission.

Schools voluntarily seek membership in ISAS. Schools must meet the Association's Standards; must conduct a thorough self-study; and must be visited by an ISAS Evaluation Committee before it will be considered for membership. After accreditation and membership are granted, the school is required to participate in a rigorous and continuous evaluation program.

The Independent Schools Association of the Southwest also conducts seminars, conferences, and institutes for school heads, teachers, trustees, first-year teachers, business managers, and middle-management administrators.

ISAS sponsors an athletic league for its students and conducts an annual Fine Arts Festival in which over 2000 students participate.

The Independent Schools Association of the Southwest is a member of the College Board, the Educational Records Bureau, and the National Association of Independent Schools.

Cistercian Preparatory School
The Episcopal School of Dallas
Fort Worth Country Day School
Good Shepherd Episcopal School
Greenhill School
The Hockaday School
Lakehill Preparatory School
The Lamplighter School
The Oakridge School
The Parish Day School of the Episcopal Church of the Transfiguration
St. John's Episcopal School
St. Mark's School of Texas
St. Philip's School and Community Center
The Selwyn School
Trinity Valley School
The Winston School

Cistercian Preparatory School

One Cistercian Road
Irving, TX 75039
(214) 438-4956

Mapsco: 32A

Fax: 214) 554-0736

Office Hours: 7:30 a.m.–4:30 p.m. Monday through Friday
School Hours: 8:25 a.m.–3:30 p.m.
School Grades Offered: 5–12
Enrollment: 324
Co-ed: Boys only
Boy/Girl Ratio: N/A
Student/Teacher Ratio: 9:1
Calendar School Year: August–May
Holidays: All major holidays plus spring break
Uniform Requirements: Yes
Founded in: 1962

Philosophy of School

The Cistercian Preparatory School was founded to prepare talented boys for the colleges of their choice by challenging their minds with an excellent academic program, molding their characters through the values of Catholic education, and offering them guidance with both understanding and discipline.

Academic Curriculum

Content: The Cistercian curriculum is a fully integrated, eight-year honors program; it is not organized according to tracks. The curriculum of English, math, laboratory science, foreign language, and social studies is identical for all students. All Christians are required to participate in the Religion/Theology program. The middle school (grades 5–8) provides the essential background in English, language arts, basic math through Algebra I, laboratory science, Latin, social studies, religion, fine arts, and computer. In the upper school, elective courses are offered in addition to the main curriculum.

Outline of Upper-School Curriculum:

Freshman
English I (classical heritage), geometry, biology, foreign language (Spanish, French, German), Western Civilization I, theology (systematic theology), elective
Sophomore
English II (British literature), Algebra II with trigonometry, chemistry, Foreign Language II, Western Civilization II, theology (moral theology), elective
Junior
English III (American literature), precalculus (elementary functions), physics, Foreign Language III, American history, theology (church history), elective
Senior
English IV (world literature), Calculus I & II, science (Biology II, Chemistry II, or Physics II), Foreign Language IV, U.S. government, theology (comparative study of religions), elective, and senior project

Grading System Used: Cistercian grades (on a 4.0 scale) are weighted by a factor of 1.2 (with the exception that A and A+ are of equal value). This grading system reflects the advanced level of course work completed by all Cistercian graduates. Progress reports and quarterly report cards are mailed to parents.
Conferences per Year: 2 scheduled and as needed
Tests Administered: Standardized tests are given early, plus additional practice PSAT and SAT tests
Method of Discipline: As stated in the handbook
Homework Policy: Approximately 2 hours per night

Enrichment Curriculum

A Cistercian student may earn college credit in two ways: (1) required senior courses are offered in conjunction with the Dallas County Community College District. These courses result in two semesters of college credit for each student in English, calculus, U.S. government, and a laboratory science (biology, chemistry, or physics); (2) students may earn credit by talking the SAT II or advanced placement tests. The curriculum allows thouse students who so choose to take the College Board AP exams in English, math, American and European history, French, Latin, Spanish, chemistry, physics, and biology.

Extracurricular Activities

Students are encouraged to participate in middle and upper school student publications, Quiz Bowl, middle and upper school drama, chess club, student council, STARS, community service projects, and other activities. Cistercian is a member of both the Southwest Preparatory Conference and the Metroplex Independent Schools Conference, competing in seven sports (football, basketball, soccer, baseball, track and cross country running, golf, swimming, and tennis).

Faculty/Staff Requirements

Qualifications of staff: All of the 10 Cistercian priests and the 24 lay men and women on the faculty are required to earn a master's degree in their teaching fields; 91% have advanced degrees, with 38% having doctorates

Qualifications of Administrator:

>The Headmaster, Fr. Bernard A. Marton, O. Cist.
>University of St. Anselm, Rome, Italy
>>Bachelor of Arts in Theology (STB)
>>Master of Arts in Theology (STM)
>>Doctor of Theology (STD)
>Southern Methodist University, Dallas, Texas
>>Master of Arts in French Literature
>Assistant Headmaster 9 years
>Headmaster since 1981
>Member of and Representative to
>>ISAS (Independent Schools Association of the Southwest)
>>NAIS (National Association of Independent Schools)
>>North Texas Principals' Association—Past President

School Information

>**Brochure Available:** Yes
>**Number of Students in Each Grade:** 32 to 44
>**Parochial:** Private, independent Catholic school
>**Organization Affiliations:** NAIS, ISAS, CASE, CEEB, NEAC, SPC, MISC
>**Accreditations:** Accredited by ISAS and TCCED
>**Parental Involvement:** Yes
>**Other Information:** Each class is assigned to a Form Master who moves with his class from one year to the next. He is personally responsible for establishing the community within which each student can develop.

Admittance

>**Whom to Contact:** Fr. Peter Verhalen, O. Cist.
>**Date to Apply:** In October we begin accepting applications for the coming year.
>**Testing Procedure per Age/Grade Level:** Testing administered by Cistercian faculty the last Saturday in January and the first Saturday in February
>**Fees Involved:** $35
>**Type of Student Preferred:** Above-average, college-bound boys
>**Forms Required:** Yes
>**Individual/Group Appointments:** Both
>**Notification Procedure:** By letter within two to three weeks after testing
>**Waiting List Policy:** Wait list is maintained through the beginning of the school year; applicant must reapply for the following year

Tuition

Approximate Tuition for 1996-97 School Year: $6450 (grades 5-8); $7175 (grades 8-12)

Methods of Payment Available: By semester (payments due July 1 and December 1); tuition plan available

Financial Assistance Offered: Yes

Cancellation Insurance Available: No

Profit/Non-profit: Non-profit

Additional Costs:

Books/Bag/Uniform: Books–approximately $200-$400 Uniform–approximately $150

Lunch Fee: Students bring their lunches.

Parents Club Dues: $25 (optional)

Annual Fund Drive: Yes

Discount for Siblings: No

Facilities/Services Provided

Computer Lab: Yes

Library: Full-time librarian, almost 47,000 items including 20,100 books, 8,500 periodicals, CD-ROM, 400 college catalogs, AV software

Snack Procedures: At breaks

Before-school Care Program Available: Beginning at 7:00 a.m.

After-school Care Program Available: Until 5:00 p.m.

Nurse on Staff: Yes

Emergency Procedure Used: Determined by staff on duty as need dicates

Transportation to and from School: Buses; families provide car pools.

Counseling and Evaluation Available: School advising; outside referrals

Graduation Information

Testing: PSAT, SAT I & II, AP preparations; preparation for college-application process begins sophomore year

Average SAT Scores: Class of 1994–composite 1301 (verbal 619, math 682)

High School Our Students Usually Attend: N/A

Percentage of Seniors Attending College: 100

Additional Information

The Episcopal School of Dallas

North Campus: 4100 Merrell Road   Mapsco: 24K
                   Dallas, TX 75229
St. Michael Campus: 8011 Douglas Ave.
                   Dallas, TX 75225   Mapsco: 25X
(214) 358-5827   Fax: 353-5872

Office Hours: Switchboard 7:30 a.m.–5:00 p.m.
              Voice Mail: 24 hours
School Hours: 8:30 a.m.–3:30 p.m.
School Grades Offered: 3-year-olds–grade 12 (North Campus–
grades 5-12; Saint Michael Campus–3-year-olds-grade 4)
Enrollment: 994
Co-ed: Yes
Boy/Girl Ratio: 50:50
Student/Teacher Ratio: 8:1
Average Class Size: 17
Calendar School Year: August–May
Holidays: Labor Day, Yom Kippur, Fair Day, Thanksgiving,
Christmas, New Year's Day, Martin Luther King Day, winter
break, spring break, Easter, Memorial Day
Uniform Requirements: Yes
Founded in: North Campus–1974, Saint Michael Campus–1950
(The Saint Michael School and The Episcopal School of Dallas
merged in 1994.)

Philosophy of School

The Episcopal School of Dallas incorporates a commitment to Judeo-Christian values
within an excellent college-preparatory curriculum. The original intent, which remains
today, was to create a learning environment in which individual achievement is
measured against standards of excellence defined personally, not collectively. We
recognize academic achievement and excellence on an individual basis and define
achievement as that which is accomplished when students realize, strive for, and reach
their own potential.

Academic Curriculum

Content: A minimum of 20 credits are required for graduation including English (4 years); mathematics (3 years–Algebra I, geometry, Algebra II); history and science (3 years history–American and world history required; 2 years science–biology and chemistry required, or 3 years science–biology and chemistry required, and 2 years history–American and world); government (1 semester); economics (1 semester); foreign language (3 years of one language); fine arts (1 year); physical education (2 years, including 1 semester of health).

In addition to the course requirements for graduation, the following are also necessary for graduation:
1) four core courses each year chosen from English, mathematics, history, science, foreign language, and religion
2) good standing in school
3) daily attendance in chapel
4) successful participation in the Wilderness Program
5) successful participation in the student-services program
6) successful participation (50 hours) in the Community Service Program

Important: These are minimum graduation requirements.

Honors courses are offered in English, geometry, Algebra II, pre-calculus, chemistry, physics, and world history. Advanced placement courses are offered in English, AB calculus, BC calculus, biology, chemistry, American history, European history, American government, art history, French, Latin, Spanish, art (general portfolio and studio art), and history of art.
Grading System Used: Preschool-grade 3–comments; grades 4-12–letter grades
Conferences per Year: Two family conferences scheduled; additional conferences as needed
Tests Administered: ERB achievement tests for grades 3-8; placement tests required to determine eligibility for some academic courses; PSAT–grades 10-11; SAT I and II–grades 11-12; ACT–grades 11-12
Homework Policy: Grades 1-12 have scheduled homework.
Method of Discipline: Assistant School Heads, grades 9-12; Honor Council

Enrichment Curriculum

Advisory system, college guidance program, community and school service programs, daily chapel, Dallas Youth Commission, Duke Talented and Gifted Program, eighth-grade Williamsburg/Washington, D.C. trip, film symposium, Hugh O'Brien Leadership Conference, Japan-United States Senate Program, literary magazine, literary festival, Megan Girard Allday Lecture Series, newspaper, Roman banquet, seventh-grade archaeology trip, Southern Methodist University Women's Symposium, Southern

Methodist University Model U.N. Program, summer travel with faculty, Thanksgiving Square Youth Commission, visiting authors, wilderness camping program, yearbook

Extracurricular Activities

Students at The Episcopal School of Dallas have an opportunity to participate in 30 clubs and organizations: Acolytes, Archaelogy Club, Computer Science Club, Ex Libris, French Honor Society, Junior Classical League, Model United Nations, National Honor Society, Students Against Drunk Driving, Student Council, Ambassadors Club, Art Club, Cultural Awareness Club, Film Club, Honor Council, Lacrosse Club, Mu Alpha Theta, Outing Club, Spanish Club, Theater Guild, Amnesty International, Chess Club, Environmental and Recycling Club, French Club, *Itinerary,* Math Team National Forensic League, Press Club, Spirit Club, Whiz Quiz

Athletics: Lifetime health and fitness, as well as the development of teamwork and individual skills, are paramount for growth into a well-rounded individual. Our athletic program is flexible enough to accommodate the novice athlete, yet competitive enough to prepare more skilled athletes for higher levels of competition. The Episcopal Eagles compete in baseball, field hockey, softball, basketball, golf, tennis, crew, gymnastics, swimming, lacrosse, track and field, cross country, soccer, and volleyball against other independent prep schools in the Southwest Preparatory Conference and MISC.

Goals for Students

The mission of The Episcopal School of Dallas is to provide a college-preparatory program. This is best accomplished by providing a co-educational, faith-centered environment which fosters intellectual, spiritual, physical, emotional, and social maturity, as well as the precepts of responsibility and giving.

The Episcopal School of Dallas was created to structure the life of the community around the precepts of the Mission Statement. The Founding tenets of The Episcopal School of Dallas were created simultaneously with the original Mission Statement and are:

DAILY WORSHIP–allows recognition of God, the teachings of the Judeo-Christian heritage, and the personal and global contemporary issues which require personal and corporate prayer and responses.

EXPERIENCES OF COMMUNITY–allows the common needs of fellow human beings to be shared, lived, and discussed in advisories, wilderness, camping, and headmaster retreats.

STUDIES IN RELIGION–allows the development and inculcation of a belief system through structured, traditional classroom settings.

SERVICE TO OTHERS–allows students to experience the giving of their time to work on campus and in various service agencies throughout the city.

The Tenets of worship, an experience of community and study, prepare members of this community for the fourth Tenet—service, the highest manifestation of God's action in our lives.

Faculty/Staff Requirements

Qualifications of Staff: Master teachers with college degrees who are creative, innovative, and willing to be involved completely with the student body. Fifty-three have master's degrees and four have Ph.D.'s. Faculty members must be committed to serving college-bound students in a faith-centered community.
Qualifications of Administrator: The Reverend Stephen B. Swann is the founding Rector/Headmaster. Father Swann has a B.A. in psychology and a Master of Divinity degree from the Church Divinity.

School Information

Brochure Available: Yes
Number of Students in Each Grade: 3-year-olds–40; 4-year-olds–45; K–60; Primer–15; 1st–54; 2nd–51; 3rd–60; 4th–52; 5th–84; 6th–85; 7th–80; 8th–80; 9th–90; 10th–70; 11th–64; 12th–59
Parochial: Affiliated with, but not governed by, The Episcopal Diocese of Dallas
Organization Affiliations: Texas Independent School Conference; National Association of Episcopal Schools; Southwestern Association of Episcopal Schools; National Association of Independent Schools; Independent Schools Association of the Southwest (ISAS); College Board
Accreditations: The Episcopal School of Dallas is accredited by the Independent Schools Association of the Southwest whose accreditation is recognized by the Texas Education Agency; Southern Association of Episcopal Schools
Parental Involvement: Parents' Association
Other Information: In November 1994, The Saint Michael School and The Episcopal School of Dallas merged, combining more than 75 years of educational excellence.

Admittance

Whom to Contact: Kay Lane, Director of Admissions, (214) 353-5827
Date to Apply: Fall of the year preceding anticipated admission
Testing Procedure for Age/Grade Level: There are scheduled testing dates for grades 5–12; additional testing dates are scheduled if openings occur. Preschool–grade 4 are tested as openings occur.

Fees Involved: $75 application fee, $56 testing fee

Type of Student Preferred: College-bound students; each student is expected to make a commitment to the founding tenets of the school: religion, self-discipline, and sound learning.

Forms Required: Yes, parent essay

Individual/Group Appointments: Campus visits by students and their parents are strongly encouraged.

Notification Procedure: Grades 5-12 notified by letter sent in March; others within two weeks of evaluation

Waiting List Policy: Students accepted to a grade with no openings are placed in a wait pool.

Tuition

Approximate Tuition for 1996-97 School Year: $5350–$9750

Methods of Payment Available: A $1000 deposit is required upon acceptance with the balance due by July; Optional Payment Plan–20% of the total tuition plus insurance costs due in May, remaining balance billed over a ten-month period with 8% interest charged on the unpaid balance

Financial Assistance Offered: Yes

Cancellation Insurance Available: Yes

Profit/Non-profit: Non-profit

Additional Costs

Books/Bag/Uniform: Books–included in tuition; bag–optional; uniform–primer-grade 12 (costs vary)

Lunch Fee: Saint Michael Campus–included in tuition; North Campus–$545 per year (optional, contracted through Parents' Association)

Parents Club Dues: $25

Annual Fund Drive: Yes

Discount for Siblings: No

Facilities/Services Provided

Computer Lab: Yes

Library: Yes

Snack Procedures: Saint Michael Campus–provided; North Campus–parent-operated snack bar open before school, during lunch, and after school

Before-school Care Program Available: Yes

After-school Care Program Available: Yes, until 6 p.m.

Nurse on Staff: No

Emergency Procedure Used: The school complies with individual family's wishes as detailed on the health forms.

Transportation to and from School: Car pool
Counseling and Evaluation Available: Yes

Graduation Information

Testing: Achievement testing; some placement testing
Average SAT Scores: 1995 graduating class: SAT range–930-1410, ACT range–20-31
High School Our Students Usually Attend: N/A
Percentage of Seniors Attending College: 100%

Additional Information

Fort Worth Country Day School

4200 Country Day Lane
Fort Worth, TX 76109
(817) 732-7718

Mapsco: 88H
(Fort Worth Mapsco)
Fax: (817) 377-3425

Office Hours: 8:00 a.m.–4:30 p.m.
School Hours: 8:20 a.m.–3:20 p.m. (k–6); 8:20 a.m.–3:40 p.m.
(7–8); 8:20 a.m.–dismissal time varies by sport (upper school)
School Grades Offered: Kindergarten–12
Enrollment: 985
Co-ed: Yes
Boy/Girl Ratio: 47:53
Student/Teacher Ratio: 10:1
Average Class Size: 15–20
Calendar School Year: Late August through May
Holidays: One week at Thanksgiving, two weeks at
Christmas, one week in March
Uniform Requirements: Yes
Founded in: 1962

Philosophy of School

The mission of Fort Worth Country Day School is to provide education of the highest
quality. In carrying out its mission, Fort Worth Country Day School strives to:

- foster and encourage its students' development through an academically
  rigorous liberal arts curriculum in grades k–12, with particular emphasis on
  preparation for college and life in a world of increasing international
  interdependence

- provide a broad and demanding academic curriculum that includes diverse
  programs in the fine arts, physical education, and athletics

97

- encourage its students to become active learners, to think critically, to question assumptions, and to take intellectual risks

- respect and nurture its students' independence and self-esteem by providing meaningful work and establishing challenging academic, physical, and personal goals for all members of its community

- value high ethical standards and appreciate human differences, social and ethnic diversity, and altruism

The heart of Fort Worth Country Day education is to make learning an exhilarating, cooperative experience that can be carried on for a lifetime.

Academic Curriculum

Content: College-preparatory curriculum with strong programs in arts, athletics, foreign language, computer (required k–12); 12 advanced-placement courses
Grading System Used: Varies by division
Conferences per Year: As needed in upper school; twice a year in lower and middle schools
Tests Administered: Standardized testing each spring (grades k–9); grades 10–12 take PSAT and SAT several times.
Homework Policy: Daily homework assignments
Method of Discipline: Not a major issue

Enrichment Curriculum

Many enrichment activities are incorporated into the school curriculum. Included are choirs, orchestras, school newspapers, ballet, jazz band, theater, technical theater, art, photography, yearbook, literary magazine, French, and Spanish.

Extracurricular Activities

More than 30 clubs and activities–AFS (foreign student exchange), Computer Club, *Cum Laude* Society, Debate Club, Falcon Force (spirit club), French Club, Natural Helpers, Outdoor Club, Ecology Club, Operation Outreach, Science Fair, Students Against Drunk Driving (SADD), Whiz Quiz, cheerleaders, various honor societies

Team sports–volleyball, field hockey, football, cross country track, basketball, soccer, wrestling, baseball, softball, track, golf, tennis

Goals for Students

College preparation; intellectual risk-taking; independence; altruism; participation in a variety of activities

Faculty/Staff Requirements

Qualifications of Staff: Four have Ph.D.'s; 72% of faculty have advanced degrees (80% of upper school faculty)
Qualifications of Administrator: S. Graham Brown, Headmaster; B.A., Hobart College; M.Ed.,Trinity College, CT

School Information

Brochure Available: Yes
Number of Students in Each Grade: Approximately 75–80 in all grade levels 65–75 (grades 6–12)
Parochial: No
Organization Affiliations: TANS, College Board, NAPSG
Accreditations: ISAS
Parental Involvement: Yes
Other Information:

Admittance

Whom to Contact: William Arnold or Barbara Jiongo, Admissions
Date to Apply: January 31 for kindergarten; the middle of March for other grades
Testing Procedure per Age/Grade Level: Jan.–Feb. for kindergarten; Feb.–March and May for grades 1–12
Fees Involved: Yes
Type of Student Preferred: Bright and motivated
Forms Required: Yes
Individual/Group Appointments: Both
Notification Procedure: Kindergarten--by letter (approximately March 1); grades 1-12 (within two weeks of completing application process)
Waiting List Policy: Yes

Tuition

Approximate Tuition for 1996-97 School Year: $7500–$8500 (depending on grade level)
Methods of Payment Available: One payment (1 1/2% discount), or two payments, or 10 payments ($50 fee)
Financial Assistance Offered: Yes

Cancellation Insurance Available: Yes
Profit/Non-profit: Non-profit

Additional Costs

Books/Bag/Uniform: Books $140–$580 (depending on grade); uniform costs vary
Lunch Fee: No
Parents Club Dues: No
Annual Fund Drive: Yes
Discount for Siblings: No

Facilities/Services Provided

Computer Lab: Three in library; one in lower school; two in middle school
Library: Large free-standing library building/technology center
Snack Procedures: Provided for kindergarten students
Before-school Care Program Available: No
After-school Care Program Available: Yes
Nurse on Staff: Yes
Emergency Procedure Used: Described in school handbooks
Transportation to and from School: From Arlington and the mid-cities
Counseling and Evaluation Available: Yes

Graduation Information

Testing: SAT, ACT, Advanced Placement
Average SAT Scores: 1190
High School Our Students Usually Attend: N/A
Percentage of Seniors Attending College: 100

Additional Information

Set on 88 acres, the Fort Worth Country Day School campus includes five classroom buildings, two gymnasiums, a cafeteria, a ballet studio, art and music buildings, an administration building, a challenge course, and extensive athletic fields. We invite and encourage prospective students and their families to visit and tour our facilities. Call for information and an appointment.

Good Shepherd
Episcopal School

Providing an excellent education while emphasizing personal ethics and individual responsibility in a close, nurturing environment.

- Pre-kindergarten through 8th grade
- Exemplary fine arts and outdoor education programs
- Accredited by I.S.A.S. and S.A.E.S.
- U.S. "Blue Ribbon School of Excellence"

We invite you to explore the possibilities of joining us!

11122 Midway Road at Northaven
Dallas, TX 75229-4119
(214)-357-1610   Fax 357-4105

Good Shepherd Episcopal School

11122 Midway Road
Dallas, TX 75229-4118
(214) 357-1610

Mapsco: 24F

Fax: (214) 357-4105

Office Hours: 7:45 a.m.–4:00 p.m.
School Hours: 8:00 a.m.–3:30 p.m.
School Grades Offered: Pre-K–grade 8
Enrollment: 520
Co-ed: Yes
Boy/Girl Ratio: 1:1
Student/Teacher Ratio: 10/12:1 (preschool); 15:1
(kindergarten); 20/21:1 (grades 1–8)
Average Class Size: 12 (pre-K); 15 (kindergarten);
20-21 (grades 1–8)
Calendar School Year: August 18, 1996–May 23, 1997
Holidays: Labor Day, Fair Day, Thanksgiving (3 days),
Christmas (2 1/2 weeks), winter break (2 days), spring
break (1 week), Good Friday (1 day), Monday after
Easter, Memorial Day
Uniform Requirements: Yes
Founded in: 1959

Philosophy of School

Mission Statement: Good Shepherd Episcopal School is a coeducational parish day school that seeks to equip students with Christian principles, a love of learning, a creative mind, and a giving spirit. The academic program is strong and serious. It aims to develop students' problem-solving and higher level thinking skills. In addition to providing a strong academic program, the education offered seeks to develop a well-rounded personality and a high standard of moral integrity attained through growth in self-discipline. Central to the mission is the concern for the development of the whole child with a commitment to an environment characterized by seriousness of purpose, love of learning, and a spirit of creativity.

Academic Curriculum

Content: The preschool is a developmental program organized into learning centers and activities involving challenging materials and experiences. The classrooms become laboratories where children explore and experiment. The centers make possible both small-group instruction areas and quiet nooks where children can work and play.

The primer class provides a step between kindergarten and first grade for those children who need this gift of time to grow. The class gives the children the freedom to develop naturally at their own developmental rates.

The elementary classes (primer through fourth grade) are self-contained. Students receive instruction in reading, language arts, spelling, handwriting, math, science, social studies, health, and safety. Specialized teachers offer art, music, physical education, and Spanish to all students.

The middle school, grades five through eight, is departmentalized. Each year a student takes one class period each of language arts, math, science, social studies, Spanish, and physical education, and one semester each of art and music.

Grading System Used: Narrative progress reports are used for preschool students; mastery notations are used for primer through second grade; letter grades are used in grades three through five; numerical grades are used in grades six through eight.
Conferences per Year: Two scheduled for preschool through fourth grades; three parent-student-teacher conferences scheduled for grades five through eight; others scheduled as necessary
Tests Administered: Educational Records Bureau achievement tests given annually
Homework Policy: Students regularly receive homework assignments which normally must be finished outside the classroom. The purpose of this homework is to prepare students for future classroom activities and to review and reinforce the lessons taught in school. Homework is also a method to develop work and study habits that will benefit students throughout their years in school.
Method of Discipline: Based on individual needs of student

Enrichment Curriculum

Daily physical education, art or music instruction, library, and Spanish are offered. Computer instruction is connected with the academic curriculum. In addition, the Classroom of the Earth, an extensive outdoor-education program that begins with day hikes in primer and culminates with a ten-day trip to Colorado in eighth grade, is an integral part of the program.

Extracurricular Activities

Student Council, National Junior Honor Society, Odyssey of the Mind, athletics, and clubs, such as Yearbook, Spanish, Service, Science, Computer, Literary, Current Events, and Art

Goals for Students

To produce students who are well-rounded spiritually, physically, and mentally and have a lifelong desire for learning

Faculty/Staff Requirements

Qualifications of Staff: Minimum: bachelor's degree and teaching certificate
Qualifications of Administrator: Mr. J. Robert Kohler, B.A., Austin College; M.A., Southern Methodist University

School Information

Brochure Available: Yes
Number of Students in Each Grade: Varies: 12 in pre-K, 15/class in kindergarten, 20-22/class in grades 1–8
Parochial: Affiliated with Episcopal Church of the Good Shepherd
Organization Affiliations: National Association of Independent Schools, Independent Schools Association of the Southwest, National Association of Episcopal Schools, Texas Association of Non-Public Schools, National Council of Teachers of Mathematics, Council for the Advancement of Support of Education, Educational Records Bureau, and Southwestern Association of Episcopal Schools
Accreditations: Independent Schools Association of the Southwest and Southwestern Association of Episcopal Schools
Parental Involvement: Yes; there are various opportunities for parents to donate their time and talents.
Other Information:

Admittance

Whom to Contact: Nancy Lawrence
Date to Apply: After September 1 for the subsequent school year
Testing Procedure per Age/Grade Level: Individualized testing for preschool and kindergarten; Children's Hospital of San Francisco Metropolitan Readiness Test for first grade; Educational Records Bureau testing for grades two through five; ISEE scores required for grades six thorugh eight
Fees Involved: A $50 application fee is nonrefundable.

Type of Student Preferred: Academically capable, motivated by a love of learning
Forms Required: Completed application, teacher recommendation form(s), current health history, school transcript including most recent grades, standardized test scores
Individual/Group Appointments: Group tours are given weekly to interested parents; student visits are arranged by appointment.
Notification Procedure: Letter and/or telephone call
Waiting List Policy: Students placed on wait list are viable candidates for admission for the next school year; you must re-apply for admission for the upcoming school year

Tuition

Approximate Tuition for 1996-97 School Year: $3916–$5308; enrollment fee (required of all new students) $350–$750
Methods of Payment Available: Annually, by semester, or monthly
Financial Assistance Offered: Yes
Cancellation Insurance Available: Yes
Profit/Non-profit: Non-profit

Additional Costs

Books/Bag/Uniform: Books–no fee; bag–no fee; uniform–$50-$100
Lunch Fee: Optional
Parents Club Dues: No fee
Annual Fund Drive: Yes
Discount for Siblings: No

Facilities/Services Provided

Computer Lab: The main computer lab is equipped with 22 Macintosh computers networked with six printers. Additionally, each classroom on the campus is equipped with a Macintosh computer; two elementary auxiliary computer labs are used to support this classroom computer use. These classroom computers and labs are used to support, enhance, and enrich the classroom curriculum. The library media lab is equipped with 8 PC workstations for library card catalog and electronic research capabilities.
Library: The goal of the library is to create a place of warmth, acceptance, learning, and excitement. A friendly facility including approximately 13,000 volumes, computerized circulation, and networked computers for card catalog and CD ROM research has been designed around these goals.
Snack Procedures: Pre-K–kindergarten: provided by school; primer–grade 8: provided by students
Before-school Care Program Available: No

After-school Care Program Available: Afternoon enrichment program for pre-kindergarten through fourth grades, from school dismissal until 6:00 p.m.
Nurse on Staff: No
Emergency Procedure Used: Medical release forms on file; parents are always contacted; paramedics summoned, if necessary
Transportation to and from School: No
Counseling and Evaluation Available: Yes

Graduation Information

Testing: N/A
Average SAT Scores: N/A
High School Our Students Usually Attend: During the past five years, our graduates have chosen to attend Bishop Lynch High School, Cistercian Preparatory School, Dallas Arts Magnet, Episcopal School of Dallas, Greenhill School, The Hockaday School, Jesuit College Preparatory School, Lakehill Preparatory School, Lutheran High School, St. Mark's School of Texas, Trinity Christian Academy, Ursuline Academy, and W.T. White High School
Percentage of Seniors Attending College: N/A

Additional Information

Good Shepherd Episcopal School offers an education serious in principles, strong in academics, and rich in the spirit of love and life. The academic program is strong and serious, preparing students for college-preparatory high school programs following graduation. Daily chapel services offer a foundation in moral integrity and values. An outstanding fine arts program helps children develop an understanding of their creative nature. Through the Classroom of the Earth, students learn skills and discover physical capabilities, make decisions and stretch their talents, and, above all, experience the fun and joy of the outdoor world.

We welcome you to our campus and encourage you to make an appointment for a tour.

Greenhill School

14255 Midway Road
Dallas, TX 75244
(214) 661-1211

Mapsco: 14P

Fax: (214) 404-8217

Office Hours: 8:00 a.m.–4:30 p.m.
School Hours: 8:00 a.m.–3:35 p.m.
School Grades Offered: Preschool (3 1/2 years)–grade 12
Enrollment: 1220
Co-ed: Yes
Boy/Girl Ratio: 51:49
Student/Teacher Ratio: 13:1
Average Class Size: 18
Calendar School Year: Follow ISAS calendar (August–May)
Holidays: Thanksgiving, 3 days; December, 2 weeks; spring break, 1 week; national holidays
Uniform Requirements: None
Founded in: 1950

Philosophy of School

Greenhill School is an independent, non-sectarian, coeducational, non-profit institution whose purpose is to provide an excellent education to select students. Greenhill School has a strong academic orientation, and its primary objective is to generate true excitement in learning for each student. Virtually all graduates of Greenhill continue their studies at the college level; therefore, Greenhill strives to offer a college-preparatory program of distinction.

Academic Curriculum

Content: Varies at grade level
Grading System Used: Through grade 4, comments; grades 5–12, letter grades and comments

Conferences per Year : Two
Tests Administered: Achievement testing; some placement testing in math and languages
Homework Policy: Through grade 4, evening review; grades 5-8, 1 1/2 hours each evening; grades 9-12, 3 hours or as needed
Method of Discipline: Conferencing; parental participation; accountabilities/ detentions; suspension; most severe–expulsion

Enrichment Curriculum

Music lessons, after-school programs (K–grade 6), Quizbowl teams, Duke Talented and Gifted Program, field trips, experiential activities at all levels, visiting authors, lecture series, visiting artists, and artists-in-residence

Extracurricular Activities

Drama, music, debate, clubs, cheerleading, literary magazines, service organizations, student government, newspapers, concerts, visiting authors

Goals for Students

Greenhill has a strong academic orientation, and its primary objective is to generate true excitement in learning for each student.

Faculty/Staff Requirements

Qualifications of Staff: Degree from accredited college; 65% of faculty hold advanced degrees, 10% have Ph.D. degrees.
Qualifications of Administrator: Same

School Information

Brochure Available: Yes
Number of Students in Each Grade: Varies from 80 to 105
Parochial: No
Organization Affiliations: No religious affiliation; member NAIS, ISAS, SSATB, ERB, NAPSG, TANS, and College Board
Accreditations: ISAS, TEA
Parental Involvement: Yes

Admittance

Whom to Contact: Thomas Perryman, Director of Admissions
Date to Apply: September through mid-February; decisions made mid-March

Testing Procedure per Age/Grade Level: Group testing December-February; testing scheduled on first-come basis

Fees Involved: $100 application fee; separate testing for grades 6–12

Type of Student Preferred: Students scoring in the top 20% on achievement tests who have a diverse range of interests, skills, or activities.

Forms Required: Application, parental/student statements, teacher (math and language arts) recommendations, transcripts; grades 5–12, one-day visit and interview

Individual/Group Appointments: Group appointments for tours, campus previews, group testing

Notification Procedure: Written correspondence in mid-March; late applications, phone calls and correspondence as soon as all information/testing is completed and admissions committees can be re-convened (approximately three weeks)

Waiting List Policy: Wait Pool for summer–re-apply; letter sent to parents

Tuition

Approximate Tuition for 1996-97 School Year: Preschool, $4685; kindergarten, $6970; primer–grade 6, $8535; grades 7–12, $10,025

Methods of Payment Available: Tuition deposit $1000 upon enrollment; remainder due by July 1

Financial Assistance Offered: Financial aid is need-based with special loan programs also available.

Cancellation Insurance Available: Yes

Profit/Non-profit: Non-profit

Additional Costs

Books/Bag/Uniform: Grades 9–12–books extra (approximately $375); Senior Assessment Fee $110 (seniors only); bag is included for grades 1-8 and optional for grades 9-12; uniforms, not required

Lunch Fee: Grades primer-6, $575/year; grades 7-12, $675/year

Parents Club Dues: $25 per year

Annual Fund Drive: Yes

Discount for Siblings: No

Facilities/Services Provided

Computer Lab: Middle and Upper School, Upper School writing lab

Library: Yes

Snack Procedures: Preschool/Lower School–snacks provided by school; snack bar in Upper School for students to purchase snacks

Before-school Care Program Available: Yes, 7:00 a.m.

After-school Care Program Available: Yes, 6:00 p.m.

Nurse on Staff: Yes
Emergency Procedure Used: Parental permission slip on file for emergency treatment
Transportation to and from School: Car pools
Counseling and Evaluation Available: Yes

Graduation Information

Testing: Achievement testing, some placement testing
Average SAT Scores: Verbal 586, math 624–median score; approximately 30 % of class receives national merit recognition
High School Our Students Usually Attend: N/A
Percentage of Seniors Attending College: 100

Additional Information

Greenhill School is considered to be the finest co-ed college preparatory school in the Southwest. Greenhill was named an "Exemplary School" by the U.S. Department of Education in June 1985. Greenhill was the first private school in North Texas to be so recognized. A number of Greenhill's educational approaches and programs have received national recognition the last 16 years: 1) pioneering grade-level team-teaching groups; 2) creative educational programs in the arts and the humanities; 3) integrating motor development in elementary curriculum; 4) leadership in the establishment of the primer class (transition between kindergarten and first grade); 5) leadership in computer education in the Metroplex.

For further information, Greenhill is also listed in the *Harvard Insiders' Guide to Prep Schools*, Bunting and Lyons, and numerous other publications.

The Hockaday School

11600 Welch Road
Dallas, TX 75229
(214) 363-6311

Mapsco: 24C

Fax: (214) 363-0942

Office Hours: 8:30 a.m.–5:00 p.m.
School Hours: 8:00 a.m.–3:45 p.m.
School Grades Offered: Preschool–grade 12
Enrollment: 986
Co-ed: No
Boy/Girl Ratio: N/A
Student/Teacher Ratio: 10:1
Average Class Size: 15
Calendar School Year: August–June
Holidays: Thanksgiving, Christmas, winter break, spring
break, Easter, and other single-day religious/school breaks
Uniform Requirements: Yes
Founded in: 1913

Philosophy of School

The Hockaday School, founded in 1913, provides a college-preparatory education for girls of strong potential who may be expected to assume positions of responsibility and leadership in a rapidly changing world.

Through small classes, individualized instruction, creative teaching, and an approach which emphasizes the process of learning, Hockaday seeks to discover unique aptitudes in and to awaken the intellectual curiosity of every student.

Through a strong physical education program and the challenge of competitive sports, Hockaday seeks to develop in each girl an enthusiastic spirit, a healthy body, and a sense of responsibility for herself and her actions.

Through continual exposure to the arts, Hockday seeks to engender an appreciation of beauty that will bring added enrichment to each girl's life.

Academic Curriculum

Content: Graduation trimester credit requirements include English,12; mathematics, 9; history, 7; foreign language, 6; laboratory science, 6; fine arts, 5; and academic electives, 6. In addition, physical education is required of every girl each year. Each student must demonstrate proficiency in using applications software, such as word processing, databases, and spreadsheets. Among the more than 78 elective courses are anthropology, creative writing, law, economics, philosophy, psychology, bioethics and biochemistry. Fine arts offerings include drama, choir, dance, art, photography, ceramics, video-media, orchestra, and d ebate. Private music instruction is available in piano, flute, violin, cello, guitar, and voice.

Grading System Used: A–F

Conferences per Year: Two, three, or four scheduled; others upon request

Tests Administered: Yes

Homework Policy: Daily, varies by grade

Method of Discipline: Honor Council

Enrichment Curriculum

Advanced placement courses are offered in English, modern European history, United States history, AB and BC calculus, physics, chemistry, biology, computer science, micro/macro economics, studio art, German, Latin, French, and Spanish. For some selected courses, Hockaday has a cooperative program with St. Mark's School of Texas, a Dallas boys' school. Opportunity for further academic exploration at Hockaday is available through an optional tutorial program based on the European system of student-conceived, teacher-directed courses. The coed summer session also offers a broad range of enrichment courses.

Extracurricular Activities

32 special-interest organizations and honor societies, English and Spanish literary and journalistic magazines, a video magazine, a newspaper, and the Hockaday yearbook; 12 varsity sports

Goals for Students

Hockaday seeks to develop in each girl a life-long love of learning. Through the provision of a challenging college preparatory program and broad elective and extracurricular opportunities, Hockaday prepares girls of strong potential for positions of leadership and responsibility in their communities.

Faculty/Staff Requirements

Qualifications of Staff: The majority of the faculty has advanced degrees; seven

have Ph.D.'s.
Qualifications of Administrator: Elizabeth M. Lee, B.A., Mount Holyoke; M.A., Columbia University; Ms. Lee has been an educator and administrator for over 25 years.

School Information
Brochure Available: Yes
Number of Students in Each Grade: Varies
Parochial: No
Organization Affiliations: National Association of Independent Schools, College Board, National Coalition of Girls' Schools, Independent Schools Association of the SW
Accreditations: Independent Schools Association of the Southwest
Parental Involvement: The Hockaday Parents' Association
Other Information:

Admittance
Whom to Contact: Ms. Jen Liggitt
Date to Apply: Fall
Testing Procedure per Age/Grade Level: Admissions testing appropriate to grade level; group testing except for pre-kindergarten and kindergarten
Fees Involved: Testing 6–12, $56; application fee, $75
Type of Student Preferred: Students with diversified interests and a high degree of motivation
Forms Required: Yes
Individual/Group Appointments: Individual appointments; campus visits encouraged; open houses; boarding visitations
Notification Procedure: In March
Waiting List Policy: Inquire with Hockaday; for further information, please contact the Office of Admissions at (214) 363-6311.

Tuition
Approximate Tuition for 1996-97 School Year: $4260–$11,470; boarding tuition, 8th-11th–$20,540; 12th–$21,000; international boarding, 8th-11th–$22,140; 12th–$22,600
Methods of Payment Available: Tuition due July 1
Financial Assistance Offered: Yes, need-based
Cancellation Insurance Available: Yes, tuition refund insurance
Profit/Non-profit: Non-profit

Additional Costs

Books/Bag/Uniform: Books–lower school: $100; middle school (5–8): $100–$200; upper school (9–12): $200–$400; Bag–N/A; uniform–cost varies, depending on grade
Lunch Fee: Lunch and fees are required, $195–$1645, misc. trips, etc.
Parents Club Dues: $15 (includes school directory)
Annual Fund Drive: Optional
Discount for Siblings: No

Facilities/Services Provided

Computer Lab: Three labs (one for lower, middle, and upper school); a total of 250 computers
Library: 50,000 volume library with separate lower/middle school library
Snack Procedures: School provides fresh fruit daily
Before-school Care Program Available: No
After-school Care Program Available: Yes, until 6:00 p.m.
Nurse on Staff: Yes
Emergency Procedure Used: Yes
Transportation to and from School: Families arrange their own transportation
Counseling and Evaluation Available: Yes

Graduation Information

Testing: No
Average SAT Scores: Verbal 530–660; math 630–680
High School Our Students Usually Attend: N/A
Percentage of Seniors Attending College: 100

Additional Information

The Hockaday School was founded in 1913 by Miss Ela Hockaday. Miss Hockaday took great care in implementing the four cornerstones of the school--character, scholarship, courtesy, and athletics--as guidelines by which the staff and students would live. They are still in place today and as vital to the school as they were 82 years ago.

Our philosophy and purpose is to provide our students with a college-preparatory education which will enable them to assume positions of responsibility and leadership in a rapidly changing world. One hundred percent of our graduates go on to college. They attend some of the most competitive colleges and universities in the country.

Our curriculum includes Advanced Placement courses in the sciences, history, mathematics, foreign languages, fine arts, and English. Hockaday offers more than 130 courses. Class size averages 15 students with an overall student-teacher ratio of 10:1. Our faculty is composed of 22 men and 82 women, the majority of whom have advanced degrees. They have an average of 17 years of teaching experience. There are 26 part-time teachers.

Our campus is located at the corner of Forest Lane and Welch Road and extends over 100 acres. Our facilities include a 50,000-volume library, and a fine arts wing with a complete ceramics studio, photography lab, painting studio, music rooms, and art gallery. To accommodate 12 competitive sports, there are two superbly equipped gyms with racquetball courts and dance studio, one indoor pool and one outdoor pool, three playing fields, and a tennis center with ten courts. The science building has extensive lab facilities, a greenhouse, and a computer lab.

Our co-ed summer programs offer a good introduction to Hockaday in a relaxed learning environment. Students may enroll in academic programs as well as art, theater, sports, English-as-a-Second-Language, and science camps.

An English-as-a-Second-Language program offers international students the opportunity to improve their English. Many students continue at Hockaday after completing this one-year program by applying for and receiving admission into the regular program. Students from ten countries attend Hockaday currently.

Each year families from all over the world send their daughters to Hockaday. They want to provide them with the best education possible in a safe and secure environment. Experienced and dedicated women provide care and guidance for the girls on the dorm halls. The nursing staff supervises the infirmary located in the dorm. The director of residence oversees the well-being of each girl and maintains ongoing communication with parents. Additional support for the boarding students is continued through the advisory and counseling programs of the school. On- and off-campus activities are offered on the weekends and on some weekday nights. Tutors provide additional support during evening study periods.
The two-story, air-conditioned residence halls have been updated with newly decorated double rooms, individual lounges, kitchens, and laundry facilities on each floor. Food service is outstanding.

We welcome you to our school and encourage you to make an appointment to tour our campus. We also encourage you to attend any of our weekend open-house programs or weekday classroom visitations beginning in October.

Lakehill Preparatory School

2720 Hillside Drive
Dallas, TX 75214
(214) 826-2931

Mapsco: 36M

Fax: (214) 826-4623

Office Hours: 7:45 a.m.–4:30 p.m.
School Hours: 8:15 a.m.–3:15 p.m.
School Grades Offered: Kindergarten–12
Enrollment: 255
Co-ed: Yes
Boy/Girl Ratio: Approximately equal
Student/Teacher Ratio: 10:1
Average Class Size: Maximum for K–16; grades 1-4–18;
middle school and high school–23
Calendar School Year: Third week in August to last week
in May
Holidays: All major holidays
Uniform Requirements: Dress code enforced; no uniforms
Founded in: 1970; first session in 1971

Philosophy of School

Traditional college-preparatory accelerated curriculum offered in a nurturing, supportive learning environment designed to optimize individual potential

Academic Curriculum

Content: College-preparatory accelerated curriculum
Grading System Used: Six-week reports; letter grades (A-F) in grades 4–12
Conferences per Year: Fall and spring formal conferences; other conferences as needed
Tests Administered: Stanford Achievement Tests, K–8; PSAT, grades 9–11; SAT, grades 11–12
Homework Policy: Appropriate homework required at every grade level
Method of Discipline: Positive reinforcement with clearly defined rules and expectations; discipline selected to guide students toward appropriate choices

Enrichment Curriculum
Field trips, activities, speakers, assemblies, literary magazine, service projects, yearbook, Middle School Adventure Club, Upper School Elective Exploration (London, 1995), Celebration of the Arts, Spring Fling, Invention Convention, Science Olympiad

Educational travel: Galveston (biology); New Mexico (ancient history); Atlanta (American history); Texas tour (Texas history).

Extracurricular Activities
Service and curricular clubs, Pan American Student Forum, drama, art, publication staff, orchestra (grades 3–8), computers, class organizations, student council, middle-school activity periods, Fall Day Out, Mu Alpha Theta; complete athletic program begins in fifth grade (no try-outs) and includes soccer, football, basketball, baseball, softball, volleyball, tennis, track, and cheerleading.

Goals for Students
To develop academically, socially, physically, and aesthetically into successful, happy adults. Academically, all students are college bound.

Faculty/Staff Requirements
Qualifications of Staff: College degree required; experience preferred
Qualifications of Administrator: Advanced degree required; experience required

School Information
Brochure Available: Yes, call (214) 826-2931.
Number of Students in Each Grade: Kindergarten classes limited to 16 students; classes in grades 1–4 are limited to 18 students; classes in grades 5–12 are limited to 23 students.
Parochial: No
Organization Affiliations: National Association of Secondary School Principals; Texas Association of Secondary School Principals; National Middle School Association; Associates for Research in Private Education; Independent School Management; many subject-area and curriculum-related affiliations; Association for Supervision and Curriculum Development; ISAS Admissions Group; Dallas Area Association of Admissions Directors
Accreditations: Independent Schools Association of the Southwest (ISAS); Southern Association of Colleges and Schools (SACS)
Parental Involvement: Parent-Faculty Club, Room Parents, field trip chaperones, annual auction, carnival, scout sponsors, coaches, annual fund drive, capital fund drive. We expect, encourage, and enjoy our parents' involvement.
Other Information:

Admittance

Whom to Contact: Dianne Harris, Assistant Head of School

Date to Apply: Primary dates for applications: September through December for next fall enrollment; rolling admissions policy

Testing Procedure per Age/Grade Level: K–morning session for group and individual assessment; grades 1–12, standardized testing session with small groups

Fees Involved: $50 application and testing fee

Type of Student Preferred: Average, above-average, and superior college-bound students with good school and behavioral records and recommendations

Forms Required: Applications, student questionnaires, essays, recommendations, school records, interview

Individual/Group Appointments: Either

Notification Procedure: Within 10 days of completing tests and application requirements

Waiting List Policy: Re-apply following year with priority status

Tuition

Approximate Tuition for 1996-97 School Year: Ranges from $5825 for kindergarten to $8075 for upper school

Methods of Payment Available: Payment in full; monthly payments with interest

Financial Assistance Offered: Need-based financial assistance available; apply by April 1st.

Cancellation Insurance Available: No

Profit/Non-Profit: Non-profit

Additional Costs

Books/Bag/Uniform: Books–cost varies from $150 to $500 yearly, depending upon grade level and courses selected; bag; p.e. uniform required

Lunch Fee: Lunch may be purchased daily or brought from home.

Uniform Requirements/Cost: Uniforms are not required, but a dress code is enforced.

Parents Club Dues: PFC dues vary depending upon the level of participation.

Annual Fund Drive: Yes, all families are expected to contribute according to their ability.

Discount for Siblings: 5%

Facilities/Services Provided

Computer Lab: An up-to-date computer lab is available for individual and class use. It operates on a Novell network, and includes CD ROM capability and multiple data-base accessibility for research and information. Computer instruction begins in middle school. Students are required to take computer classes and show programming ability prior to graduation. Advanced programming courses are available in the upper school. Multiple computers are located in each of the lower school classrooms for students' use. Seven computers are also available for use in the library. Lakehill has a ratio of one computer per six students.

Library: Lakehill maintains two libraries: one for lower school and one for middle and upper school students. Combined book collections total more than 19,000 volumes. The libraries are being computerized with completion during the 1995-96 school year. The research and study materials in the libraries are enhanced through access to multiple computerized data-bases and CD ROM software.

Snack Procedures: Kindergarten and first-grade students have daily snacks of wholesome foods. Other grades have snacks at various times.

Before-school Care Program Available: Supervision begins at 7:50 a.m. No before-school care program is offered.

After-school Care Program Available: Yes, until 6:00 p.m. An additional fee is required.

Nurse on Staff: No

Emergency Procedure Used: First aid provided; parents called; emergency form consulted

Transportation to and from School: Car pools suggested

Counseling and Evaluation Available: Yes, also referrals as needed

Graduation Information

Testing: PSAT, SAT, College Board Achievement Tests, ACT
Average SAT Scores: 1095
High School Our Students Usually Attend: N/A
Percentage of Seniors Attending College: 100%

Additional Information

Lakehill is the only kindergarten–12 college preparatory school east of Central Expressway, conveniently located between beautiful White Rock Lake and Central Expressway. The school is fully accredited by both ISAS and SACS. College board scores in 1995 averaged 1095. All graduates are college-bound, attending colleges and universities across the country. Eleven percent of the graduates since 1986 have received national merit recognition. A ten-year profile of graduating classes is available by request.

Lakehill began classes in 1971 as a school for average-to-superior students seeking an accelerated learning environment. Beginning at age 5 in kindergarten, students progress through a strong, traditional college-preparatory curriculum which culminates in their graduation from high school with a solid foundation in all subject areas.

120

Supplementing the academic curriculum, a wide variety of activities enable students to experience what they learn. These activities include school and community-service projects, class organizations, clubs, field trips, and special events. Adventure Week (Middle School) and Elective Explorations (Upper School) provide opportunities for students to travel with teachers so they might experience other cultures, traditions, and history.

A widely acclaimed athletic program in the middle and upper schools encourages all students to participate through a "no-try-out" policy. The program emphasizes physical conditioning, discipline, teamwork, and sportsmanship. Varsity teams regularly advance to district, region, and state levels.

The Lakehill faculty members believe strongly in all students' worth, dignity, and ability to achieve. They strive to provide opportunities for students not only to learn academic material, but also to develop self-confidence, self-esteem, personal responsibility, integrity, and character. The hallmark of the school is the supportive and nurturing environment that enables students to go about the business of learning.

One of our students described Lakehill this way:

> Many of my friends ask why I love Lakehill so much. My answer is: "It's small enough to get extra help when you need it; the academics are great; the preparation for college is super; the students and faculty are close; there's a chance to participate in anything you want... But there is no answer I can give to make them know how good my school is unless they come and experience it."

So, we invite you: Come and experience LPS!

The Lamplighter School

11611 Inwood Rd.
Dallas, TX 75229
(214) 369-9201

Mapsco: 24D

Fax: (214) 369-5540

Office Hours: 8:00 a.m.–4:00 p.m.
School Hours: 8:15 a.m.–3:15 p.m.
School Grades Offered: Preschool (3-year-olds)–grade 4
Enrollment: 450
Co-ed: Yes
Boy/Girl Ratio: 1:1
Student/Teacher Ratio: Preschool and kindergarten–10:1;
grades 1-4–14:1
Average Class Size: 12
Calendar School Year: Late August–end of May
Holidays: Labor Day, Yom Kippur, fall break (Columbus
Day observed), Thanksgiving, Christmas and New Year's
break, Martin Luther King Day, mid-winter break
(Presidents' Day observed), spring break, Good Friday,
Easter Monday, Memorial Day
Uniform Requirements: No
Founded in: 1953

Philosophy of School

The Lamplighter School is concerned with the worth and the potential of each individual and is dedicated to equipping its students with the knowledge necessary to understand the problems of today's world and with the skills they are encouraged to use in helping to solve these problems.

Academic Curriculum

Content: Language arts (reading, writing, spelling, composition, grammar, vocabulary, literature); mathematics (numerical concepts, computational skills); science, social studies

Grading System Used: Progress through curricula continuum reported at conferences and by parents' observation of classes via one-way glass windows into classrooms

Conferences per Year: Three per year scheduled; others as needed

Tests Administered: Individually administered readiness assessments for preschool and kindergarten; Educational Records Bureau Comprehensive Testing Program administered to grades 1-4

Homework Policy: When assigned, homework offers practice and opportunities for learning and is an exercise in accepting responsibility. Assignments may be made at all levels with consideration given to student's age, amount of time required to complete the assignment, and level of difficulty of the assignment.

Method of Discipline: Expectation of appropriate social behavior is integral to all teaching; courtesy and basic regard for others become automatic characteristics of Lamplighter students. No physical punishment is administered.

Enrichment Curriculum

Art, computer, creative dramatics, horticulture and environmental science, music, physical education/motor skills, Spanish

Extracurricular Activities

During the 1995-96 school year, Lamplighter is a pilot site for Voyager Expanded Learning, Inc., program offered for kindergarten-grade 4, three days/week, 3:15 p.m.– 6:00 p.m.

Goals for Students

Lamplighter School strives to instill in all students a feeling of self-worth and a love of learning so that each may reach the highest level of potential.

Faculty/Staff Requirements

Qualifications of Staff: All Lamplighter School faculty members have an undergraduate degree; more than half have master's degrees. While differences in personal style and approach are expected and appreciated, Lamplighter's goal is to maintain a community of stable, mature, caring adults who collectively provide a stimulating, nurturing, challenging environment for children. All are expected to have affection and genuine regard for children, have an active interest in learning, work with colleagues productively, carry on an active communication with parents and administration, and demonstrate professional attitudes and practices.

Qualifications of Administrator: As with faculty, the director has undergraduate and advanced degrees and demonstrates in her own work with faculty the qualities expected of them.

School Information

Brochure Available: Yes
Number of Students in Each Grade: Varies (45-80)
Parochial: No
Organization Affiliations: NAIS, ISAS, Educational Records Bureau
Accreditations: Accredited by TEPSAC through ISAS
Parental Involvement: Many volunteer opportunities through The Lamplighter School Parents' Association

Admittance

Whom to Contact: Dolores Evans, Admissions Director
Date to Apply: The admissions process begins during the school year prior to year for which application is being made. Applications are accepted at any time but should be on file approximately one year in advance.
Testing Procedure per Age/Grade Level: Applicants for the 3- or 4-year-old program are given an individual assessment at the time of the family visit. Applicants for kindergarten-grade 4 are scheduled to return for an individual assessment and group experience after the family visit.
Fees Involved: $100 application fee
Type of Student Preferred: The admission process is designed to attract and admit students and families who believe, with us, that learning is a lifelong and joyous endeavor. We are seeking children who will thrive in our environment. The school values a heterogenous mix of student competencies and talents. In order to provide the best possible educational experience, it is imperative there is full understanding and agreement on goals and philosophy.
Forms Required: Yes
Individual/Group Appointments: Individual
Notification Procedure: Applicants who apply for the following school year prior to the early January deadline are notified in mid-March. Later applicants are notified in a timely manner.
Waiting List Policy: A Wait Pool of applicants is maintained between mid-March and the beginning of the school year in late August.

Tuition

Approximate Tuition for 1996-97 School Year:
> 5-day Preschool (morning and afternoon programs)–$4255
> Kindergarten–$6730 (8:15 a.m.–1:15 p.m.)
> Grades 1-4–$7855

Methods of Payment Available: A deposit is due at the time of acceptance and the balance is due by July 1.
Financial Assistance Offered: Limited financial aid is available to families of currently enrolled students.

Cancellation Insurance Available: No
Profit/Non-profit: Non-profit

Additional Costs

Books/Bag/Uniform: No
Lunch Fee: Students bring lunch from home and eat in their classrooms. Milk for the year may be ordered.
Parents Club Dues: $20 per year
Annual Fund Drive: Yes
Discount for Siblings: No

Facilities/Services Provided

Computer Lab: No; computers are placed throughout the school in all class areas.
Library: A 25,000-volume media center functions as an integral part of the educational program. Featuring three fireplace alcoves, the media center's book collection and other audio-visual learning materials are bar coded for speedy computerized check-out. Students have access to the computerized card-catalog database for searches of print and non-print materials.
Snack Procedures: Provided for all students; served at either mid-morning or mid-afternoon
Before-school Care Program Available: No
After-school Care Program Available: No
Nurse on Staff: No
Emergency Procedure Used: Immediately needed first aid or CPR is provided by certified staff members followed by call to parents(s) or guardian. If they are unavailable, we call emergency contact(s) provided by parents. If no emergency contact can be reached, we follow the procedures outlined in the signed Release-and-Consent-to-Emergency-Medical-Treatment form.
Transportation to and from School: Car pools arranged through Parents' Association
Counseling and Evaluation Available: Yes

Graduation Information

Testing: Educational Records Bureau Comprehensive Testing Program scores are sent to schools to which the fourth-grade graduates apply for fifth grade. Teacher recommendation forms are also forwarded.
Average SAT Scores: N/A
High School Our Students Usually Attend: N/A (Historically, over 90% of our graduates enroll for fifth grade in other independent/private schools in the Dallas area.)

Additional Information

A nationally recognized Blue Ribbon School of Excellence, The Lamplighter School's highly integrated program manifests itself throughout the building in the form of student art on display everywhere. Motor skills activities highlight the accumulated mileage of runners who traverse the distance across Texas or the length of the Nile River from social studies activities. Creative writing merges with music and drama to produce original student-devised operas. Diverse uses of cooperative learning strategies engage the students as they experience the value of combined efforts.

Individual learning styles are recognized and accommodated at all levels. A well-organized peer-tutoring program allows students to work with and learn from one another in non-threatening and fun ways. Thematic and integrated teaching units are literature-based and are on the cutting edge of curriculum development. Computer use is a natural part of the early childhood instructional program with equipment in all the school's classrooms. A hands-on approach to the teaching of math and science is outstanding.

An exceptional program in environmental science combines horticulture (gardening in a greenhouse and in outdoor gardens), experiences with the natural world (a nature trail "out back" leads down to a creek), and animal husbandry (students tending chickens, feeding sheep, a calf, or a pig). The fourth grade "chicken and egg" corporation, Lamplighter Layers, is responsible for care and feeding of a flock of laying hens and egg gathering and selling. Elected officers regularly conduct business meetings following proper parliamentary procedures. Lamplighter students are empowered to be risk-taking learners with limitless potential.

The Oakridge School

5900 West Pioneer Parkway
Arlington, TX 76013
(817) 451-4994
Metro: (817) 654-9746

Mapsco: 81T

Fax: (817) 457-6681

Office Hours: 8:00 a.m.–4:00 p.m.
School Hours: 8:00 a.m.–3:30 p.m.
School Grades Offered: PK3–Grade 12
Enrollment: 776
Co-ed: Yes
Boy/Girl Ratio: 1:1
Student/Teacher Ratio: 10:1
Average Class Size: Varies by division
Calendar School Year: August–May
Holidays: Labor Day, Thanksgiving, winter
break, Martin Luther King Day, spring break
Uniform Requirements: Yes
Founded in: 1979

Philosophy of School

We believe the role of The Oakridge School is to provide a challenging educational
program that emphasizes the total development of each child, encompassing basic skills
as well as cultural, emotional, and physical development which prepares students for
higher education and life. We believe an environment that employs a variety of teaching
techniques and learning activities best enables each student to achieve as an individual
and as a member of a group.

We believe an orderly environment stressing personal and academic self-discipline
provides an atmosphere most conducive to success. We believe in academic excellence,
in high moral and ethical standards, in honor, in the respect of the opinions and the
rights of others, in the realization and acceptance of the consequences of an individual's
actions, and in the pursuit of knowledge as a lifelong experience.

We believe the graduates of The Oakridge School should be men and women of good character who have developed a healthy respect for self, an awareness of the privileges and obligations of citizenship, and a keen sense of empathy for, and responsibility to, fellow human beings.

Academic Curriculum
Content: College-preparatory
Grading System Used: Letter grades
Conferences per Year: Two
Tests Administered: Otis-Lennon and Stanford Achievement
Homework Policy: By academic division
Method of Discipline:

Enrichment Curriculum
Summer-in-the-Oaks program for Middle- and Upper-School students

Extracurricular Activities
Student council, full interscholastic sports program, school clubs and organizations, social activities

Goals for Students
College acceptance

Faculty/Staff Requirements
Qualifications of Staff: See school brochure.
Qualifications of Administrator: See school brochure.

School Information
Brochure Available: Yes
Number of Students in Each Grade: PK3–36; PK4–56; K5–58; T1–10; grade 1–60; grade 2–52; grade 3–55; grade 4–50; grade 5–58; grade 6–52; grade 7–65; grade 8–49; grade 9–48; grade 10–42; grade 11–46; grade 12–39
Parochial: No
Organization Affiliations: National Association of Independent Schools; Texas Association of Non-Public Schools; Texas Independent School Consortium
Accreditations: Southern Association of Colleges and Schools; Independent Schools Association of the Southwest
Parental Involvement: Yes
Other Information:

Admittance

Whom to Contact: Judy Battles, Director of Admissions
Date to Apply: Late fall
Testing Procedure per Age/Grade Level: Testing begins in first grade
Fees Involved: Application fee $50; admissions testing $75
Type of Student Preferred: Academically qualified students of superior attitude
Forms Required: Application, official transcript from prior schools, teacher recommendations
Individual/Group Appointments: Individual
Notification Procedure: Letter and phone call
Waiting List Policy: Re-apply annually

Tuition

Approximate Tuition for 1996-97 School Year: $4414–$7100
Methods of Payment Available: Single payment; ten- and twelve-month payment plans
Financial Assistance Offered: Yes (based on financial need)
Cancellation Insurance Available: Yes
Profit/Non-profit: Non-profit

Additional Costs

Books/Bag/Uniform: Books–grades 5-12; uniform–$100 or less (cost varies)
Lunch Fee: Optional
Parents Club Dues: $10
Annual Fund Drive: Yes
Discount for Siblings: 1/2 applicable tuition for 3rd student (or more); discount applied to tuition of student in the lowest grade
School Fundraisers: Parents' Club, Super Supper/Auction, Booster Club

Facilities/Services Provided

Computer Lab: Yes
Library: 15,000 volume
Snack Procedures: Preschool
Before-school Care Program Available: Yes; 7:15 a.m. - 6:00 p.m.
After-school Care Program Available: Yes; 7:15 a.m. - 6:00 p.m.
Nurse on Staff: Yes
Emergency Procedure Used: Call 911 for life-threatening situation; call parents for all other situations
Transportation to and from School: Car pool; individually contracted bus service
Counseling and Evaluation Available: Yes

Graduation Information

Testing: SAT, ACT for college admission
Average SAT Scores: N/A
High School Our Students Usually Attend: N/A
Percentage of Seniors Attending College: 100

Additional Information

The Parish Day School of the Episcopal Church of the Transfiguration

14115 Hillcrest Road
Dallas, TX 75240
(214) 239-8011

Mapsco: 15G

Fax: (214) 991-1237

Office Hours: 8:00 a.m.–4:00 p.m.
School Hours: 8:05 a.m.–3:30 p.m.
School Grades Offered: Age three years through grade 6
Enrollment: 440
Co-ed: Yes
Boy/Girl Ratio: 1:1
Student/Teacher Ratio: 18:1 (classroom teachers only)
Average Class Size: Varies from 12–20
Calendar School Year: August–May
Holidays: Labor Day, Thanksgiving, Christmas, New Year's Day, Martin Luther King Day, Easter, Memorial Day
Uniform Requirements: Yes (Parker Uniforms)
Founded in: 1972

Philosophy of School

The Parish Day School (PDS) of the Episcopal Church of the Transfiguration provides a learning environment within a Christian framework that encourages each student to develop academically, spiritually, emotionally, and physically. It is the shared belief of faculty, clergy, and parents that the education of our children is worthy of our utmost effort. Therefore, PDS strives to provide a nurturing environment in which the individual is challenged to realize the full potential of his or her abilities.

Academic Curriculum

Content: Language arts, mathematics, social studies, science, Spanish, music, P.E., art, computers, science lab, library, daily chapel services, formal religious instruction in grades K–6

Grading System Used: Narrative progress reports twice a year for pre-K and K students; narrative reporting system for grades 1 and 2 twice a year during the school year; narrative reporting system for grade 2 four times during the school year; letter grade reporting system for grades 3–6 four times during the school year

Conferences per Year: Scheduled two times a year; others as needed or requested by parents or teachers

Tests Administered: ERB for grades 3–6 (Fall 1995)

Homework Policy: Homework at The Parish Day School is assigned beginning in first grade but consists primarily of completing work not completed in class. The amount of homework required gradually increases as the student moves through the grades. The goal is to prepare the student to complete an average of two hours per night in grade 7. Beginning in third grade, students receive a detention if they have two late, missing, or incomplete assignments in a one-week period.

While homework is seen on an ascending scale as the student progresses, the parents' role is seen on a descending scale. Parents should play a lesser role and give the student more responsibility as the student grows older. The parents' role should include:

1. Setting a consistent family schedule that includes time for the student to study
2. Providing a place for the student to study
3. Removing distractions from the student (i.e.,telephone, television, radio)
4. Being available to answer the student's questions

Method of Discipline: The school follows the assertive discipline philosophy. This involves the student's knowing the rules, knowing the consequences for breaking the rules, and receiving the proper warning for inappropriate behavior.

For students in grades 3–6, a detention can be given and will be served from 3:30–4:30 p.m. on Tuesday or Thursday afternoons. If a student fails to serve an assigned detention, a second detention is assigned. Illness is the only excuse for missing a detention assignment.

Other disciplinary measures may include:
- sending a note home
- requiring the student to sit out lunch and play periods
- requiring the student to call home
- suspending the student for not more than three days
- assigning additional suspension or expulsion

A student placed on disciplinary probation may be denied privileges or participation.

Enrichment Curriculum

Kindergarten enrichment, critical and creative thinking in grades 1–3, Great Books, study skills, book club for grades 3–4

Extracurricular Activities

Odyssey of the Mind, AfterMath, CompuClub, band, PDS Chorus, girl scouts, cub scouts, Indian Guides, Indian Princesses, student forum, geography club, intramurals for grades 3–6, sports organized through area athletic associations (soccer, T-ball, baseball, softball, basketball, football, ice hockey); teams are made up of PDS students.

Goals for Students

The mission of The Parish Day School is to deliver an enriching and challenging educational experience within a Christian community of service and worship. (From PBS Statement of Institutional Mission)

Faculty/Staff Requirements

Qualifications of staff: College degree required; experience preferred
Qualifications of Administrator: Master's degree required; experience preferred

School Information

Brochure Available: Yes
Number of Students in Each Grade: 10–14 (3 and 4 years); 18 (kindergarten); 20 each in at least two sections (grades 1–6)
Parochial: Episcopal
Organization Affiliations: ISAS, SAES, NAEYC, TANS, NAES (plus membership in many professional organizations)
Accreditations: ISAS, SAES, NAEYC
Parental Involvement: Encouraged through Parents' Club activities and school volunteer programs
Other Information: Recognized as a "Blue Ribbon School of Excellence" by the U.S. Department of Education (1993-1994)

Admittance

Whom to Contact: Andrea C. Lee, Director of Admissions
Date to Apply: Immediately; the registration process begins in January.
Testing Procedure per Age/Grade Level: All students are screened or tested except those who enter as three-year-olds.
Fees Involved: $50 application fee
Type of Student Preferred: Academically able, highly motivated, well-rounded
Forms Required: Transcripts from current and previous schools; teacher-evaluation form completed by current teacher
Individual/Group Appointments: Both

Notification Procedure: Notification is made as soon as the admissions committee reviews the applicant's file. ISAS schools share a common notification date for grades 5-12.
Waiting List Policy: A continuous waiting list is maintained.

Tuition

Approximate Tuition for 1996-97 School Year: Enrollment fee and annual tuition range from $2207 to $5760.
Method of Payment Available: Tuition may be paid annually, by semester, or in 10 monthly payments.
Financial Assistance Offered: Yes
Cancellation Insurance Available: Yes
Profit/Non-profit: Non-profit

Additional Costs

Books/Bag/Uniform:
Lunch Fee: Meal tickets are available ($25 per ticket depending on items purchased).
Parents Club Dues: Varies according to grade level
Annual Fund Drive: Yes, in the fall.
Discount for Siblings: No

Facilities/Services Provided

Computer Lab: The computer lab has been updated to state-of-the-art technology with 22 Macintosh 5200 Power PC's complete with CD ROM materials, printers, Quick Take 150 camera, laserdisc player, VCR, and TV connections. Students use the lab to reinforce the curriculum especially through the use of ClarisWorks and HyperStudio multimedia presentation software. Regular weekly classes are scheduled for K-3 grades. Grades 4-6 utilize the computer as a tool for learning each curriculum area.

In early fall 1995, 25 Color PowerBooks were placed in a mobile lab to be used by the upper grade students and staff. Four additional computers will be dedicated to faculty use.

Technocrats will meet on Tuesdays alternating with outer after-school activities. Selected students will be trained in multimedia presentation techniques, and then will serve as peer consultants in the classroom.

Library: The goal of The Parish Day School Media Center (library) is to develop independent learners who are effective users of ideas and information. In keeping with this objective, the school has implemented a flexible schedule program which is characterized by collaborative planning between the school media specialists and the classroom teachers in order to totally integrate library media information skills with the curriculum. Individual classroom teachers schedule the media center as needed to offer students the opportunity to become independent in accessing, utilizing, and evaluating information.

Students have a wide variety of resources available including books, periodicals, slide presentations, educational videos, and computer programs. In addition to the fully automated circulation and cataloging system, students have access to CD ROM technology. A newly added satellite dish affords the opportunity to access cable presentations.

The value of reading and the love of reading are promoted by the total school environment. In complementing this school philosophy, the three media specialists coordinate materials for individual teachers and arrange for visiting authors who stimulate excitement and involvement with the literature and with the process of writing. Specialists also become active participants in the classroom by performing dramatic readings and skits which expose the students to creative interpretations of other literary genres. All three specialists are also active members of the Literary Committee whose primary function is to foster student love of reading and writing.

Snack Procedures: The school provides snacks for pre-kindergarten and kindergarten students.
Before-school Care Program Available: Please contact the school office.
After-school Care Program Available: Enrichment program available until 6:00 p.m.
Nurse on Staff: Yes
Emergency Procedure Used: The teacher on duty examines the student and summons the nurse and CPR-certified staff member if necessary. If the student has a severe head or spine injury, an ambulance is summoned. If the paramedics indicate hospital treatment is necessary, the student's parents are contacted and arrangements are made for transportation. The Emergency Release form is taken from the student's file, and a PDS staff member accompanies the student to the hospital to meet the parents. If it appears a bone is broken or a cut or laceration needs stitches, the parents are contacted and informed of the situation.
Transportation to and from School: Car pools (not provided by school)
Counseling and Evaluation Available: Yes

Graduation Information
Testing: Yes
Average SAT Scores: N/A
High School Our Students Usually Attend: N/A
Percentage of Seniors Attending College: N/A
Waiting List Policy:

St. John's Episcopal School

848 Harter Road   Mapsco: 37H
Dallas, TX 75218
(214) 328-9131   Fax: (214) 320-0205

Office Hours: 8.00 a.m.–4:00 p.m.
School Hours: 7:50 a.m.–3:40 p.m.
School Grades Offered: Pre-kindergarten–grade 8
Enrollment: 485
Co-ed: Yes
Boy/Girl Ratio: 1:1
Student/Teacher Ratio: 14:1 approximately
Average Class Size: 18:1 lower school; 22:1 middle school
Calendar School Year: Last week of August until first
week of June
Holidays: 2 weeks at Christmas; 1 week at spring break; 2
days at Thanksgiving; Good Friday
Uniform Requirements: Yes
Founded in: 1953

Philosophy of School

St. John's Episcopal School is dedicated to the development of the whole child through
challenging academic experiences; creative endeavors in all the arts; social and spiritual
maturity through service to each other, the family, the school and community, and a
growing awareness of the value of social, cultural, ethnic, and religious diversity in our
democratic way of life; physical fitness through exercise, good health, and nutritional
habits; opportunities for personal growth in value of self, respect for other individuals,
development of self-discipline, responsibility and an appreciation of learning as a lifelong endeavor. The program is designed to train the mind, strengthen the character, and
enrich the spirit of each student in a Christian environment.

Academic Curriculum

Content: Math, reading, language arts, science, social studies–French, (PK–5),
German, Spanish, French (6–8), art, music—twice weekly; P.E./motor

development—3 times weekly; library—once or twice weekly; computer, once weekly; honors curriculum available in middle school

Grading System Used: Not graded through third grade; reports for pre-K–grade 3; numerical subject area reports for grades 4–8; grades are sent home.

Conferences per Year: Two scheduled conferences–first and third quarters; other conferences at request of parent or teacher (except pre-K–grade 1)

Tests Administered: Stanford 8 (2–5), ERB (6–8)

Homework Policy: Students have homework in accordance with their grade and ability levels. Also, work not completed during class is finished as homework.

Method of Discipline: St. John's strives to provide the incentive for students to develop strength of character and self-discipline. Students are expected to be responsible for their own behavior and to act in an appropriate way which will reflect favorably upon themselves, their parents, and the community. Corporal punishment is never used.

Enrichment Curriculum

Music, journalism/yearbook, speech, PE and art

Extracurricular Activities

Class trips (grades 6-8), Scouts, Camp Fire, Model U.N., geography bee, spelling bee, science fair, choristers, student council, National Jr. Honor Society
Sports: available to grades 7-8; coeducational/intramural/intermural

Goals for Students

Provide for each child the ability to develop his/her full potential while providing for social/emotional development at the same time

Faculty/Staff Requirements

Qualifications of Staff: Bachelor's degree; certification in their assigned teaching field; 50% have advanced degrees

Qualifications of Administrator: Master's degree; experience in classroom and administration

Head of School: Ann Hergenrother, B.A. Beloit College, M.Ed. Tulane University

School Information

Brochure Available: Yes

Number of Students in Each Grade: Pre-K, 64; K, 58; 1st, 51; 2nd, 57; 3rd, 45; 4th, 45; 5th, 43; 6th, 42; 7th, 38; 8th, 40

Parochial: Episcopal affiliated, but an independent school
Organization Affiliations: National Association of Independent Schools, Texas Association of Non-Public Schools, Southwest Association of Episcopal Schools, National Association of the Education of Young Children/Association for Supervision and Curriculum Development
Accreditations: ISAS, TEPSAC
Parental Involvement: Parents' Association
Other Information:

Admittance

Whom to Contact: Nancy Jacobs, Admission Director; Ann Hergenrother, Head of School
Date to Apply: Immediately; Reenrollment begins in January of each year.
Testing Procedure per Age/Grade Level: Small group sessions are scheduled for Saturday mornings; preschool/primary based on developmental levels; elementary/middle school grades given standardized tests of reading, math, and a writing sample
Fees Involved: $50 testing/evaluation fee with application
Type of Student Preferred: Motivated, academically capable, wide range of interests
Forms Required: Yes
Individual/Group Appointments: Both
Notification Procedure: Earliest date is in March per agreement of ISAS schools for grades 5–8; for pre-k–grade 4, notification follows the re-enrollment of current students in February and the evaluation or testing of the applicant.
Waiting List Policy: Qualified applicants may be placed on the wait list for any possible opening at a later date if the family wishes it.

Tuition

Approximate Tuition for 1996-97 School Year: PK-$1,190-2,900, K-5 $4,100, 6-8 $4,600; semi-annual, or annual; pre-K–semi-annual or annual, 8 month payment arrangement for (K-8)
Financial Assistance Offered: For returning students primarily
Cancellation Insurance Available: Yes
Profit/Non-profit: Non-profit

Additional Costs

Books/Bag/Uniform: Book and supply fee K-8; bag optional; uniform–$75-$200
Lunch Fee: Available for choices by the day
Parents Club Dues: $12

Annual Fund Drive: Yes
Discount for Siblings: No

Facilities/Services Provided

Computer Lab: 22 Power Macintosh (5200/75LC), AV package, Quicktake Camera
Library: 8000 volumes
Snack Procedures: Provided by school for pre-kindergarten
Before-school Care Program Available: No
After-school Care Program Available: Yes; until 6:00 p.m.
Nurse on Staff: No
Emergency Procedure Used: With treatment authorization form, child is taken to Doctor's Hospital which is near school.
Transportation to and from School: None provided by school
Counseling and Evaluation Available: Upon request

Graduation Information

Testing: (2–5), Stanford 8; (6–8), ERB
Average SAT scores: N/A
High School Our Students Usually Attend: Local college-preparatory schools
Percentage of Seniors Attending College: N/A

Additional Information

In spite of rapid growth, St. John's School has retained the warm family atmosphere immediately sensed by visiting parents. Each child is known as an individual; each is treated with dignity and respect.

Individual student strengths and talents are recognized and promoted. Students at St. John's develop a sense of ownership in the school through cross-grade interaction, school spirit and community service, participation in decision-making, student government, peer tutoring, and recognition of accomplishments among peers.

St. Mark's School of Texas

10600 Preston Road
Dallas, TX 75230-4000
(214) 363-6491 ext. 172

Mapsco: 25K

Fax: (214) 373-6390

Office Hours: 8:00 a.m.–5:00 p.m.
School Hours: 8:00 a.m.–2:30 p.m. grades 1–2; 8:00
a.m.–3:45 p.m. grades 3-12
School Grades Offered: Grades 1–12
Enrollment: 783–1995-96 school year
Co-ed: No (boys only)
Boy/Girl Ratio: N/A (boys only)
Student/Teacher Ratio: 8:1
Average Class Size: 15
Calendar School Year: August to first Friday in June
Holidays: Labor Day, Yom Kippur, Thanksgiving,
Christmas, New Year's Day, Martin Luther King Day,
Good Friday, Easter
Uniform Requirements: Yes
Founded in: 1933

Philosophy of School

St. Mark's School of Texas is a nonsectarian, college-preparatory, independent day
school for boys in grades 1–12. The Charter (1950) states that the school is "designed to
afford its students well-rounded physical, intellectual, moral, and religious training and
instruction." The St. Mark's Board of Trustees intends for the school to be a diverse
community of teachers and students who share a love of learning and who strive for
high achievement in whatever they undertake.

Challenging students in the sciences, arts, and humanities form the basis of a St. Mark's
education. Teachers work to instill an enthusiasm for learning, to encourage
independent and critical judgment, and to demonstrate the methods for making sound
inquiries and for effective communication. To complement this academic experience,
St. Mark's offers boys a rich variety of opportunities for involvement and leadership in

the school community and on its playing fields. Whether academic or nonacademic, activities at St. Mark's motivate students to realize their potential, rewarding those who strive as well as those who achieve.

Academic Curriculum

Content: St. Mark's requires a minimum of 18 Carnegie units for graduation, of which 17 are earned in specific fields: English–4, mathematics–3, social studies–3, foreign language–3, sciences–3, fine arts–1, as well as a senior exhibition.

The typical course load for a student in the Upper School is five courses per trimester, which can be a combination of single-trimester and full-year courses. A full credit is earned for a year-long course and one-half credit is earned for a semester course.

In grades 10 and 11, honors courses are offered in English, Algebra I, geometry, Algebra II, and pre-calculus. Advanced placement courses are offered in American history, European history, American government and politics, AB calculus, BC calculus, English, French, German, Japanese, and Spanish. St. Mark's offers AP courses in biology, chemistry, and in two single-semester economics courses. St. Mark's also offers single-semester advanced course work in physics.

St. Mark's uses a standard letter scale (A,B,C,D, and F). Pluses and minuses are not given. St. Mark's weights the grade-point average of all students in courses designated as Honors or Advanced Placement by multiplying the grade-point equivalent (4.0, 3.0, 2.0, 1.0) by a factor of 1.25. The purpose of this weighting is to reward students for the extra work required in an Honors or A.P. class.
Conferences per Year: Two scheduled
Tests Administered: ERB
Homework Policy:
Method of Discipline:

Enrichment Curriculum

Extracurricular Activities

Students at St. Mark's are encouraged to do more than excel in their academic subjects. A boy has the opportunity to participate in speech and debate, the student council, the film society, the mathematics problem-solving club, the whiz-quiz, the school's yearbook and newspaper, the drama activities, cheerleading, the environmental club, the letterman's club, the Cum Laude Society, the Lion and Sword Society, the tutorial program, KRSM radio station, the astronomy club, the school's literary magazine, and several other activities.

Goals for Students

St. Mark's college preparatory program fosters intellectual, academic, and artistic excellence in young men and encourages development of the strengths in each boy's character and personality. The academic program is intended to be preparation for personal independence, enlightenment, and maturity. As it relates to conduct, boys are encouraged to take responsibility for their own actions. In physical education, the school is concerned with the student's neuromuscular and cardiovascular development, as well as their development and appreciation of physical fitness, through the specialty classes and intramural program. Finally, students are encouraged to do more than excel in academics; a boy has the opportunity to participate in extracurricular activities ranging from speech and debate to the environmental club.

Faculty/Staff Requirements

Qualifications of Staff: St. Mark's employs more than 98 faculty and 45 staff members. All faculty members serve as coaches and/or activity sponsors in addition to their teaching and advising duties. The 98 full-time faculty members (43 women and 55 men) hold 98 baccalaureate, 79 graduate degrees, and 9 doctoral degrees.

Qualifications of Administrator: Arnold E. Holtberg has been Headmaster of St. Mark's School since July 1993. Mr. Holtberg graduated *cum laude* from Princeton University (1970) with a baccalaureate degree in sociology. He also holds an M.A. degree (1976) in pastoral care and counseling from the Lutheran Theological Seminary in Philadelphia, Pennsylvania.

School Information

Brochure Available: Yes; write to Director of Admissions
Number of Students in Each Grade: Grade 1–32; grade 2–33; grade 3–36; grade 4–48; grade 5–70; grade 6–75; grade 7–93; grade 8–90; grade 9–85; grade 10–79; grade 11–72; grade 12–70
Parochial: No
Organization Affiliations: Its memberships include the National Association of Independent Schools, the Cum Laude Society, and the College Board.
Accreditations: St. Mark's School of Texas is accredited by the Independent Schools Association of the Southwest.
Parental Involvement: Parents are very involved and are welcome on campus at any time.
Other Information:

Admittance

Whom to Contact: Director of Admissions
Date to apply: Inquiries are welcome at any time. Group tours and individual tours are recommended. Applications should be submitted by December 15.

Testing Procedure per Age/Grade Level: First-grade testing is in November and December. Testing and interviewing are completed in February.

Fees Involved: Yes; application fee grades 1–5, $100; grades 6–12, $50

Type of Student Preferred: Highly motivated students with a keen interest in learning

Forms Required: Parents are asked to file an application, obtain a teacher's recommendation, and send a transcript of the applicant's prior work. Applicants take a general aptitude, reading comprehension, vocabulary, and mathematics tests. A writing sample and two on-campus interviews are also required.

Individual/Group Appointments: Individual appointments with the Director of Admissions or appropriate school official.

Notification Procedure: Decision letters are mailed in mid-March. A few places are available after that time.

Waiting List Policy: Students admitted to a grade where there is not an opening are placed in a waiting pool. The waiting pool is closed at the beginning of the school year, and each student must reapply and sit for entrance testing in order to reestablish his eligibility for the next school year.

Tuition

Approximate Tuition for 1996-97 School Year: Grades 1–4, $9330; grade 5, $11,155; grade 6, $11,115; grade 7, $11,900; grade 8, $11,790; grade 9, $12,785; grades 10–12, $11,985

Methods of Payment Available: $1000 deposit due at time of enrollment and balance due July 1

Financial Assistance Offered: Yes

Cancellation Insurance Available: Yes

Profit/Non-profit: Non-profit

Additional Costs

Books/Bag/Uniform: Books–grades 1–4 $55, grades 5–6 $280, grades 7–8 $365, grades 9–12 $520; Bag–no; Uniform–approximately $100

Lunch Fee: Grades 1–4 $690; grades 5–6 $765; grades 7–8 $800; grades 9–12 $845

Parents Club Dues: $25 (includes school directory fee)

Annual Fund Drive: Any donation acceptable (Fair Share Contribution $700+)

Discount for Siblings: No

Facilities/Services Provided

Computer Lab: Yes

Library: Yes; school library and Green-McDermott Library and Study Center

Snack Procedures: Snack Bar available before and after school

143

Before-school Care Program Available: No
After-school Care Program Available: Yes; Grades 1–4
Nurse on Staff: Yes; RN with four-bed infirmary
Emergency Procedure Used: RN or Trainer/RN determines student's needs
Transportation to and from School: Car pool
Counseling and Evaluation Available: School psychologist on staff

Graduation Information

Testing: The college counselor, the Head of the Upper School, and the headmaster jointly coordinate the college planning. Tenth graders are encouraged to attend "College Previews," held in September. The PSAT, SAT, and course grades are all helpful in the selection process. Several required college conferences are scheduled with the student and parent, beginning in the junior year.
Average SAT Scores: The mean SAT scores for the class of 1995 were 600 verbal and 700 math. St. Mark's graduates are attending major universities throughout the country, including Princeton, Stanford, Tulane, the University of Texas at Austin, Vanderbilt, Washington and Lee, Yale, Harvard, and Duke University.
High School Our Students Usually Attend: N/A
Percentage of Seniors Attending College: 100

Additional Information

St. Philip's School and Community Center

1600 Pennsylvania Avenue
Dallas, TX 75215
(214) 421-5221

Mapsco: 46T

Fax: (214) 428-5371

Office Hours: 8:00 a.m.–5:30 p.m.
School Hours: 7:55 a.m.–3:30 p.m.
School Grades Offered: Pre-k (age 3)–grade 4
Enrollment: 163
Co-ed: Yes
Boy/Girl Ratio: 75:88
Student/Teacher Ratio: 18:1
Average Class Size: 20
Calendar School Year: Late August 15-end of May
Holidays: Thanksgiving, Christmas, Martin Luther King Day,
Easter
Uniform Requirements: 3-yr.-olds: not required; 4-yr.-olds–
grade 4: required
Founded in: 1958

Philosophy of School

St. Philip's accepts students with many different abilities and from various
backgrounds. We recognize each child as a unique creation entitled to love, respect, and
opportunities for a safe, challenging passage through the early years. Our varied
educational techniques enhance and develop students' unique learning styles. We seek
to strengthen those qualities that produce secure, responsible adults.

Academic Curriculum

Content: Stresses African-American culture; focuses on basics–language, math,
and science
Grading System Used: Letter grades
Conferences per Year: Four or five mandatory conferences
Tests Administered: Iowa Test of Basic Skills

Homework Policy: Students are regularly assigned homework.
Method of Discipline: Students are encouraged to practice self-control.

Enrichment Curriculum
N/A

Extracurricular Activities
Drama club, choir (grades 3-4), dance, athletics (football, basketball, soccer)

Goals for Students
We want our students to be well-rounded, to know themselves, and to respect themselves and others. Upon leaving St. Philip's School, students should be ready to face academic and social challenges at any other school.

Faculty/Staff Requirements
Qualifications of Staff: K-grade 4: undergraduate degree and teacher certification
Qualifications of Administrator: Master's in Education; thorough knowledge of teaching in and supervising an elementary school

School Information
Brochure Available: Yes
Number of Students in Each Grade: 18-22
Parochial: Yes, Episcopal
Organization Affiliations: SAES (member only)
Accreditations: ISAS
Parental Involvement: Required
Other Information:

Admittance
Whom to Contact: Tammy Taylor
Date to Apply: February
Testing Procedure for Age/Grade Level: Admissions screening for all students
Fees Involved: $150 registration fee
Type of Student Preferred: Open to all students
Forms Required: Transcript, birth certificate, immunization records
Individual/Group Appointments: Yes

Notification Procedure: Letter or phone call
Waiting List Policy: First come, first served

Tuition

Approximate Tuition for 1996-97 School Year: $3312
Methods of Payment Available: Several options
Financial Assistance Offered: Yes
Cancellation Insurance Available: No
Profit/Non-profit: Non-profit

Additional Costs

Books/Bag/Uniform: Uniforms purchased through St. Agnes Uniforms; books provided by school
Lunch Fee: $40 per month
Parents Club Dues: No dues, but participation in Parents' Association fundraisers is required.
Annual Fund Drive: Yes
Discount for Siblings: Yes

Facilities/Services Provided

Computer Lab: Yes
Library: Yes
Snack Procedures: Provided for children in after-school care program
Before-school Care Program Available: Yes, 6:30 a.m.–7:55 a.m.
After-school Care Program Available: Yes, 3:30 p.m.–5:30 p.m.
Nurse on Staff: Yes
Emergency Procedure Used: Contact parents first; call 911; take patient to nearest hospital
Transportation to and from School: Provided by parents
Counseling and Evaluation Available: Referrals only

Graduation Information

Testing: Iowa Test of Basic Skills
Average SAT Scores: N/A
High School Our Students Usually Attend: N/A
Percentage of Seniors Attending College: N/A

Additional Information

Summer Camp available

The Selwyn School

3333 University Drive West
Denton, TX 76201
(817) 382-6771

Mapsco: Denton

Fax: (817) 383-0704

Office Hours: 8:00 a.m.–5:00 p.m.
School Hours: 8:00 a.m.–3:30 p.m.
School Grades Offered: Preschool–grade 8 (day school)
Enrollment: 325
Co-ed: Yes
Boy/Girl Ratio: Equal
Student/Teacher Ratio: 12:1
Average Class Size: 16
Calendar School Year: August–May
Holidays: Standard school breaks
Uniform Requirements: Yes
Founded in: 1957

Philosophy of School

The primary purpose of the The Selwyn School is to prepare students to become responsible and effective citizens in an increasingly interdependent world. The school encourages an atmosphere of caring, mutual respect, and service to others so that students may develop self-confidence, a respect for truth, and commitment to community.

Academic Curriculum

Content: Traditional (preschool); Montessori (lower grades); pre-college preparatory (middle school)
Grading System Used: A,B,C,D, (passing), F (failing)
Conferences per Year: Two
Tests Administered: Yes
Homework Policy: Yes
Method of Discipline: Standard

Enrichment Curriculum
Computer, art, swimming, camping, bee keeping, climbing, Odyssey of the Mind, rocketry, general and instrumental music, Enrichment Language (Spanish)

Extracurricular Activities
See Enrichment Curriculum
Sports: competitive teams in soccer, softball, basketball, volleyball, tennis, track

Goals for Students
We challenge students to take intellectual risks. From the Montessori program in the lower school through the middle-school program, our goal is to provide students with the tools for lifelong success and to encourage a love of learning.

Faculty/Staff Requirements
Qualifications of Staff: College degree required; experience preferred
Qualifications of Administrator: Advanced degree

School Information
Brochure Available: Yes
Number of Students in Each Grade: 20
Parochial: No
Organization Affiliations: ISAS, NAIS
Accreditations: ISAS
Parental Involvement: Yes
Other Information:

Admittance
Whom to Contact: Director of Admissions
Date to Apply: Rolling admissions
Testing Procedure per Age/Grade Level: Yes
Fees Involved: Yes
Type of Student Preferred: Average to above-average ability
Forms Required: Application, all former records, teacher references
Individual/Group Appointments: Yes
Notification Procedure: Standard
Waiting List Policy: Ongoing

Tuition
Approximate Tuition for 1996-97 School Year: $3035–$5590

Methods of Payment Available: Yes
Financial Assistance Offered: Yes
Cancellation Insurance Available: Yes
Profit/Non-profit: Non-profit

Additional Costs
Books/Bag/Uniform: No
Lunch Fee: No
Parents Club Dues: Free membership
Annual Fund Drive: Yes
Discount for Siblings: Yes

Facilities/Services Provided
Computer Lab: Yes
Library: Yes
Snack Procedures: Yes
Before-school Care Program Available: Yes; 1/2 hour before school
After-school Care Program Available: Yes; 3:00 - 6:00 p.m. daily
Nurse on Staff: No
Emergency Procedure Used: Yes
Transportation to and from School: No
Counseling and Evaluation Available: Yes

Graduation Information
Testing: Yes
Average SAT Scores: N/A
High School Our Students Usually Attend: Local, in Dallas, and in surrounding areas
Percentage of Seniors Attending College: N/A

Trinity Valley School

6101 McCart Avenue
Ft. Worth, Texas 76133
(817) 292-6060

Mapsco: 90X
(Fort Worth)
Fax: (817) 294-1958

Office Hours: 8:00 a.m.–4:00 p.m.
School Hours: 8:30 a.m.–3:30 p.m.
School Grades Offered: K–12
Enrollment: Approximately 750
Co-ed: Yes
Boy/Girl Ratio: 50:50
Student/Teacher Ratio: 12:1
Average Class Size: 20
Calendar School Year: August 23, 1996–May 29, 1997
Holidays: Labor Day, Yom Kippur, Thanksgiving (one week), Christmas break, Martin Luther King Day, Good Friday, spring break
Uniform Requirements: Boys–blue slacks, white or blue shirt; girls–blue jumper, white blouse
Founded in: 1959

Philosophy of School
To provide for above-average and superior students–from kindergarten through grade 12–an education of the highest quality

Academic Curriculum
Content: Traditional college-preparatory; all courses are full year and meet daily.
Grading System Used: A, B, C, D, F
Conferences per Year: Two scheduled for grades k-7; as requested in all grades
Tests Administered: K–Stanford; grades 1-8 ERB; grade 9–NEDT; grades 10 and 11–PSAT
Homework Policy: Determined by teacher

151

Method of Discipline: Determined by teacher; no physical punishment

Enrichment Curriculum
Physical education, Spanish, music, art, computers throughout Lower School; same offered in Upper School on elective basis with yearbook, creative writing

Extracurricular Activities
Middle and Upper School sports, camping club, drama, SADD, AFS, NHS, Student Council

Goals for Students
Fine scholarship with college attendance, development of wide constructive interests, intelligent citizenship, and spiritual and moral development which promotes lasting values

Faculty/Staff Requirements
Qualifications of Staff: Bachelor's degree and teacher certification are minimum requirements in K-7; many have graduate degrees.
Qualifications of Administrator: Headmaster Walter W. Kesler - B.S., U.S. Naval Academy, M.Div., Virginia Theological Seminary

School Information
Brochure Available: Yes
Number of Students in Each Grade: K–54; grade 1–42; grade 2–44; grade3–42; grade4–43; grade5–46; grade 6–66; grade 7–66; grade 8–70; grade 9–75; grade 10–73; grade 11–68; grade 12–68
Parochial: No
Organization Affiliations: NAIS, NACAC, ERB, SSS (Financial Aid), TISC (Texas Independent School Consortium)
Accreditations: ISAS
Parental Involvement: Parents' Club Auction, resale shop, Booster Club, room mothers, etc.
Other Information: Advanced Placement courses offered in all areas at upper levels. For further information, parents are encouraged to call for brochures. Visitors are welcome and may schedule a tour and interview by calling the Director of Admissions.

Admittance
Whom to Contact: Judith Kinser, Director of Admission; Richard F. Brennan,

Assistant Director of Admission
Date to Apply: February 9 for kindergarten; approximately March 25 for grades 1-12
Testing Procedure per Age/Grade Level: Individual testing-group observation for kindergarten in January and February; group test in late March for grades 1-12
Fees Involved: Application fee–$75; re-application fee–$25
Type of Student Preferred: Above-average to superior ability; interested in contributing to life of school community
Forms Required: Application, 3 or 4 recommendations, transcript for grades 1-12
Individual/Group Appointments: Call to schedule
Notification Procedure: By letter with contract; parents have two weeks to pay deposit.
Waiting List Policy: Re-apply and re-test annually

Tuition

Approximate Tuition for 1996-97 School Year: K-grade 6–$6825; grades 7-8–$7125; grades 9-12–$7325
Methods of Payment Available: $750 deposit; 60% by July 1 and 40% by January 15; 100% in advance or loan through school's bank
Financial Assistance Offered: Approximately 100 students receiving approximately $430,000 in 1995-96
Cancellation Insurance Available: Yes
Profit/Non-profit: Non-profit

Additional Costs

Books/Bag/Uniform: Books–included in tuition; bag–not required; uniform–approximately $200-$250
Lunch Fee: Buy or bring; no requirement to buy
Parents Club Dues: $15
Annual Fund Drive: Yes
Discount for Siblings: No

Facilities/Services Provided

Computer Lab: One lab for Upper School elective courses in computer science, one for subject-based instruction at all grade levels
Library:
Snack Procedures: Cafeteria provides snacks for additional fee in K only
Before-school Care Program Available: Yes; Clayton Child Care on site 7:00–8:30 a.m.

153

After-school Care Program Available: Yes; Clayton Child Care on site until 6:00 p.m.
Nurse on Staff: No
Emergency Procedure Used: Call parents or alternate emergency contacts; contact school-related physician if necessary.
Transportation to and from School: Not provided
Counseling and Evaluation Available: We make referrals; all students have advisors.

Graduation Information

Testing: 10 National Merit Semifinalists in class of 1995
Average SAT Scores: 1173 (1995)
High School Our Students Usually Attend: N/A
Percentage of Seniors Attending College: 100

Additional Information

The Winston School

5707 Royal Lane
Dallas, TX 75229
(214) 691-6950

Mapsco: 25E

Fax: (214) 691-1509

Office Hours: 8:00 a.m.–4:00 p.m.
School Hours: 8:10 a.m.–3:30 p.m.
School Grades Offered: Grades 1-12
Enrollment: 175
Co-ed: Yes
Boy/Girl Ratio: 4:1
Student/Teacher Ratio: 8:1
Average Class Size: 9
Calendar School Year: August 15-May 30
Holidays: Standard
Uniform Requirements: No
Founded in: 1973

Philosophy of School

Teaching differently for learning different students

Academic Curriculum

Content: Full academic program including college preparation
Grading System Used: Grades sent home every six weeks; number grades
Conferences per Year: Two; more as needed or requested by parents
Tests Administered: Individualized
Homework Policy: Reinforcement and review activities; projects
Method of Discipline: Individualized–non-corporal

Enrichment Curriculum

Drama, art, ceramics, sculpture, photography, foreign language, computer, camping, class trips

Extracurricular Activities
Soccer, basketball, softball, baseball, volleyball, tennis, golf, football, solar car, human-powered vehicle

Goals for Students
To develop individual strengths, self-confidence, compensatory skills

Faculty/Staff Requirements
Qualifications of Staff: Successful experience and training in dealing with students who learn differently
Qualifications of Administrator: Ph.D. in special education

School Information
Brochure Available: Yes
Number of Students in Each Grade: Grades 1-6, 40; grades 7-8, 40; grades 9-12, 95
Parochial: No
Organization Affiliations: ISAS, NAIS, TANS, COPSES, CASE, NACAC, ISM, TAPS
Accreditations: ISAS
Parental Involvement: Yes
Other Information:

Admittance
Whom to Contact: Ellen D. Cassidy
Date to Apply: Continual admissions for any current openings; applications encouraged in December–April for following year admission
Testing Procedure per Age/Grade Level: Testing to confirm the learning disability
Fees Involved: $150 application fee
Type of Student Preferred: Average to superior intelligence with a learning disability
Forms Required: Application, written diagnosis
Individual/Group Appointments: Individual–student visits classes for three days; group appointment with parents
Notification Procedure: After student visitation
Waiting List Policy: Re-apply annually

Tuition

Approximate Tuition for 1996-97 School Year: $9000–$11500

Methods of Payment Available: Tuition due before school begins; restricted payment plans; assistance in finding credit; Master Card or Visa

Financial Assistance Offered: Financial aid program

Cancellation Insurance Available: 4% of tuition

Profit/Non-profit: Non-profit

Additional Costs

Books/Bag/Uniform: Books and supplies–$250-$400; bag–not required; uniform–not required

Lunch Fee: Annual fee–$565 (mandatory grades 1-6), $792 (optional grades 7-12)

Parents Club Dues: $15

Annual Fund Drive: Yes

Discount for Siblings: No

Facilities/Services Provided

Computer Lab: Yes; computer center as part of the media center plus computers in every classroom

Library: Yes

Snack Procedures: N/A

Before-school Care Program Available: No

After-school Care Program Available: Yes; for grades 1-6, 3:30–6:00 p.m.

Nurse on Staff: No

Emergency Procedure Used: Yes

Transportation to and from School: Car pools; public bus

Counseling and Evaluation Available: Full-time counselor and evalution center

Graduation Information

Testing: Yes

Average SAT Scores: 1100

High School Our Students Usually Attend: N/A

Percentage of Seniors Attending College: 90-95

Additional Information

Winston provides a caring environment to foster student success.

158

LSA
The Texas District,
The Lutheran Church—
Missouri Synod

7900 E. Highway 290
Austin, TX 78724-2499
(512) 926-4272 FAX (512) 926-1006

Lutheran School Accreditation (LSA) is a process of self-evaluation to help schools improve the quality of their programs, followed by a visit of objective observers and the awarding of a certificate of accreditation. It is a completely voluntary process, which is available for every school sponsored by one or more congregations of the Texas District, The Lutheran Church–Missouri Synod. LSA is a rigorous national and district accrediting process which is designed to evaluate schools on the basis of their unique purposes as Lutheran schools. As a result, the Standard's process and awards reflect not only the quality of the academic nature of the school, but also especially the school's spiritual dimension. The standards and report forms are based on other regional accrediting agencies both secular and religious. LSA will be supervised by both a district and a national accreditation commission. The process has been authorized and approved by both the Board of Directors of the Texas District and the Board for Parish Services of the Lutheran Church–Missouri Synod. The period of accreditation is seven years.

Christ Our Savior Lutheran School, Coppell
Cross of Christ Lutheran School
Faith Lutheran School
Holy Cross Lutheran School
Lutheran High School of Dallas
Our Redeemer Lutheran School
Prince of Peace Lutheran School, Carrollton
Redeemer Lutheran School (pending)
St. Paul Lutheran School, Fort Worth
Zion Lutheran School

Christ Our Savior Lutheran School

140 Heartz   Mapsco: 1A–T
Coppell, TX 75019
(214) 393-7074 (214) 393-2875   Fax: (214) 462-0881

Office Hours: 8:00 a.m.–4:00 p.m.

School Hours: 8:30 a.m.–3:30 p.m.

School Grades Offered: 2 years through 5th grade

Enrollment: 275

Co-ed: Yes

Boy/Girl Ratio: 2:3

Student/Teacher Ratio: 9:1

Average Class Size: 18

Calendar School Year: August–May

Holidays: Labor Day, Thanksgiving, Christmas, New Year's Day, Martin Luther King Day, Good Friday, Independence Day

Uniform Requirements: Yes

Founded in: 1986

Philosophy of School

To develop and nurture Christ-centered faith by obeying the commands from Jesus in the Great Commission

Academic Curriculum

Content: Montessori and classic preschool programs; traditional program in elementary grades

Grading System Used: Grades are sent home every nine (9) weeks.

Conferences per Year: Two

Tests Administered: Stanford-Benet Achievement

160

Homework Policy: Determined by each teacher
Method of Discipline: Time out

Enrichment Curriculum
Gymnastics and piano

Extracurricular Activities
Music, chapel, computers, tennis

Goals for Students
To develop academic excellence and spiritual maturity

Faculty/Staff Requirements
Qualifications of Staff: Preschool–Montessori training, classic preschool ECE endorsement; elementary–elementary-education degree
Qualifications of Administrator: Master's degree in education; present administrator has an Ed.D. in elementary school administration

School Information
Brochure Available: Yes
Number of Students in Each Grade: Preschool, 225; elementary, 50
Parochial: Yes
Organization Affiliations: Lutheran Church Missouri Synod
Accreditations: Texas Department of Human Services, State Department of Education LCMS accreditation–extended day care before and after school
Parental Involvement: Yes, Parent-Teacher League
Other Information:

Admittance
Whom to Contact: Dr. John Troutman, Administrator
Date to Apply: Early registration, March 1
Testing Procedure per Age/Grade Level: K-5 SAT, 1-3, 5 Ottis Lennon
Fees Involved: Yes
Type of Student Preferred: No preference
Forms Required: Yes
Individual/Group Appointments: Individual
Notification Procedure: Phone call and registration
Waiting List Policy: Annually

Tuition

Approximate Tuition for 1996-97 Year: Varies–part-time preschool; full-time elementary; after-school care
Methods of Payment Available: Monthly tuition
Financial Assistance Offered: Yes
Cancellation Insurance Available: No
Profit/Non-profit: Non-profit

Additional Costs:

Books/Bag/Uniform: Students can bring back packs; girls' uniforms cost approximately $65; boys' uniforms cost approximately $47.
Lunch Fee: Included in tuition
Parents Club Dues: $5 per year
Annual Fund Drive: No
Discount for Siblings: 10%

Facilities/Services Provided

Computer Lab: Computers in classrooms
Library: Library room, volunteer librarian
Snack Procedures: School–full time; parents rotate part time
Before-school Care Program Available: Yes, beginning at 7:00 a.m.
After-school Care Program Available: Yes, ending at 6:00 p.m.
Nurse on Staff: No
Emergency Procedure Used: Teachers trained in CPR and first aid
Transportation to and from School: No–parents car pool
Counseling and Evaluation Available: Yes

Graduation Information

Testing: N/A
Average SAT Scores: N/A
High School Our Students Usually Attend: N/A
Percentage of Seniors Attending College: N/A

Cross of Christ Lutheran School

512 N. Cockrell Hill Rd., P.O. Box 306
DeSoto, TX 75123
(214) 223-9586

Mapsco: 82D

Fax: (214) 223-8432

Office Hours: 8:15 a.m.–3:15 p.m.
School Hours: 8:15a.m.–3:15 p.m.
School Grades Offered: 3-year-olds through grade 8
Enrollment: 210
Co-ed: Yes
Boy/Girl Ratio: 1:1
Student/Teacher Ratio: 20:1
Average Class Size: 20
Calendar School Year: August 16, 1996–May 31, 1997
Holidays: Labor Day, Thanksgiving, Christmas, New
Year's Day, Martin Luther King Day, Good Friday, Easter
Monday, Memorial Day
Uniform Requirements: Yes
Founded in: 1988

Philosophy of School

The Cross of Christ Lutheran Church was established 1988 to teach the good news of
free forgiveness and eternal life in Jesus Christ and to provide a program that values
each student as a loved, redeemed, unique creation of God. We are committed to
providing the best education possible to help your child become a loving Christian, a
good citizen, and a purposeful adult.

Academic Curriculum

Content: Full curriculum as prescribed by the state of Texas plus religious
training
Grading System Used: A (95–100) , B (85–94), C (75–84), D (70–74),
F (0–69)

163

Conferences per Year: At least one
Tests Administered: I.Q. tests given in grades 1, 3, and 6; Iowa Test annually
Homework Policy: Determined by each teacher
Method of Discipline: Assertive discipline

Enrichment Curriculum

Spelling bees, math contests, academic field days, computer programs, science fair, and Invent America

Extracurricular Activities

Band, basketball for grades 4–8, soccer for grades 4–6, volleyball for grades 7–8, track, class trips

Goals for Students

We strive to develop the whole child–spiritually, physically, academically, and socially. We provide an age-appropriate curriculum so students will have a positive experience in school and look forward to a lifetime of learning.

Faculty/Staff Requirements

Qualifications of Staff: College degrees and certification; dedicated Christians
Qualifications of Administrator: Master's degree in administration

School Information

Brochure Available: Yes
Number of Students in Each Grade: PS3 (12); PS4 (18); K5 (25); G1 (25); G2 (20); G3 (20); G4 (22); G5 (20); G6 (8); G7 (16); G8 (3)
Parochial: Yes
Organization Affiliations: Lutheran Church, Lutheran Education Association
Accreditations: Accredited by the Lutheran School Accreditation Commission
Parental Involvement: Active parent-teacher organization
Other Information:

Admittance

Whom to Contact: Mary Wehmiller or school office
Date to Apply: Enrollment begins March 1
Testing Procedure per Age/Grade Level: Iowa Test annually; Basic Skills (grades 1–8)

Fees Involved: Registration fee–$215 due at time of enrollment
Type of Student Preferred: We are a non-discriminatory school.
Forms Required: Yes
Individual/Group Appointments: Yes
Notification Procedure: Personal contact
Waiting List Policy:

Tuition

Approximate Tuition for 1996-97 School Year: Preschool–$1860;
grades 1-6, $2336
Methods of Payment Available: Payment can be made in nine monthly
payments.
Financial Assistance Offered: No
Cancellation Insurance Available: No

Additional Costs

Books/Bag/Uniforms: Uniforms (approximately $47 for girls and $45 for boys)
Lunch Fee: Approximately $2 per day
Parents Club Dues: $5 per year (included in registration fee)
Annual Fund Drive: None
Discount for Siblings: 10%

Facilities/Services Provided

Computer Lab: Available
Library: Available
Snack Procedures: Provided for ps3–k5
Before-school Care Program Available: Yes; 7:00 a.m.–8:00 a.m.
After-school Care Program Available: Yes; 3:30 p.m.–6:00 p.m.
Nurse on Staff: Yes
Emergency Procedure Used: Parental permission on file to secure
emergency care
Transportation to and from School: By parents
Counseling and Evaluation Available: Outside referrals are used.

Graduation Information

Testing: N/A
Average SAT scores: N/A
High School Our Students Usually Attend: Area public schools
Percentage of Seniors Attending College: N/A

Faith Lutheran School

1701 East Park Boulevard
Plano, TX 75074
(214) 423-7448

Mapsco: 659P

Fax:

Office Hours: 8:15 a.m.–4:00 p.m.
School Hours: 8:30 a.m.–3:30 p.m.
School Grades Offered: Pre-K (age 3)–grade 8
Enrollment: 350
Co-ed: Yes
Boy/Girl Ratio: 1:1
Student/Teacher Ratio: Preschool, 15:1; K–8, 22:1
Average Class Size: 22
Calendar School Year: August 15–May 31
Holidays: Thanksgiving, Christmas, spring break, Easter
Uniform Requirements: Dress code
Founded in: 1972

Philosophy of School

We exist to assist parents in bringing up their children in the nurture and admonition of the Lord. We strive to develop the whole child in a warm, caring environment that includes education, worship, evangelism, fellowship, and service.

Academic Curriculum

Content: Regular (employs Christian objectives and minimum standards)
Grading System Used: A, B, C, and Failure
Conferences per Year: Two and as needed
Tests Administered: Iowa Test of Basic Skills Achievement
Homework Policy: Individual teacher preference
Method of Discipline: Outlined in *Parents' Handbook*

166

Enrichment Curriculum
Built into the regular classroom program

Extracurricular Activities
Soccer, volleyball, basketball, track, academic contests, band, choir

Goals for Students
To present each person complete in Christ; to develop each student to his/her fullest potential

Faculty/Staff Requirements
Qualifications of Staff: All have degrees; three have master's degrees
Qualifications of Administrator: Master's degree

School Information
Brochure Available: Yes
Number of Students in Each Grade: 18–24
Parochial: Yes, Lutheran
Organization Affiliations: Lutheran Church Missouri Synod; TANS
Accreditations: State and National Lutheran Church Missouri Synod (LCMS), T.E.A.
Parental Involvement: High
Other Information:

Admittance
Whom to Contact: Principal (contact through school office)
Date to Apply: After January 1
Testing Procedure for Age/Grade Level: None for preschool; readiness for kindergarten; achievement tests for grades 1–8
Fees Involved: $200 registration and books; $2350 tuition per year for grades 1–8
Type of Student Preferred: One dedicated to learning
Forms Required: Registration, emergency care, health records
Individual/Group Appointments: Individual with principal
Notification Procedure:
Waiting List Policy:

Tuition

Approximate Tuition for 1996-97 School Year: $1500, kindergarten; $2350 for grades 1-8

Methods of Payment Available: 10 monthly payments

Financial Assistance Offered: Yes

Cancellation Insurance Available: No

Profit/Non-profit: Non-profit

Additional costs:

Books/Bag/Uniform: Individual school supplies

Lunch Fee: $2.00-$2.50 per day for hot lunch

Parents Club Dues: None

Annual Fund Drive: One fundraiser for non-budgeted items

Discount for Siblings: No

Facilities/Services Provided

Computer Lab: Yes

Library: Yes

Snack Procedures: Preschool and extended-day students

Before-school Care Program Available: Yes; 7:00 - 8:30 a.m.

After-school Care Program Available: Yes; 11:30 a.m. - 6:00 p.m.

Nurse on Staff: No

Emergency Procedure Used: Depends on problem

Transportation to and from School: No

Counseling and Evaluation Available: Yes

Graduation Information

Testing: N/A

Average SAT Scores: N/A

High School Our Students Usually Attend: Public

Percentage of Seniors Attending College: N/A

Additional Information

Holy Cross Lutheran School

11425 Marsh Lane
Dallas, TX 75229
(214) 358-4396

Mapsco: 23M

Fax: N/A

Office Hours: 8:15 a.m.-4:45 p.m.
School Hours: K-grade 6–8:30 a.m.-3:30 p.m.;
4-year-olds: Monday, Wednesday, and Friday
8:30 a.m.–11:30 a.m.; 3-year-olds–Tuesday and Thursday
8:30 a.m.–11:30 a.m.
School Grades Offered: Preschool (3- and 4-year-olds);
kindergarten; grades 1–6
Enrollment: 132
Co-ed: Yes
Boy/Girl Ratio: 50:50
Student/Teacher Ratio: 13:1–22:1
Average Class Size: 16
Calendar School Year: August 17–May 24
Holidays: Labor Day, Thanksgiving, Christmas, Easter,
Memorial Day
Uniform Requirements: Yes, K-6
Founded in: 1962

Philosophy of School

Holy Cross Lutheran School, a ministry of the church for students and their families, provides a Christian, spiritually based education and environment for meeting the needs of the whole person.

Academic Curriculum

Content: Bible study, reading, language, math, social studies, science, health, art, music, computer
Grading System Used: A–F, based on percentages
Conferences per Year: Two scheduled: end of first and third quarters; called as needed

Tests Administered: Annual achievement tests, standardized subject matter tests, and teacher-developed tests
Homework Policy: Varies by grade level
Method of Discipline: Assertive discipline model

Enrichment Curriculum
Provided on individual basis by the teacher

Extracurricular Activities
Sports: basketball offered to boys and girls grades 4–6; music (in addition to classroom program); primary and junior choirs; band (tuition–$30/month); hand chimes choir; field days for grades 1–6; metro Lutheran track meet, grades 4–6

Goals for Students
That the student develop spiritually and academically to his/her potential

Faculty/Staff Requirements
Qualifications of Staff: Bachelor's degree; Lutheran teacher's diploma
Qualifications of Administrator: Master's degree; Lutheran teacher's diploma

School Information
Brochure Available: Yes
Number of Students in Each Grade: Up to 22 in grades K–6; 16 (four-year-olds); 15 (three-year-olds)
Parochial: Lutheran
Organization Affiliations: Lutheran
Accreditations: LSAC, NLSA, TEPSAC
Parental Involvement: Yes (field trips, room mothers, special events, playground monitors, lunch duty, library)
Other Information:

Admittance
Whom to Contact: Church-school office–(214)358-4396
Date to Apply: Any time
Testing Procedure per Age/Grade Level: Grade 1–Gesell Developmental; grades 2-6–ITBS achievement testing
Fees Involved: Registration fees: three-year-olds–$120; four-year-olds–$175; kindergarten-grade 6–$375

Type of Student Preferred: Student should be working at grade level or above.
Forms Required: Application, financial agreement, health form
Individual/Group Appointments: Individual
Notification Procedure: Conference with principal or by phone
Waiting List Policy: Re-apply annually

Tuition

Approximate Tuition for 1996-97 School Year: Three-year-olds–$875; four-year-olds–$1180; kindergarten-grade 6–$3100
Methods of Payment Available: 10 monthly payments (August-May)
Financial Assistance Offered: Yes (based on financial need)
Cancellation Insurance Available: No
Profit/Non-profit: Non-profit

Additional Costs

Books/Bag/Uniform: Basic textbooks and workbooks are provided. Purchases include Bible, dictionary, sex education series, and school supplies. Student provides his/her own bag. Uniforms for students in K-6 cost approximately $150.
Lunch Fee: $2.65 for once-a-week, optional catered lunch
Parents Club Dues: $10 annually per family
Annual Fund Drive: None
Discount for Siblings: Based on financial need

Facilities / Services Provided

Computer Lab: Yes; 11 computers
Library: Yes; supervised by volunteer parents
Snack Procedures: Children bring snacks.
Before-school Care Program Available: Before-school supervision beginning at 7:00 a.m.
After-school Care Program Available: Yes; 3:30 p.m. to 5:45 p.m.
Nurse on Staff: None
Emergency Procedure Used: Yes
Transportation to and from School: No (assistance given in arranging car pools)
Counseling and Evaluation Available: Most counseling is done by referrals based on nature and intensity of need.

Graduation Information

Testing: N/A
Average SAT Scores: N/A

High School Our Students Usually Attend: Lutheran High School of Dallas
Percentage of Seniors Attending College: N/A

Additional Information

Lutheran High School of Dallas

8494 Stults Road
Dallas, TX 75243
(214) 349-8912

Mapsco: 26C

Fax: (214) 340-3095

Office Hours: 8:00 a.m.–4:00 p.m.
School Hours: 8:00 a.m.–3:30 p.m.
School Grades Offered: Grades 7–12
Enrollment: 250
Co-ed: Yes
Boy/Girl Ratio: 50:50
Student/Teacher Ratio: 17:1
Average Class Size: 22
Calendar School Year: August 22, 1996–May 31, 1997
Holidays: Thanksgiving, Christmas, Easter, spring break
Uniform Requirements: Yes (grades 7–11)
Founded in: 1976

Philosophy of School

In an academic, spiritual, and social environment, Lutheran High School provides a quality Christ-centered education that prepares students for productive Christian lives. We have a non-discrimination policy.

Academic Curriculum

Content: College-preparatory
Grading System Used: Percentages
Conferences per Year: Two scheduled; others as needed
Tests Administered: ITBS; ERB
Homework Policy: Determined by individual teacher
Method of Discipline: Practice Matthew 18: 15-16

173

Enrichment Curriculum

Study-skills program, computer, career development, journalism, music, art, drama, community-service hours

Extracurricular Activities

Interscholastic sports include boys' and girls' basketball (7–12), boys' soccer (7–12), boys' baseball (7–12), girls' volleyball (7–12), track (9–12), golf (9–12), cheerleading (7–12); other activities include band, art, yearbook, journalism, chess club, mock trial, computer club, jazz band and quiz bowl.

Goals for Students

Preparation and motivation for post-secondary education.

Faculty/Staff Requirements

Qualifications of Staff: Texas certification, bachelor's and master's degrees
Qualifications of Administrator: Principal: Master's degree in educational administration; Headmaster: Ph.D.

School Information

Brochure Available: By request
Number of Students in Each Grade: 7th–50; 8th–50; 9th–52; 10th–50; 11th–35; 12th–18
Organization Affiliations: Lutheran Church, Missouri Synod
Accreditations: TEPSAC, LSAC
Parental Involvement: Very involved
Other Information:

Admittance

Whom to Contact: Sandra Boston, Admissions Director
Date to Apply: Continual admissions
Testing Procedure per Age/Grade Level: 7-8 Gates McGinite; 9-12 Nelson Denny
Fees Involved: $350 enrollment fee; $25 testing fee
Type of Student Preferred: Average or above-average student who wants a quality education in a Christian environment
Forms Required: Yes; principal-teacher-student evaluation, medical records
Individual/Group Appointments: By appointment
Notification Procedure: Notification within seven days of testing
Waiting List Policy: Some grades on waiting list; inquire at admissions

Tuition

Approximate Tuition for 1996-97 School Year: 7-8 $4100; 9-12 $5500;
Methods of Payment Available: Full payment or 12 monthly payments
Financial Assistance Offered: Grant-in-aid; scholarship programs
Cancellation Insurance Available: No
Profit/Non-profit: Non-profit

Additional Costs

Books/Bag/Uniform: Books–cost included in tuition; workbooks may be required; $30 book deposit; bag–optional; uniform required in grades 7-11
Lunch Fee: Optional ($3.00 a day)
Parents Club Dues: No
Annual Fund Drive: Yes
Discount for Siblings: No

Facilities/Services Provided

Computer Lab: Yes; current technology
Library: Yes; 5,000+ books and Encarta, Infotract, SIRS
Snack Procedures: Only lunch provided; vending machines
Before-school Care Program Available: No
After-school Care Program Available: No
Nurse on Staff: No
Emergency Procedure Used: Notification of parents or other contacts based on parents' emergency instructions
Transportation to and from School: Car pools
Counseling and Evaluation Available: Yes; certified counselor with heavy emphasis on college and career guidance

Graduation Information

Testing: PSAT, PACT
Average SAT scores: 1050 SAT; 21 ACT
High School Our Students Usually Attend: N/A
Percentage of Seniors Attending College: 99

Additional Information

Lutheran High School offers a quality Christ-centered education. Both the regular and advanced high school diplomas are offered through mastery of the essential elements as prescribed by the Texas Education Agency. Our graduates are currently furthering their education at major colleges and universities throughout the United States.

Students: Lutheran High School students average 1 1/2 years above grade level on the nationally normed Iowa Test of Basic Skills and 100 points higher than the state average on the Scholastic Aptitude Test, used nationwide as a standard for entrance into college.

Our Redeemer Lutheran School

7611 Park Lane
Dallas, TX 75225
(214) 368-1465

Mapsco: 26S

Fax: (214) 368-1473

Office Hours: 8:00 a.m.–4:00 p.m.
School Hours: 7:00 a.m.–6:00 p.m.
School Grades Offered: Preschool (3 years)–grade 8
Enrollment: 200
Co-ed: Yes
Boy/Girl Ratio: 1:1
Student/Teacher Ratio: 18:1
Average Class Size: 20
Calendar School Year: August 21, 1996–May 30, 1997
Holidays: November 23 and 24; mid-Dec.–early-Jan.
Uniform Requirements: Yes
Founded in: 1960

Philosophy of School

Our Redeemer Lutheran School is a coeducational school dedicated to quality education in the Lutheran-Christian tradition. It presents an educational alternative for the Dallas and North Dallas communities. Our Redeemer's educational philosophy embraces the total growth of the individual. It is distinctively a Christian school and, as such, offers a program of academic excellence as well as intellectual freedom designed to encourage each student to grow and mature. Tempered by our Christian heritage, this environment is structured to animate our students' lives with the joy of learning, latitude of expression, and recognition of their individual hopes, dreams, and expectations. Within this environment, students are able to receive the personal attention that so greatly enhances academic life at every level.

Academic Curriculum

Content: Full academic curriculum, including religion, computer, art, band, and Spanish

Grading System Used: A–F; percentages

Conferences per Year: Three

Tests Administered: Iowa Test of Basic Skills; Gessell Development Readiness

Homework Policy: Maximum of 1-1/2 hrs. per night

Method of Discipline: Use natural consequences to change unacceptable behavior to acceptable behavior; application of Law and Gospel

Enrichment Curriculum

Extracurricular Activities

After-school sports program, Bell Choir, Student Council, school paper

Goals for Students

Practice self-discipline; apply good work and study habits in making full use of their God-given talents and abilities

Faculty/Staff Requirements

Qualifications of Staff: Bachelor's degrees or higher

Qualifications of Administrator: Master's degree

School Information

Brochure Available: Yes (from school office)

Number of Students in Each Grade: 20

Parochial: Lutheran

Organization Affiliations:

Accreditations: Yes, LCMS

Parental Involvement: Strongly encouraged; volunteer program

Other Information:

Admittance

Whom to Contact: David Haak, Principal, or Connie Hoggard, School Secretary

Date to Apply: January 1

Testing Procedure per Age/Grade Level: K–Gessell Development Readiness;

grades 1-8–Achievement Test Scores in Reading and Math from within the last year
Fees Involved:
Type of Student Preferred: Self-disciplined, self-motivated, Christian
Forms Required: Achievement Test Scores, copy of most recent report card, Student Referral Form
Individual/Group Appointments: Individual
Notification Procedure: Letter
Waiting List Policy: Ongoing

Tuition

Approximate Tuition for 1996-97 School Year: $3700
Methods of Payment Available: Annual, semester, 10 monthly payments
Financial Assistance Offered: Limited
Cancellation Insurance Available:
Profit/Non-profit: Non-profit

Additional costs

Books/Bag/Uniform: $30 application fee; $250 comprehensive fee; $30 activity fee; uniforms–additional cost
Lunch Fee: $2.50 per day
Parents Club Dues: $5
Annual Fund Drive: Yes
Discount for Siblings: 10%

Facilities/Services Provided

Computer Lab: Yes
Library: Yes
Snack Procedures: Provided for kindergarten and preschool students
Before-school Care Program Available: Yes, 7:00 a.m.–8:10 a.m.
After-school Care Program Available: Yes, 3:30 p.m.–6:00 p.m.
Nurse on Staff: No
Emergency Procedure Used: Contact parent or person responsible
Transportation to and from School: No
Counseling and Evaluation Available: Yes

Graduation Information

Testing: N/A
Average SAT Scores: N/A
High School Our Students Usually Attend: N/A
Percentage of Seniors Attending College: N/A

Prince of Peace Christian School

2115 Frankford Rd.
Carrollton, TX 75007
(214) 245-7564

Mapsco: 3E

Fax: (214) 245-7101

Office Hours: 8:00 a.m.–5:00 p.m.
School Hours: 8:15 a.m.–3:30 p.m.
School Grades Offered: Age 3–grade 8
Enrollment: 430
Co-ed: Yes
Boy/Girl Ratio: 1:1
Student/Teacher Ratio: 14:1–24:1
Average Class Size: Varies by class
Calendar School Year: August 14, 1996–May 23, 1997
Holidays: Traditional school holidays
Uniform Requirements: Yes, K–grade 8
Founded in: 1980

Philosophy of School
High academic standards in a caring Christian environment

Academic Curriculum
Content: Developmental preschool; academic grade school
Grading System Used: A, B, C, D, F ; E = Excellent, S = Satisfactory,
N = Needs Improvement; (non-graded preschool)
Conferences per Year: One required, one optional
Tests Administered: Achievement tests given for grades 1–8
Homework Policy: Varies by teacher
Method of Discipline: Time out, loss of privileges, or detentions, varies by
grade level

Enrichment Curriculum

Computers, music, athletics, Spanish, high-level curriculum, organizational skills, hands-on science, Read-Up Program

Extracurricular Activities

Soccer, basketball, outdoor education, school musicals, drama, field trips

Goals for Students

To become all that God created the student to be

Faculty/Staff Requirements

Qualifications of Staff: Must be certified or approved by Texas Education Agency

Qualifications of Administrator: Master's degree in education, B.S. in Education, 1991 National Distinguished Principal

School Information

Brochure Available: Yes; also video

Number of Students in Each Grade: Early Childhood Center, 125; K–grade 8 (average), 305

Parochial: Sponsored by Lutheran Church Missouri Synod

Organization Affiliations: Prince of Peace Lutheran Church

Accreditations: National Lutheran Accreditation with Texas Education Agency, Texas Department of Human Services

Parental Involvement: High and desired

Other Information:

Admittance

Whom to Contact: Grade school principal–Raymond Fricke; ECDC director–Karen Crone

Date to Apply: Year round–best probability of enrollment is to apply at least eight months in advance.

Testing Procedure per Age/Grade Level: PS-K, Geselle and PIAT R; Grades 2-8, PIAT R

Fees Involved: Yes

Type of Student Preferred: Students assessed prior to enrollment for academic and developmental readiness

Forms Required: Yes

Individual/Group Appointments: Individual

Notification Procedure: New students are notified after February 1 because current students have until then to reserve placement for the following fall.
Waiting List: Varies with grades

Tuition

Approximate Tuition for 1996-97 School Year: $3300-$3600 full-time student
Methods of Payment Available: One-time payment or 10 equal payments
Financial Assistance Offered: Yes, if qualified
Cancellation Insurance Available: No; however, a refund is given if family moves or student does not qualify.
Profit/Non-profit: Non-profit

Additional costs

Books/Bag/Uniform: Books–$100 (grades 1–5) and $125 (grades 6-8); uniform–approximately $30 each
Lunch Fee: Hot lunch service available
Parents Club Dues: None
Annual Fund Drive: Yes
Discount for Siblings: Yes

Facilities/Services Provided

Computer Lab: 12 Networked PCs (486's)
School Lunch: Yes
Snack Procedures: Provided by preschool parents on child's special day
Before-school Care Program Available: Yes; 7:00 a.m.– 8:15 a.m.
After-school Care Program Available: Yes; 3:30 p.m.–5:00 p.m.
Nurse on Staff: Yes, part-time; staff trained in CPR and first aid
Emergency Procedure Used: Parents sign release form for clinic; attempt is made to contact parents in cases of injury.
Transportation to and from School: Provided by parents and community
Counseling and Evaluation Available: Yes

Graduation Information

Testing: N/A
Average SAT scores: N/A
High School Our Students Usually Attend: N/A
Percentage of Seniors Attending College: N/A

Additional Information

New facility, near Carrollton Greenbelt; tours given to drop-in visitors; parents welcome; average achievement (test scores in top 20%)

Redeemer Lutheran School

4513 Williams Rd.
Fort Worth, TX 76116
(817) 560-0032

Mapsco: 73Y

Fax: (817) 560-0031

Office Hours: 8:00 a.m.–4:00 p.m.
School Hours: 8:30 a.m.–3:30 p.m.
School Grades Offered: Preschool (age 3)–grade 7
Enrollment: 130
Co-ed: Yes
Boy/Girl Ratio: 1:1
Student/Teacher Ratio: 18:1 or less
Average Class Size: 18
Calendar School Year: August–May
Holidays: Basically the same as F.W.I.S.D.
Uniform Requirements: None
Founded in: 1963

Philosophy of School

Redeemer Lutheran School is dedicated to serving both the congregation and the community by providing a quality program of education in a Christ-centered, safe, positive, caring environment. We strive to meet the needs of the whole child and to minister to the family.

Academic Curriculum

Content: State approved texts
Grading System Used: Percentage-based; 100-91 (A), 90-81 (B), 80-70 (C)
Conferences per Year: One scheduled; additional conferences scheduled as needed
Tests Administered: Iowa Test of Basic Skills
Homework Policy: Varies in each grade level
Method of Discipline: Canter Assertive Discipline Policy

184

Enrichment Curriculum
Spanish, computer

Extracurricular Activities
Art, drama

Goals for Students
To receive a first-class Christ-centered education

Faculty/Staff Requirements
Qualifications of Staff: College degrees; dedicated people
Qualifications of Administrator: College degrees; dedicated people

School Information
Brochure Available: Yes
Number of Students in Each Grade: Pre-K, 16; kindergarten, 16; first grade, 22; second grade, 22; third grade, 20; fourth grade, 20; fifth and sixth grade (combined class), 15
Parochial: Yes
Organization Affiliations: Lutheran Church Missouri Synod
Accreditations: Licensed by state; in process of Lutheran church accrediation which is recognized by the state of Texas; LSA (pending)
Parental Involvement: Very active group; Friends of Redeemer School (FORS)
Other Information:

Admittance
Whom to Contact: Margaret Bentrup, Principal
Date to Apply: After February 1
Testing Procedure for Age/Grade Level: All new students in grades 1–7 must take entrance exam.
Fees Involved: Registration fee (pre-k $125, kindergarten–grade 6 $175)
Type of Student Preferred: N/A
Forms Required: Health forms
Individual/Group Appointments: Individual appointments with principal and/or teacher
Notification Procedure: By phone
Waiting List Policy: Annually

Tuition

Approximate Tuition for 1996-97 School Year: $800, preschool; $1380, pre-K and kindergarten; $2300, grades 1-7

Methods of Payment Available: 9, 10, or 11 payments

Financial Assistance Offered: Limited

Cancellation Insurance Available: No

Profit/Non-profit: Non-profit

Additional Costs

Books/Bag/Uniform: None

Lunch Fee: None

Parents Club Dues: None

Annual Fund Drive: Only fundraising sales

Discount for Siblings: Yes, approximately 9%

Facilities/Services Provided

Computer Lab: Yes, Apple computers

Library: Yes, small school library and classroom libraries in each room

Snack Procedures: Provided by parents in pre-K and kindergarten; provided in after-school program

Before-school Care Program Available: Yes–beginning at 7:00 a.m.

After-school Care Program Available: Yes–until 6:00 p.m.

Nurse on Staff: No

Emergency Procedure Used: Teachers and staff trained in first aid and CPR

Transportation to and from School: No

Counseling and Evaluation Available: No

Graduation Information

Testing: N/A

Average SAT Scores: N/A

High School Our Students Usually Attend: N/A

Percentage of Seniors Attending College: N/A

Additional Information

St. Paul Lutheran School

1800 West Freeway
Fort Worth, TX 76102
(817) 332-2281

Mapsco: Ft. Worth

Fax: (817) 332-2640

Office Hours: 8:00 a.m.–5:00 p.m.
School Hours: 8:30 a.m.–3:30 p.m.
School Grades Offered: Age 4–grade 8
Enrollment: 250
Co-ed: Yes
Boy/Girl Ratio: 50:50
Student/Teacher Ratio: 20:1
Average Class Size: 24
Calendar School Year: August 14-May 31
Holidays: Thanksgiving, Christmas, spring break, Easter
Uniform Requirements: No
Founded in: 1960

Philosophy of School

To contribute to the total ministry of St. Paul Lutheran Church by: 1) teaching the truths of the Bible; 2) bringing a quality academic education to children in a loving Christian atmosphere; 3) reinforcing parents in their role as spiritual leaders in their families; 4) providing a witness to unchurched families through their children

Academic Curriculum

Content: Religion, math, social studies, science, language arts, physical education, foreign language (Spanish), fine arts (music, art, choirs, handbells)
Grading System Used: Percentages
Conferences per Year: One preschool home visit and one first quarter in school
Tests Administered: Stanford Achievement
Homework Policy: All required homework turned in by 8:30 a.m. daily
Method of Discipline: Christian love with responsibility

187

Enrichment Curriculum
Advanced courses in eighth-grade math and English

Extracurricular Activities
Sports programs for both boys and girls; grades 5-8–basketball, soccer, volleyball, track

Goals for Students

Faculty/Staff Requirements
Qualifications of Staff: All state certified; some have master's degrees.
Qualifications of Administrator: Master's degree in administration

School Information
Brochure Available: Yes
Number of Students in Each Grade: 24 maximum
Parochial: Lutheran
Organization Affiliations: Lutheran Church, Missouri Synod
Accreditations: Texas District Lutheran Schools Association
Parental Involvement: PTL very active
Other Information:

Admittance
Whom to Contact: Principal
Date to Apply: Beginning in January
Testing Procedure for Age/Grade Level: None
Fees Involved: $25 application fee
Type of Student Preferred: N/A
Forms Required: Previous tests and report cards
Individual/Group Appointments: N/A
Notification Procedure: N/A
Waiting List Policy: Annually

Tuition
Approximate Tuition for 1996-97 School Year: $3120
Methods of Payment Available: Monthly
Financial Assistance Offered: None
Cancellation Insurance Available:
Profit/Non-profit: Non-profit

Additional costs:

Books/Bag/Uniform: None
Lunch Fee: $1.75 per meal
Parents Club Dues: None
Annual Fund Drive: None
Discount for Siblings: None

Facilities/Services Provided

Computer Lab: Yes, networked Apples with printers
Library: Yes, early childhood through junior high school with computer and CD-ROM
Snack Procedures:
Before-school Care Program Available: 7:00 a.m.
After-school Care Program Available: Until 6:00 p.m.
Nurse on Staff: None
Emergency Procedure Used: Trained staff
Transportation to and from School: Cars only
Counseling and Evaluation Available: N/A

Graduation Information

Testing: N/A
Average SAT Scores: N/A
High School Our Students Usually Attend: Various
Percentage of Seniors Attending College: N/A

Additional Information

Zion Lutheran School

6121 E. Lovers Lane
Dallas, TX 75214
(214) 363-1630

Mapsco: 36C

Fax: (214) 361-2049

Office Hours: 8:00 a.m–4:30 p.m.
School Hours: 7:00 a.m–6:00 p.m.
School Grades Offered: Preschool (3 years)–grade 8
Enrollment: 225
Co-ed: Yes
Boy/Girl Ratio: 50:50
Student/Teacher Ratio: 15:1
Average Class Size: 18
Calendar School Year: August 22, 1996–June 2, 1997
Holidays: Labor Day, Thanksgiving, Christmas, New
Year's Day, Easter, Memorial Day
Uniform Requirements: Yes
Founded in: 1948

Philosophy of School

The purpose of Zion Lutheran School is to provide Christian education in partnership
with parents so that children may be provided with a comprehensive program of
education; children may be nurtured in the Word of God; children may in faith learn to
know Jesus Christ; children, by God's grace, may experience a full Christian life;
children may learn to recognize themselves as persons of worth; children may learn to
understand and appreciate their talents and gifts.

Academic Curriculum

Content: Language arts, math, science, arts (visual and performing), religious
studies, physical education, social studies, computer science
Grading System Used: Letter grades (A, B, C, F) based on numerical
percentage scale 100%–70%
Conferences per Year: Three–one pre-term, in-home conference (August) and

two progress conferences (November and March)

Tests Administered: Iowa Test of Basic Skills administered to students in grades 1-8 in March

Homework Policy: Assignments given to reinforce lessons taught in curriculum

Method of Discipline: Behaviors and appropriate consequences determined by school behavior standards

Enrichment Curriculum

Computer instruction (preschool-grade 8); outdoor education (grade 7); choir (grades 4-8; spring musical, band

Extracurricular Activities

Interscholastic sports program (grades 5-8), triennial basketball tournament (New Orleans and Houston), cheerleaders (grades 7-8), field trips related to curriculum support

Goals for Students

To be all God intended them to be

Faculty/Staff Requirements

Qualifications of Staff: Minimum degree: B.A.; state-issued teaching certificate; member of the Lutheran Church (Missouri Synod); preferred credential: certification by the Lutheran Church (Missouri Synod)

Qualifications of Administrator: Minimum degree: M.Ed. (preferred); certified by the Lutheran Church (Missouri Synod); same as above

School Information

Brochure Available: Yes

Number of Students in Each Grade: 19 (average)

Parochial: Yes

Organization Affiliations: Texas Association of Non-Public Schools (TANS), National Junior Honor Society

Accreditations: Texas Education Agency; Lutheran Church-Missouri Synod, Texas District (LCMS)

Parental Involvement: Yes, in a variety of volunteer opportunities

Other Information:

Admittance

Whom to Contact: Preschool-kindergarten/extended care–Judy Berg; grades 1-8–Douglas C. Molin

Date to Apply: New applications accepted after January 15

Testing Procedure per Age/Grade Level: None

Fees Involved: Enrollment fee $120-$280

Type of Student Preferred: Any student

Forms Required: Grade transcripts and current achievement test scores

Individual/Group Appointments: Individual interview by appointment

Notification Procedure: Acceptance letter and phone call

Waiting List Policy: Re-apply annually

Tuition

Approximate Tuition for 1996-97 School Year: $1197-$4194

Methods of Payment Available: Monthly

Financial Assistance Offered: Yes

Cancellation Insurance Available: No

Profit/Non-profit: Non-profit

Additional Costs

Books/Bag/Uniform: Books and bag–no; uniform–$200 (average cost)

Lunch Fee: Based on individual lunch order

Parents Club Dues: Yes, $10

Annual Fund Drive: No

Discount for Siblings: No

Facilities/Services Provided

Computer Lab: Self-contained computer lab equipped with 26 computer stations

Library: Over 5400 books and reference materials

Snack Procedures: Provided to preschool and kindergarten

Before-school Care Program Available: Yes; 7:00 a.m.–8:00 a.m.

After-school Care Program Available: Yes; 3:30 p.m.–6:00 p.m.

Nurse on Staff: No (teachers trained in first aid)

Emergency Procedure Used: Defined by circumstance

Transportation to and from School: None provided by school

Counseling and Evaluation Available: Yes

Graduation Information

Testing: N/A

Average SAT Scores: N/A

High School Our Students Usually Attend: Lutheran High School, Woodrow Wilson High School
Percentage of Seniors Attending College: N/A

Additional Information

For information about our parent's-day-out program, call (214) 360-0626.

NCSA
National Christian Schools
Association of America

P.O. Box 28295
Dallas, TX 75228-0295
(214) 270-5495

Definition:

Christian professionals from different schools work together to improve efforts in molding children in the image of Christ.

Eligibility for NCSA accreditation

1. A school must be a member of NCSA or a state affiliate of NCSA
2. The school must pay annual membership fees.
3. The school's board must be composed of members of churches of Christ.
4. The school must not discriminate on the basis of race, color, national, or ethnic origin.
5. A school must offer four or more consecutive grades with at least 60 students and four full-time faculty members.
6. A school will be accredited for a period of five years.

(TEPSAC) Texas Private School Accreditation Commission

In order to be accredited as a private school with Texas Education Agency, schools must meet accreditation requirements through a recognized organization. The National Christian Schools Association is one that they recognize.

There is a large book of accreditation requirements that the commission uses to accredit schools.

Dallas Christian School (see SACS)
Fort Worth Christian School (see SACS)

SACS
Southern Association of
Colleges and Schools

Southern Association of Colleges and Schools
The University of Texas at Austin
P.O. Box 7307
Austin, Texas 78713
(512) 471-6660

The Southern Association of Colleges and Schools, established in 1895, is governed by a 27-member board of trustees including an elected president. The purpose of the Southern Association is to improve education. The Association is voluntary, nonprofit, and non-governmental.

Membership is open to public and private institutions in 11 southern states and Latin America. Currently, there are more than 11,000 members enrolling nearly 10 million students. The Southern Association is composed of:
> universities
> senior colleges
> two-year colleges
> professional schools
> vocational-technical schools
> high schools
> junior high schools
> middle schools
> elementary schools
> early childhood centers and kindergartens

Accreditation is a process of helping institutions improve through a systemic program of evaluation and the application of educational standards or criteria. Accreditation means not only that minimum standards are met, but also that the school community is committed to raising the quality of its program.

Regional accreditation is comprehensive: it covers the total school, not just certain programs. Member schools must undertake exhaustive self-studies involving teachers, administrators, students, and those on governing bodies. Then there is an evaluation by a visiting committee of peers—professional educators who, serving as volunteers, give an objective and candid reaction to the self-study and make recommendations based on their assessment of the institution.

Accreditation is not a permanent status. Continuing membership in the Southern Association depends on continuing improvement demonstrated through a regular cycle of annual reports, interim reviews, and periodic re-evaluations with a self-study and visiting team. Member institutions form three commissions:

> Commission on Elementary and Middle Schools
> Commission on Secondary and Middle Schools
> Commission on Colleges

Each member institution has one vote in the delegate assembly of its commission and each assembly sets the standards or criteria for its members.

> **Akiba Academy**
> **The Alexander School (see Alternative)**
> **Arbor Acre Preparatory School (see Alternative)**
> **Bending Oaks High School (see Alternative)**
> **Bishop Lynch High School (see TCCED)**
> **Bridgeway School (see Alternative)**
> **Carrollton Christian Academy**
> **Country Day School of Arlington (pending)**
> **Dallas Academy (see Alternative)**
> **Dallas Christian School**
> **Fairhill School (see Alternative)**
> **First Baptist Academy (see ACSI)**
> **Fort Worth Christian School**
> **Happy Hill Farm Academy/Home (see Alternative)**
> **Jesuit College Preparatory School (see TCCED)**
> **Keystone Academy (see Alternative)**
> **Lakehill Preparatory School (see ISAS)**
> **Lakemont Academy**
> **Liberty Christian School**
> **The Oakridge School (see ISAS)**
> **The June Shelton School & Evaluation Center (see Alternative)**
> **Solomon Schecter Academy of Dallas**
> **Sycamore School, Inc. (see Alternative)**
> **TreeTops School International**
> **Trinity Christian Academy**
> **Tyler Street Christian Academy**
> **The Ursuline Academy of Dallas (see TCCED)**
> **Walden Preparatory School (see Alternative)**
> **White Rock North School**

Akiba Academy

6210 Churchill Way
Dallas, TX 75230
(214) 239-7248

Mapsco: 15U

Fax: (214) 239-6818

Office Hours: 7:45 a.m.–5:30 p.m.
School Hours: 8:15 a.m.–3:30 p.m.
School Grades Offered: 18 months through grade 8
Enrollment: 400
Co-ed: Yes
Boy/Girl Ratio: 1:1
Student/Teacher Ratio: 6:1
Average Class Size: 15
Calendar School Year: August–May
Holidays: Jewish holidays; winter and spring vacations
Uniform Requirements: Yes (grades 1–8)
Founded in: 1962

Philosophy of School

Akiba Academy is committed to preparing the Jewish child to successfully integrate into a complex, diverse society while at the same time developing a strong personal commitment to our American-Jewish heritage. Akiba's philosophy facilitates the emotional, intellectual, and spiritual growth of each student, guiding and motivating each child to become a responsible, informed citizen.

Academic Curriculum

Content: Language arts, math, science, social studies, Hebrew, Bible, prayer, Jewish law and holidays
Grading System Used: Preschool–narratives; 1st & 2nd–letter grades; 3rd-8th–numerical grades
Conferences per Year: Two and as needed
Tests Administered: COGAT and ITBS, ERB Writing Assessment

197

Enrichment Curriculum
Art, computer, Hebrew, music, physical education

Extracurricular Activities
Chess club, computer club, sports, drama, science club, sports teams, choir, dance, karate

Goals for Students
We want our students to emerge from Akiba with a strong grounding in their Jewish heritage, coupled with an excellent academic preparation that will enable them to become successful, active, caring members of society.

Faculty/Staff Requirements
Qualifications of Staff: Bachelor's degree or teacher's license
Qualifications of Administrator: Master's degree or equivalent

School Information
Brochure Available: Yes
Number of Students in Each Grade:
Parochial: Yes
Organization Affiliations: Torah U'Mesorah
Accreditations: SACS, NAEYC
Parental Involvement: Total
Other Information:

Admittance
Whom to Contact: Hanna Lambert, Director of Admissions
Date to Apply: Early spring (February)
Testing Procedure per Age/Grade Level: Testing, appointment, and interview (grades 1–8); interview only (preschool and kindergarden)
Fees Involved:
Type of Student Preferred: Jewish children
Forms Required: Yes, after acceptance
Individual/Group Appointments: Individual
Notification Procedure: Usually within a week; by letter or phone call
Waiting List Policy: Check with school office for specific procedures

Tuition

Approximate Tuition for 1996-97 School Year: $2000-$6200
Methods of Payment Available: Annually; semi-annually; monthly
Financial Assistance Offered: Yes
Cancellation Insurance Available: No
Profit/Non-profit: Non-profit

Additional Costs

Books/Bag/Uniform: Fees for books and uniforms
Lunch fee: Hot lunches daily (kosher) $3.50/day; can bring own kosher lunches
Parents Club Dues: PTA annual dues $15 ($7.50 single-parent family)
Annual Fund Drive: Civic Award Dinner; scholarship events
Discount for Siblings: 10% for 2nd child, 15% for 3rd child in grades kindergarten-8

Facilities/Services Provided

Computer Lab: Yes
Library: Yes
Snack Procedures: Preschool snacks distributed morning and afternoon
Before-school Care Program Available: Yes (extra fee)
After-school Care Program Available: Yes (extra fee)
Nurse on Staff: No (Preschool, kindergarten, and physical education teachers and office staff are trained in CPR and first aid.)
Emergency Procedure Used: Yes, doctor on call; all standard forms with health release on file
Transportation to and from School: Parents' car pool
Counseling and Evaluation Available: Yes

Graduation Information

Testing: N/A
Average SAT scores: N/A
High School Our Students Usually Attend: Private and public
Percentage of Seniors Attending College: N/A

Additional Information

For Jewish children only
Recipient of U.S. Department of Education Award of Excellence, 1986
Expanded facilities to accommodate increasing enrollment

Carrollton Christian Academy

1820 Pearl, P.O. Box 110204
Carrollton, TX 75011
(214) 242-6688

Mapsco: 12D

Fax: (214) 446-0203

Office Hours: 7:30 a.m. –4:00 p.m.
School Hours: 7:40 a.m. –3:30 p.m.
School Grades Offered: Age 3–grade 12
Enrollment: 975
Co-ed: Yes
Boy/Girl Ratio: 50:50
Student/Teacher Ratio: 20:1 to 25:1
Average Class Size: 22
Calendar School Year: August–May
Holidays: Thanksgiving, Christmas break, spring break
Uniform Requirements: Yes
Founded in: 1980

Philosophy of School

Carrollton Christian Academy is more than a "private school." It is uniquely a Christian school which strives to equip each student enrolled in k-12 academically, socially, emotionally, and spiritually, at a reasonable cost. The administration, faculty, and staff are committed to integrating Biblical principles into all facets of school life, curricular and extracurriular, and to help students determine God's will for their lives. We hold precious our role in preparing students who may be called into full-time ministry and work diligently to provide a gentle balance of guidance, encouragement, instruction, and example. Our continual purpose is to glorify God by offering Him our best.

Academic Curriculum

Content: Christian traditional, college prepared
Grading System Used: Letter grades
Conferences per Year: Two
Tests Administered: Stanford Achievement Test

Homework Policy: Yes; 4 to 5 nights per week
Method of Discipline: Point system

Enrichment Curriculum
Fine arts: choir, band, drama, speech, orchestra

Extracurricular Activities
All sports are available.

Goals for Students
A Christian world view and success in college

Faculty/Staff Requirements
Qualifications of Staff: Certified teachers
Qualifications of Administrator: Administrative certificate

School Information
Brochure Available: Yes
Number of Students in Each Grade: 10-25 (depends on class)
Parochial:
Organization Affiliations:
Accreditations: Southern Association of Colleges and Schools
Parental Involvement: Parent-teacher fellowship
Other Information:

Admittance
Whom to Contact: Admissions
Date to Apply: February–August
Testing Procedure per Age/Grade Level:
Fees Involved: Registration fee $200; books–$120-$140
Type of Student Preferred: Average to above average industrious students
Forms Required: Yes
Individual/Group Appointments: Individual/possibility of group appointments
Notification Procedure: Letter
Waiting List Policy: Re-apply annually

Tuition

Approximate Tuition for 1996-97 School Year: 3-year-olds–$1200; 4-year-olds–$1350; pre-K–$1600; K–$2050; 1-5–$3425; 6-8–$3800; 9-12–$4100

Methods of Payment Available: 10 monthly payments

Financial Assistance Offered: Yes

Cancellation Insurance Available: No

Profit/Non-profit: Non-profit

Additional Costs

Books/Bag/Uniform: Yes

Lunch Fee: $2.50 per day

Parents Club Dues: None

Annual Fund Drive: Yes

Discount for Siblings: Yes

Facilities/Services Provided

Computer Lab: Yes; 30 IBM compatible (mixture of 386 and 486)

Library: Yes

Snack Procedures:

Before-school Care Program Available: Yes; beginning at 7:00 a.m.

After-school Care Program Available: Yes; ending at 6:00 p.m.

Nurse on Staff: Yes

Emergency Procedure Used:

Transportation to and from School: No

Counseling and Evaluation Available: Some

Graduation Information

Testing: Yes

Average SAT Scores: 950 (only two graduating classes)

High School Our Students Usually Attend: N/A

Percentage of Seniors Attending College: 93

Additional Information

Country Day School of Arlington, Inc.

1100 Roosevelt Street
Arlington, TX 76011
(817) 275-0851

Mapsco: #83
(Fort Worth)
Fax: (817) 275-0263

Office Hours: 8:00 a.m.–4:00 p.m.
School Hours: 8:30 a.m.–3:30 p.m.
School Grades Offered: Preschool (age 2)–grade 8
Enrollment: 280
Co-ed: Yes
Boy/Girl Ratio: 50:50
Student/Teacher Ratio: Elementary homerooms 15:1
(maximum)
Average Class Size: 15
Calendar School Year: Second week of August–end of May
Holidays: Labor Day, Thanksgiving, winter break, Martin Luther
King Day, Presidents' Day, spring break
Uniform Requirements: Boys–gray slacks or shorts; girls–plaid
shorts or jumpers
Founded in: 1959

Philosophy of School

The mission of Country Day School of Arlington is to educate each student to become a proud, productive, and responsible citizen who has lifelong choices and opportunities. We seek to promote a school that functions as a diverse community of active, engaged, and reflective learners. Through rigorous studies in academics, arts, and athletics, students develop the self-discipline and confidence necessary to establish and achieve their goals.

Academic Curriculum

Content: Language arts, math, science, social studies, foreign language, computer, art, physical education, library, music

Grading System Used: A, B, C, D, F

Conferences per Year: Two conference days

Tests Administered: Stanford and Otis-Lennon

Homework Policy: Nightly homework includes work on projects and practice of new concepts

Method of Discipline: Classroom rules and consequences are established by the teacher with the students.

Enrichment Curriculum

Weekly classes in French or Spanish, art, library, music, physical education, and computers

Extracurricular Activities

Soccer, gymnastics, scouts, piano, after-school clubs (e.g. chess club, foreign language club)

Goals for Students

By giving our students an enhanced educational foundation, we instill in them the value of learning as a lifelong process.

Faculty/Staff Requirements

Qualifications of Staff: Faculty have TEA certification; many have master's degrees.

Qualifications of Administrator: Excellent educational background and administrative experience

School Information

Brochure Available: Yes

Number of Students in Each Grade: 30

Parochial: No

Organization Affiliations: TANS

Accreditations: SACS currently pending

Parental Involvement: Very active P.T.O. and involvement in classroom projects

Other Information: Summer camp–each two-week session features outdoor play, arts and crafts, field trips, and daily academic electives.

Admittance

Whom to Contact: Dr. Laura Montgomery, principal
Date to Apply: March 5 for optimal processing
Testing Procedure for Age/Grade Level: KIDS test for kindergarten applicants; Stanford for grades 1-8
Fees Involved: Processing fee ($50)
Type of Student Preferred: Admissions based on academic potential and performance, developmental readiness, and ability to contribute to class
Forms Required: Application, teacher recommendations, transcripts
Individual/Group Appointments: Individual
Notification Procedure: In writing
Waiting List Policy: Ongoing

Tuition

Approximate Tuition for 1996-97 School Year: $5530
Methods of Payment Available: Monthly; semi-annually; annually
Financial Assistance Offered: Application through School and Student Services
Cancellation Insurance Available: No
Profit/Non-profit: Non-profit

Additional Costs

Books/Bag/Uniform: Annual textbook-and-library fee ($75); parents provide uniforms.
Lunch Fee: Hot lunch available for $2.50 daily
Parents Club Dues: None
Annual Fund Drive: Contributions sought annually
Discount for Siblings: 10%

Facilities/Services Provided

Computer Lab: 17 networked PC's, laser printer, CD-ROM, Internet
Library: The library is being fully automated this year.
Snack Procedures: Preschool parents sign up on snack schedule.
Before-school Care Program Available: Available at 7:00 a.m.
After-school Care Program Available: Available until 6:00 p.m
Nurse on Staff: No
Emergency Procedure Used: Students taken to Arlington Memorial Hospital
Transportation to and from School: Bus transportation–minimum $75/month
Counseling and Evaluation Available: Students referred to outside agencies

Graduation Information

Testing: N/A
Average SAT Scores: N/A
High School Our Students Usually Attend: We have been adding a grade per year.
Percentage of Seniors Attending College: N/A

Additional Information

Sixteen acre campus; groundbreaking for new kindergarten building in winter 1996

Dallas Christian School

1515 Republic Parkway
Mesquite, TX 75150
(214) 270-5495

Mapsco: 39A–N

Fax: (214) 270-7581

Office Hours: 8:00 a.m.–4:00 p.m.
School Hours: 8:30 a.m.–3:30 p.m. (Elem); 8:15 a.m.–3:30
p.m. (JH); 8:30 a.m.–3:55 p.m. (HS)
School Grades Offered: K3–12
Enrollment: 825
Co-ed: Yes
Boy/Girl Ratio: 421:404
Student/Teacher Ratio: 22:1
Average Class Size: 24
Calendar School Year: August–May (185 days)
Holidays: Labor Day, Fair Day, Thanksgiving, Christmas,
Martin Luther King Day, spring break
Uniform Requirements: 1st–5th graders have uniforms; upper
grades have a dress code
Founded in: 1957

Philosophy of School

The mission of Dallas Christian School is to provide a thoughtful, nurturing,
educational environment and working partnership that will develop intelligent,
courteous, skillful servants prepared to carry out God's will confidently in a global
marketplace.

Academic Curriculum

Content: College preparatory
Grading System Used: Numerical grades
Conferences per Year: As needed
Tests Administered: Stanford; PSAT; PACT; SAT

Homework Policy: Teachers detemine frequency and amount.
Method of Discipline: Parent-Administration Conference; detention; corporal punishment; suspension; expulsion

Enrichment Curriculum
Yearbook, drama, computers, French, Spanish, a cappella chorus, band, Art I–IV, Origins of English, and U.S. First Engineering Competition

Extracurricular Activities
Tennis, football, golf, basketball, volleyball, soccer, track, baseball, softball, and clubs (full sports programs for boys and girls)

Goals for Students
Our goal at Dallas Christian School is for all students to reach their full potential in academics, social skills, and spiritual growth.

Faculty/Staff Requirements
Qualifications of Staff: Teaching certificate
Qualifications of Administrator: M.A. and Ph.D.; exceeds minimum qualifications required by the Southern Association of Colleges and Schools

School Information
Brochure Available: Yes
Number of Students in Each Grade: Elementary–22 per class; junior high–24 per class; senior high–27 per class
Parochial: No
Organization Affiliations: Churches of Christ
Accreditations: SACS, NCSA, and TEA
Parental Involvement: Yes, volunteers
Other Information:

Admittance
Whom to Contact: Ernestine Siddle (elementary school); Ken Ferris (secondary school)
Date to Apply: Feburary 1
Testing Procedure per Age/Grade Level: Testing is done by qualified diagnostician.
Fees Involved: $75 (preschool and kindergarten); $95 (grades 1–12); $100

enrollment fee
Type of Student Preferred: Any student desiring a Christian education
Forms Required: Transcript, application, reference forms, immunization record
Individual/Group Appointments: Individual
Notification Procedure: Administration contacts parents.
Waiting List Policy: Students must reapply annually.

Tuition

Approximate Tuition for 1996-97 School Year: One payment: preschool (two-day program)–$1059; elementary (1-5)–$4120; Jr. high (6-8)–$5077; high school (9-12)–$5487
Methods of Payment Available: Monthly by bank draft; semester payments; annual payment
Financial Assistance Offered: Yes, limited
Cancellation Insurance Available: Yes
Profit/Non-profit: Non-profit

Additional Costs

Books/Bag/Uniform: High school art fee, $25 per semester
Lunch Fee: Optional
Parents Club Dues: P.T.O. yearly dues–$5
Annual Fund Drive: Magazine sales
Discount for Siblings: After third sibling

Facilities/Services Provided

Computer Lab: Yes
Library: Yes
Snack Procedures: Parents provide snacks for preschool and kindergarten students; school provides snacks for those in after-school care program.
Before-school Care Program Available: Yes, 7:00 a.m.
After-school Care Program Available: Yes, 6:00 p.m.
Nurse on Staff: No
Emergency Procedure Used: School contacts parents.
Transportation to and from School: No
Counseling and Evaluation Available: Yes

Graduation Information

Testing: SAT required for all seniors
Average SAT Scores: 1010 average–top 50%

High School Our Students Usually Attend: N/A
Percentage of Seniors Attending College: 90+

Additional Information

Fort Worth Christian School

7517 Bogart Drive at Holiday Lane   Mapsco: 37Z/38W
North Richland Hills, TX 76180
(817) 281-6504   Fax: (817) 281-7063

Office Hours: 8:00 a.m.–4:30 p.m.
School Hours: 8:00 a.m.–3:15 p.m.
School Grades Offered: Preschool–grade 12
Enrollment: 620
Co-ed: Yes
Boy/Girl Ratio: 1:1
Student/Teacher Ratio: 17:1
Average Class Size: 18–20
Calendar School Year: August–May
Holidays: Christmas (two weeks), spring break (one week)
Uniform Requirements: None
Founded in: 1957

Philosophy of School
To provide each student with a quality education to ensure a life of faith and service

Academic Curriculum
Content: College-preparatory
Grading System Used: A (90–100), B (80–89), C (70–79), Failing (below 70)
Conferences per Year: As scheduled
Tests Administered: Stanford (K–8), PLAN (9–10), PSAT (11), ACT and SAT (12)
Homework Policy: Homework is an important part of the learning process.
Method of Discipline: Encourage students to be responsible and accountable; natural consequences suited to the offense

Enrichment Curriculum
Honors classes available in English, history, math, science

211

Extracurricular Activities
Band, chorus, gymnastics, drama, football, basketball, softball, track, volleyball, tennis, golf, baseball, interscholastic league literary meet, cheerleading, one act play

Goals for Students
To achieve spiritual growth and academic excellence

Faculty/Staff Requirements
Qualifications of Staff: Texas certificate required and bachelor's degree
Qualifications of Administrator: Texas certificate required and master's degree

School Information
Brochure Available: Yes
Number of Students in Each Grade: 40–55
Parochial: No
Organization Affiliations: Organized by members of the Church of Christ
Accreditations: Southern Association of Colleges and Schools, National Christian Schools Association
Parental Involvement: Welcomed and encouraged
Other Information:

Admittance
Whom to Contact: Sarah Schector (preschool–grade 5), Kent Hart (grades 6–8), Laura Bynum (grades 9–12)
Date to Apply: Returning students–February 1; new students–March 1
Testing Procedure per Age/Grade Level: Scheduled by appointment
Fees Involved: Yes
Type of Student Preferred: Those with C average or above; must have satisfactory conduct references
Forms Required: Yes
Individual/Group Appointments: Individual
Notification Procedure: Letter
Waiting List Policy: Re-apply

Tuition
Approximate Tuition for 1996-97 School Year: $2375–$4900
Methods of Payment Available: Payment in full upon enrollment; bank

financing available
Financial Assistance Offered: Yes
Cancellation Insurance Available: No

Additional Costs

Books/Bag/Uniform: None (except for books in special classes)
Lunch Fee: Yes, approximately $2.50
Parents Club Dues: Yes ($5 per family)
Annual Fund Drive: Yes
Discount for Siblings: Yes (10% for second child, 20% for third child, 30% for fourth child)

Facilities/Services Provided

Computer Lab: Two current labs with two under construction; additional computer facilities in all three libraries
Library: Three libraries on campus (elementary, middle school, high school), on-line Public Access Catalog
Snack Procedures: Snacks available at breaks
Before-school Care Program Available: 6:15 a.m.–8:00 a.m.
After-school Care Program Available: 2:30 p.m.–6:15 p.m.
Nurse on Staff: Yes
Emergency Procedure Used: Planned emergency procedure for fire or severe weather
Transportation to and from School: No (car pools)
Counseling and Evaluation Available: Yes

Graduation Information

Testing: Yes
Average SAT Scores: 1080
High School Our Students Usually Attend: N/A
Percentage of Seniors Attending College: 100

Additional Information

Motor-skill-development program implemented to promote mental productivity through participation in physical education classes

Lakemont Academy

3993 W. Northwest Highway
Dallas, TX 75220
(214) 351-6404

Mapsco: 24W

Fax: (214) 358-4510

Office Hours: 8:30 a.m.-5:00 p.m.
School Hours: 7:30 a.m.-6:00 p.m. (school program–
8:15 a.m.-3:30 p.m.)
School Grades Offered: 18 months-grade12
Enrollment: 120
Co-ed: Yes
Boy/Girl Ratio: Varies
Student/Teacher Ratio: 7:1–16:1
Average Class Size: 10-1
Calendar School Year: August–May
Holidays: Traditional
Uniform Requirements: Yes
Founded in: 1976

Philosophy of School

Lakemont employs Montessori methods and incorporates a Christian classics curriculum and an in-depth study into the worlds of faith, art, history, literature, and science. Our students receive a Renaissance education. Its values are traditional; its concepts are classic; its application is practical. Lakemont best serves the academically gifted, but it provides a unique, challenging setting where all competent children can excel.

Academic Curriculum

Content: Montessori, classics, and college preparatory
Grading System Used: Mastery system; grades are sent home.
Conferences per Year: Two
Tests Administered: Stanford Achievement Test (k-12)
Homework Policy: Homework from syllabus in high school; elementary

214

includes reading, spelling, and writing
Method of Discipline: Time out, parent involvement

Enrichment Curriculum

Computers, music, business entrepreneurship, extended field trips, greenhouse, foreign language, animals, gardens, and community resources

Extracurricular Activities

Sports programs; private and group lessons available in ballet, gymnastics, music, piano, and horsemanship.

Goals for Students

- To become confident learners and analytical thinkers
- To persevere at hard work until it is accomplished with integrity
- To build leadership in a context of moral and spiritual values

Faculty/Staff Requirements

Qualifications of Staff: College degree, Montessori training
Qualifications of Administrator: College degree, Montessori training

School Information

Brochure Available: Yes
Number of Students in Each Grade: Varies
Parochial: Non-denominational
Organization Affiliations: ACSI, TANS
Accreditations: SACS
Parental Involvement: Parenting classes; Montessori classes for parents; volunteer programs
Other Information:

Admittance

Whom to Contact: Edward Fidellow
Date to Apply: February 1
Testing Procedure per Age/Grade Level: Entrance exam starts with kindergarten students
Fees Involved: $250
Type of Student Preferred: Academically competent and able to become self-disciplined, independent learners

Forms Required: Yes
Individual/Group Appointments: Individual
Notification Procedure: Within two weeks of application
Waiting List Policy: Some areas

Tuition

Approximate Tuition for 1996-97 School Year: $6000–$7100
Methods of Payment Available: Yearly or monthly
Financial Assistance Offered: Yes
Cancellation Insurance Available: Yes
Profit/Non-profit: Non-profit

Additional Costs

Books/Bag/Uniform: Books $200-$400 (grades 7-12); bag not required; uniform costs vary.
Lunch Fee: Included in tuition
Parents Club Dues: N/A
Annual Fund Drive: Yes
Discount for Siblings: As requested

Facilities/Services Provided

Computer Lab: Yes
Library: Yes
Snack Procedures: Provided
Before-school Care Program Available: Yes; 7:30 a.m.–6:00 p.m. included in pre-school; $800 per year for elementary school
After-school Care Program Available: Yes; until 6:00 p.m. as indicated
Nurse on Staff: No
Emergency Procedure Used: Call parents/St. Paul Hospital
Transportation to and from School: No
Counseling and Evaluation Available: Yes

Graduation Information

Testing: SAT, ACT
Average SAT Scores: 1010
High School Our Students Usually Attend: N/A
Percentage of Seniors Attending College: 90

Additional Information

The four-acre campus provides garden space, a barnyard with chickens and rabbits, workshops, and a greenhouse for learning experiences.

Dining room tables are set each day with linens and napkins. The carpeted high school dining area has chandeliers and is set with china, crystal, and silver.

Emphasis is on serving the community. Lakemont Academy offers learning experiences both in and out of classroom settings.

Students are responsible for running their own enterprises in the Entrepreneurship Program. They learn the fundamental recipe for success: work, initiative, enthusiam responsibility, excellence, and determination. Students operate a catering company and a gourmet coffee company.

LAKEMONT ACADEMY

3993 W. Northwest Hwy **351-6404** (between Midway and Marsh)

A Christian Montessori Classics Curriculum
for the Academically Bright, Creative Child
18 Months through 12th Grade

- Critical Thinking Skills
- College Prep/Accredited
- Entrepreneurship
- Extended Day/Summer Program
- Etiquette, Travel
- Athletics

Developing independence and self-demanded excellence

Liberty Christian School

1500 South Bonnie Brae
Denton, TX 76207
(817) 565-0466

Mapsco: 346G (Fort Worth)

Fax: (817) 381-2485

Office Hours: 8:30 a.m.–4:00 p.m.
School Hours: 8:30 a.m.–3:30 p.m.
School Grades Offered: K–grade 12
Enrollment: 492
Co-ed: Yes
Boy/Girl Ratio: Approximately 50:50
Student/Teacher Ratio: Approximately 17:1
Average Class Size: 18
Calendar School Year: September-May
Holidays: Labor Day, Thanksgiving, Christmas, New Year's
Day, spring break, Good Friday
Uniform Requirements: Yes–St. Agnes Uniform Co. of Dallas
Founded in: 1982

Philosophy of School

Education can most effectively be accomplished in an environment which recognizes
that all truth is God's truth. We emphasize this fact and stress the development of an
eternal perspective of life. We strive to provide an environment in which the individual
student can mature spiritually and achieve academic excellence. Pupils are directed not
only in the acquisition of knowledge and skills, but also in the pursuit of worthy
interests, ideas, and attitudes essential for Christian maturity. We want to develop the
complete individual spiritually, mentally, physically, and socially (Luke 2:52).

Academic Curriculum

Content: Curriculum built around Christian world-view
Grading System Used: Numerical–100-point scale
Conferences per Year: One scheduled; others at parents' request
Tests Administered: Stanford Achievement Tests, PSAT, PLAN, ASVAB

Homework Policy: Required daily in academic subjects (approximately 25 minutes per subject)
Method of Discipline: Tally system and suspension

Enrichment Curriculum

Honors courses with increased requirements; others include art, foreign language (Spanish, French, introduction to Latin), choir, computer, debate, speech, drama, Christian humanities, sociology, world politics, British history, accounting

Extracurricular Activities

Sports: football, basketball, volleyball, baseball, softball, track; weight training, cheerleading, drill team, choir, debate, theater, National Honor Society, student government, National Forensic League, yearbook, dance

Goals for Students

To mature into young people who use and enjoy their God-given talents; to be prepared academically, emotionally, and socially for success in college and in life; to develop a firm foundation in Christian faith and a vital relationship with God

Faculty/Staff Requirements

Qualifications of Staff: Christian; college education and teaching certification or required number of education courses
Qualifications of Administrator: Christian; college education and teaching certification or required number of education courses

School Information

Brochure Available: Yes
Number of Students in Each Grade: K-35, 1st-51, 2nd-36, 3rd-23, 4th-27, 5th-32, 6th-28, 7th-52, 8th-43, 9th-45, 10th-46, 11th-28, 12th-41
Parochial: Inter-denominational
Organization Affiliations: Association of Christian Schools International, Texas Association of Parochial and Private Schools
Accreditations: Southern Association of Colleges and Schools
Parental Involvement: Parent-Teacher Fellowship, Parent Workrooms
Other Information: Packet of information available upon request

Admittance

Whom to Contact: Call office to make appointment with Dr. Dwight Gailey

Date to Apply: Best to apply in spring preceding fall entrance
Testing Procedure for Age/Grade Level: As needed
Fees Involved: $300 application fee
Type of Student Preferred: Christian; C minimum grade average; good conduct record
Forms Required: Enrollment application, previous report cards, achievement test scores
Individual/Group Appointments: Individual appointment preferred with parents and children
Notification Procedure: Notified by letter or telephone
Waiting List Policy: Re-enrollment for current students each spring; waiting list for grades with full enrollment

Tuition

Approximate Tuition for 1996-97 School Year: $4140-$5820
Methods of Payment Available: Annually or monthly
Financial Assistance Offered: Limited provision for financial aid and scholarships
Cancellation Insurance Available: No
Profit/Non-profit: Non-profit (not affiliated with any denomination)

Additional Costs

Books/Bag/Uniform: Textbooks included in tuition; uniforms and bus fees not included in tuition
Lunch Fee: Debit-account system (approximately $2.50 per day)
Parents Club Dues: None
Annual Fund Drive: Yes
Discount for Siblings: None

Facilities/Services Provided

Computer Lab: Yes, 14 station instruction facility
Library: More than 5000 volumes; video/VCR equipment; overhead projectors
Snack Procedures: Daily, mid-morning for grades 7-12
Before-school Care Program Available: None
After-school Care Program Available: None
Nurse on Staff: Yes
Emergency Procedure Used: Call parent; use local emergency facilities
Transportation to and from School: Bus service to Lewisville and Lake Dallas
Counseling and Evaluation Available: Entrance testing; individual K-12; academic K-12

Graduation Information

Testing: Interest Inventory, PSAT, PLAN
Average SAT Scores: 1020; ACT–21
High School Our Students Usually Attend:
Percentage of Seniors Attending College: 90

Additional Information

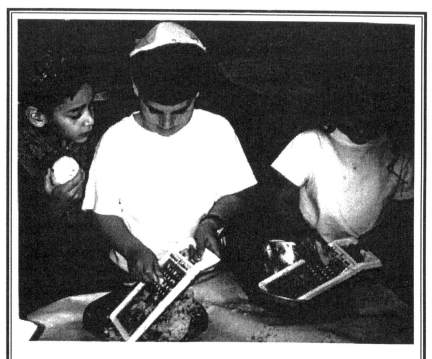

FOR THE JOY OF LEARNING

A child should find school a warm, loving place. School should nurture a child's uniqueness, helping the child to express his or her gifts. Most of all, schooling should mean the joy of learning.

At Solomon Schechter Academy, we have everything a good private school should have: a whole-language based curriculum including language arts, math, science, and social studies with opportunities for enrichment and differentiated learning, computer literacy and applications, fine arts, and athletics. We offer a comprehensive Jewish studies program in Hebrew, Bible, Jewish history, and Jewish living. But more importantly, we cherish your child's joy.

SOMOMON SCHECTER ACADEMY OF DALLAS
Day School of Congregation Shearith Israel
18011 Hillcrest Rd.
Dallas, Texas 75252
(214) 248-3032

Solomon Schechter Academy of Dallas

18011 Hillcrest Road
Dallas, TX 75232
(214) 248-3032

Mapsco: 5H

Fax: (214) 248-0695

Office Hours: 7:30 a.m.–6:00 p.m.
School Hours: 8:00 a.m.–4:00 p.m.
School Grades Offered: Preschool–grade 8
Enrollment: 533
Co-ed: Yes
Boy/Girl Ratio: 1:1
Student/Teacher Ratio: 15:1
Average Class Size: 15
Calendar School Year: August–May
Holidays: All Jewish holidays, Labor Day, Thanksgiving, winter break, Martin Luther King Day, Presidents' Day, Passover break, Memorial Day
Uniform Requirements: None
Founded in: 1979

Philosophy of School

Solomon Schechter is a Conservative Jewish Day School in which the secular and Judaic studies programs reinforce each other. The practices and beliefs of Conservative Judaism are presented positively and lived openly as an integral part of school life.

Solomon Schechter Academy offers a warm, family-oriented atmosphere--one in which children feel loved, nurtured, and motivated to learn. The school is dedicated to maintaining high standards and progressive curricula. Each child is encouraged to appreciate and express his/her own uniqueness and to function as a positive participant in a group. At Solomon Schechter, we believe the realization of the individual's potential, combined with the daily practice of relating to others, offers the child the best opportunity for learning to cope successfully in our rapidly changing world.

Academic Curriculum

Content: Full range of secular and Judaic studies
Grading System Used: Elementary, non-graded; middle school (grades 5–8), letter and numerical grades
Conferences per Year: Two parent-teacher conferences are mandatory.
Tests Administered: California Achievement Test, grades 3–8; criterion testing, grades K–2
Homework Policy: Mandatory for grades 3 and up; 45 minutes for grade 3 to approximately 2 hours per night for grade 8
Method of Discipline: We follow a discipline plan based on the concept of "logical consequences and self-responsibility" for students in grades K–8.

Enrichment Curriculum

Afternoon enrichment for preschoolers; exploratories for middle school, including photography, computers, oil painting, pottery wheel, cooking, guitar, and other art experiences

Extracurricular Activities

Basketball, soccer, and volleyball teams; choraliers; social action; student council; Vaad Tefilah; peer mediation

Goals for Students

Our mission is to:
- foster academic and ethical excellence
- stimulate a lifelong love of Judaism and learning
- promote personal and social responsibility
- enable our graduates to succeed to their maximum potential in a challenging world of diversity and rapid change

Faculty/Staff Requirements

Qualifications of Staff: Teacher certification; people educated in Jewish and general studies and committed to helping children realize their potential; (many have master's degrees)
Qualifications of Administrator: Minimum–master's degree

School Information

Brochure Available: Yes
Number of Students in Each Grade: 12-14 students in each preschool class; maximum of 16 students in each K–8 class; (preschool –5 classes; elementary–

3 or 4 classes; middle school–2 classes)
Parochial: Jewish Day School
Organization Affiliations: Day School of Congregation Shearith Israel; Texas Association of Non-Public Schools; National Solomon Schechter Day School; Association of United Synagogue of Conservatism Judaism; Beneficiary of Jewish Federation of Greater Dallas
Accreditations: Southern Association of Colleges and Schools
Parental Involvement: Active Parents' Association; we encourage participation on all school committees.

Admittance

Whom to Contact: Ms. Judi Glazer, Registrar
Date to Apply: January
Testing Procedure per Age/Grade Level: No formal testing is required for admission
Fees Involved: Application fee–$300
Type of Student Preferred: Open to all Jewish children
Forms Required: Previous school records, report cards, and medical records
Individual/Group Appointments: Appointments must be made with the appropriate administrator.
Notification Procedure: Acceptance letter sent, conditional for new students until the child's educational history is evaluated
Waiting List Policy: Selected classes

Tuition

Approximate Tuition for 1996-97 School Year: $2000–$6900
Methods of Payment Available: Monthly, semi-annually, annually; cash, checks, or credit card (Master Card or Visa)
Financial Assistance Offered: Financial aid available for grades k–8
Cancellation Insurance Available: Yes
Profit/Non-profit: Non-profit

Additional Costs

Books/Bag/Uniform: Book fee (middle school); no bag or uniform fees
Lunch Fee: Available, not compulsory
Parents Club Dues: Parents' Association dues $15
Annual Fund Drive: $600 fair share per family
Discount for Siblings: None

Facilities/Services Provided

Computer Lab: The lab consists of a classroom of multimedia computers and related instructional and demonstration hardware plus a modem for on-line services. Students attend at least weekly for direct instruction and for special projects. Computers are used to assist with the regular classroom curriculum, and special projects. All instructional activities relate to what students learn in general Jewish studies. The instructors are certified teachers in the computer field.

Library: The library is fully stocked and has a full-time librarian. This busy space is used for library instruction, book selection, special reports, and research. All students in grades k-6 attend the library weekly for classes. Students in grades 7 and 8 use the library as needed. The collection consists of over 7000 volumes.

Snack Procedures: Children provide their own snacks.

Before-school Care Program Available: 8:00 a.m.–9:00 a.m. for preschool children

After-school Care Program Available: Day care until 6:00 p.m.

Nurse on Staff: None

Emergency Procedure Used: Medics

Transportation to and from School: No bus transportation; car pools only

Counseling and Evaluation Available: Counselor available in elementary and middle school

Graduation Information

Testing: N/A

Average SAT Scores: N/A

High School Our Students Usually Attend: Greenhill, St. Mark's, D.I.S.D. magnet schools, P.I.S.D., R.I.S.D.

Percentage of Seniors Attending College: N/A

Additional Information

227

TreeTops School International

12500 South Pipeline
Euless, TX 76040
(817) 283-1771

Mapsco:

Fax: (817) 283-1771

Mailing address: D/FW Box 610734
D/FW Airport, TX 75261

Office Hours: 8:00 a.m.–4:00 p.m.
School Hours: 8:20 a.m.–3:20 p.m.
School Grades Offered: Pre-kindergarten–grade 12
Enrollment: 120
Co-ed: Yes
Boy/Girl Ratio: 1:1
Student/Teacher Ratio: Not more than 12:1
Average Class Size: 10–12
Calendar School Year: August–May
Holidays: Winter and spring breaks
Uniform Requirements: No
Founded in: 1969

Philosophy of School

To enable normal, gifted, and dyslexic students "to climb to the heights that are their own," using multiple environments to nurture the strengths of individual learners and to practice creating a caring community where respect for persons and respect for property are the basis for campus experiences and relationships.

Academic Curriculum

Content: Propaedeutic–spanning cognitive and aesthetic domains
Grading System Used: As required for accreditation
Conferences per Year: As needed
Tests Administered: Individual assessments as needed, including PSAT and PLAN

Homework Policy: Varies with course requirements and child's daily work
Method of Discipline: Student Council actions when self-discipline fails

Enrichment/Extracurricular Activities

The curriculum is not segregated into "Enrichment" or "Extracurricular," but experiences are woven together to connect disciplines, concepts, the arts, and the child's shaping of the action.

Music, dance, drama, junior historians, stock market, junior state debate, orienteering, and on-campus sports leagues are offered. The Biophilia experience is provided through trips to the school's environmental studies lodge in the Davy Crockett National Forest; international travel is also a part of the curriculum.

Goals for Students

To reach their potentials as persons, both intellectually and as caring, contributing citizens of their local community and the world community

Faculty/Staff Requirements

Qualifications of Staff: Both TEA, SACS, and Montessori credentials
Qualifications of Administrator: Ph.D., Montessori certification, educational diagnostician

School Information

Brochure Available: One-page flyer available (resources go to children)
Number of Students in Each Grade: Each cluster has 30 students, subdivided into three groups of ten.
Parochial: No
Organization Affiliations: TANS, TISC, SACS, international groups
Accreditations: Southern Association of Colleges and Schools
Parental Involvement: Required because school is organized as a co-op
Other Information: The school is organized as "Treetops Village," and each student has a role in caring for the 20-acre campus, its wandering trails, museums, and learning areas.

Admittance

Whom to Contact: Michele Solomon, Parent Services Director
Date to Apply: Prior to the term

Testing Procedure per Age/Grade Level: Individual testing
Fees Involved: None
Type of Student Preferred: Children whose joy for learning has not been polluted by pressure or surface performance goals
Forms Required: Health forms required upon admission
Individual/Group Appointments: TBA after phone inquiry
Notification Procedure: Director calls <u>after</u> parents and student visit, giving recommendations of teachers
Waiting List Policy: Not encouraged as children do not thrive with indecision, too much school switching

Tuition

Approximate Tuition for 1996-97 School Year: $3400 + fees
Methods of Payment Available: Cash in advance or FACTS payment plan
Financial Assistance Offered: N/A
Cancellation Insurance Available: N/A; recommended if moving is a possibility
Profit/Non-profit: Non-profit

Additional Costs

Books/Bag/Uniform: Books–included in supply fees; bag and uniform–not required
Lunch Fee: No
Parents Club Dues: N/A
Annual Fund Drive: N/A
Discount for Siblings: N/A, except for membership and insurance

Facilities/Services Provided

Computer Lab: Yes; also computers in classrooms
Library: 10,000 volumes
Snack Procedures: After 25 years, the Upper School now has a cold drink machine.
Before-school Care Program Available: Yes; 7:30 a.m.
After-school Care Program Available: Yes; 5:30 p.m.
Nurse on Staff: From the co-op
Emergency Procedure Used: Based on accreditation guidelines
Transportation to and from School: Parents' car pools
Counseling and Evaluation Available: Counselor on staff

Graduation Information

Testing: PSAT, PACT (PLAN), standardized achievement tests
Average SAT Scores: Varies with student
High School Our Students Usually Attend: N/A
Percentage of Seniors Attending College: 100

Additional Information

International travel is part of the curriculum, including semesters abroad. Students have won top honors for years in the state poetry awards, the National Mythology exams, video competitions, and geography exams.

Trinity Christian Academy

17001 Addison Rd.
Dallas, TX 75248
~~(214) 931-8325~~
972 931-8325

Mapsco: 4U

Fax: ~~(214)~~ *972* 931-8923

Office Hours: 8:00 a.m.–3:30 p.m.
School Hours: 8:00 a.m.–4:00 p.m.
School Grades Offered: Kindergarten–grade 12
Enrollment: 1400
Co-ed: Yes
Boy/Girl Ratio: 1:1
Student/Teacher Ratio: 14:1
Average Class Size: 18–20
Calendar School Year: August 17–May 31
Holidays: Winter break (2 weeks); spring break (5 days);
major holidays
Uniform Requirements: Yes
Founded in: 1970

Philosophy of School

The TCA mission statement is summarized by the phrase "educating and developing the whole person for the glory of God." The philosophy statement defines Trinity's goal as fostering "a dedicated faculty teaching the most challenging, Biblically integrated curriculum to a broad range of students."

Academic Curriculum

Content: College-preparatory, demanding curriculum
Grading System Used: A–F, weighted; mail grades home
Conferences per Year: Two scheduled per year; additional conferences scheduled at parent's request
Tests Administered: Grades 1-12–Stanford Achievement Test; kindergarten–Missouri KIDS test
Homework Policy: Homework at all grade levels, varies per school

232

Method of Discipline: Middle- and Lower-School students handled by heads of schools; Upper-School students led by Honor Council

Enrichment Curriculum

Integration of faith and learning; writing emphasis; AIMS program in grades 7-12 with computer-related mathematics-science applications emphasized; lower school– computer lab with regularly scheduled class time

Extracurricular Activities

Football, volleyball, track/field, cross country, tennis, wrestling, basketball, golf, baseball, softball, soccer, drill team, cheerleading, classical music band, choir, yearbook, Gallery Staff, speech, drama, international club, chess club, National Honor Society, Spanish Honor Society

Goals for Students

To develop and educate the whole person for the glory of God

Faculty/Staff Requirements

Qualifications of Staff: College degree, preferably advanced degrees; conservative, evangelical religious practice
Qualifications of Administrator: College degree; advanced degree; independent school background

School Information

Brochure Available: Yes
Number of Students in Each Grade: Varies–average 100
Parochial: N/A
Organization Affiliations: ACSI, SACS, NACAC, TACAC
Accreditations: Southern Association of Colleges and Schools
Parental Involvement: Parent-Teacher Fellowship, Booster Club, Academic Club, Fine Arts Club

Admittance

Whom to Contact: Rob Armstrong
Date to Apply: Fall for next school year
Testing Procedure per Age/Grade Level: Two scheduled testing dates (January and February)
Fees Involved: $50 application fee; $300 matriculation fee; $500 admission fee

Type of Student Preferred: College-bound from Christian homes
Forms Required: Recommendations from pastor, principal, family friend, teacher
Individual/Group Appointments: Individual
Notification Procedure: Letter
Waiting List Policy: Waiting pool–notified if accepted

Tuition

Approximate Tuition for 1996-97 School Year: $3180-$7370
Methods of Payment Available: 10 monthly payments (March to December)
Financial Assistance Offered: Yes
Cancellation Insurance Available: No
Profit/Non-profit: Non-profit

Additional Costs

Books/Bag/Uniform: Books and bag–no; uniforms–Culwell and Sons or Parker Uniforms
Lunch Fee: Cafeteria available for purchasing lunch
Parents Club Dues: No
Annual Fund Drive: Yes
Discount for Siblings: Only in admission fee after first child

Facilities/Services Provided

Computer Lab: Lower and Middle School–two equipped MAC labs; Upper School–IBM compatible.
Library: Two libraries–includes Info-trac, computer CD,
Snack Procedures: Grades 1–3 snacks from home
Before-school Care Program Available: No
After-school Care Program Available: No
Nurse on Staff: Yes
Emergency Procedure Used: Medical release forms from parents
Transportation to and from School: All car pool
Counseling and Evaluation Available: Yes

Graduation Information

Testing: SAT, ACT
Average SAT Scores: 1048
High School Our Students Usually Attend: N/A
Percentage of Seniors Attending College: 100%

Tyler Street Christian Academy

927 West Tenth Street
Dallas, TX 75208
(214) 941-9717

Mapsco: 54G

Fax: (214) 946-8126

Office Hours: 7:30 a.m.–4:15 p.m.
School Hours: 8:30 a.m.–3:30 p.m.; secondary grades–8:10 a.m.
to 3:30 p.m.
School Grades Offered: 3-year-olds; kindergarten–grade 12
Enrollment: 450
Co-ed: Yes
Boy/Girl Ratio: 229:201
Student/Teacher Ratio: 16:1
Average Class Size: Elementary: 15; ,middle school: 20; high
school: 17
Calendar School Year: August–May
Holidays: Thanksgiving (3 days); Christmas (2 weeks); Easter
(1 week)
Uniform Requirements: Yes
Founded in: 1972

Philosophy of School

To assist Christian parents in "training up a child in the way he should go" (Proverbs
22:6). The philosophy of the academy is rooted in the conviction that true wisdom
comes in revering God as we know Him in Jesus the Christ and in learning of His way
as it is recorded in the Bible.

Academic Curriculum

Content: Developmentally appropriate preschool materials; A Beka Christian
curriculum with supplemental materials in elementary grades; traditional and
college preparatory in secondary
Grading System Used: Numerical percentage grades, 90-100=A; 80-89=B;
70-79=C; below 70=Failing; report cards are sent home every six weeks.
Progress reports are sent at the end on the first three weeks in each grading

period to students failing or in danger of failing the grading period.
Conferences per Year: As needed
Tests Administered: Standard achievement tests each spring
Homework Policy: Given for reinforcement and practice and may include projects
Method of Discipline: Refer to Code of Student Conduct

Enrichment Curriculum

Fine arts, foreign language, computer, honors program

Extracurricular Activities

Physical education instruction for all grades; intramural sports for upper elementary; competitive sports for secondary students (boys and girls)–football, volleyball, basketball, track and field, and baseball; student council for elementary and secondary; choir, band, foreign language clubs with foreign travel; community service opportunities

Goals for Students

To develop spiritually, academically, intellectually, emotionally, morally, socially, and physically

Faculty/Staff Requirements

Qualifications of Staff: College degree; certification; Christian lifestyle
Qualifications of Administrator: Advanced college degree; certification

School Information

Brochure Available: Yes
Number of Students in Each Grade: 32 (average)
Parochial: TSCA is a non-denominational, non-profit Christian school.
Organization Affiliations: ACSI, TAPPS, TANS
Accreditations: TSCA is accredited by the Southern Association of Colleges and Schools.
Parental Involvement: Parent-Teacher Fellowship, school board, booster club
Other Information:

Admittance

Whom to Contact: Registrar (941-9717) Shirley Allen
Date to Apply: March–June for the following school year; other times as necessary

Testing Procedure per Age/Grade Level: Vocabulary/reading comprehension/ math (when appropriate)

Fees Involved: $20; $250 registration fee

Type of Student Preferred: Average and above average academically; TSCA's students represent a broad spectrum of racial, ethnic, religious, and socioeconomic backgrounds.

Forms Required: Yes

Individual/Group Appointments: A group or individual session with an administrator describes the programs and policies and provides a tour of the facilities. All entrance test scores and admission decisions are reviewed with parents individually.

Notification Procedure: Normally at the time of testing; done in person by an administrator

Waiting List Policy: Annually

Tuition

Approximate Tuition for 1996-97 School Year: $3000–$3400 (varies by grade level)

Methods of Payment Available: 5% discount if paid in full for the year, or 10 monthly payments beginning July 1

Financial Assistance Offered: Yes

Cancellation Insurance Available: No

Profit/Non-profit: Non-profit

Additional Costs

Books/Bag/Uniform: Books–$50-$200 (varies by grade level); bag–N/A; Uniform–$80-$100

Lunch Fee: $2.50 hot lunch (snack bar items also available)

Parents Club Dues: No fee

Annual Fund Drive: Yes

Discount for Siblings: 15% discount for second child, 33 1/3% for third child

Facilities/Services Provided

Computer Lab: Elementary and secondary

Library: Yes

Snack Procedures: Provided for preschool and kindergarten; available for older students

Before-school Care Program Available: Yes (6:30 a.m.–8:30 a.m.)

After-school Care Program Available: Yes (3:30 p.m.–6:00 p.m.)

Nurse on Staff: Full-time nurse on staff

Emergency Procedure Used: First, parent is contacted; if necessary, call for

paramedics or transport to emergency room
Transportation to and from School: No
Counseling and Evaluation Available: Yes

Graduation Information

Testing: SAT
Average SAT Scores: 978 (combined)
High School Our Students Usually Attend: N/A
Percentage of Seniors Attending College: 96

Additional Information

White Rock North School

9727 White Rock Trail　　　　　　　　　　Mapsco: 27K
Dallas, TX　75238
(214) 348-7410　　　　　　　　　　　　　Fax: (214) 348-3109

Office Hours:　7:00 a.m.–6:00 p.m.
School Hours:　8:30 a.m.–3:30 p.m.
School Grades Offered:　Grades 1-6
Enrollment:　380
Co-ed:　Yes
Boy/Girl Ratio:　6:4
Student/Teacher Ratio:　15:1
Average Class Size:　15
Calendar School Year:　Mid-August–end of May
Holidays:　Fall break (October), Thanksgiving, Christmas, spring break
Uniform Requirements:　Yes
Founded in:　1964

Philosophy of School

The mission of White Rock North School is to promote academic excellence, develop personal integrity, nurture individual artistic and imaginative expression, and create an environment conducive to learning. White Rock North School views its program as continuous learning experiences. These learning experiences are incorporated into a curriculum that provides the opportunity for intellectual and physical development, character building, and civic responsibility.

Academic Curriculum

Content:　Accelerated curriculum supported by state-of-the-art technology
Grading System Used:　A: 100-93; B: 92-85; C: 84-78; D: 77-70
Conferences per Year:　Two scheduled; others as needed
Tests Administered:　CTPIII, ISEE

Homework Policy: Kindergarten: one time per week; grade 1: two times per week; grade 2: three times per week; grade 3: three-four times per week; grades 4-6: daily
Method of Discipline: Infraction cards, detention, parent conferences, in-school suspension

Enrichment Curriculum
Odyssey of the Mind, Invention Convention, UIL indoor heated pool (swimming lessons)

Extracurricular Activities
Ballet technique, tap, jazz, modern dance, tumbling, piano, swimming, roller/in-line skating

Goals for Students
Through the efforts of caring, concerned teachers, White Rock North School seeks to build academic confidence, good self-esteem, life skills, and a sense of responsibility.

Faculty/Staff Requirements
Qualifications of Staff: Bachelor's degrees
Qualifications of Administrator: Master's degree in school administration and mid-management

School Information
Brochure Available: Yes
Number of Students in Each Grade: Grades 1-4: 15 per grade; grades 5-6: to be determined
Parochial: No
Organization Affiliations: SACS, NAEYC
Accreditations: SACS
Parental Involvement: Parents' Organization (P.O.P.S.)
Other Information:

Admittance
Whom to Contact: Amy Adams (principal); Debbie Littlefield
Date to Apply: By January 31
Testing Procedure for Age/Grade Level: Fee due, test administered, evaluation with parents

Fees Involved: Fees assessed based on grade-level student is entering
Type of Student Preferred: Self-motivated, academically accelerated
Forms Required: Application, references, previous transcripts
Individual/Group Appointments: Entrance interview with student and parent(s)
Notification Procedure: By phone or letter
Waiting List Policy: Re-apply annually

Tuition

Approximate Tuition for 1996-97 School Year: $4000
Methods of Payment Available: Annually, by semester, monthly
Financial Assistance Offered: No
Cancellation Insurance Available: No
Profit/Non-profit: Profit

Additional Costs

Books/Bag/Uniform: Uniform, fied trips, after-school care, summer camp
Lunch Fee: Lunch provided for kindergarten and younger students; lunch tickets available for grades 1-6
Parents Club Dues: $10 annually
Annual Fund Drive: Fall and spring
Discount for Siblings: No

Facilities/Services Provided

Computer Lab: Mac Lab (20 computers) with LC 575 CD-ROM with Tenet; daily classes
Library: Yes
Snack Procedures: Mornings and afternoons
Before-school Care Program Available: Yes
After-school Care Program Available: Yes
Nurse on Staff: No
Emergency Procedure Used: Yes
Transportation to and from School: No
Counseling and Evaluation Available: Yes

Graduation Information

Testing: N/A
Average SAT Scores: N/A
High School Our Students Usually Attend: N/A
Percentage of Seniors Attending College: N/A

SAES
Southwestern Association
of Episcopal Schools

5952 Royal Lane, Suite 204
Dallas, TX 75230
(214) 692-9872
Fax: (214) 692-9874
William P. Scheel, Ed.D.
Executive Director

The Southwestern Association of Episcopal Schools is a member of TEPSAC (Texas Private Schools Accrediting Commission) and is an accrediting agency for Episcopal schools. Schools in our association seeking accreditation must first make application. Following admission into the process, the school collects the various Documents for Adherence to Standards. This is followed by a thorough Self-Study which is the most important part of the whole process and takes the better part of a year to complete. An on-site visit is made to the school shortly following the completion of the study. The on-site visit lasts for at least three days and is conducted by a minimum of three qualified persons who have been designated by the Standards Committee. At the conclusion of the on-site visit, the visiting team chairman makes a report to the Standards Committee. The Standards Committee then makes a recommendation to the Executive Board of SAES to accredit or not to accredit the school. Accredited schools make regular reports to maintain their accreditation.

> **All Saints Episcopal School**
> **The Canterbury Episcopal School (pending)**
> **Epiphany Day School (pending)**
> **The Episcopal School of Dallas (see ISAS)**
> **Good Shepherd Episcopal School (see ISAS)**
> **The Parish Day School of the Episcopal Church**
> **of the Transfiguration (see ISAS)**
> **St. Alban's Episcopal School**
> **St. Andrew's Episcopal School (pending)**

All Saints' Episcopal School

8200 Tumbleweed Trail
Fort Worth, Texas 76108
(817) 246-2413

Mapsco: 73C
(Fort Worth Mapsco)
Fax: (817) 246-8320

Office Hours: 7:45 a.m.–4:15 p.m.
School Hours: 8:15 a.m.–3:30 p.m.
School Grades Offered: Kindergarten–grade 12
Enrollment: 720
Co-ed: Yes
Boy/Girl Ratio: 1:1
Student/Teacher Ratio: 12:1
Average Class Size: 20
Calendar School Year: August–June
Holidays: Thanksgiving, Christmas,
mid-winter break, spring break
Uniform Requirements: Yes
Founded in: 1951

Philosophy of School

All Saints' Episcopal School promotes academic excellence in a nurturing, Christian environment and upholds the Anglican tradition of worship.

Academic Curriculum

Content: College-preparatory
Grading System Used: A, B, C, D, F
Conferences per Year: Two scheduled; others at the discretion of the teacher
Tests Administered: SESAT, SAT, ERB
Homework Policy: Varies according to grade level, subject, and teacher
Method of Discipline:

Enrichment Curriculum

Art, music, drama

243

Extracurricular Activities

Sports (field hockey, volleyball, football, soccer, basketball, baseball, softball, tennis, golf, and track), cheerleading, yearbook, literary magazine, clubs

Goals for Students

To encourage students to become the best they can be and to prepare them for life by emphasizing moral and ethical values as well as academics

Faculty/Staff Requirements

Qualifications of Staff: College degree, certification
Qualifications of Administrator: College degree

School Information

Brochure Available: Yes
Number of Students in Each Grade: 54–69 (grades 10, 11, and 12 have fewer than 54 students at this time)
Parochial: Yes
Organization Affiliations: Southwestern Association of Episcopal Schools (SAES), NAES, TISC, NACC, TACC, CASE, ERB
Accreditations: Accredited by SAES, approved by the Texas Private School Accreditation Commission, and recognized by TEA
Parental Involvement: Yes
Other Information:

Admittance

Whom to Contact: Director of Admissions
Date to Apply: Fall, winter for kindergarten; until mid-March for grades 1–12; applications can continue on a rolling basis for grades with openings
Testing Procedure per Age/Grade Level: Kindergarten applicants test individually in January and February; applicants for grades 1–12 test on a Saturday in March and later by appointment.
Fees Involved: $50 application fee
Type of Student Preferred: Average to above-average student who appreciates a challenge
Forms Required: Application, teacher recommendations, transcript, latest report card
Individual/Group Appointments: Individual appointments (kindergarten); group testing (grades 1-12)
Notification Procedure: Letter; conference with parents
Waiting List Policy: Applicants in waiting pool notified as space becomes available; if they are not placed before school begins, applicants are

automatically moved to next year's list unless they indicate they are no longer interested.

Tuition

Approximate Tuition for 1996-97 School Year: K–5, $5400; grades 6–8, $5650; grades 9–12, $6050
Methods of Payment Available: One payment or ten payments
Financial Assistance Offered: Yes
Cancellation Insurance Available: Yes, TRP
Profit/Non-profit: Non-profit

Additional Costs

Books/Bag/Uniform: Books (grades 6-12) $300; uniforms $35-$40 each
Lunch Fee: Lunch cards available at a cost of $25 per card; most students buy part of the time and bring their lunches part of the time
Parents Club Dues: $15
Annual Fund Drive: Yes
Discount for Siblings: No

Facilities/Services Provided

Computer Lab: Yes; two labs
Library: Yes
Snack Procedures: Students in K-5 bring their own snacks; students in grade 6-12 bring their own snack or purchase from the lunchroom.
Before-school Care Program Available: Yes, Clayton Childcare; 7:00 a.m.
After-school Care Program Available: Yes, Clayton Childcare; until 6:00 p.m.
Nurse on Staff: No, first-aid person
Emergency Procedure Used: First-aid person calls outside help if needed.
Transportation to and from School: No
Counseling and Evaluation Available: No

Graduation Information

Testing: ACT, SAT, AP exams
Average SAT scores: 1060
High School Our Students Generally Attend: N/A
Percentage of Seniors Attending College: 100

Additional Information

The Canterbury Episcopal School

825 N. Cockrell Hill Rd.   Mapsco: 82H
De Soto, TX 75115
(214) 230-8851   Fax: (214) 230-8851

Office Hours: 7:45 a.m.–4:30 p.m.
School Hours: 8:00 a.m.–3:30 p.m.
School Grades Offered: Kindergarten–grade 6
(middle school scheduled to open fall 1998)
Enrollment: 100
Co-ed: Yes
Boy/Girl Ratio: 1:1
Student/Teacher Ratio: 12:1
Average Class Size: 15
Calendar School Year: August–May
Holidays: Labor Day, Columbus Day, Thanksgiving,
Christmas, winter break, Presidents' Day, spring break,
Easter
Uniform Requirements: Yes
Founded in: 1991

Philosophy of School

The Canterbury Episcopal School's foundation is its belief and tradition of the Anglican Church and its commitment to the ministry of education. We commit ourselves to educating the whole student based on Jesus Christ's example. We provide an educational program that encourages young people to love and serve God and others. We prepare young people for higher education by providing them with an academically challenging and creative learning environment. We develop within the student a love of learning, a strong sense of self-worth, and a respect for God's creation and the dignity of every human being.

Academic Curriculum

Content: Language arts, reading, math, computer, social studies, Christian education and science
Grading System Used: Non-graded through grade 3; letter grades (A–F) used in grades 4–6
Conferences per Year: Three scheduled; others upon request
Tests Administered: Stanford Achievement; Otis-Lennon Ability
Homework Policy: Daily assignments for upper grades
Method of Discipline: Positive reinforcement

Enrichment Curriculum

Spanish, music, art, physical education, service programs

Extracurricular Activities

Odyssey of the Mind, magazine and newspaper programs, service projects

Goals for Students

The Canterbury Episcopal School seeks to:
- provide an academic environment where spiritual and moral growth accompany each child's intellectual, emotional, social, aesthetic, and physical growth
- nurture each child's self-esteem and sense of fulfillment
- cultivate in each child a sense of social and moral responsibility and a genuine respect for others

Faculty/Staff Requirements

Qualifications of Staff: Bachelor's degree (minimum)
Qualifications of Administrator: Master's degree (minimum)

School Information

Brochure Available: Yes
Number of Students in Each Grade: 16 maximum (K–3); 18 (4–6)
Parochial: Episcopal
Organization Affiliations: SAES accreditation in process
Accreditations: SAES accreditation in process
Parental Involvement: High involvement
Other Information: Sponsored by four area parishes: St. Anne's (DeSoto), Good Shepherd (Cedar Hill), St. Paul's (Oak Cliff), St. Paul's (Waxahachie)

Admittance

Whom to Contact: Ron Ferguson, Headmaster
Date to Apply: December–February
Testing Procedure per Age/Grade Level: Winter/early spring testing schedule
Fees Involved: $250 application fee; $75 testing fee
Type of Student Preferred: Above-average ability; college-bound
Forms Required: Application, health
Individual/Group Appointments: Both available
Notification Procedure: Letter of acceptance issued immediately following testing and personal appointment when all documents are filed
Waiting List Policy: Yes, reapply annually

Tuition

Approximate Tuition for 1996-97 School Year: $3250 (kindergarten), $4500 (1–6)
Methods of Payment Available: Annually, by semester, or monthly
Financial Assistance Offered: Yes
Cancellation Insurance Available: No
Profit/Non-profit: Non-profit

Additional Costs

Books/Bag/Uniform: Uniform ($100-$150)
Lunch Fee: $10 monthly for special lunches
Parents Club Dues: No
Annual Fund Drive: $70,000
Discount for Siblings: No

Facilities/Services Provided

Computer Lab: Computers provided in very classroom
Library: Library materials provided: library in new school design
Snack Procedures: Provided for primary grades
Before-school Care Program Available: Yes, 7:30–7:45
After-school Care Program Available: Yes, 3:00–6:00
Nurse on Staff: No
Emergency Procedure Used: Contact parent/guardian; EMS nearby
Transportation to and from School: No
Counseling and Evaluation Available: Yes

Graduation Information

Testing: Stanford, Otis-Lennon
Average SAT Scores: N/A

High School Our Students Usually Attend: N/A
Percentage of Seniors Attending College: N/A
Additional Information: New building program; expanding to middle school in 1998-99

Additional Information

Epiphany Day School

421 Custer Road   Mapsco: 17A
Richardson, TX 75080
(214) 690-0275   Fax: (214) 644-8116

Office Hours: 8:30 a.m.–3:00 p.m.
School Hours: 9:00 a.m.–1:00 p.m. (MDO and preschool)
9:00 a.m.–3:00 p.m. (grades)
School Grades Offered: 12 months–grade 1; grade 2 (1996-97);
grade 3 (1997–98)
Enrollment: 80
Co-ed: Yes
Boy/Girl Ratio: Approximately 50:50
Student/Teacher Ratio: 1/7 (MDO); 1/10 to12, PS; 1/15, grades
Average Class Size: 12
Calendar School Year: August–May
Holidays: Same as R.I.S.D.
Uniform Requirements: No
Founded in: 1985

Philosophy of School
We believe that a child learns best when he or she is actively engaged with materials
and experiences that are developmentally appropriate for that child. The goal of
Epiphany Day School is to challenge students to construct meaning. To that end, we
provide a rich environment of materials for children to explore and abundant
opportunities for learning through discovery. Children are encouraged to learn how to
learn and to think for themselves. Our small student/staff ratios facilitate a very
individualized and child specific learning experience.

Academic Curriculum
Content: Age-appropriate math, reading, language arts, science, social studies,
art, music, physical education
Grading System Used: Pupil progress is reported through 1) regularly
scheduled parent-teacher conferences, 2) observations reported through

skills checklists, 3) 9-week report cards for grades.
Conferences per Year: Two regular and on request
Tests Administered: Metropolitan Readiness for Kindergarten; others as needed
Homework Policy: As needed
Method of Discipline: Positive reinforcement; redirection

Enrichment Curriculum
Music, Spanish, computer, chapel

Extracurricular Activities
Extended day from 1:00 p.m.–4:00 p.m. or a portion thereof available five days a week; other activities

Goals for Students
To foster a love of learning and positive self-worth so that the child develops maximum potential

Faculty/Staff Requirements
Qualifications of Staff: College degree; certification
Qualifications of Administrator: Master's degree; certification

School Information
Brochure Available: Yes
Number of Students in Each Grade: 12-24
Parochial: Episcopal
Organization Affiliations: SAES, NAEYC
Accreditations: Accreditation with SAES and NAEYC in progress
Parental Involvement: Parents' Club
Other Information: N/A

Admittance
Whom to Contact: Dr. Alexis Clayton, Director
Date to Apply: February–May
Testing Procedure for Age/Grade Level: No entrance tests
Fees Involved: $150 registration (preschool and day school); $100 registration MDO
Type of Student Preferred: EDS accepts children with a wide range of abilities

who will likely succeed at EDS.

Forms Required: Ask director

Individual/Group Appointments: Kindergarten and first-grade assessment in March

Notification Procedure: Letter by April 1

Waiting List Policy: Reapply annually

Tuition

Approximate Tuition for 1996-97 School Year: $1500 for preschool; $2300 for kindergarten (1/2 day); $3000 for grade 1; grade 2 for 1996-97

Methods of Payment Available: Annually; monthly payments

Financial Assistance Offered: Limited

Cancellation Insurance Available: No

Profit/Non-profit: Non-profit

Additional Costs

Books/Bag/Uniform: Books (no); uniform (consult director)

Lunch Fee: No

Parents Club Dues: $10

Annual Fund Drive: N/A

Discount for Siblings: 5% for second child; 7% for third child

Facilities/Services Provided

Computer Lab: Yes

Library:

Snack Procedures: Snacks provided

Before-school Care Program Available: No

After-school Care Program Available: Extended-day program

Nurse on Staff: No

Emergency Procedure Used: Parental permission slip on file for emergency treatment.

Transportation to and from School: No

Counseling and Evaluation Available: Yes

Graduation Information

Testing: N/A

Average SAT Scores: N/A

High School Our Students Usually Attend: N/A

Percentage of Seniors Attending College: N/A

St. Alban's Episcopal School

911 S. Davis
Arlington, TX 76013
(817) 460-6071

Mapsco: Y-40
Dallas/FortWorth
Fax: (817) 860-6816

Office Hours: 8:00 a.m.–4 :00 p.m.
School Hours: 8:15 a.m.–3:15 p.m.
School Grades Offered: Pre-k (3-years)–grade 6
Enrollment: 300
Co-ed: Yes
Boy/Girl Ratio: 50:50
Student/Teacher Ratio: 18:1
Average Class Size: 20
Calendar School Year: A.I.S.D. calendar school year
Holidays: Thanksgiving, Christmas, Martin Luther King
Day, Easter, spring break (one week)
Uniform Requirements: Dress and casual uniforms
Founded in: 1958

Philosophy of School

St. Alban's Episcopal School is a parochial school operating as an outreach ministry of
St. Alban's Episcopal Church. The school is co-educational and serves preschool
through sixth-grade students. A superior academic program is provided for average and
above-average students within the context of the life of this parish and its commitment
to our Lord Jesus Christ. St. Alban's School recognizes its diversity as an important
educational opportunity. St. Alban's emphasizes the development of the whole child
within a caring community grounded in Christian moral values. The school strives to
stimulate creativity, encourage a healthy curiosity in its students, and attend to the
unique needs of each child. St. Alban's Episcopal School is committed to "excellence in
all things to the glory of God."

St. Alban's Episcopal School Mission Statement:

St. Alban's Episcopal School is committed to an enriched academic program within a
safe, nurturing environment. The school seeks to serve the whole child by teaching
Christian values that develop character and the ability to serve the community.

Academic Curriculum

Content: Language arts, math, social studies, science, art, music, physical education, Spanish, computer, library science

Grading System Used: A, 90–100; B, 80–89; C, 70–79; below 70–failing

Conferences per Year: Two

Tests Administered: Stanford Achievement and Otis-Lennon for grades 2–6

Homework Policy: Students are assigned homework appropriate to grade level.

Method of Discipline: Each student is treated as an individual.

Enrichment Curriculum

Art, music, physical education, Spanish, computer, library science

Extracurricular Activities

Goals for Students

We want students to leave us with a sense of "I can do it." Our children are bright, well-rounded, caring people who have a sense of where they fit into our world and ways they can help this to be a wonderful place to be.

Faculty/Staff Requirements

Qualifications of Staff: Certified teachers

Qualifications of Administrator: B.S., M.Ed.

School Information

Brochure Available: Yes

Number of Students in Each Grade: Pre-K (3 years)–20; pre-K (4 years)–40; K–40; 1st–46; 2nd–40; 3rd–40; 4th–40; 5th–40; 6th–30

Parochial: Episcopalian

Organization Affiliations: Southwestern Association of Episcopal Schools (SAES), Texas Association of Non-Public Schools, National Association of Episcopal Schools

Accreditations: SAES

Parental Involvement: Parents are an integral part of our school. They volunteer countless hours in classrooms and at fundraising events.

Other Information:

Admittance

Whom to Contact: Pamela Epps

Date to Apply: January

255

Testing Procedure per Age/Grade Level: Pre-K–1st grade, Saturday Play Group testing; 2–6, standardized tests and classroom visit to the school
Fees Involved: Registration ($275)
Type of Student Preferred: Average and above average
Forms Required: A packet is sent.
Individual/Group Appointments: Individual
Notification Procedure: Letter
Waiting List Policy: Re-apply

Tuition

Approximate Tuition for 1996-97 School Year: $2816
Methods of Payment Available: Monthly; by semester; annually
Financial Assistance Offered: Yes
Cancellation Insurance Available: Yes
Profit/Non-profit: Non-profit

Additional Costs

Books/Bag/Uniform: Books and bag–N/A; uniform–$250 for 1 week's worth
Lunch Fee: Meals are available for $2.50.
Parents Club Dues: N/A
Annual Fund Drive: Yes
Discount for Siblings: 5%

Facilities/Services Provided

Computer Lab: State-of-the-art labs
Library: New library
Snack Procedures:
Before-school Care Program Available: 6:30 a.m.–6:00 p.m.; the school provides snacks for after care.
After-school Care Program Available: See above.
Nurse on Staff: The school secretary is a nurse.
Emergency Procedure Used: Fire and tornado plans are practiced.
Transportation to and from School: None
Counseling and Evaluation Available: Yes

Graduation Information

Testing: N/A
Average SAT Scores: N/A
High School Our Students Usually Attend: N/A
Percentage of Seniors Attending College: N/A

St. Andrews Episcopal School

727 Hill Street
Grand Prairie, TX 75050
(214) 262-3817

Mapsco: 51D

Fax: (214) 262-1788

Office Hours: 8:30 a.m.–6:00 p.m.
School Hours: 8:30 a.m.–3:30 p.m.
School Grades Offered: 3-year-olds–grade 5
Enrollment: 85
Co-ed: Yes
Boy/Girl Ratio: 38:47
Student/Teacher Ratio: 12/1
Average Class Size: 10-14
Calendar School Year: August–May
Holidays: Labor Day, Thanksgiving, Christmas, New Year's
Day, Martin Luther King Day, Good Friday, Memorial Day,
Independence Day
Uniform Requirements: Yes
Founded in: 1978

Philosophy of School

To instill in the student a respect for God's word and His people and promote an
atmosphere of caring and love for fellow beings; to provide an environment that
recognizes the uniqueness and self-worth of each child; to provide an environment that
prepares each student as an individual to live a creative, humane, and compassionate
life, and to become a contributing member of society

Academic Curriculum

Content: Phonics, hands-on math, computers, language, science, Spanish,
music
Grading System Used: Letter grades–A-F; A honor roll; A-B honor roll

257

Conferences per Year: One scheduled; others upon request
Tests Administered: C.A.T.
Homework Policy: Homework is assigned.
Method of Discipline: Positive discipline and reinforcement; we confer with parents.

Enrichment Curriculum
Plays, programs, field trips, cooking programs, around-the-world study

Extracurricular Activities
Choir, piano

Goals for Students
To be nurtured spiritually, physically, emotionally, and socially in order that they may live as intelligent, informed, creative, moral, and contributing members of today's society

Faculty/Staff Requirements
Qualifications of Staff: College degree (preschool); certification (k-5)
Qualifications of Administrator: Education background; master's degree in education/business

School Information
Brochure Available: Yes
Number of Students in Each Grade: Preschool–18; K–12; 1st–13; 2nd–14; 3rd–9; 4th–7 (no fifth grade this year)
Parochial: Episcopal
Organization Affiliations: NAES, SAES, DAEYC, TAEYC, TANS
Accreditations: In process with SAES
Parental Involvement: P.T.O. program; spirit hours worked by parents
Other Information:

Admittance
Whom to Contact: School office
Date to Apply: February 1 of each year for the next school year
Testing Procedure for Age/Grade Level: None now; will be added to program later
Fees Involved: $100 registration fee, building use fee, book rental fee

Type of Student Preferred: N/A
Forms Required: Packet of admissions forms, health forms, etc.
Individual/Group Appointments: N/A
Notification Procedure: N/A
Waiting List Policy: If enrollment is full, a waiting list is used.

Tuition

Approximate Tuition for 1996-97 School Year: Preschool–$1856; K-5–$2600
Methods of Payment Available: Smart Financial Plan–yearly, quarterly, monthly
Financial Assistance Offered: Scholarship
Cancellation Insurance Available: No
Profit/Non-profit: Non-profit

Additional Costs

Books/Bag/Uniform: Books included in book fee; students pay for their uniforms separately, but the school has a uniform exchange.
Lunch Fee: Students can bring their lunches.
Parents Club Dues: P.T.O. dues–$5.00
Annual Fund Drive: Fundraisers
Discount for Siblings: 10%

Facilities/Services Provided

Computer Lab: Computers in classrooms
Library: Yes
Snack Procedures: Morning snacks; afternoon snacks for after-school care
Before-school Care Program Available: Open at 7:00 a.m.
After-school Care Program Available: Yes, until 6:00 p.m.
Nurse on Staff: No
Emergency Procedure Used: We have notarized emergency forms on file; parents are called; if necessary, the children are taken to the nearest hospital
Transportation to and from School: No
Counseling and Evaluation Available: No

Graduation Information

Testing: N/A
Average SAT Scores: N/A
High School Our Students Usually Attend: N/A
Percentage of Seniors Attending College: N/A

TAAPS
Texas Alliance of
Accredited Private Schools

522 N. Commerce
Port Lavaca, Texas 77979
(512) 552-1900 or (512) 552-5757

The Texas Alliance of Accredited Private Schools, a non-profit accreditation association, was organized in 1985. This organization serves both traditional and non-traditional elementary and secondary schools in the state of Texas. TAAPS is a member of the Texas Private School Accredition Commission.

Schools seeking accreditation through TAAPS must have been in operation for three years before seeking an applicant visit. With a favorable applicant report, the school is encouraged to apply for the final accreditation visit. An annual report is the association's method of monitoring the school's continuing self-evaluation.

The Texas Allinace of Accredited Private Schools conducts an annual conference the last weekend of February. All member schools as well as guest schools are invited to attend.

Accredited members schools in the Dallas/ Ft. Worth area are:

Highland Park Presbyterian Day School
Hillier School of Highland Park Presbyterian Church (see Alternative)
J. Erik Jonsson Community School
Southwest Academy (pending)
Yavneh Academy of Dallas (pending)

Highland Park Presbyterian Day School

3821 University
Dallas, TX 75205
(214) 559-5353

Mapsco: 35E

Fax: (214) 559-5357

Office Hours: 8:00 a.m.–4:00 p.m.
School Hours: 8:45 a.m.–3:30 p.m.
School Grades Offered: Pre-k (age 3)–grade 4
Enrollment: 270
Co-ed: Yes
Boy/Girl Ratio:
Student/Teacher Ratio: 8:1
Average Class Size: 12
Calendar School Year: August-May
Holidays: Thanksgiving, Christmas, Easter, spring break
Uniform Requirements: Girls (red and white plaid); boys (navy)
Founded in: 1952

Philosophy of School

Highland Park Presbyterian Day School believes each child is God's creation and must be nurtured in biblically-based Christian love, acceptance, and reinforcement. We provide an enriching, productive school experience within this Christian environment.

Academic Curriculum

Content:
Grading System Used:
Conferences per Year: Three
Tests Administered: Iowa Test of Basic Skills
Homework Policy:
Method of Discipline:

Enrichment Curriculum
Music, art, Spanish, science, library, physical education, developmental tutoring, computer, storytelling

Extracurricular Activities
Integrated Arts (individualized creative arts program)

Goals for Students
To explore their own ideas, think creatively, solve problems, and work independently through experiences with music, sculpture, painting, drama, and movement

Faculty/Staff Requirements
Qualifications of Staff: All have degrees in early childhood education or elementary education.
Qualifications of Administrator: B.S. in Elementary Education; M.S. in Supervision and Administration; Ph.D. in Early Childhood Administration in progress

School Information
Brochure Available:
Number of Students in Each Grade: 14-16 (preschool); 12-16 (grades 1-4)
Parochial:
Organization Affiliations: Texas Association for Education of the Young Child; Dallas Association for Education of the Young Child; Southern Early Childhood Association
Accreditations: Texas Alliance of Affiliated Private Schools
Parental Involvement: Parents' Council
Other Information:

Admittance
Whom to Contact: Day School Office
Date to Apply: Registration is in February.
Testing Procedure for Age/Grade Level: Assessment for grades K-4
Fees Involved: Non-refundable registration fee due at time of enrollment
Type of Student Preferred: Any race, color, or ethnic origin
Forms Required: Immunization form and medical-consent form
Individual/Group Appointments:
Notification Procedure: Letter to parents
Waiting List Policy: Ongoing

Tuition

Approximate Tuition for 1996-97 School Year: $1820-$4880
Methods of Payment Available: First semester's fee due April 30; second semester's fee due July 15
Financial Assistance Offered: No
Cancellation Insurance Available: Yes
Profit/Non-profit:

Additional Costs

Books/Bag/Uniform: Uniform and book bag
Lunch Fee: Optional
Parents Club Dues: No
Annual Fund Drive: Book fair, plant sale, auction
Discount for Siblings: No

Facilities/Services Provided

Computer Lab: Yes
Library: Yes
Snack Procedures: Provided by parents
Before-school Care Program Available:
After-school Care Program Available: Church's recreation department has an after-school program.
Nurse on Staff: No
Emergency Procedure Used:
Transportation to and from School: Parents arrange car pools.
Counseling and Evaluation Available: Yes

Graduation Information

Testing: N/A
Average SAT Scores: N/A
High School Our Students Usually Attend: N/A
Percentage of Seniors Attending College: N/A

Additional Information

J. Erik Jonsson Community School

110 E. 10th Street   Mapsco: 54H
Dallas, TX 75203
(214) 941-9192   Fax: (214) 946-7140

Office Hours: 8:00 a.m.–4:40 p.m.
School Hours: 8:00 a.m.–3:00 p.m.
School Grades Offered: Grades 4–8
Enrollment: 100
Co-ed: Yes
Boy/Girl Ratio: 5:4
Student/Teacher Ratio: 10:1
Average Class Size: 20
Calendar School Year: Year round
Holidays: Usual holidays plus Martin Luther King Day
Uniform Requirements: None
Founded in: 1992

Philosophy of School

JEJCS is a co-educational, multicultural, year-round, non-profit school. Students and staff strive for excellence through an active, engaged, rich learning environment using an across-subject-area integrated curriculum. Instructional teams and collaborative student groups are a hallmark of the program. JEJCS believes it is essential to success in learning to provide an emotionally supportive and safe environment for students. A full-time, on-site, research department enables staff and students to refine and improve this model for urban eduction in the '90s.

Academic Curriculum

Content: Based on the TEA Essential Elements; varies with grade level
Grading System Used: Numerical with additional portfolio; grades mailed home
Conferences per Year: At least three; additional as requested

264

Tests Administered: ITBS
Homework Policy: Assignment sheets sent home daily
Method of Discipline: Solution-seeking strategy sessions with student

Enrichment Curriculum

Visiting artists, artists in residence; integrated fine arts across subject areas; numerous field trips; experiential learning; computer literacy with extensive educational software available

Extracurricular Activities

Athletics: basketball, soccer, volleyball, soft ball, track; student newspaper; community projects

Goals for Students

Provide strong or above-grade-level academics; practive collaborative learning; develop social skills, adopt solution-seeking attitudes; become lifelong learners

Faculty/Staff Requirements

Qualifications of Staff: Degree from accreditied college; teacher certification; approximately 20% of the staff have advanced degrees.
Qualifications of Administrator: Graduate degree in education and/or school administration

School Information

Brochure Available: Yes
Number of Students in Each Grade: 20
Parochial: No
Organization Affiliations: Salesmanship Club and Family Centers, Inc.
Accreditations: Texas Alliance of Affiliated Private Schools (TAAPS)
Parental Involvement: Integrated into classroom academic activities; parenting seminars; parent networking; on-site support; family therapy available
Other Information: Research and development program on site

Admittance

Whom to Contact: Admissions Coordinator
Date to Apply: Open admissions; February preferred for following fall
Testing Procedure per Age/Grade Level: Reading assessment; others as indicated

Fees Involved: No admittance fee
Type of Student Preferred: Those students more likely to thrive in an experientially-based, innovative teaching setting
Forms Required: Yes; previous cumulative and assessment records
Individual/Group Appointments: Individual family interview and tour; possible pre-placement visiting day for student
Notification Procedure: Personal telephone call from director
Waiting List Policy: Ongoing; annually; reapplication for following year

Tuition

Approximate Tuition for 1996-97 School Year: Sliding scale based on family income
Methods of Payment Available: Monthly tuition
Financial Assistance Offered: Flexible arrangements in financial crisis
Cancellation Insurance Available: No
Profit/Non-profit: Non-profit

Additional Costs

Books/Bag/Uniform: Basic supplies provided by family; books and other expensive items provided by school
Lunch Fee: No; students bring daily sack lunches; school provides free hot lunch once a month.
Parents Club Dues: None
Annual Fund Drive: None
Discount for Siblings: Multiple siblings can attend for one sliding-scale fee.

Facilities/Services Provided

Computer Lab: Yes, one computer per six children
Library: Yes, small but growing
Snack Procedures: Fresh fruit provided by school once a day
Before-school Care Program Available: No; students can enter supervised building as early as 7:30 a.m.
After-school Care Program Available: No; YMCA pick-up service
Nurse on staff: No
Emergency Procedure Used: Staff trained in CPR; parental permission and health form on file
Transportation to and from School: Parents, DART, car pools, limited van service
Counseling and Evaluation Available: Yes; family therapist on site

Graduation Information

Testing: N/A
Average SAT Scores: N/A
High School Our Students Usually Attend: N/A
Percentage of Seniors Attending College: N/A

Additional Information

Within-grade-level and intra-grade-level teaching; two teachers in every classroom; high family involvement

Southwest Academy

9550 Forest Lane, Suite 600   Mapsco: 17Y
Dallas, TX 75243-5933
(214) 349-7272   Fax: (214) 340-0820

Office Hours: 9:00 a.m.–4:00 p.m.
School Hours: 9:00 a.m.–3:00 p.m.
School Grades Offered: K–grade 8
Enrollment: 50
Co-ed: Yes
Boy/Girl Ratio: Approximately equal
Student/Teacher Ratio: 3:1
Average Class Size: Varies
Calendar School Year: August–May
Holidays: Thanksgiving, Christmas, spring break, teacher in-service
Uniform Requirements: None
Founded in: 1994

Philosophy of School

Southwest Academy offers a full-day program to fit the student's needs. Our faculty is a team of specially trained teachers with college degrees who share the philosophy that every child can learn in a positive, caring environment. Southwest Academy is a non-profit, coeducational, independent institution offering students a multisensory approach to education within a structured, nurturing environment where they can enhance and develop their strengths.

Academic Curriculum

Content: Talented-and-gifted curriculum
Grading System Used: K-4, letter grades; 5-8, number grades
Conferences per Year: Two (fall and spring); others available as requested
Tests Administered: Test of Written Language, Wechsler Individual Achievement Test

Homework Policy: Internally driven by individual students
Method of Discipline: Positive reinforcers; students earn points for appropriate behavior.

Enrichment Curriculum

Art, music, physical education, computer, typing, Capers for Kids, motor skills, social skills

Extracurricular Activities

Field trips, guest speakers, optional after-school program

Goals for Students

To develop a love of learning and a positive self-esteem while tapping their individual potential

Faculty/Staff Requirements

Qualifications of Staff: College degree required; graduate level training
Qualifications of Administrator: Graduate degree required

School Information

Brochure Available: Yes
Number of Students in Each Grade: Varies
Parochial: No
Organization Affiliations: TANS
Accreditations: TAAPS (pending)
Parental Involvement: Parents' Club, room mothers, parent-staff development
Other Information:

Admittance

Whom to Contact: Beverly Dooley, Ph.D.
Date to Apply: Prefer spring prior to fall enrollment; accepted throughout year
Testing Procedure for Age/Grade Level: Pre-test, post-test for grades 1,3,5,7
Fees Involved: $150
Type of Student Preferred: Average to above-average I.Q.
Forms Required: Yes
Individual/Group Appointments: Individual appointments
Notification Procedure: Parent conference
Waiting List Policy: Ongoing

Tuition

Approximate Tuition for 1996-97 School Year: $6000
Methods of Payment Available: Payment in full or monthly
Financial Assistance Offered: Applications available
Cancellation Insurance Available: No
Profit/Non-profit: Non-profit

Additional Costs

Books/Bag/Uniform: Books–cost varies depending on grade, $275-$425 yearly; bag–not required; uniform–not required
Lunch Fee: No
Parents Club Dues: No
Annual Fund Drive: Yes, scholarship fund, golf tournament for support services
Discount for Siblings: No

Facilities/Services Provided

Computer Lab: Yes
Library: Yes, in progress
Snack Procedures: Students provide
Before-school Care Program Available: No
After-school Care Program Available: Optional, 3:00–5:00 p.m.
Nurse on Staff: No
Emergency Procedure Used: Contact parents; emergency numbers on file
Transportation to and from School: Car pools arranged by parents
Counseling and Evaluation Available: Yes

Graduation Information

Testing: Yes
Average SAT Scores: N/A
High School Our Students Usually Attend: N/A
Percentage of Seniors Attending College: N/A

Additional Information

Yavneh Academy of Dallas

9401 Douglas
Dallas, TX 75225
(214) 363-7631

Mapsco: 25N

Fax: (214) 363-5684

Office Hours: 9:00 a.m.–5:00 p.m.
School Hours: 8:00 a.m.–4:48 p.m.
School Grades Offered: Grades 9–12
Enrollment: 30
Co-ed: Yes
Boy/Girl Ratio: 15:9
Student/Teacher Ratio: 1.5: 1
Average Class Size: 1–12 (varies)
Calendar School Year: August 15-June 5
Holidays: All Jewish and major American holidays
Uniform Requirements: Modest dress code
Founded in: 1993

Philosophy of School

Yavneh Academy is open to any academically qualified Jewish student regardless of level of home observance or denominational affiliation. Our Judaic courses are offered at a variety of levels. At Yavneh, we are committed to reaching out to the reform, conservative, traditional, and orthodox communities.

Academic Curriculum

Content: Major Judaic subjects, high school core and AP courses
Grading System Used: Numerical
Conferences per Year: Two
Tests Administered: ACT, PSAT, SAT, ERB Standardized
Homework Policy: Maximum of 30 minutes per subject per day
Method of Discipline: Established discipline code

Enrichment Curriculum
Boys–basketball; girls–Israeli dance, drama, chorus

Extracurricular Activities
Basketball, field trips, volleyball, theater, cultural programs

Goals for Students
To graduate with skills to enter the university and/or post-graduate rabbinical seminary of their choice

Faculty/Staff Requirements
Qualifications of Staff: Preferably master's degrees, certified
Qualifications of Administrator: At least a master's degree in administration or education and rabbinical ordination

School Information
Brochure Available: Yes
Number of Students in Each Grade: 9th–7, 10th–13, 11th–3, 12th–1
Parochial: Jewish–traditional orthodox
Organization Affiliations: Educators Council of America
Accreditations: TAAPS (pending)
Parental Involvement: Strong board and PTO, parent volunteers
Other Information:

Admittance
Whom to Contact: Rabbi Moshe Englander, Headmaster; Dr. Grant Mindle, Principal of General Studies
Date to Apply: After January 1
Testing Procedure for Age/Grade Level: Screening test; both standardized and personal interview
Fees Involved: Registration fee (before March 15 deadline, $200; after March 15, $300); tuition, book fee–$100
Type of Student Preferred: With no learning disabilities
Forms Required: Registration, health, and tuition assistance (when needed)
Individual/Group Appointments: Made upon request
Notification Procedure: By phone or by mail
Waiting List Policy: Ongoing

Tuition

Approximate Tuition for 1996-97 School Year: $6900
Methods of Payment Available: Installments (10% discount if paid in full in advance)
Financial Assistance Offered: Tuition Assistance Committee
Cancellation Insurance Available: No
Profit/Non-profit: Non-profit parochial (private) high school

Additional Costs

Books/Bag/Uniform: $100
Lunch Fee: Bag lunches; once-a-week Kosher lunch program for $4.00
Parents Club Dues: $15/year
Annual Fund Drive: None
Discount for Siblings: 5% discount for additional children

Facilities/Services Provided

Computer Lab: Yes; 486 SX and 486 DX computers with CD ROMS
Library: Yes; encyclopedia, reference books, 500+ volumes
Snack Procedures: Canteen open during breaks
Before-school Care Program Available: No
After-school Care Program Available: No
Nurse on Staff: No
Emergency Procedure Used: First aid in office; contact parents, family doctor, or hospital emergency room
Transportation to and from School: Individual car pools
Counseling and Evaluation Available: Social worker from the Jewish Family Service comes to Yavneh Academy on Mondays.

Graduation Information

Testing: ACT, PSAT, SAT
Average SAT Scores: Undetermined
High School Our Students Usually Attend: N/A
Percentage of Seniors Attending College: Undetermined

Additional Information

TCCED
Texas Catholic Conference
Education Department Diocese
of Dallas Department of
Education

3725 Blackburn Street
P.O. Box 190507
Dallas, TX 75219
(214) 528-2360
Fax: (214) 522-1753

Mission Statement

The schools of the Roman Catholic Diocese of Dallas exist as the Church's response to the Gospel message "to teach as Jesus did." Each school espouses Catholic doctrine and the spirit of Vatican II in worship, community, justice, and social concerns. For a school to be Catholic, it must be seen and it must see itself as an integral part of the Church's mission to spread God's word and bring all peoples to Christ, helping them to grow in faith and love. A school is designated "Catholic" only if it is canonically so stated by the Bishop of the Dioceses. The primary reason for Catholic schools to exist is to serve Catholic families in the Diocese of Dallas. All schools are to provide standards of religious and academic quality maintaining accreditation by the Texas Catholic Conference Education Department.

Bishop Lynch High School
Christ the King School
Cistercian Preparatory School (see ISAS)
Good Shepherd Catholic School
The Highlands School (pending)
Holy Family of Nazareth School
Holy Trinity Catholic School

Immaculate Conception School
Jesuit College Preparatory School
The Notre Dame of Dallas Schools, Inc. (see Alternative)
Prince of Peace Catholic School
St. Bernard of Clairvaux School
St. Elizabeth School
St. John the Apostle Catholic School
St. Mary of Carmel School
St. Mary's Catholic School
St. Monica School
St. Patrick School
St. Paul the Apostle School
St. Philip the Apostle Catholic School
St. Rita School
St. Thomas Aquinas School
The Ursuline Academy of Dallas

Bishop Lynch High School

9750 Ferguson
Dallas, TX 75228
(214) 324-3607

Mapsco: 38U

Fax: (214) 324-3600

Office Hours: 7:30 a.m.–3:30 p.m.
School Hours: 8:00 a.m.–3:12 p.m.
School Grades Offered: 9–12
Enrollment: 840
Co-ed: Yes
Boy/Girl Ratio: 4:6
Student/Teacher Ratio: 14:1
Average Class Size: 24
Calendar School Year: August–May
Holidays: Labor Day, Thanksgiving, Christmas, Easter, spring break, Memorial Day
Uniform Requirements: Girls–white oxford shirt, plaid skirt; boys–white oxford shirt, gray slacks, tie
Founded in: 1963

Philosophy of School

Faithful to Catholic truths and the Dominican heritage of scholarship and service, Bishop Lynch High School fosters the well-being of the total person by bringing together a diverse educational community that teaches students to seek truths and work for justice in the world.

Academic Curriculum

Content: Bishop Lynch offers a multi-faceted academic education to students who demonstrate the potential for success in a college-preparatory environment.
Grading System Used: Numerical grading system
Conferences per Year: At least two (end of first quarter, end of first semester, and by appointment)
Tests Administered: Standardized test in October

Homework Policy: 2–3 hours per night
Method of Discipline: Outlined in the student handbook; revised annually

Enrichment Curriculum

Fine Arts Day; Career Day; Guidance Fair; Science Fair; Odyssey of the Mind; math, science, and foreign language competitions; concert orchestra; fall dramatic and spring musical productions; summer study skills program

Extracurricular Activities

Organizations: National Honor Society, Student Council, Student Foundation, Choices, Peer Helpers, Amnesty International, student newspaper, yearbook, Blackfriars (theater productions)
Bands: Marching, concert, jazz, liturgical, drill team, flag corps, cheerleaders
Sports: Football, girls' and boys' basketball, girls' and boys' soccer, baseball, softball, girls' and boys' track, cross country, swimming, golf, tennis, power lifting, volleyball, golf
Clubs: FBLA, environmental club, Eucharistic Ministers, French, Latin, Spanish, Star Trek, photography/art, FTA, Scholars Club

Goals for Students

To develop well-rounded, well-balanced Christian young people who are intellectually, socially, and morally prepared to lead active, productive lives.

Faculty/Staff Requirements

Qualifications of Staff: B.A. degrees (31); M.A. degrees (23); Ph.D. degrees (2)
Qualifications of Administrator: M.A. with 14 years of service at Bishop Lynch

School Information

Brochure Available: Yes
Number of Students in Each Grade: Freshmen–231; sophomores–224; juniors–198; seniors–149
Parochial: Catholic
Organization Affiliations: Recognized by Texas Education Agency
Accreditations: Southern Association of Colleges and Schools; Texas Catholic Conference Accreditation Commission
Parental Involvement: School Board, Parents' Association, Band Boosters, Athletic Boosters
Other Information:

Admittance

Whom to Contact: Admissions office

Date to Apply: January–August

Testing Procedure per Age/Grade Level: In January of the student's eighth-grade year for ninth-grade admissions

Fees Involved: Yes

Type of Student Preferred: All students dedicated to a quest for excellence nd personal achievement

Forms Required: Application, standardized test scores, transcript, recommendation forms

Individual/Group Appointments: Individual

Notification Procedure: Freshmen–March 31st by letter

Waiting List Policy: None

Tuition

Approximate Tuition for 1996-97 School Year: $4500 (Catholics); $5355 (non-Catholics)

Methods of Payment Available: Payment in full by June 1st or guaranteed loan with local bank

Financial Assistance Offered: Catholic Diocese of Dallas Tuition Aid Program, Merit Scholars' Program, Opportunity and Achievement Scholarship Program

Cancellation Insurance Available: Tuition (minus a withdrawal fee) is refundable.

Additional Costs

Books/Bag/Uniform: Books ($200–$300 per year); uniform ($100)

Lunch fee: Plate lunch $2.25; also fresh sandwiches, hamburgers, french fries, salads, fruits, and drinks

Parents Club Dues: None

Annual Fund Drive: Over 50% of parents participate in Parents' Annual Fund Drive for Operating Budget; 15% of alumni and alumni parents support the Endowment Fund

Discount for Siblings: Yes

Facilities/Services Provided

Computer Lab: One lab– IBM 486's networked with Novell; one 486 computer networked in each classroom

Library: Automated circulation system with approximately 13,000 holdings

Snack Procedures: N/A

Before-school Care Program Available: N/A

After-school Care Program Available: N/A
Nurse on Staff: No
Emergency Procedure Used: Most teachers and all coaches are CPR–certified; parents are notified immediately; 911 called for major emergencies
Transportation to and from School: Bus transportation available for Richardson, North Dallas, Collin County, and N.W. Dallas (fee involved)
Counseling and Evaluation Available: Yes

Graduation Information

Testing: Campbell Interest and Skills Survey
Average SAT Scores: Honors curriculum 1196; regular curriculum 906
High School Our Students Usually Attend: N/A
Percentage of Seniors Attending College: 99

Additional Information

Over 37,000 hours of community service completed by Bishop Lynch students
1994 seniors offered over $2.5 million in college scholarships
1993 senior received congressional appointment to West Point; three seniors received congressional appointments to the Air Force Academy
1992 East Dallas Community Service Award
1991 Recognized School of Excellence by the U.S. Department of Education
1991 Meadow Foundation Community Service Award
85% of students participate in extracurricular activities
99% of graduates pursue higher education

National Merit Program 1980–1995
16 National Merit Scholars
25 National Merit Semi-Finalists
50 National Commended Scholars

TAPPS Sports Championships
1995, 1994, 1993, 1992, 1991 Girls' basketball state championship
1994 Football state championship
1994 Boys' swimming state championship
1994 Softball regional championship
1994, 1993 Girls' soccer regional championship
1994, 1993, 1992 Boys' and girls' cross country district championships
1993 Football bi-district championship
1993 Softball district championship
1993 Girls' golf district championship
1992 Football regional championship

1992 Boys' basketball state finalist
1991 Girls' track district championship
1991 Baseball state finalist
1991 Softball regional championship
1991, 1992, 1993 state championships in girls' basketball
1992 state finalist in boys' basketball
1992 district championships in boys' and girls' cross country
1991 district championship in girls' track
1991 state finalists in baseball
1991 regional championship in softball

Christ the King School

4100 Colgate
Dallas, TX 75225
(214) 365-1234

Mapsco: 25Y-26W

Fax: (214) 368-7419

Office Hours: 7:30 a.m.–4:00 p.m.
School Hours: 7:50 a.m.–3:30 p.m.
School Grades Offered: K–8
Enrollment: 370
Co-ed: Yes
Boy/Girl Ratio: 1:1
Student/Teacher Ratio: 18:1 in K; 22:1 in grade 1; 25:1 in grades 2–8
Average Class Size: 25
Calendar School Year: August–May
Holidays: Traditional school holidays and holy days
Uniform Requirements: Yes
Founded in: 1948

Philosophy of School

Conscious of the dignity of each student created in God's image, the primary concern of Christ the King School (CKS) is the development of the whole child. In *To Teach as Jesus Did*, the United States bishops state: "...Educational programs for the young must strive to teach doctrine, to do so within the experience of Christian community, and to prepare individuals for Christian witness and service to others." With this in mind, CKS endeavors to provide every opportunity for children to grow spiritually, intellectually, physically, and emotionally, so they can take their places as responsible members of the church, the family, and society.

Academic Curriculum

Content: Kindergartners learn to read and spell simple words, to solve basic arithmetic problems, and to use the computer. By the end of the year, they are ready academically, socially, and emotionally for first grade.

The primary grades participate in a structured traditional program that

281

emphasizes the acquisition of basic skills as well as the introduction of new concepts.

The intermediate grades are partially departmentalized with emphasis on verbal and written communication, reading comprehension, and mathematical concepts.

The departmentalized middle school's academic program emphasizes higher-order applications of knowledge and includes enrichment electives for students of average to above-average ability. All students take art, music, physical education, Spanish, and computer science.

CKS students consistently score well on standardized tests, and their superior scores have enabled many of them to participate in Duke University's Talent Identification Program and Talented and Gifted Summer Program.

Many CKS graduates receive scholarships and usually excel in the college-preparatory high schools of their choice.
Grading System Used: E, G, S (k–2); A–F (grades 3–8)
Conferences per Year: Twice and as needed
Tests Administered: Annual achievement test–National Test of Basic Skills
Homework Policy: Every night for students in grades 2–8
Method of Discipline: Clearly defined expectations with consequences outlined

Enrichment Curriculum

Field trips, reading lab, science lab, computer lab, exploratory classes for middle school, library, art, music, physical education

Extracurricular Activities

All sports, yearbook, student council, scouts, Campfire, altar servers, safety patrol

Goals for Students

CKS provides a curriculum that challenges all students to develop their intellectual, social, and spiritual capabilities to the fullest. Our goal is that each child live effectively in the present while preparing for the future.

Faculty/Staff Requirements

Qualifications of Staff: Degrees and certification
Qualifications of Administrator: Ed.D. in Private School Administration; United States Department of Education National Distinguished Principal award

School Information
Brochure Available: Yes
Number of Students in Each Grade: K,18; 1st.,22; grades 3–8,25
Parochial: Yes
Organization Affiliations: Diocese of Dallas, NCEA, TCCED
Accreditations: TCCED
Parental Involvement: Many volunteer opportunities; boards
Other Information: Named 1994 U.S. Department of Eduation National "Blue Ribbon School of Excellence"

Admittance
Whom to Contact: Ms. Gwyne Bohren, Director of Admissions
Date to Apply: Rolling admissions
Testing Procedure per Age/Grade Level: Testing in February, so register early
Fees Involved: $25
Type of Student Preferred: Academically motivated
Forms Required: Yes
Individual/Group Appointments: Both
Notification Procedure: By letter
Waiting List Policy: Ongoing; updated annually

Tuition
Approximate Tuition for 1996–97 School Year: $2200 per year for parishioners; more for non-parishioners
Methods of Payment Available: Monthly, by semester, yearly
Financial Assistance Offered: Yes
Cancellation Insurance Available: No
Profit/Non-profit: Non-profit

Additional Costs
Books/Bag/Uniform: Books (no); bag (yes); uniform (yes)
Lunch Fee: Varies by child
Parents Club Dues: $25; athletic committee, $30; activity fee: $125
Annual Fund Drive: No
Discount for Siblings: No

Facilities/Services Provided
Computer Lab: Yes
Library: Yes

Snack Procedures: K–5
Before-school Care Program Available: No; open at 7:30 a.m. with supervision
After-school Care Program Available: Yes; 3:30 - 6:00 p.m.
Nurse on Staff: Yes
Emergency Procedure Used: Emergency card on file for each student
Transportation to and from School: Car pools only; no bus or van
Counseling and Evaluation Available: Yes

Graduation Information

Testing: N/A
Average SAT Scores: N/A
High School Our Students Usually Attend: Jesuit, Ursuline
Percentage of Seniors Attending College: 99%

Additional Information

Christ the King School maintains high standards for academics and behavior and emphasizes a wide range of talents.

Good Shepherd Catholic School

214 S. Garland Avenue
Garland, TX 75040
(214) 272-6533

Mapsco: 19Y

Fax: (214) 272-0512

Office Hours: 7:30 a.m.–4:00 p.m.
School Hours: 7:55 a.m.–3:15 p.m. (pre-K–grade 4);
7:55 a.m.–3:25 p.m. (grades 5–8)
School Grades Offered: Pre-kindergarten–grade 8
Enrollment: 365
Co-ed: Yes
Boy/Girl Ratio: 50:50
Student/Teacher Ratio: 20:1
Average Class Size: 20
Calendar School Year: August–May
Holidays: Thanksgiving, Christmas, Martin Luther King Day,
Presidents' Day, Easter, spring break
Uniform Requirements: Yes
Founded in: 1954

Philosophy of School

To offer a rigorous academic program in a Catholic environment. Our three-fold
purpose is faith, knowledge, and service.

Academic Curriculum

Content: All basic subjects plus religion, art, music, computer, physical
education, Spanish; exploratory-elective program for grades 6–8
Grading System Used: Diocesan
Conferences per Year: Two (fall and spring)
Tests Administered: National Achievement Test (N.A.T.)

Homework Policy: Monday through Thursday for students in grades 1–8
Method of Discipline: Parent notification; detention

Enrichment Curriculum
Expanded academics are offered for gifted students; however, enrichment is part of the total educational goal for all students.

Extracurricular Activities
Football, volleyball, basketball, softball, soccer, track, cheerleading

Goals for Students
To achieve to their maximum educational potential and to develop spiritually in the service of God and the church

Faculty/Staff Requirements
Qualifications of Staff: Bachelor's degree and certification required; many have master's degrees.
Qualifications of Administrator: Administrator's certificate, graduate degree

School Information
Brochure Available: Yes
Number of Students in Each Grade: 22–28
Parochial: Yes, Catholic Diocese of Dallas
Organization Affiliations: National Catholic Educators' Association
Accreditations: Texas Catholic Conference
Parental Involvement: Parent-Teacher-Organization activities provide extensive involvement.
Other Information:

Admittance
Whom to Contact: School office
Date to Apply: February
Entrance Testing: Yes
Fees Involved: $20 testing fee
Type of Student Preferred: With high academic expectations and moral values
Forms Required: Registration, test scores, report cards, birth certificate, baptismal record (if Catholic)

Individual/Group Appointments: Both
Testing Procedure per Age/Grade Level: Entrance testing for students k–8
Notification Procedure: Letter within two weeks
Waiting List Policy: Reapply annually

Tuition

Approximate Tuition for 1996-97 School Year: $2100 parishioner; $2950 out-of-parish; $3400 non-Catholic
Methods of Payment Available: 10 or 11 monthly payments; 5% discount if paid in full by a specified date in June
Financial Assistance Offered: No
Cancellation Insurance Available: No
Profit/Non-profit: Non-profit

Additional Costs

Books/Bag/Uniform: Books–$100 per child; bag–none; uniform–according to Parker Uniform price list
Lunch Fee: $2.50 plate lunch
Parents Club Dues: $5
Annual Fund Drive: No
Discount for Siblings: Yes

Facilities/Services Provided

Computer: Yes, Macintosh lab
Library: Yes
Snack Procedures: Yes
Before-school Care Program Available: Yes
After-school Care Program Available: Yes
Nurse on Staff: No
Emergency Procedure Used: As directed by parent
Transportation to and from School: Parents or car pools
Counseling and Evaluation Available: No, outside referrals if needed

Graduation Information

Testing: Average test scores are above the seventy-fifth percertile.
High School Our Students Usually Attend: Usually 75 percent attend Bishop Lynch, Ursuline, or Jesuit.
Average SAT Scores: N/A
Percentage of Seniors Attending College: N/A

The Highlands School

1451 E. Northgate Drive   Mapsco: 31B-H
Irving, TX 75062
(214) 554-1980   Fax: (214) 721-1691

> *Office Hours:* 8:00 a.m.–5:00 p.m.
> *School Hours:* 8:15 a.m.–3:30 p.m.
> *School Grades Offered:* Pre-kindergarten (3-year-olds)–
> grade 12
> *Enrollment:* 440
> *Co-ed:* Yes (Pk3–grade 3); single sex (grades 4–12)
> *Boy/Girl Ratio:* 1:1
> *Student/Teacher Ratio:* 10:1
> *Average Class Size:* 13
> *Calendar School Year:* Mid-August–end of May
> *Holidays:* Christmas (2 weeks), spring break (1 week), all Holy
> Days of Obligation
> *Uniform Requirements:* Yes
> *Founded in:* 1986

Philosophy of School

The Highlands School is a private, Catholic school, directed by The Legion of Christ,
offering classes from pre-kindergarten through twelfth grade. The school is committed
to academic excellence within a Christian environment.

Faculty members are highly qualified and concerned with each student's development
and Christian maturity. Because of the small class size, the teachers get to know each
student personally. The unique combination of high academic standards and values is
implemented through the dedicated faculty members, who are expected to lead by their
example.

The Highlands School's philosophy is "*To Teach, To Educate, To Form.*" Knowledge,
beyond the mere retention of concepts, facts, and figures, is to know things in
themselves, to know their value in relation to others. Knowledge is the ability to make

proper judgments and to develop one's sense of beauty and goodness. To teach is to communicate knowledge.

Academic Curriculum
Content:

Pre-K and Kindergarten:
With the use of creative manipulatives, the child learns measuring, counting, addition, and subtraction. Major language skills of handwriting, auditory discrimination, oral language, and linguistics are developed through an extensive phonetics curriculum. Spanish is also offered.

Lower/Middle School
A strong liberal arts program is offered which includes English, math, history, geography, literature, science, computer, Spanish, Latin, religion, fine arts, choir, and physical education.

Upper School
The academic program of the Upper School receives its form from a curriculum designed to lead the Highlands student to competency in all the intellectual disciplines appropriate for pre-collegiate studies. This program reflects the desire of the Highlands to concentrate on the broad formation of the whole individual, rather than the training of a narrow specialist. Moreover, within the several disciplines by course placement and by individual instruction, the student is encouraged to set no upper limits to his development and to explore to the depth of his own intellectual abilities.

Each year the curriculum includes the study of English, literature, mathematics, and theology, as well as physical education. In addition, over the four-year course of studies, students are required to take six credits in foreign language (a combination of credit in classical and modern language), three credits in history, three credits in laboratory science, and one-half credit in politics. Successful completion of this curriculum is suitable for presentation to even the most competitive college. Many Highlands courses may be described as accelerated for purposes of college admission, and some upper courses are based upon CEEB Advanced Placement Curriculum. Class size will generally be limited to 18 students, while advanced courses are usually much smaller.

Grading System Used: A-F–grades 4-12; N (needs improvement), S (satisfactory), G (good), E (excellent)–Pk-grade 3
Conferences per Year: At least two a year, and at request of parents
Tests Administered: National Standardized Achievement Tests
Homework Policy: Varies by grade
Method of Discipline: Varies by grade

Enrichment Curriculum
Field trips, computer, Spanish at all levels, daily mass available

Extracurricular Activities
Soccer, basketball, volleyball, band, student council, boys' club, girls' club; after-school care program available until 6:30 p.m.

Goals for Students
The Highlands School aims at the perfection of the whole person, to educate not only the mind, but also the aesthetic faculties, such as an appreciation for love of beauty, harmony, and good. The Highlands School also helps form character by developing a sense of justice, responsibility, strength of will, and honesty.

Faculty/Staff Requirements
Qualifications of Staff: Bachelor's, master's, and doctoral degrees
Qualifications of Administrator: Master's degree, doctoral work in progress

School Information
Brochure Available: Yes
Number of Students in Each Grade: Pk3–two classes of 10; pk4-K–four classes of 12 (new classes added as needed); grades 1-2–three classes of 16; grade 3–two classes of 18; grades 4-12–two classes of 18
Parochial: Yes; Roman Catholic; directed by Legionaires of Christ
Organization Affiliations: N/A
Accreditations: TCCED (in progress)
Parental Involvement: Parents' Club
Other Information:

Admittance
Whom to Contact: Sylvia Najera at (214) 554-1980, ext. 235
Date to Apply: Before March 1

Testing Procedure per Age/Grade Level: Students entering K-grade 9 are required to take an entrance exam.
Fees Involved: $50 testing/application fee
Type of Student Preferred: Motivated, no discipline problems, of good moral character
Forms Required: Admission application; two letters of recommendation; transcript
Individual/Group Appointments: Family interview required; personal interview also required for students entering high school
Notification Procedure: Letters of acceptance mailed March 1
Waiting List Policy: No student placed on a waiting list until the entire admissions process has been completed and the student has been accepted for admission; waiting lists for the year of application only

Tuition

Approximate Tuition for 1996-97 School Year: $3350–$5400
Methods of Payment Available: Yearly, bi-annually, monthly (ten monthly payments)
Financial Assistance Offered: Based on financial need and academic merit
Cancellation Insurance Available: No
Profit/Non-profit: Non-profit

Additional Costs

Books/Bag/Uniform: Uniforms purchased through Parker Uniforms; registration fees–$400-$500 per student
Lunch Fee: Hot lunch program available
Parents Club Dues: N/A
Annual Fund Drive: Yes, optional participation
Discount for Siblings: 10% discount for second sibling; 15% each for third and fourth siblings; 25% discount for all other siblings

Facilities/Services Provided

Computer Lab: Yes, IBM-compatible PC's
Library: Yes
Snack Procedures: All students grades PK–grade 4 required to bring daily snack
Before-school Care Program Available: Students may be dropped off at 7:45 a.m. (no fee)
After-school Care Program Available: 3:30 p.m.–6:30 p.m.
Nurse on Staff: Yes
Emergency Procedure Used: We follow each student's emergency

291

authorization card.

Transportation to and from School: Not available at this time

Counseling and Evaluation Available: Yes

Graduation Information

Testing: Yes, P.S.A.T. and S.A.T.

Average SAT Scores: 1200

High School Our Students Usually Attend: N/A

Percentage of Seniors Attending College: 100

Additional Information

Holy Family of Nazareth School

2323 Cheyenne
Irving, TX 75062
(214) 255-0205

Mapsco: 31M

Fax: (214) 252-5523

Office Hours: 7:30 a.m.–4:00 p.m.
School Hours: 7:55 a.m.–3:15 p.m.
School Grades Offered: Pre-k–grade 8
Enrollment: 400
Co-ed: Yes
Boy/Girl Ratio: 50:50
Student/Teacher Ratio: 25:1
Average Class Size: 25
Calendar School Year: August–May
Holidays: Holy days, in-service days, Labor Day, Fair
Day, parent-teacher conferences, Thanksgiving holiday,
Christmas vacation, Martin Luther King Day, spring break,
Easter holiday, Memorial Day
Uniform Requirements: Yes
Founded in: 1965

Philosophy of School

We at Holy Family of Nazareth School see each child as an uniquely important
individual who is a vital part of a caring school community. We strive to supply a safe,
comfortable environment where the education of children can take place. We hope to
balance their education and satisfy the intellectual, physical, and spiritual needs of each
child as an individual and as a member of the school family. We want to prepare our
students and faculty to face the complex and challenging world of the 21st century.

Academic Curriculum

Content: Religion, language arts, mathematics, social studies, music, art,
computer science, physical education; curriculum approved by the Diocese of

Dallas and the Texas Catholic Conference Education Department for the use in accredited schools; electives offered in the middle schools are: Life Skills, Journalism, Yearbook, Peace and Justice, Spanish, Young Authors
Grading System Used: Diocese of Dallas
Conferences per Year: Two
Tests Administered: Comprehensive testing program; in spring, standardized achievement tests administered in kindergarten–grade 8
Homework Policy: Assignments given to provide opportunities to extend knowledge and develop independent study habits; no set pattern; deadlines set by teachers must be met punctually.
Method of Discipline: See *Discipline Code of Conduct* in school office.

Enrichment Curriculum
Enrichment programs and educational field trips; resources of the library and audio-visual media are available; art, drama, Odyssey of the Mind, band, student council

Extracurricular Activities
Soccer, basketball, volleyball, track and field, cheerleading, football, and DECATS (DeBusk Center for Academically Talented Students); the parish sponsors boy scouts, cub scouts, girl scouts, brownie troops

Goals for Students
To prepare students to live effectively in the present as Christian young people and in the future as Christian adults; to develop the whole child–academically, spiritually, and emotionally.

Faculty/Staff Requirements
Qualifications of Staff: Bachelor's degree and/or master's degree
Qualifications of Administrator: M.A. ED. in Administration and Supervision

School Information
Brochure Available: Yes
Number of Students in Each Grade: 50
Parochial: Yes
Organization Affiliations: Holy Family of Nazareth Parish; Diocese of Dallas
Accreditations: Texas Educational Association (TEA); Texas Catholic Conferences Education Department (TCCED)
Parental Involvement: Yes, very active home and school association; room parents

Other Information: Awarded Exemplary School Award by the U.S. Department of Education

Admittance

Whom to Contact: Micki McCutcheon, Development Director
Date to Apply: Annual registration begins the last weekend of February.
Testing Procedure per Age/Grade Level: Yes; for placement
Fees Involved: Due at registration; registration fee, book-and-activity fee, snack fee for pre-K and kindergarten
Type of Student Preferred: Inquire
Forms Required: Application for enrollment, birth certificate, baptismal certificate (for baptized Catholics), former school records, health history form including physical and current immunization record
Individual/Group Appointments: Individual
Notification Procedure: Letter or phone call in May
Waiting List Policy: Annually

Tuition

Approximate Tuition for 1996-97 School Year: Please call office for rates.
Methods of Payment Available: Monthly or by semester with 5% discount
Financial Assistance Offered: Yes
Cancellation Insurance Available: No
Profit/Non-profit: Non-profit

Additional Costs

Books/Bag/Uniform: Book-and-activity fee includes books and field trips. Uniforms are purchased from Parker School Uniforms. School supplies and book bags are additional. Lists are mailed to students during the summer.
Lunch Fee: Hot lunch available for $1.50; may bring sack lunch; government-subsidized reduced-cost or free lunch program available to those who qualify
Parents Club Dues: No
Annual Fund Drive: Yes
Discount for Siblings: Yes

Facilities/Services Provided

Computer Lab: Yes; our lab is equipped with Apple and IBM compatible computers and staffed by a full time computer teacher.
Library: Yes; Library is fully automated and is staffed by a full-time librarian.
Snack Procedures: Snack fee due for pre-K and kindergarten; grades 1-8– teacher's discretion

Before-school Care Program Available: No
After-school Care Program Available: Yes; from school's dismissal until 6:00 p.m. on school days only (fee)
Nurse on Staff: Yes
Emergency Procedure Used: Fire drill evacuation plan in force; emergency call buttons in classrooms
Transportation to and from School: Bus available for Grapevine, Trophy Club, and Hackberry Creek
Counseling and Evaluation Available: Master's Level Guidance Counselor

Graduation Information

Testing: Comprehensive testing program; standardized achievement tests administered in the spring
Average SAT Scores: N/A
High School Our Students Usually Attend: Ursuline Academy, Jesuit College Preparatory School, Cistercian Preparatory School, Nolan High School, Bishop Dunn High School, or their neighborhood public school
Percentage of Seniors Attending College: Information available at the school

Additional Information

Holy Trinity Catholic School

3815 Oak Lawn Avenue
Dallas, TX 75219
(214) 526-5113

Mapsco: 35X

Fax: (214) 526-3477

Office Hours: 7:30 a.m.–4:30 p.m.
School Hours: 7:45 a.m.–3:30 p.m.
School Grades Offered: Preschool (age 3)–grade 8
Enrollment: 215
Co-ed: Yes
Boy/Girl Ratio: 2:3
Student/Teacher Ratio: 18:1
Average Class Size: 20
Calendar School Year: Mid-August to end of May
Holidays: Labor Day, Thanksgiving, Christmas, spring
break, Easter break, Holy Days
Uniform Requirements: Yes
Founded in: 1914

Philosophy of School

The mission at Holy Trinity Catholic School is to provide each student the highest
quality foundation of Catholic education. The school enriches the minds, bodies, and
spirits of the children. The school produces students who are competitive in Catholic
secondary schools, and who ultimately become productive citizens and wise leaders in
society. In our rapidly changing urban community, the school reaches out to include and
welcome those from the emerging cultural and ethnic diversity around us. The school's
uniquely personal educational process encourages and motivates each student to strive
for excellence.

Academic Curriculum

Content: Traditional curriculum of English, math, science, social studies plus
art, music, drama, and computer
Grading System Used: Letter grades of E, G, S, and N in primary grades;

297

A-F in upper grades
Conferences per Year: Scheduled after first and third marking periods; others scheduled as needed
Tests Administered: ACT Achievement Tests
Homework Policy: Yes
Method of Discipline: Time out; loss of privileges

Enrichment Curriculum
Art, music, band, drama, public speaking, and computer

Extracurricular Activities
Soccer, girls volleyball, student council, yearbook, newspaper, band

Goals for Students
To teach religion as a way of life; to promote a positive attitude in the face of change; to develop school spirit, civic pride, good sportsmanship, and leadership qualities

Faculty/Staff Requirements
Qualifications of Staff: College degree and teacher certification
Qualifications of Administrator: Master's degree in educational administration

School Information
Brochure Available: Yes
Number of students in each grade: PS–18; PK–20; K–25; 1st–24; 2nd–25; 3rd–22; 4th–20; 5th–22; 6th–13; 7th–15; 8th–11
Parochial: Catholic
Organization Affiliations: National Catholic Education Association and Texas Catholic Conference Education Department (TCCED)
Accreditations: TCCED
Parental Involvement: PTO, volunteerism, and fundraising

Admittance
Whom to Contact: School principal or school secretary
Date to Apply: Mid-February through May of each year
Testing Procedure per Age/Grade Level: Placement test given for grades 1-7
Fees Involved: Registration fee of $150
Type of Student Preferred: Motivated; wants to learn; self-disciplined
Forms Required: Birth certificate, baptismal certificate for Catholics, recent

report card, recent achievement test scores

Individual/Group Appointments: Individual

Notification Procedure: Letter, phone call, or in person

Waiting List Policy: Priority is given first to siblings, then Catholic parishioners, Catholic non-parishioners, and lastly to non-Catholics.

Tuition

Approximate Tuition for 1996-97 School Year: Parishioner–$1800; Non-Parishioner–$2500; Non-Catholic–$2800

Methods of Payment Available: Annually, semi-annually, or monthly

Financial Assistance Offered: Yes, but very limited

Cancellation Insurance Available: No

Profit/Non-profit: Non-profit

Additional Costs

Books/Bag/Uniform: Books–no; bag–yes; uniforms–yes

Lunch Fee: $2.00-$2.50

Parents Club Dues: None

Annual Fund Drive: Yes

Discount for Siblings: Yes

Facilities/Services Provided

Computer Lab: Yes

Library: Yes

Snack Procedures: Preschool through kindergarten bring morning snacks.

Before-school Care Program Available: No

After-school Care Program Available: Yes, until 6:30 p.m.

Nurse on Staff: Yes

Emergency Procedure Used: Emergency form on file

Transportation to and from School: No

Counseling and Evaluation Available: No

Graduation Information

Testing: N/A

Average SAT Scores: N/A

High School Our Students Usually Attend: Bishop Dunne, Bishop Lynch, Jesuit, Ursuline, and DISD Magnet Schools

Percentage of Seniors Attending College: N/A

Immaculate Conception School

400 N. E. 17th Street
Grand Prairie, TX 75081
(214) 264-8777

Mapsco: 51A-C

Fax: (214) 264-7742

Office Hours: 8:00 a.m.–4:30 p.m.
School Hours: 8:00 a.m.–3:30 p.m.
School Grades Offered: Prekindergarten–grade 8
Enrollment: 225
Co-ed: Yes
Boy/Girl Ratio: 50:50
Student/Teacher Ratio: 20:1
Average Class Size: 20
Calendar School Year: August–May
Holidays: Labor Day, Thanksgiving, Christmas, Easter,
Memorial Day, Holy days of obligation
Uniform Requirements: Yes (Parker Uniform Company)
Founded in: 1953

Philosophy of School
The student is a unique individual having his/her own special talents and abilities. It is our responsibility to educate the whole person, not only academically, but also spiritually, emotionally, psychologically, socially, and physically.

Academic Curriculum
Content: Religion, English, math, reading, social studies, science, Spanish, health, computer science, music, art, physical education
Grading System Used: A, B, C, D, F
Conferences per Year: One
Tests Administered: ACT College Testing
Homework Policy: Homework is assigned in grades 1–8. It is the student's responsibility to complete it in a timely, accurate fashion.

Method of Discipline: Discipline through discipleship–a positive approach without corporal punishment

Enrichment Curriculum

Two experienced resource teachers; reading-support program; music-education program; pre-kindergarten program; computer education program; art

Extracurricular Activities

Band, choir, cheerleading, basketball, volleyball, soccer, track, art club, yearbook, geography club, scouts, speech team

Goals for Students

Our primary goal is the continuous formation of the Christian person. We encourage the spiritual, intellectual, social, cultural, and physical development of the student.

Faculty/Staff Requirements

Qualifications of Staff: Certification
Qualifications of Administrator: M.A. in Humanities; professional mid-management certification

School Information

Brochure Available: Yes
Number of Students in Each Grade: 20 (average)
Parochial: Private Catholic school
Organization Affiliations: National Catholic Education Association, Grand Prairie Chamber of Commerce, Dallas Parochial League, Dallas Hispanic Chamber of Commerce
Accreditations: TCCED
Parental Involvement: Parent-volunteer program (15 hours per year)
Other Information: Awarded "Excellence-in-Education Exemplary Award" from the U.S. Department of Education

Admittance

Whom to Contact: School office
Date to Apply: Open enrollment year round
Testing Procedure for Age/Grade Level: ACT testing in February
Fees Involved: Registration fee $100; testing fee $5; tuition-program fee $35
Type of Student Preferred: All students are welcome; Catholic students

receive first consideration.

Forms Required: Registration form, emergency form, parish-support agreement

Individual/Group Appointments: Both available

Notification Procedure: Phone call

Waiting List Policy: Ongoing; we welcome students all year.

Tuition

Approximate Tuition for 1996-97 School Year: $2140

Methods of Payment Available: Prepaid or monthly coupon book

Financial Assistance Offered: Limited funds available for those who qualify

Cancellation Insurance Available: N/A

Profit/Non-profit: Non-profit

Additional Costs

Books/Bag/Uniform: Parker Uniform Company

Lunch Fee: $15 lunch card available

Parents Club Dues: Home-and-School Association annual fee $3

Annual Fund Drive: School board's annual night-out fundraiser

Discount for Siblings: 50% discount

Facilities/Services Provided

Computer Lab: Yes

Library: Yes

Snack Procedures: Mid-day snack for prekindergarten–grade 5

Before-school Care Program Available: Supervision 7:30 a.m.–7:45 a.m. (no charge)

After-school Care Program Available: 3:30 p.m.–6:00 p.m. ($6)

Nurse on Staff: No

Emergency Procedure Used: Parents notified immediately

Transportation to and from School: No

Counseling and Evaluation Available: Available through G.P.I.S.D.

Graduation Information

Testing: N/A

Average SAT Scores: N/A

High School Our Students Usually Attend: N/A

Percentage of Seniors Attending College: N/A

Additional Information

The school's status as a nationally recognized Exemplary School continues to build enrollment.

Jesuit College Preparatory School

12345 Inwood Road
Dallas, TX 75244
(214) 387-8700

Mapsco: 14V

Fax: (214) 661-9349

Office Hours: 8:00 a.m.–4:30 p.m.
School Hours: 8:00 a.m.–3:30 p.m.
School Grades Offered: Boys, grades 9–12
Enrollment: 820
Co-ed: No
Boy/Girl Ratio: Boys only
Student/Teacher Ratio: 11:1
Average Class Size: 20–25
Calendar School Year: August–May
Holidays: Christmas (2 weeks), spring break (1 week), summer (12 weeks)
Uniform Requirements: Dress code
Founded in: 1942

Philosophy of School

St. Ignatius of Loyola, who founded the Jesuit order over four centuries ago, believed in the importance of developing the self as a prerequisite to an enriching life in the world. Building on this 400-year-old belief, Jesuit College Preparatory School is committed to the intellectual, psychological, physical, social, and spiritual growth of each student.

Academic Curriculum

Content: College preparatory
Grading System Used: A–F; grades are sent home.
Conferences per Year: Scheduled four times a year, or by request at any time
Tests Administered: Mid-quarter

Homework Policy: 2-3 hours per night
Method of Discipline: Positive, developmental discipline

Enrichment Curriculum
See extracurricular activities.

Extracurricular Activities
Varsity, junior varsity, and freshman teams in eleven sports; compete with public and private schools; member Texas Christian Interscholastic League; over 30 extracurricular clubs and organizations

Goals for Students
To prepare for higher education; to obtain an intellectual and moral foundation necessary for success in the modern world

Faculty/Staff Requirements
Qualifications of Staff: Almost 75% of the faculty have master's degrees with at least 10 years of teaching experience
Qualifications of Administrator: Principal has M.Ed. from Boston College; both assistant principals have master's degrees.

School Information
Brochure Available: Yes
Number of Students in Each Grade: Grade 9–210; grade 10–200; grade 11–190; grade 12–180
Parochial: Operated by The Society of Jesus (Jesuit Fathers)
Organization Affiliations: NASSP, JSEA, NCEA, TCIL
Accreditations: Southern Association of Colleges and Schools; TCCED; TEPSAC
Parental Involvement: Parent Executive Board; volunteer programs
Other Information:

Admittance
Whom to Contact: Principal, Rev. Paul Deutsch, S.J.
Date to Apply: Late fall for following school year
Testing Procedure per Age/Grade Level: Yes, for grades 9 and 10
Fees Involved: Yes
Type of Student Preferred: Jesuit is open to male, qualified students of all

faiths, denominations, race; candidates are considered for their academic ability and character.

Forms Required: Yes

Individual/Group Appointments: Individual

Notification Procedure: Usually March/April for early applicants; six to eight weeks after applying (applies to applications received after April)

Waiting List Policy: N/A

Tuition

Approximate Tuition for 1996-97 School Year: $5775

Methods of Payment Available: Half payment beginning of each semester

Financial Assistance Offered: Financial aid, scholarships, and work-grants are available to those who qualify academically and/or economically.

Cancellation Insurance Available: No

Profit/Non-Profit: Non-profit

Additional Costs

Books/Bag/Uniform: Yes

Lunch Fee: No

Parents Club Dues: N/A

Annual Fund Drive: Yes

Discount for Siblings: No

Facilities/Services Provided

Computer Lab: Yes

Library: Yes

Snack Procedures: N/A

Before-school Care Program Available: N/A

After-school Care Program Available: N/A

Nurse on Staff: N/A

Emergency Procedure Used: Published in student handbook

Transportation to and from School: Public, bus, car pool

Counseling and Evaluation Available: Yes

Graduation Information

Testing: 51 percent of the 1995 class received scholarships totaling over $2,750,933.

Average SAT Scores: 1124 (mean)

High School Our Students Usually Attend: N/A

Percentage of Seniors Attending College: 100%

Additional Information

One of the first schools in the nation to introduce a community service program over 18 years ago, Jesuit College Preparatory School requires all seniors to do 100 hours of service. A need-based financial aid program is available for qualified students. Jesuit is one of the few high schools in the nation with its own museum, with over 350 pieces of art throughout the corridors and classrooms. Each year the school sponsors "Issues Week" focusing upon a particular region of the world. Students and faculty attend lectures, workshops, and panel discussions throughout the week.

Prince of Peace Catholic School

5100 Plano Parkway West	Mapsco: 656Y
Plano, TX 75093	
(214) 380-5505	Fax: (214) 380-5162

Office Hours: 8:00 a.m.–4:00 p.m.
School Hours: 8:30 a.m.–3:30 p.m.
School Grades Offered: Pre-K (age 3)–grade 4 (The school will add one grade each year until it reaches the eighth grade.)
Enrollment: 326
Co-ed: Yes
Boy/Girl Ratio: 50:50
Student/Teacher Ratio: 16:1
Average Class Size: 3K/4K–15; K-grade 3–22; grade 4-5-25
Calendar School Year: August-May
Holidays: Holy Days, Christmas break, fall and spring breaks, Easter
Uniform Requirements: Begins in kindergarten
Founded in: 1991

Philosophy of School

The Prince of Peace Catholic School provides a nurturing and dynamic environment that facilitates the development of lifelong learning skills and the formation of the whole person within the Catholic Christian value system. We foster peacemaking and the awareness of the presence of God in human growth. We see ourselves as an integral part of the church's mission to spread God's work and bring all people to Christ, helping them to grow in faith, love, and wisdom.

Academic Curriculum

Content: Full core curriculum(interdisciplinary, literature-based)
Grading System Used: Portfolio; M (met/achieved objectives),

P (progressing), N (needs help); grades 6-8–letter grades
Conferences per Year: Three
Tests Administered: American College Testing
Homework Policy: Homework provides practice, enrichment, and/or extension opportunities of newly formed skills and concepts that relate what is learned in school to children's lives outside of school connecting school learning with the real world.
Method of Discipline: An important life skill to learn is self-discipline. The staff disciplines children in a kind, firm manner emphasizing mutual courtesy and respect for the rights of all people. To become a Peacemaker, your child is encouraged to discuss ("Use your words, please") and work out solutions to conflicts that arise with others. Self-discipline is the goal for each student.

Enrichment Curriculum
Peacemaker Press–publishing center; Spanish program; daily integrated computer program; music program

Extracurricular Activities
Parish athletics, Odyssey of the Mind, scouts, Indian guides and princesses

Goals for Students
To become lifelong learners integrating their faith life into daily living so they may make wise decisions and act as "Peacemakers"

Faculty/Staff Requirements
Qualifications of Staff: All of the professional staff have degrees; 50% have post-graduate degrees
Qualifications of Administrator: Post-graduate degrees with emphasis on school administration

School Information
Brochure Available: Registration packet
Number of Students in Each Grade: 3K–30; 4K–45; K–grade 3–44; grade 4–25
Parochial: Yes
Organization Affiliations: NCEA
Accreditations: TCCED, TEA
Parental Involvement: 25 active volunteer committees
Other Information:

Admittance

Whom to Contact: Anne Battes Kirby or school office
Date to Apply: February
Testing Procedure for Age/Grade Level: Interview with principal
Fees Involved: Registration fee, technology fee, tuition
Type of Student Preferred: Reviewed on an individual basis
Forms Required: Registration packet
Individual/Group Appointments: School information meetings–3 per year
Notification Procedure:
Waiting List Policy: Ongoing waiting list (See registration packet.)

Tuition

Approximate Tuition for 1996-97 School Year: Parishioner–1 child $2270, 2 children $3860, 3 children $4770, 4 children $5450; non-parishioner $3200
Methods of Payment Available: 10 monthly payments
Financial Assistance Offered: Tuition Assistance Program for currently enrolled families
Cancellation Insurance Available: No
Profit/Non-profit: Non-profit

Additional Costs

Books/Bag/Uniform: Uniforms required for students in kindergarten and above; available from Parker Uniform Co.
Lunch Fee: $2.50 per day (optional)
Parents Club Dues: $10.00
Annual Fund Drive: Fall Auction; Spring International Affair
Discount for Siblings: Yes

Facilities/Services Provided

Computer Lab: Building scheduled for 1997-98
Library: Media Center
Snack Procedures: Provided by school and families
Before-school Care Program Available: 8:00 a.m.
After-school Care Program Available: Until 6:00 p.m.
Nurse on Staff: R.N.
Emergency Procedure Used: Provided in school handbook
Transportation to and from School: Provided by parents
Counseling and Evaluation Available: Student and family formation available

Graduation Information

Testing: N/A
Average SAT Scores: N/A
High School Our Students Usually Attend: N/A
Percentage of Seniors Attending College: N/A

Additional Information

St. Bernard of Clairvaux

1420 Old Gate Lane
Dallas, TX 75218
(214) 321-2897

Mapsco: 37R

Fax: (214) 321-4060

Office Hours: 7:30 a.m.–3:30 p.m.
School Hours: 7:50 a.m.–3:15 p.m.
School Grades Offered: Kindergarten–grade 8
Enrollment: 360
Co-ed: Yes
Boy/Girl Ratio: 1:1
Student/Teacher Ratio: 20:1
Average Class Size:
Calendar School Year: August–May
Holidays: Thanksgiving, Christmas, spring break, Easter
Uniform Requirements: Yes
Founded in: 1948

Philosophy of School

We believe each child is a unique, loving, and spiritual individual. Each possesses the potential for learning and the ability to share these innate gifts.

At St. Bernard of Clairvaux School, we strive to create an open, loving atmosphere that will promote the growth of the whole child—spiritual, emotional, intellectual, physical, and social.

To achieve these philosophical goals, St. Bernard of Clairvaux School sets forth the following objectives:
1. To teach religion as a way of life and provide Christian role models.
2. To provide opportunities to develop spirituality through worship, prayer, and service.
3. To promote a healthy self-image by giving positive reinforcement and consistency.
4. To meet individual academic and personal needs with warmth and love.
5. To promote appreciation of others by sharing cultural and traditional enrichments.

Once a student is registered and accepted into St. Bernard of Clairvaux School, it is understood that the student and parent agree to cooperate with the school's regulations and policies.

Academic Curriculum

Content: Approved by Diocese and Texas Education Agency
Grading System Used: Letter grades
Conferences per Year: Three
Tests Administered: ACT
Homework Policy: Every night except Fridays
Method of Discipline: No corporal punishment

Enrichment Curriculum

Art, music, speech/drama: 6–8; Spanish, computer science, library science, and sensory-motor; remedial reading; talented and gifted enrichment

Extracurricular Activities

Speech, drama, sports, student council, choir, yearbook, newspaper

Goals for Students

Behavioral goals in curriculum areas; they are evaluated by the community each year and then updated.

Faculty/Staff Requirements

Qualifications of Staff: College degree; 27% have master's degrees or higher
Qualifications of Administrator: Must have at least a master's degree with three years teaching experience and an emphasis in administration

School Information

Brochure Available: Yes
Number of Students in Each Grade: 17–28
Parochial: Yes, Catholic
Organization Affiliations: National Catholic Education Association, TANS, Dallas Parochial League
Accreditations: TCCED
Parental Involvement: Home and School Association
Other Information:

Admittance

Whom to Contact: Mr. Jack R. LaMar
Date to Apply: February
Testing Procedure per Age/Grade Level: Kindergarten–grade 7
Fees Involved: $125-$200 (Registration fee $125; books; activity fee $30)
Type of Student Preferred: Evaluated one-on-one
Forms Required: Registration packet
Individual/Group Appointments: Individual
Notification Procedure: Notification is usually done in person or by phone. If someone is not accepted, the principal works with parents for placement.
Waiting List Policy: There is a waiting list; it is best to register on the appointed registration dates.

Tuition

Approximate Tuition for 1996-97 School Year: Parishioners–$2090 with a reduction for more than one child; non-parishioners–$2825; non-Catholic–$3100
Methods of Payment Available: Prepaid tuition; may pay the school directly or take a signature loan through the approved bank
Financial Assistance Offered: Limited
Cancellation Insurance Available: Inquire at school office
Profit/Non-profit: Non-profit

Additional Costs

Books/Bag/Uniform: Uniform
Lunch Fee: $1.50 per day hot lunch
Parents Club Dues: Home and School Association
Annual Fund Drive: Three drives–magazines, casino
Discount for Siblings: Yes

Facilities/Services Provided

Computer Lab: Yes
Library: Yes
Snack Procedures: Snacks for kindergarten classes only
Before-school Care Program Available: No
After-school Care Program Available: Yes, 3:00 p.m.–6:00 p.m.
Nurse on Staff: Trained staff person
Emergency Procedure Used: On registration forms
Transportation to and from School: No
Counseling and Evaluation Available: Yes–referrals made

Graduation Information

Testing: N/A
Average SAT scores: N/A
High School Our Students Usually Attend: N/A
Percentage of Seniors Attending College: 90

Additional Information

St. Elizabeth of Hungary Catholic School

4019 S. Hampton
Dallas, TX 75224
(214) 331-5139

Mapsco: 63H

Fax: (214) 467-4346

Office Hours: 7:30 a.m.–4:00 p.m.
School Hours: 7:50 a.m.–3:40 p.m.
School Grades Offered: Kindergarten–grade 8
Enrollment: 420
Co-ed: Yes
Boy/Girl Ratio: 186:231
Student/Teacher Ratio: 25:1
Average Class Size: 23
Calendar School Year: August–May
Holidays: Christmas (2 weeks), spring break (1 week), summer
Uniform Requirements: Yes
Founded in: 1957

Philosophy of School

We help each child develop and achieve to his/her greatest potential in a secure, caring, stimulating Christian environment.

Academic Curriculum

Content: Traditional curriculum of English, reading, math, social studies, science, and religion; art, music, physical education, and computer are also taught. Curriculum is approved by the Diocese of Dallas and TCCED.
Grading System Used: Report cards issued four times each year using Diocesan system of letter grades
Conferences per Year: Two

Tests Administered: National Achievement Test

Homework Policy: Homework is an important part of instruction.

Method of Discipline: Our students are well-behaved. We spend very little time dealing with discipline problems. We teach self-responsibility, and we expect our students to behave appropriately.

Enrichment Curriculum

Art, band, music, physical education, library, computer

Extracurricular Activities

Student Council, NJHS, Environmental Club, yearbook, volleyball, basketball, softball, cheerleading, track, speech, choir, band

Goals for Students

We strive to develop academic excellence and a love for lifelong learning within a Christian atmosphere. We encourage students to become independent thinkers and responsible citizens.

Faculty/Staff Requirements

Qualifications of Staff: Bachelor's degree and teacher certification required

Qualifications of Administrator: M.Ed. with administrative and teaching experience

School Information

Brochure Available: Yes

Number of Students in Each Grade: 50

Parochial: Yes

Organization Affiliations: NCEA, TCCED

Accreditations: TCCED

Parental Involvement: Strong!

Other Information:

Admittance

Whom to Contact: John Ringhauser, Principal

Date to Apply: February

Testing Procedure per Age/Grade Level: Grade-level testing for placement

Fees Involved: $15 testing fee, $150 registration fee

Type of Student Preferred: Motivated students with a strong desire to learn

Forms Required: Registration form, birth certificate, shot records, school records

Individual/Group Appointments: Individual

Notification Procedure: Telephone/mail

Waiting List Policy: Annually

Tuition

Approximate Tuition for 1996-97 School Year: Please call for tuition schedule.

Methods of Payment Available: Annually, semi-annually, monthly

Financial Assistance Offered: Limited (for parishioners only)

Cancellation Insurance Available: N/A

Profit/Non-profit: Non-profit

Additional costs

Books/Bag/Uniform: Uniform approximately $150

Lunch Fee: Students may buy their lunch or bring their own.

Parents Club Dues: $5.00

Annual Fund Drive: No

Discount for Siblings: Yes

Facilities/Services Provided

Computer Lab: Yes

Library: Yes

Snack Procedures: For kindergarten and first grade

Before-school Care Program Available: Day care center on premises

After-school Care Program Available: Day care center on premises

Nurse on Staff: Clinic open during all school hours; staffed by trained parent volunteers

Emergency Procedure Used: Emergency form on file

Transportation to and from School: No

Counseling and Evaluation Available: No

Graduation Information

Testing: N/A

Average SAT Scores: N/A

High School Our Students Usually Attend: Bishop Dunne, Jesuit, Ursuline, Bishop Lynch, public high schools

Percentage of Seniors Attending College: N/A

Additional Information

Please call or visit for additional information.

St. John the Apostle Catholic School

7421 Glenview Drive
Fort Worth, TX 76180
(817) 284-2228

Mapsco: 52N

Fax: (817) 284-1800

Office Hours: 7:45 a.m.–3:45 p.m.
School Hours: 8:00 a.m.–3:00 p.m.
School Grades Offered: K3–grade 8
Enrollment: 623
Co-ed: Yes
Boy/Girl Ratio: 50:50
Student/Teacher Ratio: 22:1
Average Class Size: 25
Calendar School Year: August–May
Holidays: Thanksgiving, Christmas, spring break, Easter
Uniform Requirements: Yes
Founded in: 1965

Philosophy of School

St. John the Apostle Catholic School provides learning conditions that enable each child to develop to his/her full potential, encouraged by realistic goals and motivated by relevant curriculum. Students are given spiritual, intellectual, cultural, social, and physical opportunities, structured to encourage and even challenge growth in all facets of their personality.

Academic Curriculum

Content: Follow TEA guidelines; diocesan curriculum
Grading System Used: Use report cards
Conferences per Year: Two scheduled; others as needed
Tests Administered: Stanford Achievement Test; Otis-Lennon School Ability
Homework Policy: Yes
Method of Discipline: Lee Cantor's Assertive Discipline

Enrichment Curriculum
EAGLE, Spanish, computer

Extracurricular Activities
Sports, grades 6-8; band, grades 4-8; elective classes, grades 7-8; student council; cheerleading

Goals for Students
1. To build awareness of each child's uniqueness that he/she might grow in dignity and self-esteem and to extend this dignity and respect toward others, loving each other as Jesus did
2. To teach individual responsibility for making choices and to understand how these choices affect others
3. To prepare students for adulthood by fostering within them:
    (a) the skills that enable them to do God's work
    (b) a sense of connection to and with a community
    (c) a hope-filled attitude based on the belief that their God is a faithful God

Faculty/Staff Requirements
Qualifications of Staff: Bachelor's degree required
Qualifications of Administrator: Master's degree with administrative and teaching experience required

School Information
Brochure Available: Yes
Number of Students in Each Grade: 25 per homeroom; grades 1-3 have both a teacher and a teacher assistant.
Parochial: Yes
Organization Affiliations: NCEA
Accreditations: Texas Catholic Conference
Parental Involvement: Yes
Other Information:

Admittance
Whom to Contact: Dr. Bronte Gonsalves, Principal
Date to Apply: Ongoing
Testing Procedure per Age/Grade Level: N/A
Fees Involved: Application fee; registration fee
Type of Student Preferred: Nondiscriminatory

Forms Required: Birth certificate, shot record, school records
Individual/Group Appointments: Individual
Notification Procedure: Letter/phone call
Waiting List Policy: Ongoing

Tuition

Approximate Tuition for 1996-97 School Year: Parishioner–$1990 (one child, K-8); non-parishioner–$2990 (one-child, K-8)
Methods of Payment Available: Monthly
Financial Assistance Offered: Yes
Cancellation Insurance Available: No
Profit/Non-profit: Non-profit

Additional Costs

Books/Bag/Uniform: Books and bag–none; uniform–$100 (approximate)
Lunch Fee: None
Parents Club Dues: $5
Annual Fund Drive: No
Discount for Siblings: Yes

Facilities/Services Provided

Computer Lab: Yes
Library: Yes
Snack Procedures: Yes
Before-school Care Program Available: Yes, through parish organization
After-school Care Program Available: Yes, through parish organization
Nurse on Staff: Yes
Emergency Procedure Used: Parent or guardian contacted
Transportation to and from School: No (carpools)
Counseling and Evaluation Available: Yes, by referral

Graduation Information

Testing: N/A
Average SAT Scores: N/A
High School Our Students Usually Attend: Nolan High School
Percentage of Seniors Attending College: N/A

Additional Information

St. Mary of Carmel School

1716 Singleton Blvd.
Dallas, TX 75212
(214) 748-2934

Mapsco: 44N

Fax: (214) 760-9052

Office Hours: 8:00 a.m.–3:00 p.m.
School Hours: 7:50 a.m.–3:00 p.m.
School Grades Offered: Pre-k–grade 8
Enrollment: 209
Co-ed: Yes
Boy/Girl Ratio: 1:1
Student/Teacher Ratio: 16:1
Average Class Size: 25
Calendar School Year: August-May
Holidays: Labor Day, Thanksgiving, Christmas, spring break, Catholic Holy Days
Uniform Requirements: Yes
Founded in: 1944

Philosophy of School

Education is the lifelong growth and development of all aspects of each individual. To attain the reality of "made in the image and likeness of the Lord," each person strives for fulfillment in intellect, physicality, and equality. The growth journey encompasses the fundamental formation molded by family, faith leaders, and educators. With unity of purpose, these contributors bring about the fulfillment of the whole individual. With confidence in faith and knowledge, the educated youth emerge as true Christian citizens, productive contributors to the world community.

Academic Curriculum

Content: Math, science, English, literature, history, religion, computer
Grading System Used: A (100-94), B (93-85), C (84-76), D (75-70), and F (69 and below)
Conferences per Year: Two

323

Tests Administered: National Achievement Test
Homework Policy: 2 hours or more (junior high); 1-2 hours (grades 4-6); 30 minutes (primary grades)
Method of Discipline: "Golden Rule"; Lee Cantor's Assertive Discipline

Enrichment Curriculum
Eighth grade tutorial for those students wanting to attend Catholic high schools

Extracurricular Activities
Sports, yearbook, newspaper, speech

Goals for Students
To be productive citizens who practice Gospel values

Faculty/Staff Requirements
Qualifications of Staff: Texas teacher certification; bachelor's degree
Qualifications of Administrator: Master's degree in educational administration

School Information
Brochure Available: No
Number of Students in Each Grade: Approximately 22–25
Parochial: Catholic
Organization Affiliations: NCEA, Texas Catholic Conference Education Department (TCCED)
Accreditations: TCCED
Parental Involvement: Parent-Teacher Organization; parent volunteers
Other Information: Parish-Partnership Program with St. Rita parish

Admittance
Whom to Contact: School office
Date to Apply: Spring
Testing Procedure for Age/Grade Level: Yes, grade level
Fees Involved: Registration fee $150 for first child; decreases $10 with each additional child
Type of Student Preferred: Student who is willing to work and wants to learn
Forms Required: Birth certificate; baptismal certificate; physical, health, and emergency forms

Individual/Group Appointments: Individual
Notification Procedure: Interview
Waiting List Policy: Ongoing

Tuition

Approximate Tuition for 1996-97 School Year: $1500 for one child
(parishioner), $2250 (non-parishioner)
Methods of Payment Available: Monthly
Financial Assistance Offered: Yes
Cancellation Insurance Available: No
Profit/Non-profit: Non-profit

Additional Costs

Books/Bag/Uniform: Uniform/athletic fee
Lunch Fee: $2.00 per day
Parents Club Dues: No
Annual Fund Drive: Several fundraisers; parents required to participate
Discount for Siblings: No

Facilities/Services Provided

Computer Lab: Yes
Library: Yes
Snack Procedures: Snack for pre-kindergarten students
Before-school Care Program Available: No
After-school Care Program Available: No
Nurse on Staff: Yes
Emergency Procedure Used: Contact parents
Transportation to and from School: No
Counseling and Evaluation Available: Counselor available once a week

Graduation Information

Testing: N/A
Average SAT Scores: N/A
High School Our Students Usually Attend: Jesuit, Ursuline, Bishop Dunne,
DISD
Percentage of Seniors Attending College: N/A

Additional Information

St. Mary's Catholic School

713 South Travis
Sherman, TX 75090
(903) 893-2127

Mapsco: Sherman

Fax: (903) 813-5489

Office Hours: 7:30 a.m.–4:00 p.m.
School Hours: 8:30 a.m.–3:30 p.m.
School Grades Offered: Pre-K (age 3)–grade 6
Enrollment: 150
Co-ed: Yes
Boy/Girl Ratio: 82:68
Student/Teacher Ratio: 22:1
Average Class Size: 22
Calendar School Year: August-June
Holidays: Feast of the Assumption (August 15), Labor Day, fall
break, All Saints Day (November 1), Thanksgiving, Christmas,
Martin Luther King Day, Presidents' Day, spring break, Easter
break, Ascension Thursday, Memorial Day
Uniform Requirements: See handbook (page 12).
Founded in: 1877

Philosophy of School

Catholic education has its essential elements: message, community, and service. St.
Mary's seeks the integration of this threefold dimension with the total educational
process so the child may grow in the knowledge and love of God and in awareness of
and commitment to the basic Christian values of love and service to neighbor.

Academic Curriculum

Content: See handbook (page 6).
Grading System Used: See handbook (page 10).
Conferences per Year: Two
Tests Administered: Spring

Homework Policy: See handbook (page 8).
Method of Discipline: See handbook (page 13).

Enrichment Curriculum
SRA, SSS, math lab, social study lab

Extracurricular Activities
Karate, music

Goals for Students
See handbook (philosophy–page 1).

Faculty/Staff Requirements
Qualifications of Staff: Bachelor's degree in elementary education
Qualifications of Administrator: B.S. in Elementary Education, M.Ed.

School Information
Brochure Available: Yes
Number of Students in Each Grade: P3–12; P4 (3-day)–6; P4 (5-day)–12; K–24; grade 1–22; grade 2–22; grade 3–22; grade 4–18; grade 5–18; grade 6–14
Parochial: Yes
Organization Affiliations: TANS, NCEA
Accreditations: Texas Catholic Conference
Parental Involvement: Home and school association
Other Information:

Admittance
Whom to Contact: Frances Baird
Date to Apply: Spring
Testing Procedure for Age/Grade Level: N/A
Fees Involved: $200 registration-book fee
Type of Student Preferred: N/A
Forms Required: Birth certificate, shot record, baptismal certificate
Individual/Group Appointments: Individual
Notification Procedure: Letter
Waiting List Policy: Annually

Tuition

Approximate Tuition for 1996-97 School Year: Catholic contributing–$2100; Catholic non-contributing–$2550; non-Catholic–$2600
Methods of Payment Available: Monthly
Financial Assistance Offered: Yes
Cancellation Insurance Available: No
Profit/Non-profit: Non-profit

Additional Costs

Books/Bag/Uniform: Uniform
Lunch Fee: Preschool-grade 1 $1.35; grades 2-6–$1.85
Parents Club Dues: N/A
Annual Fund Drive: Yes
Discount for Siblings: Yes

Facilities/Services Provided

Computer Lab: Yes, 15 486 IBM compatible
Library: Yes
Snack Procedures: At morning break
Before-school Care Program Available: Yes, 6:45 a.m.–8:00 a.m.
After-school Care Program Available: Yes, 3:30 p.m.–6:00 p.m.
Nurse on Staff: No
Emergency Procedure Used: Call parents
Transportation to and from School: Car
Counseling and Evaluation Available: Yes

Graduation Information

Testing: N/A
Average SAT Scores: N/A
High School Our Students Usually Attend: Sherman High School
Percentage of Seniors Attending College: N/A

Additional Information

St. Monica School

4140 Walnut Hill
Dallas, TX 75229
(214) 351-5688

Mapsco: 24Q

Fax: (214) 352-2608

Office Hours: 7:30 a.m.–4:00 p.m.
School Hours: 8:00 a.m.– 3:30 p.m.
School Grades Offered: K–grade 8
Enrollment: 795
Co-ed: Yes
Boy/Girl Ratio: Approximately 50:50
Student/Teacher Ratio: 22:1 (K); 25:1 (grades 1–8)
Average Class Size: 25
Calendar School Year: August–May
Holidays: Christmas break, spring break
Uniform Requirements: Yes–Parker Uniform Co.
Founded in: 1955

Philosophy of School

The educational mission of St. Monica Catholic School is to provide for the harmonious development of our students in their physical, moral, spiritual, and intellectual growth. It is our wish that St. Monica School offer our school families a clearly Catholic experience in a sound educational environment. We have established high academic standards that encourage each student to develop his/her greatest potential.

Academic Curriculum

Content: Religion, language arts, math, science, social studies, electives
Grading System Used: Diocese of Dallas grading system
Conferences per Year: Two
Tests Administered: Yes
Homework Policy: Grade 1–30 mins.; grade 2–40 mins.; grade 3–45 mins.; grade 4–one hour; grades 5-6–1 1/2 hours; grades 7-9–2+ hours
Method of Discipline: No corporal punishment; sign-ups leading to detention

Enrichment Curriculum

K-8–computer, Spanish, music, library, physical education, art, Exploratory Electives Program in grades 7–8 to include theatre arts, expanded art and music programs, etiquette, CPR and chess

Extracurricular Activities

Football, basketball, drill team, cheerleading, volleyball, choir, computer club, scouts, academic fair, continental math, Odyssey of the Mind, Duke University program and stamp club.

Goals for Students

To create an environment in which students encounter God within themselves and discover their unconditional worth as children of God; to equip each student with tools for lifelong learning; to provide a growth plan that recognizes the dynamic society in which we live and offers continued development for all staff members; to provide quality education as it relates to learning the core curriculum that includes religious education in the context of Catholic traditions; to model the Christian concept of unity through community interaction.

Faculty/Staff Requirements

Qualifications of Staff: Teaching certificate
Qualifications of Administrator: Master's degree

School Information

Brochure Available: Yes
Number of Students in Each Grade: Approximately 25
Parochial: Yes
Organization Affiliations: Texas Catholic Conference; National Catholic Education Association
Accreditations: TCCED
Parental Involvement: Yes
Other Information:

Admittance

Whom to Contact: Dr. Joan Wagner
Date to Apply: Late January
Testing Procedure per Age/Grade Level: K,Gesell Testing; grades 1–8, Achievement Testing
Fees Involved: $150 registration fee (subject to change)

Type of Student Preferred: N\A
Forms Required: Birth certificate, baptismal certificate (if Catholic), immunization records, evaluation and grades from previous school
Individual/Group Appointments: When necessary
Notification Procedure: Letter
Waiting List Policy: Re-apply

Tuition

Approximate Tuition for 1996-97 School Year: Parishioner(one child plus fees)–$2250; Catholic, non-parishioner–$3100; non-Catholic–$3400
Methods of Payment Available: Annual, semi-annually, monthly
Financial Assistance Offered: Only for Catholic families
Cancellation Insurance Available: No
Profit/Non-profit: Non-profit

Additional Costs

Books/Bag/Uniform: $170 per student
Lunch Fee: Plate lunch ($2.50); students may bring their lunches.
Parents Club Dues: Included in academic fee
Annual Fund Drive: Two major fund drives
Discount for Siblings: Yes

Facilities/Services Provided

Computer Lab: One Apple lab, one IBM lab
Library: Yes
Snack Procedures: For the lower grades
Before-school Care Program Available: No
After-school Care Program Available: Yes; 3:30 p.m. - 6:15 p.m.
Nurse on Staff: Yes
Emergency Procedure Used: Emergency forms given to nurse and followed when necessary
Transportation to and from School: No
Counseling and Evaluation Available: No

Graduation Information

Testing: Yes
Average SAT Scores: N/A
High School Our Students Usually Attend: Jesuit, Ursuline Academy, Bishop Lynch High School
Percentage of Seniors Attending College: N/A

St. Patrick School

9635 Ferndale   Mapsco: 27R
Dallas, TX 75238
(214) 348-8070   Fax: (214) 503-7230

Office Hours: 8:00 a.m.–4:30 p.m.
School Hours: 8:00 a.m.–3:20 p.m.
School Grades Offered: Preschool–grade 8
Enrollment: 525
Co-ed: Yes
Boy/Girl Ratio: 1:1.5
Student/Teacher Ratio: 22:1
Average Class Size: 26
Calendar School Year: August–May
Holidays: Labor Day, Thanksgiving, Christmas, Martin
Luther King Day, Easter, Memorial Day
Uniform Requirements: Yes
Founded in: 1964

Philosophy of School

St. Patrick School is an integral and contributing body within our Catholic community.
Rooted in the tradition of our Church, St. Patrick School strives to be a visible
instrument and servant of Christ in the formation and education of its students.

Created in the image of God, the student is seen as a whole person–spirit, intellect, and
body–worthy of our respect and deserving of our efforts. We believe education is a
process of continual growth. We are concerned with developing each student's abilities
and talents–spiritually, morally, intellectually, physically, emotionally, and socially.

We share our ministry with the parents whom we recognize as the primary educators of
their children. To them we look for support and guidance as we work toward a mutual
goal–the development of the whole person and a sense of personal worth.

The Gospels call each of us to a life of Christian witness, community, and service based
on the ministry of Jesus. Our Christian and political heritage remind us that we are not

islands of ourselves but members of an ever-broadening world. The Eucharistic celebration, the classroom, the extra-curricular activities are all vehicles for teaching responsible citizenship, concern for our brothers and sisters, and an appreciation for the richness and variety of our culture. We call upon our students to live ethical and moral lives and to challenge their society to do the same.

In our efforts to attain our goals, we as administrators, teachers, parents, and students of St. Patrick School community will occasionally fall. Let us be willing to admit and forgive shortcomings. At the same time, let us rejoice in each other's successes. Our ministry becomes a Christian reality when our students are able to make wise choices in faith and love.

Academic Curriculum

Content: The educational process at St. Patrick School aims to meet the needs and challenge the potential of the individual student. The core curriculum guide provided by the Diocese of Dallas serves as a basic guide to insure proper sequencing and scope of skills and content. Teachers are encouraged to be sensitive to individual differences in learning and to design learning experiences that will address these differences.

"The intellectual dimension is met through a comprehensive offering of a variety of learning experiences that assist the student in attaining the goals of the various areas of instruction, to prepare to cope with societal demands, to understand and participate in civic and governmental activities, and to appreciate the worth of each person and his culture." (Mission Statement— Catholic Schools of Texas)

The daily schedule includes instruction in religion, English, language arts, science, mathematics, social studies, and physical education. Art, music, health, computer literacy, and computer-assisted instruction are also included in the weekly schedule. Electives for grades 5—8 include: choir, band, journalism, speech, and drama. Foreign language (Spanish) is taught in grades 7-8.

Religion Program:
The primary goal of St. Patrick's religious education is "the continuous formation of the Christian person," as set forth in the Mission Statement of the Catholic Schools of Texas. Its aim includes the individual's spiritual, moral, intellectual, social, cultural, and physical development.

Grading System Used: Report cards are issued four times a year; however, students in kindergarten and first grade do not receive their first report card until the end of the first semester. All report cards should be reviewed, signed by parents/guardians, and returned within one week.

Progress reports are issued to all students mid-way during the first quarter (after 4 1/2 weeks of school). Other interim progress reports are issued mid-way during each quarter to students with low or failing grades.

Conferences per Year: At least one

Tests Administered: Standardized (Ability Test–grades 2, 4, 6, 8; Achievement Test–all grades) annually

Homework Policy:

Method of Discipline:

Enrichment Curriculum

See Academic Curriculum.

Extracurricular Activities

Extra-curricular activities include cheerleaders and drill team, choir, band, speech and drama, journalism, athletic financial committee, athletics.

Goals for Students

The goal in all co-curricular and extra-curricular activities is to provide students opportunities for enjoyment and fun, opportunities for developing talents, skills, and qualities of responsibility, self-discipline, and creativity.

Faculty/Staff Requirements

Qualifications of Staff: Degree, certification

Qualifications of Administrator: Master's degree in education administration

School Information

Brochure Available: Yes

Number of Students in Each Grade: Pre–18; k–25; grades 1-8–26

Parochial: Yes

Organization Affiliations: Texas Catholic Conference, N.C.E.A.

Accreditations: TCCED

Parental Involvement: Yes (volunteers–classroom, playground, cafeteria)

Other Information:

Admittance

Whom to Contact: School office

Date to Apply: January

Testing Procedure per Age/Grade Level: At the request of the principal

Fees Involved: N/A
Type of Student Preferred: N/A
Forms Required: Yes
Individual/Group Appointments: Individual
Notification Procedure: Telephone/mail
Waiting List Policy: Yes

Tuition

Approximate Tuition for 1996-97 School Year: One student $1600
(parishioner); $2600 (non-parishioner)
Methods of Payment Available: Full payment/bank loan
Financial Assistance Offered: On a limited basis
Cancellation Insurance Available: N/A
Profit/Non-profit: Non-profit

Additional Costs

Books/Bag/Uniform: Books and bag–no; uniform–approximately $60
Lunch Fee: Separate; card purchased or daily payment
Parents Club Dues: $5
Annual Fund Drive: Yes
Discount for Siblings: Yes (for parishioners)

Facilities/Services Provided

Computer Lab: Computer lab facilities
Library: Multi-media lab and library
Snack Procedures: Younger students bring own
Before-school Care Program Available: For preschool children: 8:00 a.m.–
9:00 a.m., 12:00 p.m.–6:00 p.m.
After-school Care Program Available: Yes
Nurse on Staff: Part-time
Emergency Procedure Used: Yes
Transportation to and from School: None
Counseling and Evaluation Available: Use community resources

Graduation Information

Testing: N/A
Average SAT Scores: N/A
High School Our Students Usually Attend: Bishop Lynch
Percentage of Seniors Attending College: N/A

St. Paul the Apostle School

720 S. Floyd
Richardson, TX 75080
(214) 235-3263

Mapsco: 16H

Fax: (214) 690-1542

Office Hours: 7:30 a.m.–4:00 p.m.
School Hours: 7:50 a.m.–3:20 p.m.
School Grades Offered: Kindergarten—8th grade
Enrollment: 500
Co-ed: Yes
Boy/Girl Ratio: 1:1
Student/Teacher Ratio: 22:1 approximately
Average Class Size: 22
Calendar School Year: August–May
Holidays: Christmas–2 weeks; spring break–1 week,
summer 2–3 months; Holy Days
Uniform Requirements: Yes
Founded in: 1957

Philosophy of School

St. Paul the Apostle School is committed to the development of the whole child and shares with parents the responsibility for the religious, intellectual, moral, physical, aesthetic, and social formation of the children.

Academic Curriculum

Content: Diocesan-approved curriculum in all areas—core areas as well as areas of enrichment subjects
Grading System Used: 9-weeks grading periods; every 4 1/2 weeks progress reports are sent; every 9 weeks report cards are sent.
Conferences per Year: Two–1st and 3rd quarters
Tests Administered: Standardized Achievement Tests
Homework Policy: Grades 1–6 approximately 15-20 minutes; grades 7–8, two hours

336

Method of Discipline: Each student is responsible for his/her actions; positive reinforcement for responsible behavior

Enrichment Curriculum

Spanish, computer, music, art, physical education, media center

Extracurricular Activities

All sports, boy/girl scouts, choir, yearbook; grades 4-8 boys: football, softball, basketball, track, volleyball, baseball; younger grades: soccer, T-Ball

Goals for Students

To endow each student with a sense of personal worth, to impart strength of character and principles, and to develop strong faith

Faculty/Staff Requirements

Qualifications of Staff: Degrees and certification
Qualifications of Administrator: Master's in administration; certification in administration

School Information

Brochure Available: Yes
Number of Students in Each Grade: Kindergarten, 25 per class (with full-time aide); grades 1-3, 25 per class; grades 4-8, 30 per class
Parochial: Catholic
Organization Affiliations: National Catholic Education Association, Texas Catholic Conference Education Department (TCCED), Middle School Teachers, Council for Exceptional Children
Accreditations: TCCED
Parental Involvement: Yes
Other Information:

Admittance

Whom to Contact: Principal, Mary C. Williams
Date to Apply: Usually in February or March of each year; applications taken year round
Testing Procedure per Age/Grade Level: N/A
Fees Involved: $125 registration fee
Type of Student Preferred: Students who are responsible and willing to work

to the best of their ability and achieve high goals
Forms Required: Registration and application
Individual/Group Appointments: Individual
Notification Procedure: Immediately upon registration
Waiting List Policy: Re-apply each year

Tuition

Approximate Tuition for 1996-97 School Year: Parishioner (one child)–
$2448; non-parishioner (one child)–$2784; non-Catholic (one child)–$3228
Methods of Payment Available: Variety of payment options
Financial Assistance Offered: Limited through Parish
Cancellation Insurance Available: No
Profit/Non-profit: Non-profit

Additional Costs

Books/Bag/Uniform: Books–included in registration fee ($125); bag–none;
uniform–yes
Lunch Fee: $2 per day if child elects to purchase lunch at school
Parents Club Dues: $15 annually; included at time of registration
Annual Fund Drive: N/A
Discount for Siblings: Yes

Facilities/Services Provided

Computer Lab: Yes
Library: Yes
Snack Procedures: N/A
Before-school Care Program Available: Yes; 7:00 a.m.–7:50 a.m.
After-school Care Program Available: Yes; 3:20 p.m.–6:00 p.m.
Nurse on Staff: Yes
Emergency Procedure Used: Call parents and/or 911 for emergency
Transportation to and from School: No
Counseling and Evaluation Available: Yes, through outside agencies

Graduation Information

Testing: N/A
Average SAT Scores: N/A
High School Our Students Usually Attend: Ursuline Academy, Jesuit College
Preparatory School, Bishop Lynch High School
Percentage of Seniors Attending College: N/A

St. Philip the Apostle Catholic School

8151 Military Parkway
Dallas, TX 75227
(214) 381-4973

Mapsco: 48A

Fax: None

Office Hours: 7:30 a.m.–4:00 p.m.
School Hours: 7:45 a.m.–3:00 p.m.
School Grades Offered: Kindergarten–grade 8
Enrollment: 230
Co-ed: Yes
Boy/Girl Ratio: 1:1
Student/Teacher Ratio: 25:1
Average Class Size: 25
Calendar School Year: August–May
Holidays: Martin Luther King Day, Presidents' Day
Uniform Requirements: Yes
Founded in: 1955

Philosophy of School

St. Philip the Apostle School is a community of faith where we believe each child is a unique creation of God, blessed with a special set of talents and gifts. Each child deserves to approach life with a sense of self-worth and respect for others while developing a sense of one's own personal relationship with God.

We believe each child deserves the opportunity to develop his/her God-given potential to the fullest. Our mission is to guide each child toward the fulfillment of this potential in all areas of the child's life: spiritual, intellectual, social, psychological, and physical. We seek to enrich and deepen each student's faith by promoting good self-esteem, self-discipline, skills, and knowledge.

St. Philip the Apostle School affirms that parents are the first and primary educators of their children. Through a spirit of understanding and cooperation, we strive to create an atmosphere in which teachers, students, and parents can join together with the total faith community to come alive, to grow, and to learn.

As a Catholic school, we strive to influence students and families to be dynamic agents of change in society in the areas of social and racial justice, human dignity, freedom, and peace. We provide an environment that fosters a belief in the sacredness of the human person and an awareness that we are born into one worldwide human family.

At St. Philip the Apostle School, we create an atmosphere for learning that combines structure and creativity while fostering enthusiasm for lifelong learning. Toward this end, we strive to maintain a joyous, happy environment which promotes love, understanding, and acceptance of self and others.

Academic Curriculum

Content: All subject areas covered
Grading System Used: A, B, C's
Conferences per Year: Two scheduled; others as needed
Tests Administered: ACT
Homework Policy: Recommended for grades 1-4: 1/2 hr.-1 1/2 hrs.; grades 5-8: 1 hr.-2 1/2 hrs. (per day)
Method of Discipline: Parental Support

Enrichment Curriculum

Odyssey of the Mind; speech team; spelling bee; geography bee

Extracurricular Activities

Sports program; Odyssey of the Mind

Goals for Students

To reach their maximun potential in all areas–spiritually, academically, emotionally, physically, and socially

Faculty/Staff Requirements

Qualifications of Staff: All have degrees.
Qualifications of Administrator: Master's degree

School Information

Brochure Available: No (in process)

Number of Students in Each Grade: 25 (average)
Parochial: Yes
Organization Affiliations: ASCD, NCEA, IRA
Accreditations: TCCED
Parental Involvement: Yes
Other Information:

Admittance

Whom to Contact: Principal
Date to Apply: February
Testing Procedure for Age/Grade Level: Students in grades 2-8 are tested; $10 per student
Fees Involved: Total registration fees: $261
Type of Student Preferred: Students interested in learning
Forms Required: Test results, report card, birth certificate, immunization records, baptism certificate
Individual/Group Appointments: Individual appointments
Notification Procedure: Phone/letter
Waiting List Policy: Re-apply annually

Tuition

Approximate Tuition for 1996-97 School Year: $2750
Methods of Payment Available: Monthly
Financial Assistance Offered: No
Cancellation Insurance Available: No
Profit/Non-profit: Non-profit

Additional Costs

Books/Bag/Uniform: Books included in registration fees; students buy their supplies and uniforms.
Lunch Fee: Can bring lunch or purchase ($2.00 per day average cost)
Parents Club Dues: $20 (included in registration fees)
Annual Fund Drive: Candy sale; Fun Fest Carnival
Discount for Siblings: Yes

Facilities/Services Provided

Computer Lab: Yes
Library: Yes
Snack Procedures: None
Before-school Care Program Available: No

After-school Care Program Available: Yes, 3:00 p.m.–6:00 p.m.
Nurse on Staff: Yes
Emergency Procedure Used: Yes
Transportation to and from School: No
Counseling and Evaluation Available: No

Graduation Information

Testing: Done at high school of choice
Average SAT Scores: N/A
High School Our Students Usually Attend: Bishop Lynch, Mesquite, Skyline
Percentage of Seniors Attending College: N/A

Additional Information

St. Rita School

12525 Inwood Road
Dallas, TX 75244
(214) 239-3203

Mapsco: 14Z

Fax: (214) 934-0657

Office Hours: 7:30 a.m.–4:30 p.m.
School Hours: 7:50 a.m.–3:15 p.m.
School Grades Offered: Kindergarten–grade 8
Enrollment: 517
Co-ed: Yes
Boy/Girl Ratio: 281: 242
Student/Teacher Ratio: 16:1
Average Class Size: 25
Calendar School Year: August–May
Holidays: Thanksgiving, Christmas, spring break, Easter
Uniform Requirements: Blue shorts/pants, white shirts for boys; plaid shorts/skirt/jumper, white shirts for girls
Founded in: 1964

Philosophy of School

The guiding philosophy of St. Rita School is to provide a safe and caring environment in which optimum learning can take place. In this atmosphere, students are encouraged to develop fully in the spiritual, intellectual, physical, and artistic domains. Basic to the educational program at St. Rita School is a deep conviction that each child is a unique individual. Therefore, the school seeks to provide conditions in which each child's needs can be addressed. In addition, the school stresses the formation of character, leadership, and concern for social justice and environmental issues. The school's primary aim is to prepare responsible Christian citizens for a challenging and complex world.

Academic Curriculum

Content: See the philosophy statement.
Grading System Used: Diocesan system; grades are sent home quarterly.
Conferences per Year: One in the fall (Oct.) and one in the spring (Feb.)
Tests Administered: February (Achievement Test)

Homework Policy: Expected daily (how much depends on grade level)
Method of Discipline: Positive academic atmosphere

Enrichment Curriculum
Special field trips each year; participation in Odyssey of the Mind

Extracurricular Activities
Yes, teams fielded for football (grades 5–8), basketball (grades 4–8), track (all grades), volleyball (grades 6–8), baseball (grades 5–8), softball (grades5–8), drama competition (grades 6–8)

Goals for Students
St. Rita School is a Catholic coeducational parish school for children in grades kindergarten through 8, operated under the auspices of St. Rita Parish Community and the direction of the education department of the Diocese of Dallas. The mission of the school is to be committed to the religious, intellectual, psychological, physical, and social growth of each student and to provide an atmosphere of academic challenge and religious commitment, the primary goal being the ongoing formation and development of the Christian person.

Faculty/Staff Requirements
Qualifications of Staff: Degrees and certification
Qualifications of Administrator: Degree and certification

School Information
Brochure Available: Yes
Number of Students in Each Grade: K, 1,2–three classes of 20 each; grades 3–8, two classes of 28 each
Parochial: Yes
Organization Affiliations: NCEA, ASCD, Diocese of Dallas, NMSA
Accreditations: TCCED-TEA (Texas Catholic Conference Education Department) recognized by Texas Educational Department
Parental Involvement: Yes, encouraged
Other Information:

Admittance
Whom to Contact: Pam Neville
Date to Apply: Begin in February for next school year

Testing Procedure per Age/Grade Level: For kindergarten, a diagnostic test is administered; for grades 1–8, a placement test is administered.
Fees Involved: Yes
Type of Student Preferred: Catholic
Forms Required: Yes
Individual/Group Appointments: Both
Notification Procedure: March and April
Waiting List Policy: Waiting list is active for one school year, and applicants have to re-apply for the next school year.

Tuition

Approximate Tuition for 1996-97 School Year: Parishioner (one child)–$3024; non-parishioner (one child)–$3500
Methods of Payment Available: Tuition
Financial Assistance Offered: Yes
Cancellation Insurance Available: N/A
Profit/Non-profit: Non-profit

Additional Costs

Books/Bag/Uniform: Book and computer fee–$135; bag–yes; uniform–$150
Lunch Fee: Yes, K–3 $2.35 with drink; grades 4–8 $2.85 with drink; sack lunch $1.70 without drink; salad $1.70 without drink; baked potato $2.00 without drink; drinks $.50 (We use a lunch card.)
Parents Club Dues: Yes
Annual Fund Drive: Yes
Discount for Siblings: Yes

Facilities/Services Provided

Computer Lab: Yes
Library: Yes
Snack Procedures: Verify with school
Before-school Care Program Available: No
After-school Care Program Available: Yes; 3:30 p.m. - 6:00 p.m.
Nurse on Staff: Yes, full time
Emergency Procedure Used: Health Room
Transportation to and from School: No
Counseling and Evaluation Available: Yes; Counselor on staff, at school 2 days a week

Graduation Information

Testing: N/A
Average SAT Scores: N/A
High School Our Students Usually Attend: Jesuit College Prepatory School, Ursuline Academy, Bishop Lynch High School
Percentage of Seniors Attending College: N/A

Additional Information

St. Thomas Aquinas School

3741 Abrams Rd.
Dallas, TX 75214
(214) 826-0566

Mapsco: 36L

Fax: (214) 826-0251

Office Hours: 7:30 a.m.–4:00 p.m.
School Hours: 7:55 a.m.–3:30 p.m.
School Grades Offered: Pre-K (age 3)–grade 8
Enrollment: 571
Co-ed: Yes
Boy/Girl Ratio: 1:1
Student/Teacher Ratio: PK3–6:1, PK4–8:1, K–22:1, grades 1-8–30:1
Average Class Size: 26
Calendar School Year: August-May
Holidays: Usual holidays and Holy Days
Uniform Requirements: Yes
Founded in: 1947

Philosophy of School

St. Thomas Aquinas School is dedicated to fostering a wholesome atmosphere of Christian respect that pervades relationships among students, school officials, and parents. We emphasize responsibility in behavior, in actions, and above all, in showing Christian concern and compassion for others.

Academic Curriculum

Content:
Grading System Used: Nine-week
Conferences per Year: Two
Tests Administered: National Achievement Test
Homework Policy: Yes; minimums determined by grade level
Method of Discipline: Assertive discipline

347

Enrichment Curriculum
Optimal match, stock market contest, spelling bee

Extracurricular Activities
Athletics, drama, music, speech, band, Odyssey of the Mind, scouts

Goals for Students

Faculty/Staff Requirements
Qualifications of Staff: Bachelor's degree (minimum requirement); many have master's degrees.
Qualifications of Administrator: Master's degree in administration; Ph.D. Early Childhood Education

School Information
Brochure Available: Yes
Number of Students in Each Grade: Average 26-28
Parochial: Yes, Catholic
Organization Affiliations: TCCED, NCEA, ACD
Accreditations: TCCED
Parental Involvement: Yes
Other Information:

Admittance
Whom to Contact: Dr. Carole C. Stabile
Date to Apply: After February
Testing Procedure for Age/Grade Level: None
Fees Involved: Tuition, registration fee
Type of Student Preferred: N/A
Forms Required: Birth certificate, baptismal certificate (if Catholic), immunizations, former school records (grades 1-8)
Individual/Group Appointments: Individual
Notification Procedure: Letter
Waiting List Policy: Re-apply

Tuition
Approximate Tuition for 1996-97 School Year: $2100-$3700
Methods of Payment Available: Monthly

Financial Assistance Offered: To parishioners
Cancellation Insurance Available: No
Profit/Non-profit: Non-profit

Additional Costs

Books/Bag/Uniform: Uniforms (fee determined by parents), registration fee $150-$200 per child
Lunch Fee: No; lunches available for purchase ($2.50/day)
Parents Club Dues: $7.50 per year
Annual Fund Drive: Yes
Discount for Siblings: Yes, for parishioners

Facilities/Services Provided

Computer Lab: Yes; IBM PS/1 computers (approximately 30 computers in the lab)
Library: Yes; approximately 7,000 volumes in acquisition; computerized; reference section in primary library
Snack Procedures: Yes, in grades K-2
Before-school Care Program Available: Yes; 7:00 a.m.–7:45 a.m.
After-school Care Program Available: Yes; 3:30 p.m.–6:00 p.m.
Nurse on Staff: Yes
Emergency Procedure Used: Yes
Transportation to and from School: No
Counseling and Evaluation Available: Yes

Graduation Information

Testing: N/A
Average SAT Scores: N/A
High School Our Students Usually Attend: Bishop Lynch, Jesuit, Ursuline
Percentage of Seniors Attending College: N/A

Additional Information

The Ursuline Academy of Dallas

4900 Walnut Hill Lane
Dallas, TX 75229
(214) 363-6551

Mapsco: 24Q

Fax: (214) 363-5524

Office Hours: 8:00 a.m.–5:00 p.m.
School Hours: 800 a.m.–3:50 p.m.
School Grades Offered: Grades 9–12
Enrollment: 710
Co-ed: No (Girls only)
Boy/Girl Ratio: Girls only
Student/Teacher Ratio: 15:1
Average Class Size: 10–25
Calendar School Year: Mid-August–late May
Holidays: Standard
Uniform Requirements: Yes
Founded in: 1874

Philosophy of School

For over a century, Ursuline Academy of Dallas has continued to educate young women in the tradition of excellence and high standards of scholarship. At the core of Ursuline's philosophy is belief in an openness to truth, in whatever form it may be found, and the student's total growth and development–moral, spiritual, intellectual, social, and physical.

Academic Curriculum

Content: The academic program at Ursuline is challenging. To be eligible for graduation, students are required to earn credits as follows: English, 4; mathematics, 4; social studies, 4; foreign language, 3; science, 3; physical education, 1; computer science, 1; fine arts, 1; health, 1/2; speech, 1/2; electives, 2; and theology, 4. Honors courses are offered to qualified students in all major subject areas except theology.

350

Community service is required of all students. Seniors are required to complete 60 hours of community service during one semester. Students work in public and private schools with learning-disabled students, in community hospitals, in convalescent centers, and in social agencies.

Electives are offered in all academic subjects. In mathematics and science, students may take advanced studies that include precalculus, calculus, botany, genetics, environmental science and chemistry, philosophy of history, physics, trigonometry, and biology. Students with advanced language skills may choose to take a fourth year of French, Spanish, or Latin. Advanced Placement U.S. history and European history, psychology, government, economics, and contemporary issues are offered through the Social Science Department. The Fine Arts Department offers aesthetics, art appreciation, choral, band, string ensemble, design, drawing, painting, photography, pottery, theater arts, and acting as electives. The English Department provides students with yearbook, speech, debate, competitive speech, journalism classes, literature, American Southern fiction, desktop publishing, as well as Advanced Placement courses. Driver's education is also offered to interested students.

Grading System Used: Percentage system–(65-100); additional points given for honors and advanced placement courses
Conferences per Year: Yes
Homework Policy: N/A
Method of Discipline: N/A

Enrichment Curriculum

Electives are offered in all academic subjects. Summer school is also offered for grades 7-adults.

Extracurricular Activities

Visits to art and science museums, government centers, and theaters, and attendance at lectures and concerts provide the students with opportunities to broaden their academic experiences. Special programs include the Presidential Classroom, which enables girls to spend a week in Washington, D.C., theater trips to New York City, and art trips to Europe.

Most students participate actively in a number of groups and organizations that the school has provided to meet their special interests. Among these are the academic clubs (including languages and mathematics clubs), yearbook, literary magazine, Ursuline Ambassadors, Student Council, academic competitions, National Honor Society chapter, Student Reach-out Service Club, cheerleaders, band, color guard, Clown Ministry, Astronomy Club, Art Club, Drama Club, Environmental Club, Outdoors Club, Video Yearbook, newspaper, and Faculty-Student Senate.

Goals for Students

Founded in 1874, the Ursuline Academy of Dallas, under the sponsorship of the Ursuline Sisters of Dallas, Texas, is a private Catholic college-preparatory high school for young women. The Academy encourages each student to develop her individual interests and potential through programs focused on academic excellence, spiritual formation, physical development, leadership, community-building, and service in a caring and challenging environment of students, parents, and educatiors. Ursuline Academy with its valued traditions prepares young women to think critically and act responsibly in a global society.

Faculty/Staff Requirements

Qualifications of Staff: 64 faculty members, 72% have advanced degrees; faculty members are chosen on the basis of their academic credentials and certification, teaching ability, and interest in the total growth of their students in and out of the classroom

Qualifications of Administrator: Master's degrees and doctorates

School Information

Brochure Available: Yes

Number of Students in Each Grade: 9th–194; 10th–175; 11th–151; 12th–141

Parochial: Yes

Organization Affiliations: NCEA, TAPPS, CASE, TANS

Accreditations: Southern Association of Colleges and Schools (SACS), Texas Catholic Conference (TCCED)

Parental Involvement: Yes

Other Information: 1992-93 Blue Ribbon School (national award)

Admittance

Whom to Contact: Lisa Bond

Date to Apply: One year prior to fall entrance

Testing Procedure per Age/Grade Level: Test given: Independent School Entrance Exam (ISEE)

Fees Involved: Testing fee, application fee

Type of Student Preferred: College-bound

Forms Required: Application, teacher recommendations, transcripts, test scores

Individual/Group Appointments: Tour days–most Tuesdays by appointment; campus visit days–scheduled

Notification Procedure: Common notification in March

Waiting List Policy: Must re-apply each year; contact school for more information

Tuition

Approximate Tuition for 1996-97 School Year: $6180; laptop computers are required for freshman class.

Methods of Payment Available: Semi-annually; special monthly plan

Financial Assistance Offered: Yes

Cancellation Insurance available: No

Profit/Non-profit: Non-profit

Additional Costs

Books/Bag/Uniform: Books–approximately $300; bag–optional; uniform cost–approximately $200–$300 (includes blazer)

Lunch Fee: Optional

Parents Club Dues: $45

Annual Fund Drive: Yes

Discount for Siblings: No

Facilities/Services Provided

Computer Lab: Yes; IBM and Macintosh labs, some computers in classrooms

Library: Yes, fully automated

Snack Procedures: N/A

Before-school Care Program Available: N/A

After-school Care Program Available: N/A

Nurse on Staff: N/A

Emergency Procedure Used: Yes

Transportation to and from School: Car pools arranged by families

Counseling and Evaluation Available: Yes

Graduation Information

Testing: N/A

Average SAT Scores: Ursuline students continue to exceed national SAT average by more than 100 points and surpass the national female average by almost 200 points. In the past 5 years, Ursuline has had 15 National Merit Finalists, 20 Semi-Finalists, 69 Letters of Commendation plus 17 students recognized in the National Hispanic Program.

High School Our Students Usually Attend: N/A

Percentage of Seniors Attending College: 99

Additional Information

Ursuline does not discriminate on the basis of race, color, national or ethnic background. The student body, made up of approximately 700 students in grades 9-12,

Additional Information (continued)

is approximately 75% Catholic and 25% non-Catholic. Minority students comprise 16% of Ursuline students, and 19% of the student body receives some form of financial aid.

TSDA
Texas Conference of
Seventh-Day Adventists

P.O. Box 800
Alvarado, TX 76009-0800
(817) 783-2223

The Seventh-Day Adventist School System began in the late 1800s and has developed into a world-wide system of education.

There are three schools located in the Dallas area: Dallas Adventist Junior Academy (4025 North Central Expressway, Dallas, Texas 75204) and Richardson Adventist School (1201 West Beltline Road, Richardson, Texas 75080). There is one school in Arlington: Burton Adventist Academy, 4611 Kelly-Elliot Road, Arlington, Texas 76017.

Each school is accredited through the Adventist Accrediting Association—the accrediting organization of Seventh-Day Adventist schools. New schools are evaluated during the second year of operation, and if they meet the requirements, they receive accreditation.

Each school is presented as an accredited school through the Texas SDA School System to the Texas Private School Accreditation Commission (TEPSAC). Each of these schools is then recognized by Texas Education Agency (TEA) in Austin as an accredited school.

The teachers of Seventh-Day Adventist schools are certified by the Seventh-Day Adventist Office of Education. Requirements must be met in order to receive this certification. These requirements are comparable to the requirements for state certification.

Therefore, each of the above-mentioned schools is accredited and has certified teachers. Students receive an education comparable to that required by TEA and religious instruction.

Richardson Adventist School

Richardson Adventist School

1201 W. Beltline Road
Richardson, Texas 75080
(214) 238-1183

Mapsco: 16B

Fax: (214) 231-3280

Office Hours: 7:30 a.m.–5:00 p.m.
School Hours: 8:30 a.m.–3:30 p.m.
School Grades Offered: Grades 1–10
Enrollment: 85
Co-ed: Yes
Boy/Girl Ratio: 1:1
Student/Teacher Ratio: 15:1
Average Class Size: 15
Calendar School Year: July–May
Holidays: Thanksgiving, Christmas, Martin
Luther King Day, Presidents' Day, Easter
Uniform Requirements: None
Founded in: 1984

Philosophy of School

The Richardson Adventist School is dedicated to providing all students with a Christ-centered educational experience designed to help them reach their fullest potential spiritually, mentally, physically, socially, and morally. We value the infinite worth of every individual and seek to provide a climate in which the development of personal excellence is practiced. Our mission is to prepare each student to be a lifelong seeker of knowledge and to live purposefully in service of God and man.

Academic Curriculum

Content: General Conference of Seventh-Day Adventist Schools
Grading System Used: Grades 1–3 E, S, N (non-letter); 4–8 A, B, C, etc. (90, 80, etc.)
Conferences per Year: Two (October and March or as needed)
Tests Administered: Achievement testing in October, Iowa Tests of Basic Skills

356

Homework Policy: Lower grades–20 minutes/night; upper grades–45-90 minutes/night
Method of Discipline: Individual conferences with students and parents

Enrichment Curriculum
Spanish, piano, music, computers, peer mediation

Extracurricular Activities
Overnight field trips, presentation of dramas and musical programs, many field trips, guest speakers, outreach activities, summer activities

Goals for Students
To work individually with each student to reach his/her potential academically, socially, physically, and spiritually

Faculty/Staff Requirements
Qualifications of Staff: College degree; state and denominational certifications
Qualifications of Administrator: College degree; state and denominational certifications

School Information
Brochure Available: Yes
Number of Students in Each Grade: 15 (average)
Parochial: Seventh-Day Adventist Church
Organization Affiliations: Texas Conference of Seventh-Day Adventist Schools
Accreditations: Texas Education Agency, Board of Regents of General Conference of Seventh-Day Adventist
Parental Involvement: Home and School (PTA) very active; volunteer program
Other Information:

Admittance
Whom to Contact: Doris Sorenson, Principal (238-1183)
Date to Apply: Any time (early registration January–April)
Testing Procedure per Age/Grade Level: Individual
Fees Involved: $150 annual registration fee
Type of Student Preferred: Open enrollment

Forms Required: Application form, immunizations
Individual/Group Appointments: With Principal
Notification Procedure: Letter or telephone call
Waiting List Policy: N/A

Tuition

Approximate Tuition for 1996-97 School Year: $2500/$250 per month/10 months
Methods of Payment Available: Smart Tuition Plan/monthly
Financial Assistance Offered: For worthy student
Cancellation Insurance Available: N/A
Profit/Non-profit: Non-profit

Additional Costs

Books/Bag/Uniform: N/A
Lunch Fee: $2.25 per lunch per day
Parents Club Dues: N/A
Annual Fund Drive: August
Discount for Siblings: 10% discount for second child; 20% discount for third child; 35% discount for fourth child

Facilities/Services Provided

Computer Lab: In classrooms
Library: Grades 1–8
Snack Procedures: N/A
Before-school Care Program Available: Students of the school may enter the before-school program. There is no charge for this program; 7:00 a.m.–8:15 a.m.
After-school Care Program Available: Students of the school may enter after-school program for $20 per week or $5 per day. Payments are due each Monday; 3:45 p.m.–6:00 p.m.
Nurse on Staff: No
Emergency Procedure Used: Notify parents first; school follows procedure parents have specified on consent-to-treatment form.
Transportation to and from School: None available through school; car pools used
Counseling and Evaluation Available: Recommendations provided

Graduation Information

Testing: N/A
Average SAT scores: N/A

High School Our Students Usually Attend: Burton Adventist Academy; area high schools
Percentage of Seniors Attending College: N/A

Additional Information

Our greatest asset is a loving, family-type environment which fosters learning. The classrooms are structured, yet flexible for special projects. We also strive to integrate our Christian beliefs into all areas of life.

The *Pure & Natural* Story

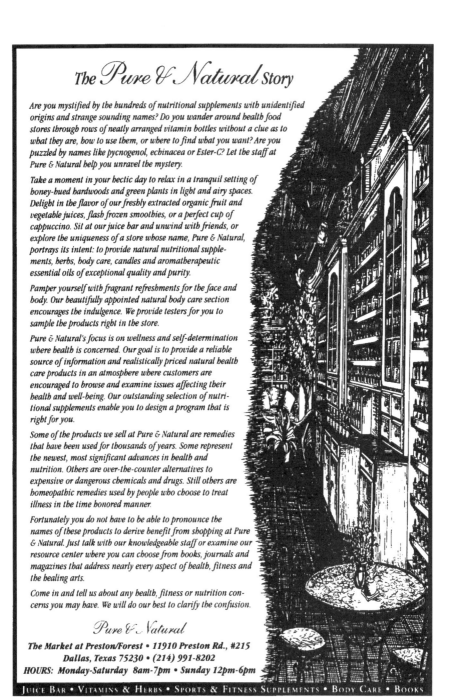

Are you mystified by the hundreds of nutritional supplements with unidentified origins and strange sounding names? Do you wander around health food stores through rows of neatly arranged vitamin bottles without a clue as to what they are, how to use them, or where to find what you want? Are you puzzled by names like pycnogenol, echinacea or Ester-C? Let the staff at Pure & Natural help you unravel the mystery.

Take a moment in your hectic day to relax in a tranquil setting of honey-hued hardwoods and green plants in light and airy spaces. Delight in the flavor of our freshly extracted organic fruit and vegetable juices, flash frozen smoothies, or a perfect cup of cappuccino. Sit at our juice bar and unwind with friends, or explore the uniqueness of a store whose name, Pure & Natural, portrays its intent: to provide natural nutritional supplements, herbs, body care, candles and aromatherapeutic essential oils of exceptional quality and purity.

Pamper yourself with fragrant refreshments for the face and body. Our beautifully appointed natural body care section encourages the indulgence. We provide testers for you to sample the products right in the store.

Pure & Natural's focus is on wellness and self-determination where health is concerned. Our goal is to provide a reliable source of information and realistically priced natural health care products in an atmosphere where customers are encouraged to browse and examine issues affecting their health and well-being. Our outstanding selection of nutritional supplements enable you to design a program that is right for you.

Some of the products we sell at Pure & Natural are remedies that have been used for thousands of years. Some represent the newest, most significant advances in health and nutrition. Others are over-the-counter alternatives to expensive or dangerous chemicals and drugs. Still others are homeopathic remedies used by people who choose to treat illness in the time honored manner.

Fortunately you do not have to be able to pronounce the names of these products to derive benefit from shopping at Pure & Natural. Just talk with our knowledgeable staff or examine our resource center where you can choose from books, journals and magazines that address nearly every aspect of health, fitness and the healing arts.

Come in and tell us about any health, fitness or nutrition concerns you may have. We will do our best to clarify the confusion.

Pure & Natural

The Market at Preston/Forest • 11910 Preston Rd., #215
Dallas, Texas 75230 • (214) 991-8202
HOURS: Monday-Saturday 8am-7pm • Sunday 12pm-6pm

JUICE BAR • VITAMINS & HERBS • SPORTS & FITNESS SUPPLEMENTS • BODY CARE • BOOKS

Star-Quality Shoes

The finest selection of quality kid's shoes in Dallas

Texas Kids
NorthPark Center
(214) 369-8953

363

Texas Medical & Surgical Associates

8440 Walnut Hill Lane
Dallas, Texas 75231

Don E. Cheatum, M.D., F.A.C.P., F.A.C.R.
Rheumatology

Fellow of the American College of Physicians
Fellow of the American College of Rheumatology
Diplomate of the American Specialty Board of Internal Medicine
Diplomate of the American Subspecialty Board of Rheumatology

(214) 345-1408   Refill: 345-1411   Fax: 345-5732

Raymond R. Johnson, M.D., F.A.A.P.
Pediatrics

Special Interests:
Allergy/Asthma, Attention Deficit

(214) 345-1461   Fax: 345-1462

Presley M. Mock, M.D.
Otolaryngology - Head & Neck Surgery
Diseases of the Ear, Nose & Throat
Facial Plastic & Reconstructive Surgery
Allergy

Diplomate of the American Board of Otolaryngology

(214) 345-1494   (214) 494-6764

Second Location: 777 Walter Reed
Garland, TX 75042

364

365

366

Additional Schools

These schools are not currently licensed or accredited. It is important to remember that accreditation is NOT MANDATORY in Texas. It is a voluntary process for the schools to select accreditation from an organization that meets their needs.

St. Therese Academy
YouthCrossing Academy

St. Therese Academy

2215 N. Britain Road
Dallas, TX 75062
(214) 252-3000

Mapsco: 31 B-L

Fax: (214) 252-3000/
Make a voice call prior to
sending a fax.

Office Hours: 8:00 a.m. –4:00 p.m.
School Hours: 8:00 a.m.–3:15 p.m.
School Grades Offered: Montessori pre-k, k–grade 12
Enrollment: 75
Co-ed: Yes
Boy/Girl Ratio: 50/50
Student/Teacher Ratio: 12:1
Average Class Size: 12
Calendar School Year: Labor Day to Memorial Day
Holidays: Thanksgiving, Christmas,
Presidents' Day, Easter
Uniform Requirements: Yes, St. Agnes Uniforms
Founded in: 1989

Philosophy of School

The emphasis at St. Therese Academy is on the tradition of 2000 years of Western
Christian civilization, with special focus on the tradition of the Roman Catholic
Church.

Academic Curriculum

Content: Basics emphasized: phonics, reading, writing, spelling, grammar,
math, science, history, geography
Grading System Used: Letter grades
Conferences per Year: Two
Tests Administered: National Achievement Test
Homework Policy: Nightly, but not on weekends except for extended projects/
papers

Method of Discipline: Each teacher is responsible for maintaining discipline in his/her classroom.

Enrichment Curriculum

The enrichment curriculum includes art, music, literature, Spanish, Latin, computer, and religion.

Extracurricular Activities

Monthly field trips, band, sports

Goals for Students

Mastery of the basic learning tools and development of character and moral virtue

Faculty/Staff Requirements

Qualifications of Staff: Devoted Christians who have college degrees
Qualifications of Administrator: Degree in child development; 7 years of experience

School Information

Brochure Available: Yes
Number of Students in Each Grade: 12
Parochial: Christian with an emphasis on Catholicism
Organization Affiliations: N/A
Accreditations: N/A
Parental Involvement: Manditory
Other Information: Students attending St. Therese consistantly score two grade levels or more above the national standard for private and parochial schools as reported by the National Achievement Test.

Admittance

Whom to Contact: Ms. Cheryl Woolnough or Ms. Ellen Thomas
Date to Apply: May 1
Testing Procedure per Age/Grade Level: Per grade level
Fees Involved: $200 registration/tuition fee, $50 testing fee
Type of Student Preferred: Students with no learning disabilities
Forms Required: Application, immunization, emergency release, transcript
Individual/Group Appointments: Individual
Notification Procedure: By personal contact
Waiting List Policy: Apply after July 15

Tuition

Approximate Tuition for 1996-97 School Year: $1800 per year for one child; $3600 for two or more children
Methods of Payment Available: Monthly for ten months
Financial Assistance Offered: Yes
Cancellation Insurance Available: No
Profit/Non-profit: Non-profit

Additional Costs

Books/Bag/Uniform: Books–$100 (grades K-6), $125 (grades 7-10); bag–no; uniform costs vary.
Lunch Fee: Students bring their lunches.
Parents Club Dues: None
Annual Fund Drive: Silent auction and dinner
Discount for Siblings: After the second child, only registration and book fees are due for additional children.

Facilities/Services Provided

Computer Lab: On campus
Library: On campus
Snack Procedures: Provided by parents
Before-school Care Program Available: Only upon request and availability of teacher
After-school Care Program Available: Only upon request and availability of teacher
Nurse on Staff: No
Emergency Procedure Used: Contact parents
Transportation to and from School: No
Counseling and Evaluation Available: No

Graduation Information

Testing: N/A
Average SAT Scores: N/A
High School Our Students Usually Attend: St. Therese Academy
Percentage of Seniors Attending College: N/A

Additional Information

YouthCrossing Academy

3500 I-30, #300 E
Mesquite, TX 75150
(214) 686-0685

Mapsco: 39X

Fax: (214) 613-2453

Office Hours: 8:00 a.m.–5:00 p.m.
School Hours: 10:00 a.m.–1:00 p.m.
School Grades Offered: Grades 7-12
Enrollment: 10
Co-ed: Yes
Boy/Girl Ratio: Varies
Student/Teacher Ratio: 5:1
Average Class Size: 10
Calendar School Year: Usual
Holidays: Usual
Uniform Requirements: None
Founded in: 1995

Philosophy of School

YouthCrossing Academy provides each student with an individualized curriculum at
his/her current educational levels while encouraging self-confidence and self-esteem.
Each student should be afforded the best possible education to help develop maximum
potential.

Academic Curriculum

Content: Mostly Alpha Omega; others as requested and needed
Grading System Used: Percent mastery
Conferences per Year: As needed
Tests Administered: Upon request only
Homework Policy: As needed
Method of Discipline: Redirection, time out

374

Enrichment Curriculum
Self-paced; each child's curriculum is enriched individually

Extracurricular Activities

Goals for Students
To learn to take pride in their efforts

Faculty/Staff Requirements
Qualifications of Staff: M.A., R.N.
Qualifications of Administrator: M.A. degree; secondary certification

School Information
Brochure Available: Yes
Number of Students in Each Grade: Mixed
Parochial: No
Organization Affiliations:
Accreditations: TDPRS, through Summit Christian Academy
Parental Involvement: Yes
Other Information: Unless parents specify otherwise, Summit Christian Academy handles our testing, curriculum, and transcripts.

Admittance
Whom to Contact: Eleanor Scott
Date to Apply: Any time
Testing Procedure for Age/Grade Level: Individualized placement in each subject area
Fees Involved: $35 for testing; $3000 yearly tuition (approximate)
Type of Student Preferred: Ages 12-18
Forms Required: Yes
Individual/Group Appointments: Yes
Notification Procedure: Phone
Waiting List Policy: Ongoing; no waiting list presently

Tuition
Approximate Tuition for 1996-97 School Year: Approximately $2800
Methods of Payment Available: Credit card, cash

Financial Assistance Offered: None
Cancellation Insurance Available: No
Profit/Non-profit: Profit

Additional Costs

Books/Bag/Uniform: Books–included in tuition; uniform–none
Lunch Fee: Not included
Parents Club Dues: No
Annual Fund Drive: No
Discount for Siblings: Yes

Facilities/Services Provided

Computer Lab: Computer-assisted instruction (CAI)
Library: Use outside sources
Snack Procedures: Vending machines
Before-school Care Program Available: No
After-school Care Program Available: N/A
Nurse on Staff: Yes
Emergency Procedure Used: Affiliated with hospital
Transportation to and from School: Yes (for an additional fee)
Counseling and Evaluation Available: Yes (for an additional fee);
(YouthCrossing Academy is part of YouthCrossing Adolescent Treatment Center).

Graduation Information

Testing: N/A (YouthCrossing Academy is too new to have this information.)
Average SAT Scores: N/A (YouthCrossing Academy is too new to have this information.)
High School Our Students Usually Attend: N/A (YouthCrossing Academy is too new to have this information.)
Percentage of Seniors Attending College: N/A (YouthCrossing Academy is too new to have this information.)

Additional Information

Alternative Schools

An alternative school is an educational facility that implements an individualized or alternative curriculum to meet the specific needs of its students. ASESA and SAILS are recognized accrediting organizations for these schools.

The Alexander School
Arbor Acre Preparatory School
Autistic Treatment Center
Bending Oaks High School
Brideway School
Dallas Academy
Dallas Learning Center
Fairhill School and Diagnostic Assessment Center
Glen Lakes Academy
Happy Hill Farm Academy/Home
Highland Academy
Hillier School of Highland Park Presbyterian Church
Keystone Academy
Meadowview School
The Notre Dame of Dallas Schools, Inc.
Oak Hill Academy
Preston Hollow Presbyterian Week Day School
The June Shelton School and Evaluation Center
Sycamore School, Inc.
Vanguard Preparatory School
Walden Preparatory School
The Winston School (see ISAS)

The Alexander School

409 International Pkwy.   Mapsco: 17D
Richardson, TX 75081
(214) 690-9210   Fax: (214) 690-9284

Office Hours: 8:00 a.m.–4:30 p.m. (Mon.–Thurs.)
9:00 a.m.–12:00 p.m. (Fri.)
School Hours: 8:00 a.m.–4:30 p.m. (Mon.–Thurs.)
9:00 a.m.–3:00 p.m. (Fri.)
School Grades Offered: 8–12
Enrollment: 75
Co-ed: Yes
Boy/Girl Ratio: 1.5:1
Student/Teacher Ratio: 4:1 (average); 7:1 (maximum); 1:1
(available)
Calendar School Year: Mid-August to the end of May; two
summer school sessions
Holidays: Labor Day, fall break, Thanksgiving, Christmas,
Martin Luther King Day, winter break, Easter/spring break
Uniform Requirements: No
Founded in: 1975

Philosophy of School

The Alexander School is dedicated to the personal growth and academic success of the
individual student. Open to all students, it is the only high school in north Texas using
the one-teacher-to-one-student instruction method. The students enjoy a relaxed,
attractive atmosphere that encourages them to realize their full potential. The one-to-
one instruction and small classes allow the students to form friendships and
interpersonal relationships often missing in the large classroom. Limited enrollment
ensures that each student receives the individual attention all young people deserve. In
this smaller school setting, the originality and integrity of the individual is encouraged
at all times.

The Alexander School serves a diverse student population and strives to enhance the social and intellectual growth of each student. The traditional, yet flexible, curriculum is designed to strengthen weak areas while facilitating the student's success in college. A feeling of belonging and a true camaraderie among students and teachers distinguish the Alexander School from the larger school.

Academic Curriculum

Content: The Alexander School requires 24 credits for graduation and 26 credits for the college-preparatory program. The required credits include English (4), mathematics (3), social studies (3), physical education (2), computer science (1), and electives (8). The college-preparatory program requires an additional two credits in a foreign language.
(College-preparatory students may graduate with honors if they earn five credits in honors/AP courses.) Students earn one full credit for a year-long course and one-half credit for a semester course. Most students enroll for six credits per year. AP and honors courses are offered in biology, chemistry, physics, calculus, English, U.S. history, and European history.

Grading System Used: Numerical; 100–0 (70 lowest passing grade).

Conferences per Year: At request of parent or administration; open house once per semester

Tests Administered: California Achievement Test/5; extended-time SAT and ACT

Homework Policy: Daily

Method of Discipline: Non-corporeal punishment

Enrichment Curriculum

Friday study sessions and science labs; summer school; daily teacher conference periods available for all students

Extracurricular Activities

Students are encouraged to participate in athletics (golf, tennis, basketball, volleyball), debate, photography, the school yearbook and newspaper, and the international club.

Goals for Students

The Alexander School's objective is to guide and assist each student in obtaining his or her full academic and personal potential. In addition to preparing the student for the post-high school academic challenges, the school fosters the student's self-reliance and responsibility.

Faculty/Staff Requirements

Qualifications of Staff: Degrees and/or certification in their teaching fields

379

Qualifications of Administrator: B.S.Ed.–Texas Tech University, 1973; M.Ed.–University of North Texas, 1985

School Information

Brochure Available: Yes
Number of Students in Each Grade: N/A
Parochial: No
Organization Affiliations: T.A.P.P.S.
Accreditations: Southern Association of Colleges and Schools in 1978, TEA in 1983
Parental Involvement: N/A
Other Information:

Admittance

Whom to Contact: David B. Bowlin
Date to Apply: Year-round enrollment
Testing Procedure per Age/Grade Level: Standardized testing done upon enrollment and at end of the school year (all students)
Fees Involved: None
Type of Student Preferred: Those wanting to improve their academic performance
Forms Required: Application and school records (transcripts, health, etc.)
Individual/Group Appointments: Individual
Notification Procedure: Pending interview and test results
Waiting List Policy: Ongoing, when school is full

Tuition

Approximate Tuition for 1996-97 School Year: $9000–$12000
Methods of Payment Available: 1/4 down at time of enrollment, 3 payments of 1/4 each
Financial Assistance Offered: None
Cancellation Insurance Available: No
Profit/Non-profit: Profit

Additional Costs

Books/Bag/Uniform: Books–invoiced: approximately $300 per year; fees: science labs, art, photography–$50 to $100 per course
Lunch Fee: None
Parents Club Dues: N/A
Annual Fund Drive: No fund drives
Discount for Siblings: Yes

Facilities/Services Provided

Computer Lab: 9 IBM compatable with printers
Library: Over 3,000 volumes
Snack Procedures: Vending machines
Before-school Care Program Available: No
After-school Care Program Available: No
Nurse on Staff: No
Emergency Procedure Used: Private emergency clinic four blocks from school
Transportation to and from School: No
Counseling and Evaluation Available: Yes

Graduation Information

Testing: Administration coordinates standardized testing; extended-time SAT and ACT available
Average SAT Scores: 1100
High School Our Students Usually Attend: N/A
Percentage of Seniors Attending College: 95

Additional Information

Concurrent enrollment and summer school are available to outside students with their home school's permission.

Arbor Acre Preparatory School

8000 South Hampton Rd.　　　　　　　Mapsco: 73D
Dallas, TX 75232
(214) 224-0511　　　　　　　　　　　Fax: 224-0511

Office Hours: 8:00 a.m. to 4:30 p.m.
School Hours: 8:00 a.m. to 3:10 p.m.
School Grades Offered: Kindergarten (4-year-olds)–
grade 8
Enrollment: 100
Co-ed: Yes
Boy/Girl Ratio: 3:1 (Varies)
Student/Teacher Ratio: 12:1
Average Class Size: 12
Calendar School Year: Third week in August–May
Holidays: Traditional national holidays; Christmas; spring
break at Easter
Uniform Requirements: Yes; red polo shirts with blue
pants; skirts, jumpers
Founded in: 1964

Philosophy of School

To provide educational services to children with average or above-average I.Q's; to
provide a successful learning situation for language-learning-different children

Arbor Acre is dedicated to creating a positive learning atmosphere within a well-
rounded, comprehensive program that encourages students to develop their potential
intellectually, emotionally, socially, and physically.

Academic Curriculum

Content: Arbor Acre individualizes its curriculum using state-approved textbooks and
the Scottish Rite Dyslexia Training Program's intensive phonics program and effective
remedial methods and concepts.

Grading System Used: A,B,C,F (grades K–4); 100–70 (grades 5–8); three-week reports; six-week report cards
Conferences per Year: Scheduled as needed
Tests Administered: Standardized achievement tests (fall and spring)
Homework Policy: Reading is required; unfinished classwork is sent home.
Method of Discipline: Positive reinforcement for good work and behavior;
K–4: Time-out; loss of privileges; all work must be completed before the student is allowed to participate in the Fun-Friday-Afternoon activities.
5–8: Loss of privileges; student is assigned to detention hall to complete make-up work.

Enrichment Curriculum
All grades are given field trips to take advantage of museums in the Dallas–Fort Worth area. The seventh grade takes a trip to Texas historical points, including San Antonio, Austin, and NASA in Houston. The eighth grade travels to Washington, D.C., and nearby historical areas in Louisiana and Mississippi.

Extracurricular Activities
Puppet Team; gardening

Goals for Students
To develop their potential intellectually, emotionally, socially, and physically

Faculty/Staff Requirements
Qualifications of Staff: Teachers with college degrees and experience
Qualifications of Administrator: Master's degree; LLD certification; language therapist

School Information
Brochure Available: Yes
Number of Students in Each Grade: 15
Parochial: No
Organization Affiliations: Texas Association for Children with Learning Differences; Texas Association of Non-Public Schools
Accreditations: Southern Association of Colleges and Schools; T.E.A. approved
Parental Involvement: Yes
Other Information: Arbor Acre accepts students with average or above-average ability who have dyslexia or attention-deficit problems. The structure of the small classrooms and the Alphabetic-Phonics method of teaching reading and language skills have proven successful for these children. Our students are readily accepted into both private and public high schools.

383

Admittance

Whom to Contact: Mary B. Cunningham
Date to Apply: March–July
Testing Procedure per Age/Grade Level: Testing for applicants for grades 1–8
Fees Involved: $400 enrollment fee ($200 applies to tuition)
Type of Student Preferred: Average to above-average ability, creative, gifted
Forms Required: Application, health records
Individual/Group Appointments: Both
Notification Procedure: Phone call approximately one week after testing
Waiting List Policy: Current students have first choice of places for the new school year. The remaining positions are assigned based on date of application and testing.

Tuition

Approximate Tuition for 1996-97 School Year: K: $2500; grades 1–8: $3500
Methods of Payment Available: Monthly
Financial Assistance Offered: Scholarships (sliding scale)
Cancellation Insurance Available: No
Profit/Non-Profit: Non-profit educational corporation (501 c 3)

Additional Costs

Books/Bag/Uniform: Art fee, computer fee
Lunch Fee: Approximately $2–$2.50 per day or bring lunch
Parents Club Dues: $10
Annual Fund Drive: Yes, golf tournament
Discount for Siblings: 20%

Facilities/Services Provided

Computer Lab: 15 Apple computers and printers; keyboarding taught in 4th grade; word processing taught; lab open before and after school for reference books and general reading (5800 books)
Library: Yes
Snack Procedures: Mid-morning and late afternoon
Before-school Care Program Available: Yes, 7:00 a.m.
After-school Care Program Available: Yes, 3:00–6:00 p.m.
Nurse on staff: No
Emergency Procedure Used: Follow parent's request
Transportation to and from School: Car pools
Counseling and Evaluation Available: Yes

Graduation Information

Testing: N/A

Average SAT Scores: N/A

High School Our Students Usually Attend: Local private, public, and parochial

Percentage of Seniors Attending College: Approximately 80% of our students attend college after they graduate from high school.

Additional Information

Autistic Treatment Center

10503 Forest Lane, Suite 100
Dallas, TX 75243
(214) 644-2076 (V/TDD)

Mapsco: 18W

Fax: (214) 644-5650

Office Hours: 9:00 a.m.–4:30 p.m.
School Hours: 9:00 a.m.–4:00 p.m.
School Grades Offered: N/A
Enrollment: Varies
Co-ed: Yes
Boy/Girl Ratio: 4:1
Student/Teacher Ratio: 3 or 4:1
Average Class Size: 3 or 4
Calendar School Year: Year-round
Holidays: One week in April, August, and December
Uniform Requirements: No
Founded in: 1976

Philosophy of School

Mission Statement: The Autistic Treatment Center will assist people who are disabled to live in the community, achieve educational goals, be gainfully employed, and experience personal satisfaction and happiness.

Academic Curriculum

Content: Cognitive, self-help, social, and recreational skills
Grading System Used: N/A
Conferences per Year: Annually and as needed
Tests Administered: None
Homework Policy: N/A
Method of Discipline: N/A

Enrichment Curriculum

N/A

Extracurricular Activities
Camp, swimming, outings for meals, area amusement parks and facilities, Equest horseback riding

Goals for Students
Listed in "Philosophy of School"

Faculty/Staff Requirements
Qualifications of Staff: Varies according to position
Qualifications of Administrator: Varies according to position

School Information
Brochure Available: Yes
Number of Students in Each Grade: N/A
Parochial: No
Organization Affiliations: TRC, TEA, TDMHMR, TDPRS
Accreditations: N/A
Parental Involvement: Parent training offered

Admittance
Whom to Contact: Ms. Kris Beard
Date to Apply: Year round
Testing Procedure per Age/Grade Level: N/A
Fees Involved: N/A
Type of Student Preferred: Diagnosed developmental disabilities, autism pervasive developmental disorder, or mental retardation
Forms Required: Diagnostic packet
Individual/Group Appointments: Contact Kris Beard for information
Notification Procedure: Referral contact is notified of availability.
Waiting List Policy: Ongoing after applicant is accepted by the Admissions Committee

Tuition
Approximate Tuition for 1996-97 School Year: $13,200
Methods of Payment Available: Negotiable
Financial Assistance Offered: Negotiable
Cancellation Insurance Available: No
Deposit Required: No
Profit/Non-profit: Private non-profit

Additional Costs

Books/Bag/Uniform: N/A
Lunch Fee: Sack lunch must be brought from home.
Parents Club Dues: N/A
Annual Fund Drive: N/A
Discount for Siblings: N/A

Facilities/Services Provided

Computer Lab: N/A
Library: N/A
Snack Procedures: Provided by the center
After-school Care Program Available: No
Before-school Care Program Available: No
Nurse on Staff: Yes
Emergency Procedure Used: 911, area hospitals
Transportation to and from School: Must be provided by family or ISD
Counseling and Evaluation Available: Yes

Graduation Information

Testing: N/A
Average SAT Scores: N/A
High School Our Students Usually Attend: N/A
Percentage of Seniors Attending College: N/A

Additional Information

Bending Oaks High School

11884 Greenville Avenue
Dallas, TX 75243
(214) 669-0000

Mapsco: 16Z

Fax: (214) 669-8149

Office Hours: 9:00 a.m.–4:00 p.m.
School Hours: 9:00 a.m.–3:30 p.m.
School Grades Offered: 9–12
Enrollment: 75
Co-ed: Yes
Boy/Girl Ratio: 1:1
Student/Teacher Ratio: Approximately 6:1
Average Class Size: 6
Calendar School Year: August–June
Holidays: (Same as public schools) Fair Day, Christmas,
winter and spring breaks, Good Friday, and Memorial Day
Uniform Requirements: None
Founded in: 1985

Philosophy of School

Bending Oaks High School was founded by a group of teachers who believe many
students cannot reach their full potential in a large classroom setting. They designed the
school for limited enrollment to ensure the availability of the teacher's assistance
without sacrificing the sharing of ideas in the classroom.

Academic Curriculum

Content: Math, science, language arts, art, computer science, social studies,
foreign languages, electives
Grading System Used: A (90–100), B (80–89), C (70–79), F (below 70); grades
are sent home every three weeks.
Conferences per Year: Two; additional as needed
Tests Administered: Timed and untimed P.S.A.T.; untimed S.A.T.; untimed
A.C.T.; S.A.T. (at area locations)

Homework Policy: Assigned regularly as required by the subject matter; the class schedule provides extra study time.

Method of Discipline: Handled individually by the principal with the parents and the student; the purpose is to motivate the student academically and to evaluate the student's commitment to school.

Enrichment Curriculum:

Yearbook, photography lab, astronomy, art, field trips, college-credit courses for seniors at area community colleges

Extracurricular Activities:

National Honor Society, prom committee, community service

Goals for Students

Our focus is on guiding students towards academic achievement and personal growth.

Faculty/Staff Requirements

Qualifications of Staff: Texas certification or advanced degree

Qualifications of Administrator: Principal–Ph.D. and extensive teaching experience in private and public schools

School Information

Brochure Available: Yes

Number of Students in Each Grade: Approximately 25

Parochial: No

Organization Affiliations: Recognized by Texas Education Agency, National Association of Secondary School Principals, College Board, Texas Association of College Admissions Counselors

Accreditations: Southern Association of Colleges and Schools

Parental Involvement: Welcomed and encouraged

Other Information: Summer school (two sessions in which students may earn two complete credits)

Admittance

Whom to Contact: Admissions office

Date to Apply: Year-round enrollment

Testing Procedure per Age/Grade Level: Educational Diagnostic Testing, if necessary

Type of Student Preferred: Average and above-average students with satisfactory behavioral background who believe they can learn better in a smaller classroom; students with mild learning differences who can benefit from smaller class sizes
Forms Required: School records, transcripts, health records
Individual/Group Appointments: Individual
Notification Procedure: Varies, as space is available
Waiting List Policy: Yes, when maximum enrollment is obtained

Tuition

Approximate Tuition for 1996-97 School Year: $8000–$9000
Methods of Payment Available: Payment in full upon enrollment; budgeting program available
Financial Assistance Offered: No
Cancellation Insurance Available: No
Profit/Non-Profit: Profit

Additional Costs

Books/Bag/Uniform: Included in tuition
Lunch Fee: N/A
Parents Club Dues: N/A
Annual Fund Drive: No
Discount for Siblings: No

Facilities/Services Provided

Computer Lab: Computers are utilized for keyboarding and computer literacy. Additional assistance is provided through a variety of software, including CD-ROM.
Library: A small library serves as a learning resource, together with Forest Green Public Library.
Snack Procedures: N/A
Before-school Care Program Available: No
After-school Care Program Available: No
Nurse on Staff: No
Emergency Procedure Used: Procedure followed as listed in school handbook
Transportation to and from School: No
Counseling and Evaluation Available: Yes

Graduation Information

Testing: Yes
Average SAT Scores: 1050

High School Our Students Usually Attend: N/A
Percentage of Seniors Attending College: 90

Additional Information

Bending Oaks High School seeks to establish a close parent-teacher-student relationship based on cooperation, communication, and respect.

Bridgeway School

7808 Clodus Fields Drive
Dallas, TX 75251
(214) 770-0845

Mapsco: 16W

Fax: (214) 991-2417

Office Hours: 8:00 a.m.–5:00 p.m.
School Hours: 8:30 a.m.–2:15 p.m.
School Grades Offered: 7–12
Enrollment: Year-round
Co-ed: Yes
Boy/Girl Ratio: N/A
Student/Teacher Ratio: 10:1
Average Class Size: 8
Calendar School Year: Year-round
Holidays: Same as public schools: Labor Day, Fair Day for private schools, Thanksgiving, Friday after Thanksgiving, Christmas, winter and spring breaks, Good Friday, Memorial Day, Independence Day (two complete summer sessions)
Uniform Requirements: No
Founded in: 1988

Philosophy of School

Bridgeway School provides a therapeutic academic program for adolescents who may be experiencing emotional problems or have learning difficulties and need a structured academic environment to enable them to return to optimal functioning.

Academic Curriculum

Content: Core curriculum plus electives (computer, languages, etc.)
Grading System Used: A (90–100), B (80–89), C (70–79), F (below 70)
Conferences per Year: At grading periods and as needed
Tests Administered: As needed

Homework Policy: Based upon each student's individualized instructional program

Method of Discipline: Therapeutic approach; structured classrooms; limit setting; individualized behavior modification; level system

Enrichment Curriculum

Reading improvement, computer graphics/art, cultural outings, etc.

Extracurricular Activities

Special outings, Reality-Oriented Physical Experiential Services (R.O.P.E.S), plays, area cultural events, community service

Goals for Students

To maintain or improve the academic performance of students who are experiencing emotional, behavioral, and/or learning difficulties

Faculty/Staff Requirements

Qualifications of Staff: College degree (master's degree preferred; most have master's degrees); teacher certification and/or work-related experience

Qualifications of Administrator: Principal–M.Ed. in educational administration; state-certified; alternative-education experience

School Information

Brochure Available: Yes

Number of Students in Each Grade: Varies

Parochial: No

Organization Affiliations: TAPH, AAPH, Dallas–Ft. Worth Hospital Council, DBGH

Accreditations: Southern Association of Colleges and Schools

Parental Involvement: Parent-teacher reporting conferences

Other Information: Students must be in a therapeutic treatment program or counseling while attending Bridgeway School.

Admittance

Whom to Contact: Tami Whitington or Margie English

Date to Apply: Year-round

Testing Procedure per Age/Grade Level: Individualized and as needed; all students must have a drug test before enrolling at Bridgeway School.

Fees Involved: Tuition
Type of Student Preferred: Students with special needs; i.e., learning difficulties and behavior problems
Forms Required: Previous school records; immunization records; previous academic and/or psychological testing results; drug testing results
Individual/Group Appointments: Family/student orientations
Notification Procedure: N/A
Waiting List Policy: Not currently

Tuition

Approximate Tuition for 1996-97 School Year: $700 per month plus fees
Methods of Payment Available: Deposit plus monthly payment
Financial Assistance Offered: None
Cancellation Insurance Available: No
Profit/Non-profit: Profit

Additional Costs

Books/Bag/Uniform: $50 book-usage fee and $50 activity fee
Lunch Fee: No
Parents Club Dues: None
Annual Fund Drive: None
Discount for Siblings: N/A

Facilities/Services Provided

Computer Lab: PC's utilized in the classrooms for instructional reinforcement of core subjects, keyboarding, word processing, and graphic arts
Library: Research/ resources available through modem access to outside electronic sources and use of community libraries
Snack Procedures: Provided by Bridgeway
Before-school Care Program Available: No
After-school Care Program Available: No
Nurse on Staff: Yes
Emergency Procedure Used: Contact parents
Transportation to and from School: No
Counseling and Evaluation Available: All students are required to be in a therapeutic program or counseling while attending Bridgeway School. The staff communicates with each student's counselor on an as-needed basis.

Graduation Information

Testing: N/A
Average SAT Scores: N/A

High School Our Students Usually Attend: N/A
Percentage of Seniors Attending College: Most students return to their neighborhood school districts before graduation.

Additional Information

To enable its students to succeed, Bridgeway School seeks to:
- improve attention skills
- enhance learning skills
- modify behavior
- improve self-esteem
- increase school attendance
- control impulsive behavior
- develop interpersonal communication skills

Bridgeway School provides an alternative educational program for students with emotional problems or learning difficulties that prevent them from functioning well in a traditional academic setting.

Bridgeway School provides a transition for secondary-school students who are in out-patient therapy (individual and/or family counseling) and need a school program that emphasizes close interaction with teachers in small, structured classes with individualized instruction. When students are ready to return to their home schools, Bridgeway School's liaison assists the students and parents in contacting the home school to make the transition as comfortable and successful as possible.

Dallas Academy

950 Tiffany Way
Dallas, TX 75218
(214) 324-1481

Mapsco: 37H

Fax: (214) 328-1272

Office Hours: 8:15 a.m.–3:30 p.m.
School Hours: 8:30 a.m.–3:00 p.m.
School Grades Offered: 7–12
Enrollment: 115
Co-ed: Yes
Boy/Girl Ratio: 2:1
Student/Teacher Ratio: 9:1
Average Class Size: 9
Calendar School Year: August–May (same as R.I.S.D.)
Holidays: R.I.S.D. schedule
Uniform Requirements: Shirts
Founded in: 1965

Philosophy of School

Dallas Academy's basic philosophy is to offer a structured, caring environment to all students. The Academy offers an extremely structured multisensory program for students (grades 7–12) with diagnosed learning disabilities. Structure is the main factor in student success at the Academy. We believe that students who have trouble in school with concentration and attention span need a quiet, structured, nurturing environment to achieve their maximum potential. Structure aids students in academic areas and develops positive personal and social skills as well.

Academic Curriculum

Content: Individualized college preparatory
Grading System Used: A–F
Conferences per Year: Yes, 7
Tests Administered: WISC, WRAT, Woodcock-Johnson

397

Homework Policy: Approximately one hour per night
Method of Discipline: In-school suspension (ISS); standard discipline policy

Enrichment Curriculum

Drawing, arts and crafts, drama, Spanish, social-skills classes, humanities, journalism, sports, homemaking, marine biology, chemistry

Extracurricular Activities

Sports (football, baseball, basketball, tennis, golf, volleyball, track), cheerleading, homecoming, chili cook-off, Halloween dance, TGIF field trips, junior-senior prom

Goals for Students

We want students to graduate with good self-esteem and positive directions in their lives. Ninety percent of our students attend college following graduation. Many of our students attend the Academy for one or two years and then return to public or private schools.

Faculty/Staff Requirements

Qualifications of Staff: Our staff have these degrees: B.S., M.A., M.S., Ph.D.; all have state certification.
Qualifications of Administrator: M.S. in Special Education; supervisor and administration certification

School Information

Brochure Available: Yes
Number of Students in Each Grade: 22
Parochial: No
Organization Affiliations: Texas Association of Private Schools (Class A, Dist. 1); National Association of Private Schools for Exceptional Children (Founding Member); Southern Association of Colleges and Schools; Association for Children with Learning Disabilities; Council for Exceptional Children
Accreditations: SACS; TEA-approved
Parental Involvement: Yes (Booster Club, Parent Group)

Admittance

Whom to Contact: Jim Richardson, Director, or Dr. Annette Fulton
Date to Apply: January
Testing Procedure per Age/Grade Level: Call for appointment

Fees Involved: Yes
Type of Student Preferred: LD, ADD, dyslexic
Forms Required: Yes
Individual/Group Appointments: Individual
Notification Procedure: Depends on waiting list
Waiting List Policy: Ongoing

Tuition

Approximate Tuition for 1996-97 School Year: $7500
Methods of Payment Available: 12 months; 9 months; single payment
Financial Assistance Offered: Yes
Cancellation Insurance Available: No
Profit/Non-profit: Non-profit

Additional Costs

Books/Bag/Uniform: Shirts–approximately $17 each
Lunch Fee: Buy your own
Parents Club Dues: $15
Annual Fund Drive: Yes
Discount for Siblings: Yes

Facilities/Services Provided

Computer Lab: 13 IBM 486 computers, Internet, computers in classes
Library: 2,000 volumes, Internet, IBM 486 computer, printer
Snack Procedures: N/A
Before-school Care Program Available: No
After-school Care Program Available: No
Nurse on Staff: No
Emergency Procedure Used: As stated in brochure
Transportation to and from School: Yes, North Dallas-Plano-Richardson
Counseling and Evaluation Available: Yes

Graduation Information

Testing: SAT, ITBS
Average SAT Scores: Available upon request
High School Our Students Usually Attend: N/A
Percentage of Seniors Attending College: 90

Dallas Learning Center

301 S. Sherman, Suite 116
Richardson, TX 75081
(214) 231-3723

Mapsco: 17E
Fax: 231-3860
(Call before faxing)

Office Hours: 9:00 a.m.–4:30 p.m.
School Hours: 9:00 a.m.–3:00 p.m.
School Grades Offered: 9–12 (Alternative School)
Enrollment: 35
Co-ed: Yes
Boy/Girl Ratio: 2:1
Student/Teacher Ratio: 5:1
Average Class Size: 1:1 and 5:1
Calendar School Year: August–May (Summer school–June and July)
Holidays: Labor Day, Fair Day, Thanksgiving, Christmas, spring break
Uniform Requirements: No
Founded in: January 1991

Philosophy of School

The Dallas Learning Center is dedicated to providing students with positive learning experiences that emphasize the needs of the individual. The Dallas Learning Center achieves this by offering a structured, yet comfortable, environment that promotes academic and personal growth.

Academic Curriculum

Content: Individualized, college-preparatory curriculum through the University of Nebraska–Lincoln Independent Study High School
Grading System Used: Numerical
Conferences per Year: At request of parent or administration
Tests Administered: Wide-Range Achievement Test; SAT

Homework Policy: Homework is required only when students have late work.
Other Information: Behavior modification and in-school suspension

Enrichment Curriculum
Weekly field trips, daily study halls, computer programs, college guidance program, accelerated programs

Extracurricular Activities
Student council, environmental recycling group, community service

Goals for Students
The goal of the Dallas Learning Center is to guide each student in maximizing his/her academic and personal growth.

Faculty/Staff Requirements
Qualifications of Staff: College degrees, certification, or experience in working with learning-differenced students
Qualifications of Administrator: Master's degree and 10 years of teaching experience

School Information
Brochure Available: Yes
Number of Students in Each Grade: Varies (approximately 8)
Parochial: No
Organization Affiliations: None
Accreditations: The University of Nebraska–Lincoln Independent Study High School is accredited through the North Central Association of Colleges and Schools
Other Information: Students may accelerate through our high school and graduate up to two years early.

Admittance
Whom to Contact: Kathleen Herrin-Kinard
Date to Apply: Open enrollment year-round
Testing Procedure per Age/Grade Level: At time of enrollment and/or upon request; SAT offered on campus once a year
Fees Involved: None
Type of Student Preferred: All types of students are welcome; we specialize in learning-differenced students as well as students who wish to accelerate.

Forms Required: Application, contract, and school records
Individual/Group Appointments: Group appointment with student and parent(s); individual student visit one school day prior to enrollment
Notification Procedure: In person within one day of student's school visit
Waiting List Policy: Ongoing; more availability during fall semester; no waiting list for summer program

Tuition

Approximate Tuition for 1996-97 School Year: $4500 per semester
Methods of Payment Available: Full tuition or interest-free monthly financing
Financial Assistance Offered: One scholarship per year
Cancellation Insurance Available: No
Profit/Non-profit: Profit

Additional Costs

Books/Bag/Uniform: N/A
Lunch Fee: N/A
Parents Club Dues: N/A
Annual Fund Drive: N/A
Discount for Siblings: No

Facilities/Services Provided

Computer Lab: The lab consists of four MacIntosh computers available for student use at all times.
Library:
Snack Procedures: Vending machines
Before-school Care Program Available: No
After-school Care Program Available: No
Nurse on Staff: No
Emergency Procedure Used: Richardson Medical Center (located within five miles of the school)
Transportation to and from School: D.L.C. will aid in coordinating car pools.
Counseling and Evaluation Available: Yes

Graduation Information

Testing: Yes
Average SAT Scores: Available upon request
High School Our Students Usually Attend: N/A
Percentage of Seniors Attending College: 75

Additional Information

Dallas Learning Center is an alternative for students who find the traditional school environment does not meet their individual needs. Dallas Learning Center offers accelerated programs which allow students to graduate in a more timely manner. The Dallas Learning Center summer school program permits students to take up to four classes per session. Many students from other schools use the Dallas Learning Center's summer program.

Diagnostic Assessment Center

Grades one through twelve

Fully accredited

Co-educational
day school

For students with learning
differences

214/233-1026

16150 Preston Road at Keller Springs
Dallas, Texas 75248

Fairhill School and Diagnostic Assessment Center

16150 Preston Road
Dallas, TX 75248
(214) 233-1026

Mapsco: 5T

Fax: (214) 233-8205

Office Hours: 7:30 a.m.–4:30 p.m.
School Hours: 8:15 a.m.–3:15 p.m.
School Grades Offered: 1–12
Enrollment: 200
Co-ed: Yes
Boy/Girl Ratio: 4:1
Student/Teacher Ratio: 8:1
Average Class Size: 10 (grades 1–4); 12 (grades 5–12)
Calendar School Year: Traditional school calendar
Holidays: Traditional school holidays
Uniform Requirements: Yes
Founded in: 1971

Philosophy of School

Fairhill is dedicated to providing the best possible education to learning different students, emphasizing each student's unique pattern of information acquisition, processing, and expression. To accomplish this, Fairhill focuses upon academic, social, and emotional development. Fairhill is also dedicated to transferring this knowledge through training programs for professionals in the learning disabilities field. Fairhill guides its students in LEARNING TO LEARN and trains other professionals to do so as well.

Academic Curriculum

Content: Our traditional curriculum, geared to each student's level, emphasizes the basic skills of reading, language arts, writing, and mathematics. At the same time, the student receives appropriate grade-level instruction in the content and enrichment areas. The Fairhill curriculum is not bound by a particular teaching method; the needs and unique talents of each student determine teaching strategies.

Grading System Used: Comprehensive report cards and detailed progress reports

Conferences per Year: Three

Tests Administered: Standford Achievement Test

Homework Policy: Designed to teach responsibility and enhance curriculum

Method of Discipline: Various techniques are used to develop age-appropriate, responsible behavior

Enrichment Curriculum

Organizational/study skills, social skills, creative dramatics, physical education, visual art, music, library skills, computer

Extracurricular Activities

Lower school: competitive sports, Reading Club, Arts and Crafts Club, environmental study trip for grades 5 and 6

Middle school: competitive sports, Student Council, Science Fair, Journalism Club, Texas history trip for grade 7, earth science trip for grade 8

Upper school: competitive sports, Student Council, National Honor Society, Odyssey of the Mind, Homecoming, Junior/Senior Prom, volunteer community service programs, annual upper-school trip (Boston, Montreal, Washington, D.C.)

Goals for Students

Individual goals are set for each student in partnership with the student, the parent, and the faculty.

Faculty/Staff Requirements

Qualifications of Staff: College degree; certification; suitable experience

Qualifications of Administrator: College degree; certification; suitable experience

School Information

Brochure Available: Yes

Number of Students in Each Grade: 10–26

Parochial: No

Organization Affiliations: CASE, COPSES, SACS, Orton Society
Accreditations: Southern Association of Colleges and Schools; Texas
Education Agency
Parental Involvement: Fairhill Parents' Council; encouraged
Other Information:

Admittance

Whom to Contact: Carla Stanford (grades 1–7); Kay Wendell (grades 8–12)
Date to Apply: Enrollment begins in January
Testing Procedure per Age/Grade Level: Testing at end of grading periods
and end of semesters (grades 5-12)
Fees Involved: N/A
Type of Student Preferred: Students with average to above-average intellect
who have been diagnosed as having a learning difference
Forms Required: Yes
Individual/Group Appointments: Individual appointments
Notification Procedure: Telephone call and formal letter
Waiting List Policy: Reapply annually

Tuition

Approximate Tuition for 1996-97 School Year: Grades 1–5, $7900;
6–8, $8000; 9–12, $8200
Methods of Payment Available: Due in full prior to July 15 for
upcoming year
Financial Assistance Offered: Limited
Cancellation Insurance Available: No
Profit/Non-profit: Non-profit

Additional Costs

Books/Bag/Uniform: Books furnished
Lunch Fee: N/A
Parents Club Dues: Yes
Annual Fund Drive: Yes
Discount for Siblings: No

Facilities/Services Provided

Computer Lab: Yes; network with full lab plus individual classroom
instruction and drill and practice
Library: Yes, fully equipped library with approximately 3000 volumes
Snack Procedures: N/A

Before-school Care Program Available: N/A
After-school Care Program Available: N/A
Nurse on Staff: No
Emergency Procedure Used: Notify parents; call 911
Transportation to and from School: N/A
Counseling and Evaluation Available: Yes; psychologist on staff; Diagnostic Assessment Center on campus

Graduation Information

Testing: Information available upon request
Average ACT Scores: 21 (1995)
High School Our Students Usually Attend: N/A
Percentage of Seniors Attending College: 98% (1995)

Additional Information

The Fairhill Diagnostic Assessment Center provides the community (ages 5 to adult) with a professional, full-service facility that evaluates educational, psychological, and speech-and-language skills. We emphasize the patterns of functioning that affect learning. Our staff first identifies each individual's unique talents and skills and then designs a program to help the individual realize his or her potential for learning and psychological development. In 1995 the Diagnostic Assessment Center proudly announced its merger with Bobbie Hamilton Jones and Associates.

Glen Lakes Academy

6000 Custer Road
Plano, TX 75074
(214) 383-2614

Mapsco: 658E

Fax: (214) 360-0253

Office Hours: 8:00 a.m.–5:00 p.m.
School Hours: 8:30 a.m.–3:30 p.m.
School Grades Offered: K–grade 8
Enrollment: 117
Co-ed: Yes
Boy/Girl Ratio: Unknown
Student/Teacher Ratio: 10:1
Average Class Size: 13 (maximum)
Calendar School Year: September–end of May
Holidays: P.I.S.D. holidays
Uniform Requirements: Strict dress code
Founded in: 1996 by Steven Steen (M.S., L.P.C., psychotherapist in private practice)

Philosophy of School

Glen Lakes Academy seeks to combine therapeutic practice with education to create a new model of training for children and youth. The school is committed to helping individuals who exhibit the symptoms of ADD/ADHD. (Please see "Additional Information.")

Academic Curriculum

Content: Taken from the Highland Park School District
Grading System Used:
Conferences per Year: One every eight weeks
Tests Administered:
Homework Policy: Homework should be completed at school.
Method of Discipline: Each case reviewed individually

409

Enrichment Curriculum
Social Skills Group (for all children) meets three times per week.

Extracurricular Activities
Karate, Suzuki Violin School, drama, Odyssey of the Mind

Goals for Students
To develop good self-esteem and succeed academically

Faculty/Staff Requirements
Qualifications of Staff: All are certified; most have master's degrees or higher.
Qualifications of Administrator: Ph. D. degree

School Information
Brochure Available: Yes
Number of Students in Each Grade: 13
Parochial: No
Organization Affiliations:
Accreditations: Applying for accreditation
Parental Involvement: Yes
Other Information:

Admittance
Whom to Contact: Steven Steen, MS LPC
Date to Apply: Rolling admissions
Testing Procedure for Age/Grade Level: ADD, ADHD, psychological evaluation, interview
Fees Involved: $50 application fee
Type of Student Preferred: Intelligent student with ADD/ADHD who does not perform well in the public-school system or in a large classroom
Forms Required: Previous transcripts
Individual/Group Appointments: Yes
Notification Procedure: After interview, by mail
Waiting List Policy: Ongoing

Tuition
Approximate Tuition for 1996-97 School Year: $8900
Methods of Payment Available: $3000 deposit; $675 per month (August-May)

Financial Assistance Offered: No
Cancellation Insurance Available: No
Profit/Non-profit: Profit

Additional Costs

Books/Bag/Uniform: Varies
Lunch Fee: Yes, varies
Parents Club Dues: No
Annual Fund Drive: N/A
Discount for Siblings: Yes

Facilities/Services Provided

Computer Lab: Yes
Library: Public library is next door.
Snack Procedures: N/A
Before-school Care Program Available: No
After-school Care Program Available: Yes; 3:00 p.m.-6:30 p.m.
Nurse on Staff: No
Emergency Procedure Used: Notify parents
Transportation to and from School: No
Counseling and Evaluation Available: Yes

Graduation Information

Testing: N/A
Average SAT Scores: N/A
High School Our Students Usually Attend: N/A
Percentage of Seniors Attending College: N/A

Additional Information

In addition to a challenging curriculum, Glen Lakes Academy offers a low student-teacher ratio, after-school tutorials, a phonetics program, multisensory learning, parent support groups, outside ADD/ADHD speakers, and continuous monitoring of progress. We also offer art classes, music classes, computer classes, and tri-weekly sessions addressing concerns, such as anger management, impulse control, listening skills, social behavior, following directions, making and keeping friends, and coping with frustration.

Happy Hill Farm Academy/Home

Star Route, Box 56
Granbury, TX 76048
(817) 897-4822

Mapsco: N/A

Fax: (817) 897-7650

Office Hours: 8:30 a.m.–5:00 p.m. (Monday–Friday)
School Hours: 8:30 a.m.–3:05 p.m.
School Grades Offered: K–12
Enrollment: 100
Co-ed: Yes
Boy/Girl Ratio: 1:1
Student/Teacher Ratio: 6:1
Average Class Size: 6–8
Calendar School Year: Year-round; residential facility
Holidays: Boarding school schedule–Thanksgiving, Christmas, Easter (spring break), other weekend breaks
Uniform Requirements: Yes
Founded in: 1975

Philosophy of School

Happy Hill Farm Academy/Home is a year-round, residential treatment center, child-care facility, offering a unique boarding school environment for children and adolescents. Though interdenominational in approach, there are strong moral, ethical, and spiritual underpinnings to the entire academic and vocational programs.

Academic Curriculum

Content: The Academy's full curriculum meets all state guidelines and objectives. Twenty-two credits are required for graduation.

Grading System Used: A (90-100); B (80-89); C (70-79); grades are reported quarterly.

Conferences per Year: Four; progress reports and parent conferences are scheduled routinely.

Tests Administered: ACT, 1/4 SAT, SAT, Standard Achievement
Homework Policy: Study time each night mandatory in living units
Method of Discipline: Discipline–no corporal punishment

Enrichment Curriculum

Academic competitions; fine arts department offers choral, hand bells, instruments, painting, pottery; Gifted-Talented Program

Extracurricular Activities

Student council, cheerleading, volleyball, football, baseball, softball, tennis, swimming, track, basketball, horseback riding, 4-H, cross country, field trips, music

Goals for Students

The objectives at Happy Hill Farm Academy/Home emphasize a balance of the spiritual, academic, and the practical to prepare students to become happy, productive members of society while engaged in their chosen professions or vocations.

Faculty/Staff Requirements

Qualifications of Staff: Teaching degree; Texas certification
Qualifications of Administrator: Bachelor's degree, master's degree, and administrative certification

School Information

Brochure Available: Yes
Number of Students in Each Grade: Average of 6-15
Parochial: Christian, but no denominational affiliation
Organization Affiliations: TALCS, TAPPS, TANPS, T.P.H.S.
Accreditations: Southern Association of Colleges and Schools
Parental Involvement: Yes
Other Information: Located 40 miles south of FortWorth on State Highway 144

Admittance

Whom to Contact: Office, social worker
Date to Apply: Continual admissions
Testing Procedure per Age/Grade Level:
Fees Involved: $1250 per month; scholarships available
Type of Student Preferred: Children and adolescents with average to above-

413

average intelligence who have emotional and/or school-related problems
Forms Required: Family history; admissions application
Individual/Group Appointments: Available
Notification Procedure: Usually three to four weeks; in writing
Waiting List Policy: N/A

Tuition

Approximate Tuition for 1996-97 School Year: Verify with school office
Methods of Payment Available: Arrangements available
Financial Assistance Offered: Scholarships available
Cancellation Insurance Available: N/A
Profit/Non-profit: Non-profit

Additional Costs

Books/Bag/Uniform: All fees included
Lunch Fee: All fees included
Parents Club Dues: N/A
Annual Fund Drive: N/A
Discount for Siblings: N/A

Facilities/Services Provided

Computer Lab: Yes
Library: Yes
Snack Procedures: After school
Before-school Care Program Available: 24-hour, year-round, boarding school program
After-school Care Program Available: Yes, 24-hour residential facility
Nurse on Staff: Yes
Emergency Procedure Used: Clinic on campus; local hospital emergency room
Transportation to and from School: Located on campus
Counseling and Evaluation Available: Ph.D., M.S.W.; group and individual counseling available

Graduation Information

Testing: SAT, TSAP, ACT
Average SAT Scores: 1000
High School Our Students Usually Attend: N/A
Percentage of Seniors Attending College: 85

Additional Information

Happy Hill Farm Academy/Home's program offers 20 years' experience in helping children and adolescents with emotional and/or school-related problems.

Highland Academy

1231 W. Belt Line Rd.   Mapsco: 16B
Richardson, TX 75080
(214) 238-7567   Fax:

Office Hours: 8:00 a.m.–3:00 p.m.
School Hours: 8:30 a.m.–2:30 p.m.
School Grades Offered: K–grade 8
Enrollment: 65
Co-ed: Yes
Boy/Girl Ratio: 7:3
Student/Teacher Ratio: 6:1
Average Class Size: 6
Calendar School Year: Late August–May 31
Holidays: Same as R.I.S.D.
Uniform Requirements: Yes
Founded in: 1980

Philosophy of School

To provide a complete elementary education for intelligent children with language-learning difficulties and A.D.D.

Academic Curriculum

Content: Full academics, intensive language, computerized phonics
Grading System Used: Progress reporting
Conferences per Year: Three or more
Tests Administered: WRAT, Woodcock-Johnson, ITBS
Homework Policy: Homework assigned in academic subjects four days weekly
Method of Discipline: Anticipatory-preventive, discipline by example, positive approach using Lee Canter methods

Enrichment Curriculum

Arts, computer lab, science lab

Extracurricular Activities

Aerobics, athletics, debates, drama, bowling, roller skating, musical production

Goals for Students

Re-entry into mainstream

Faculty/Staff Requirements

Qualifications of Staff: Teacher certification, special education degrees
Qualifications of Administrator: Master's degree in special education, academic language-therapy certification, certified educational diagnostician

School Information

Brochure Available: Yes
Number of Students in Each Grade: 6–10
Parochial: No
Organization Affiliations: Orton Dyslexia Society, ALTA, ASESA
Accreditations: ASESA (Association for Specialized Elementary School Accreditation)
Parental Involvement: Parents' Association, hot lunch, field trips, class parties
Other Information:

Admittance

Whom to Contact: Director
Date to Apply: Year-round
Testing Procedure per Age/Grade Level: Annual achievement testing
Fees Involved: Included in tuition
Type of Student Preferred: Intelligent children with special learning needs
Forms Required: Yes
Individual/Group Appointments: Both
Notification Procedure: Phone call
Waiting List Policy: Ongoing

Tuition

Approximate Tuition for 1996-97 School Year: $6900–$7500
Methods of Payment Available: Annually; semi-annually; monthly

417

Financial Assistance Offered: Limited
Cancellation Insurance Available: No
Profit/Non-profit: Inquire with school

Additional Costs

Books/Bag/Uniform: Books, bag--no fees; uniform–approximately $100
Lunch Fee: Twice monthly
Parents Club Dues: No
Annual Fund Drive: No
Discount for Siblings: No

Facilities/Services Provided

Computer Lab: IBM PC; annual technology update
Library: More than 1000 literature/reference volumes
Snack Procedures: Kindergarten and first grade
Before-school Care Program Available: No
After-school Care Program Available: After-school tutorials
Nurse on Staff: No
Emergency Procedure Used: Emergency numbers provided by parents
Transportation to and from School: No
Counseling and Evaluation Available: Referrals

Graduation Information

Testing: N/A
Average SAT Scores: N/A
High School Our Students Usually Attend: Varies
Percentage of Seniors Attending College: N/A

Additional Information

Hillier School of Highland Park Presbyterian Church

3821 University Boulevard
Dallas, TX 75205-1781
(214) 559-5363

Mapsco: 35F

Fax: (214) 559-5311

Office Hours: 8:00 a.m.–3:30 p.m.
School Hours: 8:30 a.m.–3:00 p.m.
School Grades Offered: 1–7
Enrollment: 61
Co-ed: Yes
Boy/Girl Ratio: 3:1
Student/Teacher Ratio: 6:1
Average Class Size: 6
Calendar School Year: August–May
Holidays: Labor Day, Thanksgiving, Christmas, Martin Luther King Day, spring break, Easter, Memorial Day
Uniform Requirements: Yes
Founded in: 1965

Philosophy of School

The Hillier School provides special curriculum which meets the needs of dyslexic (language-learning differences) students within the context of a Christian environment.

Academic Curriculum

Content: Multisensory teaching techniques
Grading System Used: Progress reports (reflecting progress in specific academic skills) are given three times per year.
Conferences per Year: Two scheduled (one in the fall and one in the spring); parents encouraged to request additional conferences as needed
Tests Administered: Testing is not emphasized. Students are regularly evaluated in "review situations." Standardized achievement tests are given each

419

spring.

Homework Policy: Moderate amount of carefully selected assignments

Method of Discipline: Behavior modification; parental involvment

Enrichment Curriculum

Field trips, guest speakers

Extracurricular Activities

Science Fair, Pet Day, school plays, basketball, Field Day

Goals for Students

Our goal is to prepare our students to enter the mainstream of education as soon as they are able. On the average, this requires three years.

Faculty/Staff Requirements

Qualifications of Staff: College degrees

Qualifications of Administrator: B.S. in Education; academic language therapist

School Information

Brochure Available: Yes

Number of Students in Each Grade: 10–16

Parochial: Non-denominational Christian School

Organization Affiliations: TANS, COPSES

Accreditations: TAAPS

Parental Involvement: Parents' Club

Admittance

Whom to Contact: Regina Garrett

Date to Apply: Year round

Testing Procedure per Age/Grade Level: Done by other agencies who refer students to our school

Fees Involved: $235 registration fee

Type of Student Preferred: Dyslexic (language-learning differences)

Forms Required: Copy of educational testing

Individual/Group Appointments: Parent-principal interview

Notification Procedure: Call from principal

Waiting List Policy: N/A

Tuition

Approximate Tuition for 1996-97 School Year: $6400 (includes registration fee)
Methods of Payment Available: Monthly payments (9 months)
Financial Assistance Offered: Partial or full scholarships
Cancellation Insurance Available: No
Profit/Non-profit: Non-profit

Additional Costs

Books/Bag/Uniform: Books–no additional costs; bag–n/a; uniform–$125
Lunch Fee: Parents' Club determines each year the price of Friday's hot lunch.
Parents Club Dues: $10
Annual Fund Drive: N/A
Discount for Siblings: No

Facilities/Services Provided

Computer Lab: Yes
Library: Yes
Snack Procedures: N/A
Before-school Care Program Available: No
After-school Care Program Available: Yes; 3:00 p.m.–5:00 p.m.
Nurse on Staff: No
Emergency Procedure Used: Standard first-aid procedures
Transportation to and from School: No
Counseling and Evaluation Available: Yes

Graduation Information

Testing: Standardized achievement tests
Average SAT Scores: N/A
High School Our Students Generally Attend: N/A
Percentage of Seniors Attending College: N/A

Additional Information

The Hillier School does not discriminate on the basis of race, color, national, or ethnic origin in the administration of its educational or admissions policies.

Keystone Academy

6506 Frankford Rd.
Dallas, TX 75252
(214) 250-4455

Mapsco: 5F

Fax: N/A

Office Hours: 8:30 a.m.–4:00 p.m.
School Hours: 8:30 a.m.–3:00 p.m.
School Grades Offered: Pre-kindergarten–grade 8
Enrollment: 60
Co-ed: Yes
Boy/Girl Ratio: 4:1
Student/Teacher Ratio: 7:1
Average Class Size: 6 or 7
Calendar School Year: August–May
Holidays: Labor Day, Christmas, Presidents' Day, Easter, one week in March
Uniform Requirements: Yes
Founded in: 1982

Philosophy of School

Keystone Academy is a school for the child of average or above-average ability who has learning differences such as attention-deficit, dyslexia, or other language-learning delays. We believe every child has the right to a program suited to meet his/her individual needs.

Academic Curriculum

Content: Alphabet Phonics Program; individual student programming and perceptual motor development curriculum
Grading System Used: Grades k-3, letter grades; grades 4-8, numerical grades
Conferences per Year: Required after first and last 9 weeks; as needed
Tests Administered: Brigance testing administered every spring
Homework Policy: Used to further the learning in the classroom; reinforcement
Method of Discipline: Time out; miss special activities; parent conference

422

Enrichment Curriculum

Art, music, motor-perceptual training in physical education classes, computer lab, living science center

Extracurricular Activities

Goals for Students

To help the student reach his/her potential, be mainstreamed, and become a successful citizen.

Faculty/Staff Requirements

Qualifications of Staff: Lead teachers are certified.
Qualifications of Administrator: Chief administrator–M.D., Behavioral Pediatrics

School Information

Brochure Available: Yes
Number of Students in Each Grade: N/A
Parochial: No; private school with Biblical teaching
Organization Affiliations: ACSI, COPSES, Orton Dyslexic Society, TANS
Accreditations: Southern Association of Colleges and Schools
Parental Involvement: Greatly encouraged
Other Information: Monthly seminars open to the public; summer school; academic testing available in summer; director speaks at various functions

Admittance

Whom to Contact: Helen B. Werner, Director
Date to Apply: New student application process begins March 1.
Testing Procedure per Age/Grade Level: In-class evaluation (pre-kindergarten–grade 1); Brigance Comprehensive Test (all other grades)
Fees Involved: $350 first-time enrollment fee; tuition
Type of Student Preferred: Students with average or above-average ability or potential
Forms Required: Previous test scores (within the last two years)
Individual/Group Appointments: Individual
Notification Procedure: By letter after board approval
Waiting List Policy: Ongoing

Tuition

Approximate Tuition for 1996-97 School Year: Prekindergarten and kindergarten–$7000; grades 1-8–$8200; mainstream grades 1-2–$3500
Methods of Payment Available: 10 monthly payments (June 1–March 1)
Financial Assistance Offered: Yes
Cancellation Insurance Available: No
Profit/Non-profit: Non-profit

Additional Costs

Books/Bag/Uniform: Uniforms required
Lunch Fee: Optional Friday hot lunch $2
Parents Club Dues: $15
Annual Fund Drive: Parent participation encouraged
Discount for Siblings: Yes, at discretion of Board

Facilities/Services Provided

Computer Lab: Yes
Library: Yes
Snack Procedures: Mid-morning and 2:00 p.m. apple break; students bring fruit from home.
After-school Care Program Available: No
Before-school Care Program Available: No
Nurse on Staff: No
Emergency Procedure Used: (1) Contact parent for instructions; (2) call family doctor
Transportation to and from School: None
Counseling and Evaluation Available: Please call

Graduation Information

Testing: N/A
Average SAT Scores: N/A
High School Our Students Usually Attend: Depends on the student's needs
Percentage of Seniors Attending College: N/A

Additional Information

Parent in-service meetings are held five times each year (in addition to scheduled conferences) to further coordinate home and school for the benefit of the student.

Meadowview School

2419 Franklin
Mesquite, TX 75150
(214) 289-1831

Mapsco: 49A-F

Fax: (214) 289-8730

Office Hours: 8:00 a.m.–4:00 p.m.
School Hours: 8:00 a.m.–3:00 p.m.
School Grades Offered: Grades 1–8
Enrollment: 60
Co-ed: Yes
Boy/Girl Ratio: 45:15
Student/Teacher Ratio: 10:1
Average Class Size: 10
Calendar School Year: August–May
Holidays: Labor Day, Fair Day, Thanksgiving, Christmas,
spring break, Good Friday, other special days
Uniform Requirements: Yes
Founded in: 1983

Philosophy of School

Meadowview School provides a full academic program for intelligent students with
learning disabilities. Meadowview recognizes and stresses the uniqueness of each
student within an environment that continually affirms the worth and diversity of all
students. A student is allowed to progress at his/her own rate and receives instruction
suited to the student's learning style.

Academic Curriculum

Content: Multisensory teaching techniques with skills taught in a
developmental sequence
Grading System Used: Report cards issued each six weeks
Conferences per Year: Minimum of two
Tests Administered: Developmental testing in academic areas and annual
achievement tests
Homework Policy: Students who fail to complete homework are sent to a

special study hall and required to complete the assignment.
Method of Discipline: "Guidelines for Addressing Inappropriate Student Behavior" are available for review.

Enrichment Curriculum
Computer classes are provided for all grades.

Extracurricular Activities
All seventh- and eighth-grade girls are cheerleaders and play competitive volleyball and softball. All seventh- and eighth-grade boys participate in competitive soccer, basketball, and softball.

Goals for Students
Meadowview School strives to provide an educational program to help students become productive, responsible citizens who believe in themselves and desire to grow academically, socially, and emotionally.

Faculty/Staff Requirements
Qualifications of Staff: Most certified in learning disabilities with many years of teaching experience
Qualifications of Administrator: Master's degree in education with certifications in learning and language disabilities

School Information
Brochure Available: Yes
Number of Students in Each Grade: Approximately 10 in each classroom
Parochial: No
Organization Affiliations: No
Accreditations: ASESA
Parental Involvement: Very strong, active parent-teacher organization
Other Information:

Admittance
Whom to Contact: Beverly Presley, Director of Meadowview School
Date to Apply: March 1
Testing Procedure per Age/Grade Level: Available at any time
Fees Involved: Diagnostic evaluations $150–$425
Type of Student Preferred: Students with average to above-average

intelligence who have specific learning disabilities
Forms Required: Yes
Individual/Group Appointments: Individual
Notification Procedure: Varies
Waiting List Policy: Waiting lists for some grades; applications considered in order received

Tuition

Approximate Tuition for 1996-97 School Year: $6950 (discounted if paid in full by August 1)
Methods of Payment Available: Ten payments of $695 if paid monthly
Financial Assistance Offered: Partial scholarships available on a limited basis; award based on financial need
Cancellation Insurance Available: No
Profit/Non-profit: Non-profit

Additional Costs

Books/Bag/Uniform: Books and bag–n/a; uniforms cost approximately $100; seventh- and eighth-grade students also buy physical-education uniforms.
Lunch Fee: Approximately $20 per month
Parents Club Dues: $3 annually
Annual Fund Drive: Yes; currently in the process of establishing one
Discount for Siblings: No

Facilities/Services Provided

Computer Lab: Yes
Library: Yes
Snack Procedures: Inquire with Meadowview
Before-school Care Program Available: No
After-school Care Program Available: No
Nurse on Staff: No
Emergency Procedure Used: Medical release forms are signed by parents so medical treatment can be obtained; first aid available at school or on school vans
Transportation to and from School: No
Counseling and Evaluation Available: Yes

Graduation Information

Testing: N/A
Average SAT Scores: N/A
High School Your Students Usually Attend: N/A
Percentage of Seniors Attending College: N/A

The Notre Dame of Dallas Schools, Inc.

2018 Allen Street
Dallas, TX 75204
(214) 720-3911

Mapsco: 45B

Fax: (214) 720-3913

Office Hours: 8:00 a.m.–4:00 p.m.
School Hours: 8:30 a.m.–3:00 p.m.
School Grades Offered: Ungraded; ages 3–21
Enrollment: 100
Co-ed: Yes
Boy/Girl Ratio: 3:2
Student/Teacher Ratio: 5:1
Average Class Size: 8
Calendar School Year: August–May
Holidays: Traditional school holidays
Uniform Requirements: No
Founded in: 1963

Philosophy of School

The mission of Notre Dame School is twofold: to provide quality, individualized education to students with mental disabilitites and to maximize their integration into society.

Academic Curriculum

Content: Academics; vocational skills
Grading System Used: Individual Educational Progress (IEP), progress reports, and portfolio assessment
Conferences per Year: Two
Tests Administered: Yes
Homework Policy: Depends on class
Method of Discipline: N/A

Enrichment Curriculum
No specific programs listed

Extracurricular Activities
Dances, plays, field trips, Special Olympics Track and Field, bowling team, Saturday Social Program

Goals for Students
The Notre Dame of Dallas Schools believe each student is a unique individual who should have the opportunity to develop his/her fullest potential academically, vocationally, and socially.

Faculty/Staff Requirements
Qualifications of Staff: Certified in special education
Qualifications of Administrator: Master's degree in special education and 20 years' experience with special-needs population

School Information
Brochure Available: Yes
Number of Students in Each Grade: Ungraded
Parochial: No
Organization Affiliations: NAPSEC, CEC
Accreditations: Texas Catholic Conference Education Department (TCCED); approved by TEA
Parental Involvement: Yes, volunteer work at school and for fundraisers
Other Information:

Admittance
Whom to Contact: Theresa Francis, Principal
Date to Apply: Thoughout the year
Testing Procedure per Age/Grade Level: Spring (students currently enrolled)
Fees Involved: $100 registration fee
Type of Student Preferred: Those with developmental disabilities
Forms Required: Placement application, medical and educational records
Individual/Group Appointments: Individual
Notification Procedure: By letter
Waiting List Policy: Ongoing

Tuition

Approximate Tuition for 1996-97 School Year: $3300
Methods of Payment Available: 10- or 12-month schedule
Financial Assistance Offered: Yes
Cancellation Insurance Available: No
Profit/Non-profit: Non-profit

Additional Costs

Books/Bag/Uniform: None
Lunch Fee: Hot lunch–$1.75; milk–$.50
Parents Club Dues: $5
Annual Fund Drive: Yes
Discount for Siblings: N/A

Facilities/Services Provided

Computer Lab: Computer lab and computers in each classroom
Library: Yes
Snack Procedures: N/A
Before-school Care Program Available: 7:30 a.m.–8:15 a.m.
After-school Care Program Available: After-school care until 6:00 p.m. for students ages 5 to 14
Nurse on Staff: No
Emergency Procedure Used: Refer to emergency card on file
Transportation to and from School: Yes
Counseling and Evaluation Available: Yes

Graduation Information

Testing: Vocational testing
Average SAT Scores: N/A
High School Our Students Usually Attend: N/A
Percentage of Seniors Attending College: N/A

Additional Information

Oak Hill Academy

6464 E. Lovers Lane
Dallas, TX 75214
(214) 368-0664

Mapsco: 36D

Fax: (214) 368-0664

Office Hours: 8:00 a.m.–4:00 p.m.
School Hours: 8:30 a.m.–3:15 p.m.
School Grades Offered: Preschool–grade 8
Enrollment: 105
Co-ed: Yes
Boy/Girl Ratio: 3:1 (varies)
Student/Teacher Ratio: 7:1
Average Class Size: 6-7 for basic skills; 10-12 in homerooms
Calendar School Year: August–May
Holidays: Labor Day, Thanksgiving, winter vacation, spring break, Memorial Day
Uniform Requirements: Yes
Founded in: 1987

Philosophy of School

Oak Hill Academy emphasizes multisensory, interactive learning experiences within a structured environment. The curriculum for basic skills, reading, writing, spelling, and math is individualized. The program also emphasizes organizational/study skills and language development. The staff offers students positive reinforcement in all activities.

Academic Curriculum

Content: Phonics-reading, language arts, computers and word processing, math, science, social studies, art, drama, physical education, study skills, language development

Grading System Used: Progress notes for all academics; report cards for grades 7 and 8

Conferences per Year: Three

431

Tests Administered: California Achievement Tests (speech-language, motor)
Homework Policy: Homework assigned for grades 1-8 four nights per week
Method of Discipline: Time out; loss of privilege; much positive reinforcement

Enrichment Curriculum

Art, drama, music

Extracurricular Activities

Sports program: soccer, basketball, softball, track

Goals for Students

Mainstream

Faculty/Staff Requirements

Qualifications of Staff: College degree; many have master's degrees and various certifications in learning disabilities, special education, academic language therapy, speech-language therapy, and adaptive physical education
Qualifications of Administrator: Executive Director–25 years in special education, master's degree, Montessori certification, certification in language disorders; Associate Director–12 years in special education, master's degree, certification in language disorders

School Information

Brochure Available: Yes
Number of Students in Each Grade: 10-12
Parochial: No
Organization Affiliations: ASESA, LDA, ODS
Accreditations: ASESA
Parental Involvement: Parents' organizaton–very active and involved
Other Information:

Admittance

Whom to Contact: Pam Quarterman or Carole Hill
Date to Apply: Anytime there are openings
Testing Procedure per Age/Grade Level: Diagnostic testing accepted from outside sources
Fees Involved: $600 registration/supply fee
Type of Student Preferred: Student with average IQ's who have language-

learning differences

Forms Required: Testing, report cards, therapy progress notes (if applicable)

Individual/Group Appointments: Individual

Notification Procedure: Telephone conference and registration packet

Waiting List Policy: Ongoing

Tuition

Approximate Tuition for 1996-97 School Year: $5400–$8100 (includes registration fee)

Methods of Payment Available: Annually, semi-annually, or monthly

Financial Assistance Offered: Limited (12 students)

Cancellation Insurance Available: No

Profit/Non-profit: Incorporated

Additional Costs

Books/Bag/Uniform: Supply list averages $14; uniform costs approximately $250

Lunch Fee: Hot-lunch program optional ($100 per semester)

Parents Club Dues: $15

Annual Fund Drive: No

Discount for Siblings: Frequently

Facilities/Services Provided

Computer Lab: Yes

Library: Yes

Snack Procedures: Preschool snacks provided; lower-school students bring a snack

Before-school Care Program Available: 8:00 a.m.–8:30 a.m. supervision

After-school Care Program Available: No (day care in area picks up)

Nurse on Staff: No

Emergency Procedure Used: Yes, outlined in staff policy manual

Transportation to and from School: Parents–many car pools

Counseling and Evaluation Available: Yes, on a limited basis

Graduation Information

Testing: N/A

Average SAT Scores: N/A

High School Our Students Usually Attend: Public and private schools

Percentage of Seniors Attending College: N/A

Preston Hollow Presbyterian Week Day School

9800 Preston Road
Dallas, TX 75230
(214) 368-3886

Mapsco: 25P

Fax: (214) 368-6312

Office Hours: 8:00 a.m.–3:45 p.m.
School Hours: 8:15 a.m.–2:45 p.m. (grades 1-3);
  8:15 a.m.–3:15 p.m. (grades 4-6)
School Grades Offered: Grades 1-6
Enrollment: 87
Co-ed: Yes
Boy/Girl Ratio: 2/3 boys, 1/3 girls
Student/Teacher Ratio: 6:1
Average Class Size: 8-9
Calendar School Year: Late August–late May
Holidays: Normal
Uniform Requirements: None
Founded in: 1962

Philosophy of School

To provide a positive, nurturing, individualized teaching approach to remediate children's weaknesses, build on their strengths, and teach them compensating skills. Ours is a structured, multisensory program geared to maximize the learning potential of bright children diagnosed with learning differences. Ours is a full academic program which addresses all aspects of grade-level curriculum.

Academic Curriculum

Content: Full academic program—multisensory in nature; our reading program is multimodal—a structured multisensory phonics program combined with a whole- word sight approach. Our instructional program also includes spelling, handwriting, process writing, English, math, science, social studies, organization and study skills, computer skills (keyboarding and word processing), perceptual motor skills, and library skills.

434

Grading System Used: Progress reports with detailed information on all skills (grades 1-4); report cards with A-F system (grades 5-6)

Conferences per Year: Three scheduled

Tests Administered: ITBS Achievement Tests and other standardized reading tests

Homework Policy: Grades 1-6 have homework Monday through Thursday nights; all students read for a specific amount of time each night.

Method of Discipline: Follow natural consequences. System with expectations for behaviors set out in advance.

Enrichment Curriculum

Art (once weekly), music (twice weekly), physical education (three times weekly), computer lab (three times weekly plus all classrooms have two computers for students to use throughout the day), drama (Artist-in-Residence Program through Dallas Children's Theatre)

Extracurricular Activities

After-school sports for fourth-grade boys and girls (soccer); fourth-, fifth-, and sixth-grade boys and girls (soccer, basketball, softball, track, and field), cub scouts, brownies, annual sixth-grade 4-day trip to Mo Ranch (Environmental Leadership Program), cheerleading for fifth- and sixth-grade girls

Goals for Students

Our school program is designed to help each child grow academically, personally, and socially. PHPS focuses on the development of improved self-esteem and interpersonal skills as well as academic skills. Our goal is to return children to the mainstream of education as quickly as possible with the necessary tools for a happy, successful experience.

Faculty/Staff Requirements

Qualifications of Staff: Degree and certification in special education with a concentration in learning disabilities

Qualifications of Administrator: M.Ed. in L.D. and E.D. and 28 years' experience in the L.D. field (21 years at Preston Hollow)

School Information

Brochure Available: Yes

Number of Students in Each Grade: 8-9

Parochial: No

Organization Affiliations: Learning Disabilities Association, Attention-Deficit Disorder Association, Texas Computer Education Association, Council for Exceptional Children (the division for learning disabilities)
Accreditations: ASESA
Parental Involvement: Very active parents' club which sponsors three parent meetings with speakers, an annual family sock hop, an annual fundraiser, a school directory publication, a school yearbook publication, a library organization, and daily cafeteria servers
Other Information:

Admittance

Whom to Contact: Sheila Phaneuf, Director; or Kay Burns, Administrative Assistant
Date to Apply: Beginning in November prior to fall semester you wish to enroll
Testing Procedure per Age/Grade Level: Each applicant interviews with the director or assistant director.
Fees Involved: None
Type of Student Preferred: Students of average or above-average intelligence who have identified learning differences
Forms Required: Copy of diagnostic testing, school records, and teacher-recommendation form
Individual/Group Appointments: Individual
Notification Procedure: By telephone or in person
Waiting List Policy: Students are placed from waiting list according to match of student with available class

Tuition

Approximate Tuition for 1996-97 School Year: $7300
Methods of Payment Available: 10 monthly payments
Financial Assistance Offered: No
Cancellation Insurance Available: No
Profit/Non-profit: Non-profit

Additional Costs

Books/Bag/Uniform: Books–no; bag–optional; uniform–no
Lunch Fee: $3.00 per day (optional); students may bring their lunches.
Parents Club Dues: Yes (optional)
Annual Fund Drive: Occasionally (optional)
Discount for Siblings: No

Facilities/Services Provided

Computer Lab: Ten MacIntosh computers (one for each child and the teacher)

Library: Full library with all books color-coded by grade-level

Snack Procedures: Provided in grade 1; others may bring nutritious snacks.

Before-school Care Program Available: No

After-school Care Program Available: No

Nurse on Staff: No

Emergency Procedure Used: Forms completed and signed by parents are kept on file and taken on all field trips and sports outings.

Transportation to and from School: School assists with information for parents to arrange car pools.

Counseling and Evaluation Available: No

Graduation Information

Testing: N/A

Average SAT Scores: N/A

High School Our Students Usually Attend: N/A

Percentage of Seniors Attending College: N/A

Additional Information

Serving Learning
Different Children
Preschool through
10th Grade

Shelton School & Evaluation Center

5002 West Lovers Lane (Grades 5–10)
Dallas, Texas 75209

9407 Midway Rd. (Grades EC–4)
Dallas, Texas 75220

(214) 352-1772   Fax 352-1851

The June Shelton School and Evaluation Center

5002 West Lovers Lane (grades 5-10)
Dallas, TX 75209
(214) 352-1772

Mapsco: 34B

Fax: (214) 352-1851

9407 Midway Rd. (grades EC-4)
Dallas, TX 75220
(214) 353-9030

Mapsco 24X

Fax: (214) 353-2711

Office Hours: 8:00 a.m.–4:00 p.m.
School Hours: 8:10 a.m.–3:20 p.m. (Monday-Thursday),
8:10 a.m.–2:20 p.m. (Friday)
School Grades Offered: Preschool–grade 10
Enrollment: 340
Co-ed: Yes
Boy/Girl Ratio: 2:1
Student/Teacher Ratio: 5:1
Average Class Size: 10
Calendar School Year: Mid-August–May
Holidays: Ten days in December/January, five days in spring
Uniform Requirements: Yes
Founded in: 1976

Philosophy of School

The June Shelton School is an independent, nonsectarian, coeducational, nonprofit school that seeks to provide excellence in education to learning-different children (preschool–grade 10). The School offers this population a full, broad-based curriculum with a strong academic orientation and a nurturing family atmosphere which considers the physical, social, emotional, and social growth of each student.

Academic Curriculum

Content: Language therapy, reading, writing, spelling, English, multisensory math, science, social studies
Grading System Used: K-3, level of mastery–grades Satisfactory or Needs Attention; grades 4-10, numerical grades and written comments; k-5, grades sent three times per year; grades 7-10, grades sent every six weeks
Conferences per Year: Three and upon request
Tests Administered: Stanford Achievement Test; individual testing/evaluation yearly
Homework Policy: Homework required at all levels
Method of Discipline:

Enrichment Curriculum

Social skills, organizational/study skills, computer, library skills, art, drama, physical education, remedial motor skills, speech-language therapy as needed, handwriting

Extracurricular Activities

Student council, intramural sports–grades 7–10 (fall–soccer, volleyball; winter–basketball; spring–field hockey, baseball, softball, track)

Goals for Students

To equip students–through a highly individualized curriculum–with skills to enable them to succeed in spite of their particular learning differences; many students develop academic skills allowing them to return to a conventional school setting.

Faculty/Staff Requirements

Qualifications of Staff: Bachelor's degree (or above) plus specialized multisensory training
Qualifications of Administrator: Master's degree and over 25 years' experience in teaching, therapy, testing, and administrative work

School Information

Brochure Available: Yes
Number of Students in Each Grade: Varies from 17 to 50
Parochial: No
Organization Affiliations: TANS, COPSES, TACLD, Orton Dyslexia Society, ALTA
Accreditations: SACS, SAIS
Parental Involvement: Parent Council, Dads' Club, parent-education courses
Other Information:

Admittance

Whom to Contact: Diann Slaton, Director of Admission–(214) 352-1772

Date to Apply: Year round if there is an opening; most apply between November and March

Testing Procedure per Age/Grade Level: Psycho-educational diagnostic testing required for grades 1 and up

Fees Involved: $50 application fee

Type of Student Preferred: Average to above-average intelligence with a diagnosed learning difference

Forms Required: Verify with school

Individual/Group Appointments: Call admissions office for information.

Notification Procedure: Within one week after a 3-day student visit; by phone call or conference

Waiting List Policy: Yes, re-apply annually

Tuition

Approximate Tuition for 1996-97 School Year: Preschool-$5450; T/1-10–$9995

Methods of Payment Available: $950 deposit due in Feb.; balance due in July

Financial Assistance Offered: Yes, limited

Cancellation Insurance Available: Yes

Profit/Non-profit: Non-profit

Additional Costs

Books/Bag/Uniform: Books–ninth graders pay additional $325 book fee; bag–no; uniform–approximately $75

Lunch Fee: Optional $3/day

Parents Club Dues: $10 per family

Annual Fund Drive: Yes

Discount for Siblings: No

Facilities/Services Provided

Computer Lab: 3 labs

Library: 2

Snack Procedures: Children bring mid-morning snacks.

Before-school Care Program Available: No

After-school Care Program Available: Yes; until 6:00 p.m.

Nurse on Staff: No

Emergency Procedure Used: Cards on file with pertinent information on each student

Transportation to and from School: No

Counseling and Evaluation Available: Yes; speech therapy also provided if needed

Graduation Information

Testing: Stanford Achievement Test; individual achievement testing
Average SAT Scores: N/A
High School Our Students Usually Attend: Bishop Lynch, Lutheran High School, First Baptist
Percentage of Seniors Attending College: N/A

Additional Information

The June Shelton School and Evaluation Center provides assessment services for the comprehensive evaluation and referral of children, youth, and adults.

Children (from age three) and adults are evaluated to establish a developmental learning and behavioral profile which includes measures of intellectual ability, pre-academic and academic achievement, sensory function, perceptual-motor integration, and personality indicators.

The June Shelton and Evaluation Center frequently sees students with the following learning conditions:

1. Dyslexia
2. Attention deficit disorder (ADD) (with or without hyperactivity)
3. Neurological impairment
4. Maturational lag (social or emotional)
5. Generalized (cognitive or physical) development lag

The Shelton Speech, Language, and Hearing Clinic, a division of the June Shelton School and Evaluation Center, serves adults and children in need of evaluation and therapy for difficulties with: articulation, fluency, voice, and language. For those experiencing hearing problems, we also provide audiological evaluations and referrals. Speech and language therapists at both campuses work with Shelton students who need this service.

Students enrolled at Shelton benefit from both of the above centers. The Director of the Evaluation Center is available for "spot" testing during the school year when teachers feel it would be helpful and appropriate. The services of the Speech, Language, and Hearing Clinic are also available. A full-time professional staff member works with Shelton students daily.

Both of these resources are available to Shelton students at no additional cost.

Sycamore School, Inc.

3400 Charleston Ave.
Fort Worth, TX 76123
(817) 292-3434

Mapsco: 103R

Fax: (817) 294-9420

Office Hours: 8:00 a.m.–4:00 p.m.
School Hours: 8:30 a.m.–3:30 p.m.
School Grades Offered: Kindergarten–grade 12
Enrollment: 45
Co-ed: Yes
Boy/Girl Ratio: 4:1
Student/Teacher Ratio: 10:1
Average Class Size: 10
Calendar School Year: September–July 15
Holidays: Same as public school's
Uniform Requirements: Khaki skirts/slacks and white shirts
Founded in: 1986

Philosophy of School
We want your child to know the rewards and enjoyment of learning.

Academic Curriculum
Content: Reading, math, English, science, social studies
Grading System Used: E (excellent); S (satisfactory); N (needs improvement); U (unsatisfactory); I (incomplete) for grades K-6; number grades (based on 100 percent) for grades 7-12
Conferences per Year: Three scheduled; more as needed
Tests Administered: Stanford Achievement Tests given in spring
Homework Policy: 30-45 minutes Monday-Thursday; none on weekends
Method of Discipline: Incentives (points) earned and spent by students; time out and/or losing points for consequences

444

Enrichment Curriculum
Fine arts, computer, physical education

Extracurricular Activities
Field trips and recreational activities arranged by individual staff

Goals for Students
To complete high school diploma with necessary skills to enter workplace or college

Faculty/Staff Requirements
Qualifications of Staff: Bachelor's degree minimum; most are certified Texas teachers.
Qualifications of Administrator: B.A. in Elementary Education with endorsement in learning disabilities; M.S., R.N.; 15 years business and administrative experience

School Information
Brochure Available: Yes
Number of Students in Each Grade: Approximately 5
Parochial: No
Organization Affiliations: Private-school consortium
Accreditations: SACS
Parental Involvement: Volunteer assistance
Other Information: Summer six weeks open to any student

Admittance
Whom to Contact: Beverly Erskine, Director
Date to Apply: All year
Testing Procedure per Age/Grade Level: Skill testing done by individual instructors
Fees Involved: $25
Type of Student Preferred: ADD, learning disabilities, general academic problems, dyslexia
Forms Required: Application, health, academic and testing records
Individual/Group Appointments: Individual
Notification Procedure: Phone
Waiting List Policy: Ongoing

Tuition

Approximate Tuition for 1996-97 School Year: $5500
Methods of Payment Available: Monthly
Financial Assistance Offered: Yes
Cancellation Insurance Available: No
Profit/Non-profit: Non-profit

Additional Costs

Books/Bag/Uniform: Books–$350; bag–not required; uniform–approximately $40 per outfit
Lunch Fee: No
Parents Club Dues: None
Annual Fund Drive: To be arranged
Discount for Siblings: 1/2 tuition

Facilities/Services Provided

Computer Lab: Yes; daily computer lab classes
Library: Yes; and CompuServe on computer
Snack Procedures: Morning break
Before-school Care Program Available: Yes; 7:00 a.m.
After-school Care Program Available: Yes; 6:00 p.m.
Nurse on Staff: Yes
Emergency Procedure Used: Routine fire and safety procedures
Transportation to and from School: None provided
Counseling and Evaluation Available: Limited as done by teachers and director

Graduation Information

Testing: N/A
Average SAT Scores: N/A
High School Our Students Usually Attend: Public or private
Percentage of Seniors Attending College: Unknown–percentage of graduates is small

Additional Information

Sycamore School also offers tutoring services and Irlen Screening for Dyslexia.

Vanguard Preparatory School

13750 Omega Drive
Dallas, TX 75244
(214) 404-1616

Mapsco: 14L

Fax: (214) 404-1641

Office Hours: 8:05 a.m.–4:00 p.m.
School Hours: 8:30 a.m.–3:30 p.m.
School Grades Offered: Pre-k–grade 8
Enrollment: 55
Co-ed: Yes
Boy/Girl Ratio: 7:1
Student/Teacher Ratio: 4:1
Average Class Size: 8
Calendar School Year: August 1 (year-round school)
Holidays: Traditional–year-round school
Uniform Requirements: None
Founded in: 1993

Philosophy of School

Vanguard Preparatory School serves children of normal intelligence who are
experiencing social, emotional, behavioral, or academic delays. We offer a highly
individualized program in a therapeutic milieu that emphasizes development of
academic skills, and behavioral and social abilities to build successful relationships
and foster scholastic achievement.

Academic Curriculum

Content: Based on student need; follow TEA essential elements
Grading System Used: Progress on individual objectives reported on progress
note each nine weeks
Conferences per Year: Minimum of two; frequent (daily or weekly) informal
contact
Tests Administered: Woodcock-Johnson Psycho-educational Battery (revised)
Homework Policy: Individualized; based on student need

447

Method of Discipline: Individualized (example: token system, level system); therapeutic milieu in every classroom

Enrichment Curriculum

Focus is on basic academics at child's own level; weekly language group; social skills group for elementary and preschool; daily social skills group for the middle school; weekly art therapy

Extracurricular Activities

Parents are encouraged to utilize neighborhood resources.

Goals for Students

To develop academic, social, and emotional coping skills to seek and find identity, success, and purpose

Faculty/Staff Requirements

Qualifications of Staff: College degree; certification; minimum of three years' experience

Qualifications of Administrator: Master's degree in special-education administration; minimum of five years' experience with special populations

School Information

Brochure Available: Yes
Number of Students in Each Grade: Ungraded; multi-age classrooms
Parochial: No
Organization Affiliations:
Accreditations: Association for Specialized Elementary School Accreditation
Parental Involvement: Active parent-support group
Other Information: Therapist on staff; consulting speech pathologist; occupational therapists, psychologists, and psychiatrist available; family therapy and diagnostics available

Admittance

Whom to Contact: Director–Rosalind Funderburgh, M.Ed.
Date to Apply: April 1
Testing Procedure for Age/Grade Level: Individualized
Fees Involved: $300 registration plus tuition
Type of Student Preferred: Those with learning differences, social/emotional/

or behavioral problems
Forms Required:
Individual/Group Appointments: Individual
Notification Procedure: Individual conference with parents
Waiting List Policy: After student visit, parental request

Tuition
Approximate Tuition for 1996-97 School Year: $755/month, preschool; $775/month, elementary; $1055/month, middle school
Methods of Payment Available: Annually, by semester, or monthly
Financial Assistance Offered: Limited scholarships
Cancellation Insurance Available: No
Profit/Non-profit: Profit

Additional Costs
Books/Bag/Uniform: No
Lunch Fee: $2.50 per day (optional)
Parents Club Dues: No
Annual Fund Drive: No
Discount for Siblings: No

Facilities/Services Provided
Computer Lab: One computer per 6 children
Library: Yes, small but growing
Snack Procedures: Preschool–morning and afternoon snacks; elementary–morning snacks; no refined sugar
Before-school Care Program Available: No
After-school Care Program Available: No
Nurse on Staff: No
Emergency Procedure Used: Call EMS or transport to nearest medical facility
Transportation to and from School: No
Counseling and Evaluation Available: Yes, diagnostician on staff; licensed therapist on staff

Graduation Information
Testing: N/A
Average SAT Scores: N/A
High School Our Students Usually Attend: N/A
Percentage of Seniors Attending College: N/A

Walden Preparatory School

14552 Montfort Drive
Dallas, TX 75240
(214) 233-6883

Mapsco: 15E

Fax: N/A

Office Hours: 8:00 a.m.–4:00 p.m.
School Hours: 8:30 a.m.–3:20 p.m.
School Grades Offered: Grades 9–12
Enrollment: 60–65
Co-ed: Yes
Boy/Girl Ratio: 35:25
Student/Teacher Ratio: 10:1
Average Class Size: 8-10
Calendar School Year: Traditional school calendar
Holidays: Traditional holidays
Uniform Requirements: No
Founded in: 1970

Philosophy of School

Small classes or individualized instruction with special accelerated programs

Academic Curriculum

Content: Traditional and self-paced programs
Grading System Used: A–90-100; B–80-89; C–70-79
Conferences per Year: Yes
Tests Administered: Stanford Achievement Test in October
Homework Policy: We do not believe in assigning "busy work" to occupy students' time, but classwork can be done at home.
Method of Discipline: Natural consequences of the student's actions

Enrichment Curriculum

Accelerated and college-preparatory classes

Extracurricular Activities
None

Goals for Students
High school graduation for students who might not succeed in larger school environments

Faculty/Staff Requirements
Qualifications of Staff: College degrees
Qualifications of Administrator: College degrees

School Information
Brochure Available: Yes
Number of Students in Each Grade: 9th–15; 10th–10; 11th–10; 12th–25
Parochial: No
Organization Affiliations: Southern Association of Colleges and Schools
Accreditations: Southern Association of Colleges and Schools
Parental Involvement: Parents' organization
Other Information:

Admittance
Whom to Contact: Pamela Stone
Date to Apply: Ongoing enrollment
Testing Procedure per Age/Grade Level: No testing for admission
Fees Involved: No
Type of Student Preferred: High school students seeking smaller classes and individualized approach
Forms Required: Application; high school transcripts
Individual/Group Appointments: Individual
Notification Procedure: All done during initial interview
Waiting List Policy: Not at this time

Tuition
Approximate Tuition for 1996-97 School Year: $6550
Methods of Payment Available: Monthly ($700 enrollment fee; $550 per month)
Financial Assistance Offered: None available
Cancellation Insurance Available: No
Profit/Non-profit: Non-profit

Additional Costs

Books/Bag/Uniform: No
Lunch Fee: No
Parents Club Dues: No
Annual Fund Drive: No
Discount for Siblings: No

Facilities/Services Provided

Computer Lab: Computers located in classrooms
Library: No
Snack Procedures: No
Before-school Care Program Available: No
After-school Care Program Available: No
Nurse on Staff: No
Emergency Procedure Used: Parents notified
Transportation to and from School: No
Counseling and Evaluation Available: Yes

Graduation Information

Testing: PSAT; information available on SAT and ACT
Average SAT Scores: Not available
High School Our Students Usually Attend: N/A
Percentage of Seniors Attending College: 85

Additional Information

Curriculum Alternatives

A curriculum alternative is an educational facility that implements a specialized curriculum which is unique to that school.

Academic Achievement Associates
The Carlisle School
Coughs & Cuddles - Care for Mildly Ill Children
Dallas International School (French National Ministry of Education)
The Highlander School (Carden)
Study Skills Course (SMU)
Summer Accelerated Language Training (SMU)

Academic Achievement Associates

12820 Hillcrest Road, Ste. 124
Dallas, TX 75230
(214) 490-6399

Mapsco: 15R

Fax: (214) 490-6416

Office Hours: 8:00 a.m.–6:00 p.m. plus evening tutoring or counseling appointments
School Hours: 9:00 a.m.–4:00 p.m.
School Grades Offered: Kindergarten–adult
Enrollment: Varies
Co-ed: Yes
Boy/Girl Ratio: Varies
Student/Teacher Ratio: 1:1 or small groups
Average Class Size: One-on-one
Calendar School Year: Students are treated individually; therefore, they can begin throughout the year.
Holidays: Traditional
Uniform Requirements: None
Founded in: 1985

Philosophy of School

Academic Achievement Associates is a group of teachers and counselors who work with individuals of all ages to overcome obstacles blocking them from achievement. We take students who need time out from a traditional educational setting and work with them to return to such a setting.

Academic Curriculum

Content: Everyone has an individual lesson plan.
Grading System Used: Varies with each student
Conferences per Year: As needed

Tests Administered: A complete psycho-educational is available. Other tests include WRAT, Gilmore, and Woodcock-Johnson
Homework Policy: When necessary
Method of Discipline: Varies with situation

Enrichment Curriculum
CD-Rom computers, Josten Learning Lab

Extracurricular Activities
None

Goals for Students
Our goal is to enable students to reach their greatest potential academically, socially, and emotionally.

Faculty/Staff Requirements
Qualifications of Staff: College degree; teacher certification.
Qualifications of Administrator: Teacher certification; Licensed Professional Counselor; Licensed Marriage and Family Therapist

School Information
Brochure Available: Yes
Number of Students in Each Grade: Varies
Parochial: No
Organization Affiliations: Association of Educational Therapists; Orton Dyslexia Society
Accreditations: No
Parental Involvement: Yes
Other Information: We work closely with schools for the welfare of our students. We stay informed about other schools, so we can make good referrals.

Admittance
Whom to Contact: Dorothy Baxter, M.Ed., LPC, LMFT
Date to Apply: Open
Testing Procedure per Age/Grade Level: When appropriate
Fees Involved: Varies
Type of Student Preferred: Students who have had difficulty in other schools and realize this is transitory.

Forms Required: Varies with situation
Individual/Group Appointments: Yes
Notification Procedure: N/A
Waiting List Policy: N/A

Tuition

Approximate Tuition for 1996-97 School Year: Varies with service
Methods of Payment Available: Monthly
Financial Assistance Offered: No
Cancellation Insurance Available: No
Profit/Non-profit: Profit

Additional Costs

Books/Bag/Uniform: No
Lunch Fee: No
Parents Club Dues:
Annual Fund Drive:
Discount for Siblings:

Facilities/Services Provided

Computer Lab: Josten Educational CD-ROM software
Library:
Snack Procedures: Vending machines, snack bar
Before-school Care Program Available: No
After-school Care Program Available: No
Nurse on Staff: No
Emergency Procedure Used: Parents notified
Transportation to and from School: No
Counseling and Evaluation Available: Yes

Graduation Information

Testing:
Average SAT Scores: N/A
High School Our Students Usually Attend:
Percentage of Seniors Attending College:

Additional Information

Our facility combines the hand-in-hand disciplines of education and counseling. High school students are able to receive a high school diploma through the Texas Tech guided education program.

The Carlisle School

4705 W. Lovers Lane
Dallas, TX 75209
(214) 351-1833

Mapsco: 34B

Fax: (214) 351-1833

Office Hours: 7:30 a.m.–5:45 p.m.
School Hours: Before-school care: 7:30 a.m.–9:00 a.m.; class:
9:00 a.m.–3:00 p.m.; after-school care: 3:00 p.m.–6:00 p.m.
School Grades Offered: Pre-kindergarten–kindergarten
Enrollment: 17
Co-ed: Yes
Boy/Girl Ratio: Equal
Student/Teacher Ratio: Age 2: 4/1; age 3: 6/1; others: 10/1
Average Class Size: Ratio determined
Calendar School Year: Year-round program: September–May;
June–August
Holidays: Labor Day, Thanksgiving, winter break, spring break
(day care provided), Independence Day, Memorial Day
Uniform Requirements: Yes
Founded in: 1979

Philosophy of School

The Carlisle School provides a caring environment for the learning process which
serves each child individually as a bridge between home and the more institutional
structures of both private and public elementary schools. We use our combined 50
years of teaching to rise above the current stagnation in American education. In short,
we are grounded in the traditional values of education.

Academic Curriculum

Content: Full academic program with enrichment in music, theater, visual arts
Grading System Used: No grades; each child's work is individually critiqued.
Conferences per Year: We maintain an open-door policy; parents consult as
needed.

457

Tests Administered: Individualized evaluation of reading, writing, math skills
Method of Discipline: If necessary, a child is instructed to sit aside during an activity in which he/she is being disruptive

Enrichment Curriculum

In addition to music appreciation and theatrical expression, regular field trips to museums, galleries; outdoor activities included; bilingual, multicultural instruction throughout program

Extracurricular Activities

Ballet, gymnastics, fencing for older children; summer program in opera and ballet for older children

Goals for Students

Each Carlisle student should leave us fully prepared to overcome the situation posed by the generally mediocre educational system in this country; we want children to read for enjoyment and to study for the same reason.

Faculty/Staff Requirements

Qualifications of Staff: College degree, Montessori training
Qualifications of Administrator: B.A., M.A., Ph.D. degrees; 30+ years of experience

School Information

Brochure Available: Yes, call 351-1833
Number of Students in Each Grade: Age 2, 7; age 3, 8; ages 4–6, 19
Parochial: No
Organization affiliations:
Accreditations:
Parental involvement:

Admittance

Whom to Contact: Dr. Richard Carlisle
Date to Apply: Open applications, year-round
Testing Procedure per Age/Grade Level: By interview; we do not "screen" potential students.
Fees involved: Admission: $150; paper fee: $75
Type of Student Preferred:

Forms Required: Health certificate, application form, enrollment agreement
Individual/Group Appointments: By telephone: 351-1833
Notification Procedure: Personal notification
Waiting List Policy: Depends upon level of entry

Tuition

Approximate Tuition for 1996-97 School Year: Partial, $400/month; academic only, $425/month; full, $450/month
Method of Payment Available: Annually (discounted); semester (discounted); monthly
Financial Assistance Offered: Occasional scholarships available
Profit/Non-profit: Non-profit

Additional Costs

Books/Bag/Uniform: Uniforms–girls: $30; boys: $20 (approximate costs); diapering fee: $50/month
Lunch Fee:
Parents Club Dues:
Annual Fund Drive: N/A
Discount for Siblings: 10%

Facilities/Services Provided

Computer Lab: No computers
Library: Yes
Snack Procedures: Before school, at 3:00 p.m., and at 5:00 p.m.
Before-school Care Program Available: 7:30 a.m.–9:00 a.m.
After-school Care Program Available: 3:00 p.m.–6:00 p.m.
Nurse on Staff:
Emergency Procedure Used: Parent/guardian called immediately
Transportation to and from School: Available within immediate area
Counseling and Evaluation Available: Yes

Graduation Information

Testing: N/A
Average SAT Scores: N/A
High School Our Students Usually Attend: N/A
Percentage of Seniors Attending College: N/A

Additional Information

Challenging programs in reading, social studies, humanities, and math for grades K through 6, June–August each summer; Spanish throughout curriculum

Coughs and Cuddles Care for Mildly ill Children

6120 West Parker Rd.
Plano, TX 75093
(214) 608-8585

Mapsco: 655F

Fax: (214) 608-8587

Office Hours: 6:30 a.m.–5:00 p.m.
School Hours: 6:30 a.m.–7:30 p.m
School Grades Offered: 6 weeks–16 years
Enrollment: N/A
Co-ed: N/A
Boy/Girl Ratio: N/A
Student/Teacher Ratio: N/A
Average Class Size: N/A
Calendar School Year: N/A
Holidays: N/A
Uniform Requirements: N/A
Founded in: N/A

Philosophy of School
N/A

Academic Curriculum
Content: N/A
Grading System Used: N/A
Conferences per Year: N/A
Tests Administered: N/A
Homework Policy: N/A
Method of Discipline: N/A

Enrichment Curriculum
N/A

Extracurricular Activities
N/A

Goals for Students
N/A

Faculty/Staff Requirements
Qualifications of Staff: Teacher and nurse–college degrees
Qualifications of Administrator: College degree

School Information
Brochure Available: Yes
Number of Students in Each Grade: N/A
Parochial: N/A
Organization Affiliations: N/A
Accreditations: N/A
Parental Involvement: N/A
Other Information: N/A

Admittance
Whom to Contact: Misti Kester
Date to Apply: As needed
Testing Procedure for Age/Grade Level: N/A
Fees Involved: N/A
Type of Student Preferred: N/A
Forms Required: N/A
Individual/Group Appointments: N/A
Notification Procedure: N/A
Waiting List Policy: N/A

Tuition
Approximate Tuition for 1996-97 School Year: $4 per hour; $32 per day
Methods of Payment Available: Cash, check, credit cards–Visa, MasterCard, American Express, Discover
Financial Assistance Offered: N/A

Cancellation Insurance Available: N/A
Profit/Non-profit: N/A

Additional Costs

Books/Bag/Uniform: N/A
Lunch Fee: None
Parents Club Dues: N/A
Annual Fund Drive: N/A
Discount for Siblings: N/A

Facilities/Services Provided

Computer Lab: N/A
Library: N/A
Snack Procedures: N/A
Before-school Care Program Available: N/A
After-school Care Program Available: N/A
Nurse on Staff: Yes
Emergency Procedure Used: N/A
Transportation to and from School: N/A
Counseling and Evaluation Available: N/A

Graduation Information

Testing: N/A
Average SAT Scores: N/A
High School Our Students Usually Attend: N/A
Percentage of Seniors Attending College: N/A

Additional Information

If your child isn't feeling well or has an injury that prevents attendance at a regular childcare facility, call Coughs and Cuddles at Presbyterian Hospital of Plano. We provide a warm, comfortable atmosphere where your child can receive attention from nurses and other trained childcare providers.

Dallas International School

6039 Churchill Way
Dallas, TX 75230
(214) 991-6379

Mapsco: 25G

Fax: (214) 991-6608

Office Hours: 7:30 a.m.–5:00 p.m.
School Hours: 8:30 a.m.–3:30 p.m.
School Grades Offered: Preschool–12
Enrollment: 200
Co-ed: Yes
Boy/Girl Ratio: Varies by grade level
Student/Teacher Ratio: 10:1
Average Class Size: 15
Calendar School Year: End of August–mid-June
Holidays: One-week vacation every eight weeks;
American holidays
Uniform Requirements: Yes
Founded in: 1987

Philosophy of School

Dallas International School seeks to provide an excellent education based on French-American biculturalism. Meeting people of different nationalities teaches students to respect others and gives them a broad perspective of the world from an early age. Our work is guided primarily by secular and humanistic ideals. Based on biculturalism, our program brings young people of different races and nationalities together and prepares them for the future.

Academic Curriculum

Content: Bilingual curriculum (French-English)
Grading System Used: French
Conferences per Year: Four
Tests Administered: Yes
Homework Policy: Homework given to be corrected in class; extra curricular

464

workshops available after school for homework assistance
Method of Discipline: Time-outs for younger grades; detention for older students

Enrichment Curriculum
Remedial tutoring; continuing education classes

Extracurricular Activities
Sports, computers, drama, oil painting, ballet, tennis, orchestra, choir

Goals for Students
To be well prepared for tomorrow's world of international affairs

Faculty/Staff Requirements
Qualifications of Staff: French instructors must meet French qualifications; American teachers must have degrees.
Qualifications of Administrator: Certified by the French National Ministry of Education

School Information
Brochure Available: Yes
Number of Students in Each Grade: Varies
Parochial: No
Organization Affiliations: Dallas Accueil Le Cercle Francais, American Association of Teachers of French, Mission Laique Francais, French-American Chamber of Commerce, Greater Dallas Chamber of Commerce, Hispanic Chamber of Commerce, AFSA (American French Schools Association)
Accreditations: French National Ministry of Education
Parental Involvement: Yes (encouraged and appreciated)
Other Information: Tours of school available by appointment

Admittance
Whom to Contact: Jeanne Jeannin
Date to Apply: As soon as possible; students are accepted on a space-available basis.
Testing Procedure per Age/Grade Level: Yes
Fees Involved: $130 registration fee due after student is accepted
Type of Student Preferred: Students with a strong desire to become bilingual

and multicultural
Forms Required: Yes
Individual/Group Appointments: Individual
Notification Procedure: By telephone
Waiting List Policy: Ongoing

Tuition

Approximate Tuition for 1996-97 School Year: $2500 (preschool); $4800 (grade school); $5700 (high school)
Methods of Payment Available: Yearly or monthly
Financial Assistance Offered: Yes, to French citizens
Cancellation Insurance Available: No
Profit/Non-profit: Non-profit

Additional Costs

Books/Bag/Uniform: Books ($100 per student); bag required; uniform ($85)
Lunch Fee: $12.50/week (preschool); $15/week (grade school); $17.50/week (high school)
Parents Club Dues: Yes, $25 per family
Annual Fund Drive: Yes
Discount for Siblings: No

Facilities/Services Provided

Computer Lab: Computers with both French and English software
Library: Multi-language library for all grades
Snack Procedures: Scheduled snack times for preschool students
Before-school Care Program Available: Yes (7:30 a.m.–8:30 a.m.)
After-school Care Program Available: Yes (4:00 p.m.–6:00 p.m.)
Nurse on Staff: No–teachers and staff are trained in CPR and certified in first aid.
Emergency Procedure Used: Contact parents or call 911
Transportation to and from School: Parents
Counseling and Evaluation Available: Yes

Graduation Information

Testing: Yes
Average SAT Scores: N/A
High School Our Students Usually Attend: N/A
Percentage of Seniors Attending College: N/A

Additional Information

Dallas International School offers adult language classes throughout the year and summer language classes.

The Highlander School

9120 Plano Road
Dallas, TX 75238
(214) 348-3220

Mapsco: 28J

Fax: N/A

Office Hours: 8:00 a.m.–4:00 p.m.
School Hours: 8:15 a.m.–3:15 a.m.
School Grades Offered: Pre-K through grade 6
Enrollment: 300+
Co-ed: Yes
Boy/Girl Ratio: 50:50
Student/Teacher Ratio: 8:1–20:1
Average Class Size: 17
Calendar School Year: August–May
Holidays: Same as R.I.S.D.
Uniform Requirements: Yes
Founded in: 1966

Philosophy of School

It is a wise teacher who makes learning a joy, but an even wiser one who makes each of God's children feel special.

Academic Curriculum

Content: Carden Curriculum-whole language approach that integrates spelling, reading, language, and social studies
Grading System Used: Grade 1(S,I,U); grades 2 and 3 (A,B,C); grades 4, 5, and 6 (70–100)
Conferences per Year: Two
Tests Administered: ITBS
Homework Policy: According to grade level
Method of Discipline: Conference with parents

Enrichment Curriculum

Art appreciation, newspaper done by fourth, fifth, and sixth graders, computers, plays (Christmas play and spring program)

Extracurricular Activities

Parent-sponsored activities in soccer, baseball, and basketball; field trips during school hours; field day (k-6 grade)

Goals for Students

To experience success

Faculty/Staff Requirements

Qualifications of Staff: Minimum of bachelor's degree with additional Carden Curriculum training
Qualifications of Administrator: Ph.D. in Elementary Education and Computer Science

School Information

Brochure Available: Yes
Number of Students in Each Grade: PK II–8; PK I–12; K–18; E–20
Parochial: No
Organization Affiliations: ACSD, ATE, TATE, and Phi Delta Kappa
Accreditations: Carden
Parental Involvement: Parents' Club
Other Information:

Admittance

Whom to Contact: Betty G. Woodring, Ph.D.
Date to Apply: After January 1
Testing Procedure per Age/Grade Level: K (learning styles); grades 1–6 (ITBS)
Fees Involved: $35–$50
Type of Student Preferred: Those with parents interested in education
Forms Required: Health, enrollment, directory, emergency form, field trip form
Individual/Group Appointments: Both
Notification Procedure: Phone call
Waiting List Policy: Annually

Tuition

Approximate Tuition for 1996-97 School Year: Grades 1-3, $3300;
grades 4-6, $3400
Methods of Payment Available: Yearly, by semester, or monthly
Financial Assistance Offered: No
Cancellation Insurance Available: No
Profit/Non-profit: Profit

Additional Costs

Books/Bag/Uniform: Books and supplies ($200);
uniform (approximately $50–$75)
Lunch Fee: Yes
Parents Club Dues: None
Annual Fund Drive: Carnival, Parents' Club
Discount for Siblings: Yes

Facilities/Services Provided

Computer Lab: Yes; Macintosh computers, one computer per child
Library: Yes; scheduled library period for each class
Snack Procedures: School provides for pre-kindergarten and kindergarten, not
for elementary students
Before-school Care Program Available: No
After-school Care Program Available: No
Nurse on Staff: No
Emergency Procedure Used: Refer to parent's emergency form and release
Transportation to and from School: No
Counseling and Evaluation Available: Yes

Graduation Information

Testing: N/A
Average SAT Scores: N/A
High School Our Students Usually Attend: Lake Highlands High School
Percentage of Seniors Attending College: N/A

Additional Information

Study Skills Course

Southern Methodist University
6404 Airline, P.O. Box 750384
Dallas, TX 75275-0384
(214) 768-2223

Mapsco: 35H

Fax: (214) 768-1071

Office Hours: 8:30 a.m.–5:00 p.m.
School Hours: Scheduled classes
School Grades Offered: For students entering grades 7–12
Enrollment: 12 per session (maximum)
Co-ed: Yes
Boy/Girl Ratio: N/A
Student/Teacher Ratio: 12:1
Average Class Size: 12
Calendar School Year: Classes scheduled in summer, fall, spring
Holidays: N/A
Uniform Requirements: N/A
Founded in: 1994 (this particular class offering)

Philosophy of School

Study skills and learning strategies are offered to assist students in developing their academic potential. Many students limit their progress in school because of their disorganization, poor study habits, and/or inability to work with teachers. This course addresses these problems.

Academic Curriculum

Content: Skills in organization, listening, note-taking, class participation, textbook study, test prep, working with teachers, developing good study habits
Grading System Used: N/A
Conferences per Year: Group parent meeting
Tests Administered: N/A

471

Homework Policy: N/A
Method of Discipline: Student signs a contract.

Enrichment Curriculum
N/A

Extracurricular Activities
N/A

Goals for Students
N/A

Faculty/Staff Requirements
Qualifications of Staff: Certified academic language therapists with study-skills training
Qualifications of Administrator: M.Ed., certified academic language therapist

School Information
Brochure Available: Yes
Number of Students in Each Grade: 12 in each class (maximum)
Parochial: No
Organization Affiliations: N/A
Accreditations: N/A
Parental Involvement: N/A
Other Information:

Admittance
Whom to Contact: Pam Leutz
Date to Apply: January, May, September
Testing Procedure for Age/Grade Level: N/A
Fees Involved: $100 deposit
Type of Student Preferred: Student who is not reaching academic potential because of disorganization or a lack of effective study skills
Forms Required: Registration form
Individual/Group Appointments: Group meeting for parents
Notification Procedure: Letter sent to verify student is in class.
Waiting List Policy: If class is full, student is put on next class list after parents are notified.

Tuition

Approximate Tuition for 1996-97 School Year: Class tuition–$245 (includes materials)
Methods of Payment Available: Visa, Master Card, check, cash
Financial Assistance Offered: No
Cancellation Insurance Available: No
Profit/Non-profit: Non-profit

Additional Costs

Books/Bag/Uniform: Supplies included in tuition
Lunch Fee: N/A
Parents Club Dues: N/A
Annual Fund Drive: N/A
Discount for Siblings: N/A

Facilities/Services Provided

Computer Lab: N/A
Library: N/A
Snack Procedures: 15-minute break to use snack machines
Before-school Care Program Available: No
After-school Care Program Available: No
Nurse on Staff: No
Emergency Procedure Used: Health center
Transportation to and from School: N/A
Counseling and Evaluation Available: N/A

Graduation Information

Testing: N/A
Average SAT Scores: N/A
High School Our Students Usually Attend: N/A
Percentage of Seniors Attending College: N/A

Additional Information

Summer Accelerated Language Training

Southern Methodist University
6404 Airline, P.O. Box 750384
Dallas, TX 75275-0384
(214) 768-2223

Mapsco: 35H

Fax: (214) 768-1071

Office Hours: 8:50 a.m.–5:00 p.m.
School Hours: Sessions scheduled for 6 weeks each summer
School Grades Offered: For students entering grades 6–12
Enrollment: Approximately 30
Co-ed: Yes
Boy/Girl Ratio: 2:1
Student/Teacher Ratio: 8:1 maximum
Average Class Size: 6
Calendar School Year: 6 weeks beginning the first week in June
Holidays: Independence Day
Uniform Requirements: N/A
Founded in: 1985

Philosophy of School

Many capable learners who are not reaching their academic potential in the written-language areas can be helped by a fast-paced course that will strengthen their basic skills. Summer Accelerated Language Training (SALT) is designed to establish an academic foundation using a structured, sequential, phonetic, multisensory, Orton-Gillingham approach that emphasizes reading, word attack, handwriting, spelling, and strategies for reading comprehension and written composition.

Academic Curriculum

Content: Accelerated Orton-Gillingham presentations in reading, handwriting, and spelling

474

Grading System Used: Individual conference with student and parent
Conferences per Year: Initial group meeting with parents to introduce the course goals; final individual conference with student and parent to discuss course progress and make academic suggestions
Tests Administered: Bench Mark measure administered in student orientation and during final week of course
Homework Policy: 10-15 minutes Monday-Thursday
Method of Discipline: Students sign a behavioral contract.

Enrichment Curriculum
N/A

Extracurricular Activities
N/A

Goals for Students
The goal of the curriculum is for students to strengthen their basic written language skills as they continue secondary education.

Faculty/Staff Requirements
Qualifications of Staff: Experienced, certified academic language therapists
Qualifications of Administrator: M.Ed. with Reading Specialization, certified academic language therapist

School Information
Brochure Available: Yes
Number of Students in Each Grade: Students are usually placed with classmates within two years of age.
Parochial: N/A
Organization Affiliations: N/A
Accreditations: N/A
Parental Involvement: N/A
Other Information:

Admittance
Whom to Contact: Pam Leutz, Administrative Coordinator
Date to Apply: Applications preferred by April for grouping
Testing Procedure for Age/Grade Level: Bench Mark level for reading and

spelling taken at student orientation and during final week of course
Fees Involved: $100 application fee (refundable by June 1)
Type of Student Preferred: Capable learner who is not reaching academic potential primarily in the written-language area
Forms Required: Application
Individual/Group Appointments:
Notification Procedure:
Waiting List Policy: Re-apply annually

Tuition

Approximate Tuition for 1996-97 School Year: $750
Methods of Payment Available: Visa, Master Card, check, cash
Financial Assistance Offered: N/A
Cancellation Insurance Available: N/A
Profit/Non-profit: Non-profit

Additional Costs

Books/Bag/Uniform: Supplies included in tuition
Lunch Fee: Students may bring money for snack machines.
Parents Club Dues: N/A
Annual Fund Drive: N/A
Discount for Siblings: N/A

Facilities/Services Provided

Computer Lab: N/A
Library: N/A
Snack Procedures: Students have a 15-minute break during two-hour class to use snack machines.
Before-school Care Program Available: No
After-school Care Program Available: No
Nurse on Staff: No
Emergency Procedure Used: University clinic
Transportation to and from School: No
Counseling and Evaluation Available: No

Graduation Information

Testing: N/A
Average SAT Scores: N/A
High School Our Students Usually Attend: N/A
Percentage of Seniors Attending College: N/A

DALLAS MONTESSORI TEACHER PROGRAMS

offered through El Centro
College Continuing Education

- **Pre-Primary**
  3–6 years

- **Elementary**
  6–9 years
  9–12 years

The Dallas Montessori Teacher Programs are designed to educate private and public school teachers in Montessori strategies and philosophy.

Dr. Maria Montessori insisted that the purpose of education is LIFE. In accordance with this principle, the Dallas Montessori Teachers Program prepares teachers to assist children in the development of the human mind through academic and aesthetic study, and the development of social skills in preparation for their roles in society.

- *Classes begin in June*   • *Fall evening classes also available*

For additional information, call or write:
Directors: James and Dina Paulik
Dallas Montessori Teacher Programs

5757 Samuell Blvd. Dallas, TX 75228
(214) 388-0091   Fax: (214) 388-3415

All classes are held at Dallas Montessori Academy.

Affiliated with the American Montessori Society and accredited by the Montessori Accreditation Council for Teacher Education. Educational opportunities are offered by the Dallas County Community College District without regard to race, color, age, national origin, religion, sex, or disability.

477

Montessori Schools

What is the Montessori method?

1. The method is a means of scientific assistance to the total development of the child: social, intellectual, psychic, physical. Academic development is not a concern of the method, for it follows naturally in the child who has the experiences essential to the fulfillment of the aforementioned aspects of development.

2. The environment is carefully prepared so that the child's sense of order is fulfilled by having a special place for each item, with apparatus arranged in categories. There are no distracting decorations or excess materials to clutter the room.

3. Activities with scientifically designed learning apparatus take place in the "prepared environment." Use of these didactic materials is demonstrated by the teacher to each child individually. Once a demonstration has been given, self-teaching is possible as the child uses the apparatus which has built-in control of error, allowing self-correction. There are special materials for care of the environment (practical life), education of the senses, language (reading, grammar, vocabulary), mathematics, geography, history, handwork, natural and experimental science.

4. Concentration develops through work with the hands, leading to self-discipline and independence through self-direction. "Normalization" is the term used by Montessori.

5. There is freedom of choice within well-defined limits. The child may choose to:
    - work alone or with others
    - select any activity after a lesson has been given
    - continue an activity as long as desired with any material
    - pursue a wide range of activities according to individual interests and needs
    - socialize with children of several ages
    - exercise self-discipline in an atmosphere of trust and faith in the child
    - solve his/her own problems
    - meet challenges through the exercise of independence and self-reliance which enhances the development of exercise self-esteem.

What are the goals of Montessori education?

The proper application of Montessori's method permits the child to develop a positive self-concept, self-discipline, respect for others, respect for the environment, and to maintain the innate natural love of learning.

What are the qualities of the ideal Montessori teacher?

The teacher knows Montessori's principles of child development as well as those of other major theorists; understands the uses, purposes and sequences of materials in all areas of learning; observes objectively to be able to give the appropriate lesson at the proper time; presents short, interesting lessons and demonstrations; sets appropriate limits and always enforces them equally; provides beautiful learning materials and maintains the simple, orderly environment; respects the personal dignity of each child; and displays a sense of humility, keeping one's own personality in abeyance.

What are the characteristics of Montessori education?

1. Learning is active, not passive.

2. Teacher control is replaced by the child's self-control.

3. The natural interests of each child are followed rather than subjecting an entire class to a pre-determined syllabus or daily lesson plan.

4. Acquisition of teacher-determined facts by rote memory is replaced by understanding of concepts through work with the Montessori learning materials.

5. Montessori education is concerned with the total development of each individual child rather than accenting academic achievement.

Jane Dutcher
President
Montessori Educators International, Inc.
P.O. Box 143
Cordova, TN 38018

Montessori schools included in this text are listed below:

A Child's Garden Montessori
Branch Schools
Dallas Montessori Academy

The Dallas North Montessori School
East Dallas Community School
Good Shepherd Montessori
Highland Meadow Montessori Academy
The Hillcrest Academy (preschool only, see TDPRS)
Lakemont Academy (see SACS)
Meadowbrook Private School
Montessori Children's House and School, Inc.
Montessori Episcopal School
Montessori of Las Colinas
Montessori School of North Dallas
Montessori School of Park Cities
Montessori School–Pleasant Grove
Montessori School of Westchester
Redeemer Montessori School
The St. Alcuin Montessori School
St. James Episcopal Montessori School
Treetops School International (see SACS)
Trinity Episcopal Preschool (see TDPRS)
West Plano Montessori School
Westwood Montessori School
White Rock Montessori School
White Rock Montessori School (satellite location)
Windsong Montessori School

A Child's Garden Montessori School

1935 Old Denton Rd.
Carrollton, TX 75006
(214) 446-2663

Mapsco: 2T

Fax: (214) 247-3299

Office Hours: 8:00 a.m.–4:00 p.m.
School Hours: 8:30 a.m.–3:00 p.m.
School Grades Offered: Age 2–grade 3
Enrollment: 100
Co-ed: Yes
Boy/Girl Ratio: Varies; usually 1:1
Student/Teacher Ratio: Age 2–6:1; ages 3-9–12:1
Average Class Size: 20-22
Calendar School Year: September–May
Holidays: Yes
Uniform Requirements: No
Founded in: 1983

Philosophy of School

A Child's Garden Montessori School seeks to provide an environment where children can explore and discover the world. The clasrooms are equipped with Montessori materials that follow the natural development of the child.

Academic Curriculum

Content: Montessori
Grading System Used: Individual
Conferences per Year: Three
Tests Administered: CTBS
Homework Policy: None
Method of Discipline: Time out; withdrawal of privileges

Enrichment Curriculum
Orff music, Spanish, art, gymnastics, ballet

Extracurricular Activities

Goals for Students
To give all students the opportunity to understand and apply life skills and to provide an educational foundation for further learning

Faculty/Staff Requirements
Qualifications of Staff: Teachers–Montessori certification for pre-primary; college degree for elementary
Qualifications of Administrator: College degree, Montessori cerification, administrative training or five years' experience

School Information
Brochure Available: Yes
Number of Students in Each Grade: Grouped (three year ages)
Parochial: No
Organization Affiliations: AMS
Accreditations: M.A.C.T.E.
Parental Involvement: Yes
Other Information:

Admittance
Whom to Contact: Lynda Landreth
Date to Apply: Year-round
Testing Procedure for Age/Grade Level: K-3–CTBS in May
Fees Involved: $50 application fee; $30 per semester supply fee
Type of Student Preferred:
Forms Required: Health, emergency, questionnaire of child's history
Individual/Group Appointments: Individual
Notification Procedure: All students are evaluated and then discussed with parent(s) before admittance.
Waiting List Policy: Ongoing for new enrollment; current students re-enroll in March.

Tuition

Approximate Tuition for 1996-97 School Year: $3800–$4800
Methods of Payment Available: Monthly
Financial Assistance Offered: Limited scholarships
Cancellation Insurance Available: No
Profit/Non-profit: Profit

Additional Costs

Books/Bag/Uniform: No
Lunch Fee: Hot-lunch program available at extra cost ($1.70/day)
Parents Club Dues: No
Annual Fund Drive: No
Discount for Siblings: Yes, 10%

Facilities/Services Provided

Computer Lab: Computers in all classes
Library: In classrooms
Snack Procedures: Morning snacks provided by parents
Before-school Care Program Available: Yes, 7:00–8:30 a.m.
After-school Care Program Available: Yes, 3:00–6:00 p.m.
Nurse on Staff: No
Emergency Procedure Used: Yes; call emergency number, parent, or designated person
Transportation to and from School: No
Counseling and Evaluation Available: Referrals

Graduation Information

Testing: CTBS
Average SAT Scores: N/A
High School Our Students Usually Attend: CFBISD, Coppell, Lewisville
Percentage of Seniors Attending College: N/A

Additional Information

Branch Schools

6144 Prospect Ave.
Dallas, TX 75214
(214) 826-5717

Mapsco: 36Y

Fax: (214) 827-8165

Office Hours: 9:00 a.m.–11:30 a.m.
School Hours: 9:00 a.m.–11:30 a.m.
School Grades Offered: Preschool (children who walk well through age 3)
Enrollment: 12
Co-ed: Yes
Boy/Girl Ratio: 1:1
Student/Teacher Ratio: 6:2
Average Class Size: 12
Calendar School Year: Year-round school
Holidays: Labor Day, Thanksgiving weekend, Christmas break, spring break
Uniform Requirements: No
Founded in: 1988

Philosophy of School

We offer Montessori education for toddlers in a home-like environment. Our teachers are Montessori certified. We offer language development, gross motor-skill development, practical life skills, music, art, cooking, and gardening. We accept children from the time they walk well through age three.

Academic Curriculum

Content: Individual and group lessons; developmentally appropriate
Grading System Used: None
Conferences per Year: Two
Tests Administered: N/A
Homework Policy: N/A
Method of Discipline: Distraction in most cases; occasionally sitting aside

Enrichment Curriculum

Our Montessori curriculum is enriched and appropriate for toddlers. Lessons include practical life skills, sensorial stimulation, fine and large motor-skill exercises, language development, music, and art projects.

Extracurricular Activities

Monthly theme crafts, cooking, gardening, movement games, physical education, nature-study activities, swimming (warm weather)

Goals for Students

Our goal is to help each child meet his or her full potential in all developmental areas–physical, social, emotional, academic, and spiritual.

Faculty/Staff Requirements

Qualifications of Staff: Montessori certification
Qualifications of Administrator: Montessori certification (Association of Montessori International)

School Information

Brochure Available: Yes
Number of Students in Each Grade: 12
Parochial: No
Organization Affiliations: Association of Montessori International (A.M.I.)
Accreditations:
Parental Involvement: Very involved; Parents' Club; parent-education classes
Other Information: Optional: parent and baby classes for parents and children under 12 months; consultations available for creating a home environment that meets your child's developmental needs

Admittance

Whom to Contact: Hart Robinson, director
Date to Apply: Year-round
Testing Procedure per Age/Grade Level: N/A
Fees Involved: Enrollment fee (10% of tuition)
Type of Student Preferred: Those who need love and have very involved, supportive parents
Forms Required: Introduction packet; enrollment packet
Individual/Group Appointments: Parent-introduction meetings on Saturdays at 12:00 p.m., 2:00 p.m., and 4:00 p.m. by reservation

Notification Procedure: After the current students reapply for next year, the remaining spaces are filled from the waiting list.
Waiting List Policy: Ongoing

Tuition

Approximate Tuition for 1996-97 School Year: $2700 (Sept.–May)
Methods of Payment Available: Annually, by semester, or monthly
Financial Assistance Offered: N/A
Cancellation Insurance Available: N/A
Profit/Non-profit: Profit

Additional Costs

Books/Bag/Uniform: N/A
Lunch Fee: Parents provide snacks.
Parents Club Dues: N/A
Annual Fund Drive: N/A
Discount for Siblings: N/A

Facilities/Services Provided

Computer Lab: N/A
Library: N/A
Snack Procedures: Parents provide snacks.
Before-school Care Program Available: 7:30 a.m.–9:00 a.m.
After-school Care Program Available: 11:30 a.m.–6:00 p.m.
Nurse on Staff: N/A
Emergency Procedure Used: Staff trained and certified in Red Cross procedures; we contact parents or individuals listed on the emergency release form.
Transportation to and from School: No
Counseling and Evaluation Available: Referrals given; parent-education classes offered

Graduation Information

Testing: N/A
Average SAT Scores: N/A
High School Our Students Usually Attend: N/A
Percentage of Seniors Attending College: N/A

Additional Information

The toddler school for children walking through age three (3) is only one of the

Montessori experiences we provide. We specialize in Montessori education for children from birth to age three (3). In addition to our toddler school, we provide parent-and-baby classes to assist new parents, and we consult with parents on setting up their home environment to meet their children's developmental needs. We also offer parent-education and discussion classes in English and Spanish.

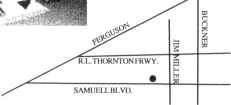

488

Dallas Montessori Academy

5757 Samuel Boulevard (parallel to I-30)   Mapsco: 48F
Dallas, TX 75228
(214) 388-0091   Fax: (214) 388-3415

Office Hours: 8:00 a.m.–5:00 p.m.
School Hours: 8:30 a.m.–3:00 p.m.
School Grades Offered: Pre-primary (ages 3-6)–grade 8
Enrollment: 150
Co-ed: Yes
Boy/Girl Ratio: 1:1
Student/Teacher Ratio: Pre-primary, 12:1; elementary, 15:1
Average Class Size: Pre-primary, 24; elementary, 21
Calendar School Year: August–May and summer school
Holidays: Winter break (2 weeks), spring break (1 week)
Uniform Requirements: Elementary students only
Founded in: 1984

Philosophy of School

The Dallas Montessori Academy educates children from preschool through eighth grade. We adhere to the psychology, philosophy, and pedagogy of Dr. Maria Montessori. The goal of Montessori education is to assist the child in the positive development of a flexible personality. We prepare children to meet tomorrow's challenges in a culturally diverse global society.

Academic Curriculum

Content: Montessori curriculum
Grading System Used: Multi-age grouping (3-6, 6-9, 9-12, 12-14)
Conferences per Year: Two
Tests Administered: ERB (only administered to students ages 9, 12, and 13)
Homework Policy: None; children read only for information or enjoyment; they complete projects.
Method of Discipline: Time out; parent conference

489

Enrichment Curriculum
Classroom music, art, gymnastics, computer

Extracurricular Activities
Private lessons in piano and violin; private art lessons

Goals for Students
To acquire a love for learning and academic excellence; use each child's potential, independence, and self-discipline to develop a flexible personality

Faculty/Staff Requirements
Qualifications of Staff: College degree; AMS certification
Qualifications of Administrator: AMS certification; M.Ed.

School Information
Brochure Available: Yes
Number of Students in Each Grade: Multi-age classes
Parochial: No
Organization Affiliations: AMS
Accreditations: AMS
Parental Involvement: Yes; room parents, Parents' Support Group, scouts
Other Information: The Academy is located on the site of the Dallas Montessori Teacher Program (AMS).

Admittance
Whom to Contact: James or Dina Paulik
Date to Apply: February
Testing Procedure for Age/Grade Level: N/A
Fees Involved: $75 application fee; $200 supply fee
Type of Student Preferred: Curious; self-motivated
Forms Required: Previous school reports
Individual/Group Appointments: Individual interview
Notification Procedure: Conference with parents and child
Waiting List Policy: Siblings receive top priority; next, students admitted in order of application

Tuition
Approximate Tuition for 1996-97 School Year: $3600–3900
Methods of Payment Available: Yearly or 10 monthly payments

Financial Assistance Offered: N/A
Cancellation Insurance Available: N/A
Profit/Non-profit: Profit

Additional Costs

Books/Bag/Uniform: Book fee/supply fee–$200; uniforms–Parker Uniform Company
Lunch Fee: Signature-Service lunches at $40/month
Parents Club Dues: N/A
Annual Fund Drive:
Discount for Siblings: Yes

Facilities/Services Provided

Computer Lab: Computers in each room; lap-top computer for each middle-school student
Library:
Snack Procedures: School provides
Before-school Care Program Available: Yes, 7:00 a.m.–8:30 a.m.
After-school Care Program Available: Yes, 3:00 p.m.–6:00 p.m.
Nurse on Staff: No
Emergency Procedure Used: Call parent; contact nearest hospital
Transportation to and from School: No
Counseling and Evaluation Available: Yes

Graduation Information

Testing: N/A
Average SAT Scores: N/A
High School Our Students Usually Attend: Bishop Lynch High School, Ursuline Academy, public schools
Percentage of Seniors Attending College: N/A

Additional Information

Summer camp and enrichment programs available

The Dallas North Montessori School

1149 Rockingham
Richardson, TX 75080
(214) 669-3322

Mapsco: 7W

Fax: N/A

Office Hours: 8:30 a.m.–3:00 p.m.
School Hours: 7:00 a.m.–6:00 p.m.
School Grades Offered: Preschool through grade 3
Enrollment: 50
Co-ed: Yes
Boy/Girl Ratio: 1:1
Student/Teacher Ratio: 12:1
Average Class Size: Preschool–25; elementary–25
Calendar School Year: Mid-August–May (plus summer program)
Holidays: Same as Richardson Independent School District
Uniform Requirements: N/A
Founded in: 1986

Philosophy of School

To provide the best possible physical and emotional environment for the children–one that is conducive to superior learning and that gives consideration to the educational abilities of all the children

Academic Curriculum

Content: Montessori
Grading System Used: Montessori
Conferences per Year: Two
Tests Administered: Elementary only; CAT-5 each spring
Homework Policy: Elementary only
Method of Discipline: Sit aside (time-out)

Enrichment Curriculum
Orff music program, art, science, Spanish

Extracurricular Activities
Private dance lessons are available after school.

Goals for Students
To develop independence, self-confidence, social skills, creativity and imagination, sensory motor skills, improved concentration skills, and a positive attitude toward others

Faculty/Staff Requirements
Qualifications of Staff: College and Montessori degrees
Qualifications of Administrator: S.A.A.

School Information
Brochure Available: Yes
Number of Students in Each Grade: 25 (preschool, grades 1–3)
Parochial: N/A
Organization Affiliations:
Accreditations: State license
Parental Involvement: Yes
Other Information: N/A

Admittance
Whom to Contact: Jennifer Lane
Date to Apply: Year-round registration
Testing Procedure per Age/Grade Level: N/A
Fees Involved: $50 registration fee
Type of Student Preferred: N/A
Forms Required: Yes
Individual/Group Appointments: Yes
Notification Procedure: Yes
Waiting List Policy: Ongoing; students are enrolled whenever space is available.

Tuition
Approximate Tuition for 1996-97 School Year: $2525–$3650

Methods of Payment Available: Monthly installments or an annual payment
Financial Assistance Offered: No
Cancellation Insurance Available: No
Profit/Non-profit: Profit

Additional Costs

Books/Bag/Uniform: Supply fee; books per year: $80 (preschool), $100 (elementary)
Lunch Fee: N/A
Parents Club Dues: No
Annual Fund Drive: Yes (minimal)
Discount for Siblings: 15%

Facilities/Services Provided

Computer Lab: Computers in classrooms
Library: Yes
Snack procedures: School provides morning snack.
Before-school Care Program Available: Yes; 7:00 a.m.–8:30 p.m.
After-school Care Program Available: Yes; 3:00–6:00 p.m.
Nurse on Staff: No
Emergency Procedure Used: Yes
Transportation to and from School: No
Counseling and Evaluation Available: No

Graduation Information

Testing: N/A
Average SAT Scores: N/A
High School Our Students Usually Attend: N/A
Percentage of Seniors Attending College: N/A

East Dallas Community School

924 Wayne Street
Dallas, TX 75223
(214) 824-8950

Mapsco: 46D

Fax: (214) 827-7683

Office Hours: 8:30 a.m.–4:00 p.m.
School Hours: 7:00 a.m.–6:00 p.m.; half-day program
available
School Grades Offered: Preschool–grade 3
Enrollment: 75
Co-ed: Yes
Boy/Girl Ratio: 1:1 (approximately)
Student/Teacher Ratio: 12:1
Average Class Size: 24
Calendar School Year: August–May
Holidays: Closed winter vacation, spring break, summer
Uniform Requirements: No
Founded in: 1978

Philosophy of School

All children–regardless of income level or ethnicity–can and do succeed educationally
in a challenging, supportive educational program.

Academic Curriculum

Content: Montessori
Grading System Used: None–parent is informed of child's current
mastery and activity level
Conferences per Year: Two scheduled; more as needed
Tests Administered: ITBS in winter of third grade
Homework Policy: Small amounts assigned beginning in first grade, consisting
mainly of reading, spelling, unfinished work
Method of Discipline: Explanation of rules; natural/logical consequences;
sitting aside

Enrichment Curriculum

A variety of activities, according to availabliity of volunteers
(Art is part of regular curriculum.)

Extracurricular Activities

No specific classes or sports program; after-school program with a large variety of informal activities; some special programs with visiting artists

Goals for Students

1. Have a strong sense of self-concept
2. Be independent, self-motivated learners
3. Succeed in fourth grade and beyond

Faculty/Staff Requirements

Qualifications of Staff: Montessori training
Qualifications of Administrator: College degree

School Information

Brochure Available: Yes
Number of Students in Each Grade: 6 in toddler class; 24-26 in primary classes (3-6 years old); 22-24 in elementary class (6-9 years old)
Parochial: No
Organization Affiliations: NAEYC, AMITOT, Child Care Partnership
Accreditations: NAEYC
Parental Involvement: Yes (Most parents pay part of their tuition through work.)
Other Information:

Admittance

Whom to Contact: Carol Wolfe
Date to Apply: Any time, but apply as soon as possible; long waiting list
Testing Procedure per Age/Grade Level: N/A
Fees Involved: Registration fee after admittance
Type of Student Preferred: All kinds welcome; school has mixture of income levels and ethnic backgrounds.
Forms Required: Yes
Individual/Group Appointments: Both
Notification Procedure: In spring or any time there's an opening; children remain on the waiting list until space is available.
Waiting List Policy: Ongoing

496

Tuition

Approximate Tuition for 1996-97 year: Top tuition $3708 for 7:00 a.m.–6:00 p.m. program (sliding scale)
Methods of Payment Available: Monthly or weekly
Financial Assistance Offered: Yes
Cancellation Insurance Available: No
Profit/Non-profit: Non-profit

Additional Costs

Books/Bag/Uniform: None
Lunch Fee: Bring own lunch
Parents Club Dues: No
Annual Fund Drive: No
Discount for Siblings: No

Facilities/Services Provided

Computer Lab: No, but a few computers in elementary classrooms and after-school program
Library: Yes; modest but growing and each class has a classroom library
Snack Procedures: Health food snacks provided
Before-school Care Program Available: Yes; 7:00–8:00 a.m.
After-school Care Program Available: Yes; 3:00–6:00 p.m.
Nurse on Staff: No
Emergency Procedure Used: Yes, as stated in staff-orientation manual
Transportation to and from School: No
Counseling and Evaluation Available: Yes, to a limited degree

Graduation Information

Testing: N/A
Average SAT Scores: N/A
High School Our Students Usually Attend: Mostly D.I.S.D. schools, including magnet schools
Percentage of Seniors Attending College: N/A

Additional Information

We welcome and encourage visits and class observations before enrollment; we offer orientations for new students.

Good Shepherd Montessori School

7701 Virginia Parkway
McKinney, TX 75070
(972) 547-4767

Mapsco: 659P

Fax: N/A

Office Hours: 8:30 a.m.–4:00 p.m.
School Hours: 7:30 a.m.–6:00 p.m.
School Grades Offered: 18 months–grade 6
Enrollment: 84
Co-ed: Yes
Boy/Girl Ratio: 1:1
Student/Teacher Ratio: Toddlers, 6:1; primary, 11:1;
elementary, 15:1
Average Class Size: Toddler, 12; primary, 21; elementary, 15
Calendar School Year: August–May and summer camp
Holidays: McKinney ISD calendar
Uniform Requirements: 5 years and over–St. Agnes Uniform
Company
Founded in: 1996-1997

Philosophy of School

Good Shepherd Montessori School has three distinctive features: 1) We are a Christian school with a curriculum dedicated to introducing children to a loving and joyous relationship with Jesus Christ. 2) Our Montessori approach to education provides hands-on learning for the development of each child in a multi-age setting. 3) We recognize the parent's role as the child's most important teacher, and we support this with open communication, parent education, and opportunities for parental involvement.

Academic Curriculum

Content: Montessori and Christian
Grading System Used: Trimester evaluations

498

Conferences per Year: Two
Tests Administered: Elementary students only
Homework Policy: Minimal
Method of Discipline: Positive approach

Enrichment Curriculum
Music and Movement classes

Extracurricular Activities
We invite speakers to discuss a wide range of topics. Only elementary students take various field trips and participate in community service projects.

Goals for Students
Good Shepherd Montessori School focuses on the development of each child academically, socially, physically, and spiritually. Our goal is to instill in children a love of learning that will last a lifetime.

Faculty/Staff Requirements
Qualifications of Staff: College degree; Montessori training (AMS or AMI)
Qualifications of Administrator: College degree; Montessori training (AMS or AMI)

School Information
Brochure Available: Yes
Number of Students in Each Grade: N/A (new school)
Parochial: Independent Christian school
Organization Affiliations: American Montessori Society; participate in ACSI
Accreditations:
Parental Involvement: Encouraged
Other Information: Good Shepherd Montessori School is located north of Stonebridge community on 1.6 acres between McKinney and Frisco. It's an easy drive from Allen and Plano.

Admittance
Whom to Contact: Business office
Date to Apply: February
Testing Procedure for Age/Grade Level: Interview/evaluation
Fees Involved: Registration fee, supply fee, book fee (elementary students only)

Type of Student Preferred: Montessori develops **every** child to his/her potential.
Forms Required: Registration, student information, medical, emergency
Individual/Group Appointments: Student-and-family visit required
Notification Procedure: Formal notice after student visits
Waiting List Policy: Ongoing

Tuition

Approximate Tuition for 1996-97 School Year: 1/2 day–$2500; full-day$3750–$4500
Methods of Payment Available: Monthly, annually
Financial Assistance Offered: No
Cancellation Insurance Available: No
Profit/Non-profit: Profit

Additional Costs

Books/Bag/Uniform: Book fee (elementary students only); uniforms
Lunch Fee: Presently, students bring their lunches.
Parents Club Dues: N/A
Annual Fund Drive: N/A
Discount for Siblings: Yes

Facilities/Services Provided

Computer Lab: Each class
Library: Each class
Snack Procedures: Provided by school and parents
Before-school Care Program Available: Yes, 7:30 a.m.–8:45 a.m.
After-school Care Program Available: Yes, 3:30 p.m.–6:00 p.m.
Nurse on Staff: No
Emergency Procedure Used: Standard emergency procedures
Transportation to and from School: No
Counseling and Evaluation Available: No

Graduation Information

Testing: N/A
Average SAT Scores: N/A
High School Our Students Usually Attend: N/A
Percentage of Seniors Attending College: N/A

Additional Information

Parents' meetings, registration, and interviews have begun. The school will open for the 1996-97 school year.

Highland Meadow Montessori Academy

1060 Highland St.
Southlake, TX 76092
(817) 488-2138

Mapsco:

Fax:

Office Hours: 8:30 a.m.–3:00 p.m. (M-F)
School Hours: 8:30 a.m.–3:00 p.m. (class); extended care (7:30 a.m.-6:00 p.m.)
School Grades Offered: 2 years–grade 6
Enrollment: 120
Co-ed: Yes
Boy/Girl Ratio: 1:1
Student/Teacher Ratio: 10 or 11:1
Average Class Size: 22
Calendar School Year: August-May
Holidays: Thanksgiving, Christmas, spring break
Uniform Requirements: Yes
Founded in: 1980

Philosophy of School

Montessori

Academic Curriculum

Content: Montessori
Grading System Used: Individualized
Conferences per Year: Two
Tests Administered: SAT
Homework Policy: Upper elementary only
Method of Discipline: Time out; conference

Enrichment Curriculum
Computer, physical education, music, Spanish, art

Extracurricular Activities
Gymnastics, dance, art

Goals for Students

Faculty/Staff Requirements
Qualifications of Staff: College degree, Montessori certification
Qualifications of Administrator: Business degree , Montessori certification

School Information
Brochure Available: Yes
Number of Students in Each Grade: Toddler–10; ages 3-5–66; ages 6-12–43
Parochial: No
Organization Affiliations: MACTE, AMS
Accreditations: AMS
Parental Involvement: Yes; many volunteer programs
Other Information:

Admittance
Whom to Contact: Pat McCormick
Date to Apply: Year-round
Testing Procedure for Age/Grade Level:
Fees Involved: Annual tuition; extended care; extra-curricular activities; new student registration fee–$100
Type of Student Preferred:
Forms Required: Immunization
Individual/Group Appointments: Both
Notification Procedure: Mail
Waiting List Policy: Ongoing

Tuition
Approximate Tuition for 1996-97 School Year: Range $2300-$4800
Methods of Payment Available: Total; 12-month plan
Financial Assistance Offered: No

Cancellation Insurance Available: No
Profit/Non-profit: Non-profit

Additional Costs

Books/Bag/Uniform: Uniform
Lunch Fee: Students bring their lunches.
Parents Club Dues: None
Annual Fund Drive: Annual giving program; fundraisers
Discount for Siblings: No

Facilities/Services Provided

Computer Lab: Yes
Library: Yes
Snack Procedures: Provided
Before-school Care Program Available: Yes, 7:30 a.m.–8:30 a.m.
After-school Care Program Available: Yes, 11:30 a.m.–3:00 p.m. / 3:00–6:00
Nurse on Staff: No
Emergency Procedure Used: Administer first aid; call 911
Transportation to and from School: No
Counseling and Evaluation Available: Yes

Graduation Information

Testing: SAT
Average SAT Scores: 95%
High School Our Students Usually Attend: Public (Southlake, Carroll, Grapevine, Northwest)
Percentage of Seniors Attending College: N/A

Additional Information

Meadowbrook Private School

5414 Northwest Highway
Dallas, TX 75220
(214) 369-4981

Mapsco: 24Y

Fax:

Office Hours: 9:00 a.m.–3:00 p.m.
School Hours: 9:00 a.m.–11:45 a.m.; 12:15 p.m.–3:00 p.m.
School Grades Offered: Preschool–kindergarten
Enrollment: 110
Co-ed: Yes
Boy/Girl Ratio: Varies
Student/Teacher Ratio: 9:1
Average Class Size: 18
Calendar School Year: Day after Labor Day–end of May
Holidays: Thanksgiving, Christmas, Easter, Martin Luther
King Day
Uniform Requirements: None
Founded in: 1970 by Trisha M. Fusch

Philosophy of School

Meadowbrook is an academic facility modeled after the English traditional school using Montessori materials. It is dedicated to giving children a firm academic foundation with a special focus on the three R's. It is an individualized program that works on self-esteem and a meaningful relationship among child, teacher, and parent. It offers children a choice within a controlled environment.

Academic Curriculum

Content: Academic background including early foundation in phonics, mathematics, and reading
Grading System Used: Conference plus written evaluation
Conferences per Year: Can be held at teacher's or parent's request throughout the year
Tests Administered: Metropolitan General Readiness Test given in January to students in kindergarten

505

Homework Policy: N/A
Method of Discipline: Individualized according to child's needs (examples: verbal reprimand; time out; communication with home)

Enrichment Curriculum
Music taught two times per week (30-minute classes); Spanish two times per week for kindergarten (30-minute classes); field trips once a month for kindergarten

Extracurricular Activities
After-school science program; art course; soccer team outside of school organized by parents; summer camp 9:00 a.m.–1:00 p.m. the month of June

Goals for Students
To provide students with a solid foundation so they will successfully enter a variety of public and private schools

Faculty/Staff Requirements
Qualifications of Staff: College degree; certification; trained by Meadowbrook
Qualifications of Administrator: B.S. and master's degrees

School Information
Brochure Available: Yes
Number of Students in Each Grade: 18 students per 2 teachers
Parochial: No
Organization Affiliations: Montessori
Accreditations: Texas Department of Human Services
Parental Involvement: Parents' Club
Other Information:

Admittance
Whom to Contact: Sharon Goldberg
Date to Apply: Any time during the school year
Testing Procedure per Age/Grade Level: No tests for first-year program; admission tests for second- and third-year program
Fees Involved: Registration fee $475
Type of Student Preferred: Self-motivated with a desire to learn
Forms Required: Registration form; medical emergency form
Individual/Group Appointments: Small-group orientation for perspective Meadowbrook parents

Notification Procedure: Telephone call; registration form mailed
Waiting List Policy: Siblings have first priority; other applicants are placed on waiting list according to the date of their telephone call and follow-up visitation.

Tuition

Approximate Tuition for 1996-97 School Year: Preschool $3300; kindergarten–half day $3550
Methods of Payment Available: Registration fee due by February 1 to reserve space in the class; tuition due by April 1
Financial Assistance Offered: Tuition-plan arrangements can be made with the headmistress.
Cancellation Insurance Available: None
Profit/Non-profit: Profit; privately owned by Trish M. Fusch

Additional Costs

Books/Bag/Uniform: Books provided by school; bag $8; uniform not required
Lunch Fee: N/A
Parents Club Dues: $25 per year; $35 for two children
Annual Fund Drive: None
Discount for Siblings: N/A

Facilities/Services Provided

Computer Lab:
Library: No
Snack Procedures: Room mothers provide snack lists.
Before-school Care Program Available: None
After-school Care Program Available: None
Nurse on Staff: No
Emergency Procedure Used: Staff trained in CPR; individual emergency card on file for each student
Transportation to and from School: Car pools; (car-pool coffee in May provides zip code list.)
Counseling and Evaluation Available: Referred to specialists outside school

Graduation Information

Testing: N/A
Average SAT Scores: N/A
High School Our Students Usually Attend: N/A
Percentage of Seniors Attending College: N/A

Montessori Children's House & School, Inc.

7335 Abrams Road
Dallas, TX 75231
(214) 348-6276

Mapsco: 27S

Fax: (214) 348-6628

Office Hours: 8:00 a.m.–3:00 p.m.
School Hours: 8:15 a.m.–11:30 a.m. or 8:15 a.m.–2:30 p.m. or 7:30 a.m.–6:00 p.m.
School Grades Offered: 3–6 years old (includes kindergarten)
Enrollment: 75
Co-ed: Yes
Boy/Girl Ratio: 37:38
Student/Teacher Ratio: 12:1
Average Class Size: 25
Calendar School Year: September-May for Montessori classes; June, July, August for summer school; before- and after-school care year round
Holidays: Two weeks in December; last two weeks of August
Uniform Requirements: No
Founded in: 1970

Philosophy of School
Montessori

Academic Curriculum
Content: Montessori curriculum (i.e., math, language, geography, science, practical life, sensorial, art, and music)
Grading System Used: N/A
Conferences per Year: At least twice a year
Tests Administered: None
Homework Policy: None

508

Method of Discipline: Logical consequences working toward self-discipline; conflict resolution with peers by conversation and compromise

Enrichment Curriculum
Integrated within academic curriculum

Extracurricular Activities
After-school class options

Goals for Students
Independence, concentration and attention span, intellectual development through individual lessons, emotional development, social growth–the total child

Faculty/Staff Requirements
Qualifications of Staff: College degrees and Montessori AMI certification
Qualifications of Administrator: College degree and Montessori certification

School Information
Brochure Available: Yes
Number of Students in Each Grade: 25 children in multi-age class
Parochial: No
Organization Affiliations: Association of Montessori Internationale (AMI)
Accreditations: AMI
Parental Involvement: Monthly parent-teacher evening
Other Information: Our after-school care is licensed by the Texas Department of Protective and Regulatory Services.

Admittance
Whom to Contact: Administrator, Pat Slavich
Date to Apply: By February for the next fall
Testing Procedure per Age/Grade Level: None
Fees Involved: $100 registration fee paid when child is accepted
Type of Student Preferred: Any child who is 3 years old and potty trained
Forms Required: Yes–application
Individual/Group Appointments: Parents observe students in class and meet with school administrator.
Notification Procedure: By letter in March
Waiting List Policy: Ongoing

Tuition

Approximate Tuition for 1996-97 School Year: $2700 for 8:15 a.m.–11:30 a.m. Montessori class; before- and after-school class is an additional cost.
Methods of Payment Available: By semester or monthly
Financial Assistance Offered: Yes; apply in early January
Cancellation Insurance Available: No
Profit/Non-profit: Non-profit

Additional Costs

Books/Bag/Uniform: Supply fee $60
Lunch Fee: N/A
Parents Club Dues: N/A
Annual Fund Drive: N/A
Discount for Siblings: $10 per month for before- and after-school care

Facilities/Services Provided

Computer Lab: N/A
Library: N/A
Snack Procedures: School provides
Before-school Care Program Available: 7:30 a.m.-8:15 a.m.
After-school Care Program Available: 11:30 a.m.-6:00 p.m.
Nurse on Staff: No
Emergency Procedure Used: Parents sign emergency medical form and school acts accordingly.
Transportation to and from School: No
Counseling and Evaluation Available: No

Graduation Information

Testing: N/A
Average SAT Scores: N/A
High School Our Students Usually Attend: N/A
Percentage of Seniors Attending College: N/A

Montessori Episcopal School

602 North Old Orchard Lane
Lewisville, TX 75067
(214) 221-3533

Mapsco: 650K

Fax: (214) 221-3532

Office Hours: 8:00 a.m.–4:00 p.m.
School Hours: 8:30 a.m.–2:45 p.m.
School Grades Offered: 2-year-olds–grade 2
Enrollment: 155
Co-ed: Yes
Boy/Girl Ratio: 1:1 (77:78)
Student/Teacher Ratio: 12:1; 15:2
Average Class Size: 13
Calendar School Year: Same as L.I.S.D. (mid-August–Memorial Day)
Holidays: Labor Day, Thanksgiving, Christmas, spring break, Easter, in-service days
Uniform Requirements: Only for kindergarten and elementary students (optional for preschoolers)
Founded in: 1968

Philosophy of School

Mission Statement: To provide quality education for children and their families within a Christian environment using Montessori methods. The Montessori curriculum creates an environment that stimulates children to explore and discover for themselves according to their own interests and readiness. Freedom to choose is balanced with structure and order that demand respect and growth. The teacher acts as a guide who aids children in their educational journey.

Academic Curriculum

Content: Montessori materials make up our curriculum
Grading System Used: Progress reports and parent conferences replace grades.
Conferences per Year: Two (fall and spring)

Tests Administered: Stanford Achievement Test (elementary students)
Homework Policy: As needed; at teacher's discretion
Method of Discipline: Re-direction, time out, loss of privilege, positive re-inforcement; assertive discipline card system used with older students

Enrichment Curriculum

Art, physical education, music, computer, library, chapel, field trips, Good Shepherd religious curriculum and hands-on Bible stories

Extracurricular Activities

None

Goals for Students

The primary goal is to foster the healthy development of the whole child and to help children develop self-discipline, self-understanding, and independence in a loving Christian environment

Faculty/Staff Requirements

Qualifications of Staff: College degree; Montessori training required for lead teachers
Qualifications of Administrator: College degree and experience in teaching and business management

School Information

Brochure Available: Yes
Number of Students in Each Grade: 87–preschool; 40–kindergarten; 28–elementary
Parochial: Yes
Organization Affiliations: SAES
Accreditations: None
Parental Involvement: Encouraged to become members of Parent-Teacher Fellowship (PTF)
Other Information: Tours are conducted by appointment or drop-in. Observations can be scheduled.

Admittance

Whom to Contact: Carolyn Ely or Eleanor Edwards
Date to Apply: January/February for the following school year

Testing Procedure for Age/Grade Level: No pre-admittance testing
Fees Involved: Registration fee equal to one month's tuition
Type of Student Preferred: Eager learners of all ages and abilities
Forms Required: Yes
Individual/Group Appointments: Individual
Notification Procedure: Within two weeks of registration
Waiting List Policy: Re-apply each January

Tuition

Approximate Tuition for 1996-97 School Year: $1140–$3200
Methods of Payment Available: Monthly by check or cash
Financial Assistance Offered: Limited scholarships available
Cancellation Insurance Available: No
Profit/Non-profit: Non-profit

Additional Costs

Books/Bag/Uniform: Back pack recommended; uniform required for kindergarten and elementary students
Lunch Fee: Students bring their lunches.
Parents Club Dues: $10 per family per year
Annual Fund Drive: Small fundraisers throughout the year
Discount for Siblings: 10% for second and subsequent children

Facilities/Services Provided

Computer Lab: Individual computer in each classroom
Library: Over 7000 books
Snack Procedures: Daily in classrooms–juice and crackers; special snacks
Before-school Care Program Available: Yes, 7:30 a.m.-8:30 a.m.
After-school Care Program Available: Yes, 2:45 p.m.-6:30 p.m.
Nurse on Staff: Part-time volunteer
Emergency Procedure Used: Call child's emergency phone numbers; fire station and parmedics one mile from school
Transportation to and from School: No
Counseling and Evaluation Available: Referrals made

Graduation Information

Testing: N/A
Average SAT Scores: N/A
High School Our Students Usually Attend: N/A
Percentage of Seniors Attending College: N/A

Additional Information

In the Christian school, the child is invited to experience the fullness of life in companionship with the Lord Jesus Christ. Religious education, a part of the daily regime, is both instructional and experiential. Worship services are conducted once a week in the chapel and once a week in the class.

Montessori School
of Las Colinas

4961 N. O'Connor Blvd.   Mapsco: 21B-X
Irving, TX 75062
(214) 717-0417   Fax: None

Office Hours: 6:30 a.m.–6:30 p.m., M–F
School Hours: 6:30 a.m.–6:00 p.m., M–F
School Grades Offered: Infants, toddlers, preschool, kindergarten
Enrollment: 130
Co-ed: Yes
Boy/Girl Ratio: 1:1
Student/Teacher Ratio: Preschool 13:1
Average Class Size: 24-26
Calendar School Year: Year-round
Holidays: Six major holidays
Uniform Requirements: None
Founded in: 1987

Philosophy of School

Our philosophy is the Montessori philosophy that focuses on the whole child with emphasis on grace and courtesy; this is the foundation of the school. The individual child is recognized and cultural differences are encouraged. The goals are independence, confidence, and a love for learning. The Montessori method offers a strong academic curriculum.

Academic Curriculum

Content: Practical life, sensorial, math, language, geography, history, art, music
Grading System Used: Progress reports; no grades
Conferences per Year: Two (minimum)

515

Tests Administered: None (CAT if requested by parents)
Homework Policy: None
Method of Discipline: Positive discipline; choices and re-direction

Enrichment Curriculum

Music is expressive music as well as music appreciation. Art is expressive as well as art appreciation.

Extracurricular Activities

Tennis, gymnastics, music, computer

Goals for Students

To develop independence, confidence, a love for learning, and a strong academic foundation for elementary years

Faculty/Staff Requirements

Qualifications of Staff: Montessori certification
Qualifications of Administrator: B.S. degree, Montessori certification, 3-5 years' teaching experience

School Information

Brochure Available: Yes
Number of Students in Each Grade: 24-26 preschool and kindergarten
Parochial: No
Organization Affiliations: International Montessori Institute
Accreditations: International Montessori Institute Training Center
Parental Involvement: Monthly parents' meetings
Other Information: Montessori of Las Colinas is also a training center for Montessori teachers.

Admittance

Whom to Contact: Ruth Myers
Date to Apply: Year-round–fall registration held in May
Testing Procedure for Age/Grade Level: None; personal interview
Fees Involved: $100 registration fee
Type of Student Preferred: 3-6 years old
Forms Required: Medical and family information
Individual/Group Appointments: Interview with director

Notification Procedure: Phone call
Waiting List Policy: Ongoing

Tuition

Approximate Tuition for 1996-97 School Year: $485 (full day); $395 (8:30 a.m.-2:30 p.m.); $370 (8:30 a.m.-12:30 p.m.)
Methods of Payment Available: Monthly
Financial Assistance Offered: Corporate discounts
Cancellation Insurance Available: N/A
Profit/Non-profit: Profit

Additional Costs

Books/Bag/Uniform: All school supplies furnished by school
Lunch Fee: None (breakfast and lunch served)
Parents Club Dues: None
Annual Fund Drive: None
Discount for Siblings: 10%

Facilities/Services Provided

Computer Lab: Computers in each classroom
Library: In classrooms
Snack Procedures: Serving table
Before-school Care Program Available: Yes (Montessori all-day concept)
After-school Care Program Available: Yes (Montessori all-day concept)
Nurse on Staff: No
Emergency Procedure Used: School provides
Transportation to and from School: No
Counseling and Evaluation Available: No

Graduation Information

Testing: N/A
Average SAT Scores: N/A
High School Our Students Usually Attend: N/A
Percentage of Seniors Attending College: N/A

Additional Information

Montessori School of North Dallas

18303 Davenport
Dallas, TX 75252
(214) 985-8844

Mapsco: 5G

Fax: (214) 867-6929

Office Hours: 7:00 a.m.–6:00 p.m.
School Hours: 7:00 a.m.–6:00 p.m.
School Grades Offered: Preschool–grade 1
Enrollment: 210
Co-ed: Yes
Boy/Girl Ratio: 1:1
Student/Teacher Ratio: Toddler 7:1; primary and elementary 13:1
Average Class Size: Toddlers 14-16 with 2 teachers; primary and elementary 24-26 with 2 teachers
Calendar School Year: August-May
Holidays: All major holidays observed
Uniform Requirements: None
Founded in: 1990

Philosophy of School

The main purpose in establishing the Montessori School of North Dallas was to provide a carefully planned, stimulating environment which will help our children develop within themselves an excellent foundation for creative learning. Each child is guided individually in each subject according to his/her own individual requirements.

Academic Curriculum

Content: Language, math, geography, history, science, practical life-and-sensorial study
Grading System Used: None
Conferences per Year: Two (fall and spring)
Tests Administered: Continued application and review

518

Homework Policy: Mostly done in school
Method of Discipline: See school policies and guidelines.

Enrichment Curriculum
Spanish, music, art, and computer classes

Extracurricular Activities
Ballet, gymnastics, dance, and creative art classes

Goals for Students
In brief, the school's purpose is to help students develop the fundamental habits, attitudes, skills, appreciation, and ideas essential for a lifetime of creative learning.

Faculty/Staff Requirements
Qualifications of Staff: Certified Montessori teachers
Qualifications of Administrator: Bachelor's or master's degree and Montessori certification

School Information
Brochure Available: Yes
Number of Students in Each Grade: Depends on class
Parochial: No
Organization Affiliations: American Montessori Society
Accreditations: American Montessori Society
Parental Involvement: Yes
Other Information: Programs offered: half-day (8:30 a.m.–11:30 a.m.); extended-day (8:30 a.m.–3:00 p.m.); full-day (7:00 a.m.–6:00 p.m.)

Admittance
Whom to Contact: Reena Khandpur
Date to Apply: Open
Testing Procedure per Age/Grade Level: Any time prior to enrollment
Fees Involved: Registration and supply fee
Type of Student Preferred: Open
Forms Required: Registration, medical, emergency
Individual/Group Appointments: Individual
Notification Procedure: Personal contact
Waiting List Policy: Ongoing

Tuition

Approximate Tuition for 1996-97 School Year: Depends on program selected
Methods of Payment Available: Monthly, by semester, or yearly
Financial Assistance Offered: No
Cancellation Insurance Available: No
Profit/Non-profit: Profit

Additional Costs

Books/Bag/Uniform: None
Lunch Fee: None
Parents Club Dues: None
Annual Fund Drive: None
Discount for Siblings: None

Facilities/Services Provided

Computer Lab: Computer classes offered to all students ages 4 and above
Library: Excellent selection of books, cassettes and computer software available at on-site computer room and library
Snack Procedures: Morning and afternoon snacks provided
Before-school Care Program Available: Yes; 7:00 a.m.–8:30 a.m.
After-school Care Program Available: Yes; 3:00 p.m.–6:00 p.m.
Nurse on Staff: Staff trained in first aid and CPR
Emergency Procedure Used: Call 911 and notify parents; call parents in non-emergency situations
Transportation to and from School: No
Counseling and Evaluation Available: Yes

Graduation Information

Testing: N/A
Average SAT Scores: N/A
High School Our Students Usually Attend: N/A
Percentage of Seniors Attending College: N/A

Additional Information

Montessori School of Park Cities

4011 Inwood
Dallas, TX 75209
(214) 350-2503

Mapsco: 34H

Fax: N/A

Office Hours: 9:00 a.m.–3:00 p.m.
School Hours: 7:00 a.m.–6:00 p.m.
School Grades Offered: 6 weeks to 6 years
Enrollment: 92
Co-ed: Yes
Boy/Girl Ratio: N/A
Student/Teacher Ratio: Varies
Average Class Size: N/A
Calendar School Year: Year-round
Holidays: Major holidays, Christmas (1 week), spring
break (1 week), summer break (1 week)
Uniform Requirements: No
Founded in: 1975

Philosophy of School
To provide a nurturing atmosphere where academics and individualized instruction are
stressed

Academic Curriculum
Content: Montessori
Grading System Used: N/A
Conferences per Year: Two
Tests Administered: N/A
Homework Policy: N/A
Method of Discipline: Positive rewards; time out; redirection

Enrichment Curriculum
Gymnastics, art, music

Extracurricular Activities

Goals for Students
To progress at their own rate

Faculty/Staff Requirements
Qualifications of Staff: Experience and Montessori training
Qualifications of Administrator: Bachelor of Science and Master of Arts degrees

School Information
Brochure Available: Yes
Number of Students in Each Grade: 12 (infants and toddlers); 14 (two-year-olds); 44 (three-, four-, and five-year-olds)
Parochial: No
Organization Affiliations: NAEYC, DAEYC
Accreditations: TDHR Licensing
Parental Involvement: Parents' Board of Directors

Admittance
Whom to Contact: School office
Date to Apply: Year round
Testing Procedure per Age/Grade Level: N/A
Fees Involved: $225 registration fee
Type of Student Preferred: Any type
Forms Required: Application and doctor's statement
Individual/Group Appointments: Either
Notification Procedure: Letter or phone call
Waiting List Policy: Ongoing

Tuition
Approximate Tuition for 1996-97 School Year: $500/month (average)
Methods of Payment Available: Monthly
Financial Assistance Offered: No
Cancellation Insurance Available: No
Profit/Non-profit: Non-profit

Additional Costs

Books/Bag/Uniform: N/A
Lunch Fee: Optional for catering service
Parents Club Dues: N/A
Annual Fund Drive: Yes (donations)
Discount for Siblings: No

Facilities/Services Provided

Computer Lab: N/A
Library: N/A
Snack Procedures: Parents bring morning snacks; school provides afternoon snacks
Before-school Care Program Available:
After-school Care Program Available: K-grade 1, 11:15 a.m.–2:45 p.m. (Highland Park schools only)
Nurse on Staff: No
Emergency Procedure Used: Card on file
Transportation to and from School: K–grade 1 (Highland Park only)
Counseling and Evaluation Available: Yes

Graduation Information

Testing: N/A
Average SAT Scores: N/A
High School Our Students Usually Attend: N/A
Percentage of Seniors Attending College: N/A

Additional Information

Montessori School—Pleasant Grove

1655 Jim Miller
Dallas, TX 75217
(214) 391-2176

Mapsco: 58S

Fax:

Office Hours: 6:00 a.m.–6:00 p.m.
School Hours: 6:00 a.m.–6:00 p.m.
School Grades Offered: Kindergarten
Enrollment: 59
Co-ed: Yes
Boy/Girl Ratio: 50:50
Student/Teacher Ratio: 15:1 (and up)
Average Class Size: 15
Calendar School Year: Year-round
Holidays: Memorial Day, Independence Day, Labor Day
Uniform Requirements: No
Founded in: 1983

Philosophy of School

Allowing each child to develop at his/her own pace neither pushing them ahead or holding them back; hands-on manipulative learning activities for early years

Academic Curriculum

Content: Appropriate for age and development
Grading System Used: Parent conference
Conferences per Year: As desired
Tests Administered: N/A
Homework Policy: N/A
Method of Discipline: Logical consequences

Enrichment Curriculum
Multi-cultural program and experiences

Extracurricular Activities
Computer, dance, music, art

Goals for Students
For each child to be successful in his/her own right

Faculty/Staff Requirements
Qualifications of Staff: Some have degrees.
Qualifications of Administrator: Master's degree and 30 years' experience

School Information
Brochure Available: Yes
Number of Students in Each Grade: Varies
Parochial: No
Organization Affiliations: CCMS, P/C
Accreditations:
Parental Involvement: Yes

Admittance
Whom to Contact: Hazel LeFall or Shawn Carr
Date to Apply: Year-round
Testing Procedure per Age/Grade Level: N/A
Fees Involved: Yes
Type of Student Preferred: All are welcome. Disruptive behaviors, though, are not acceptable.
Individual/Group Appointments: Either
Notification Procedure: Parent called
Waiting List Policy: No waiting list at present

Tuition
Approximate Tuition for 1996-97 School Year: Please call for rates
Methods of Payment Available: In advance: weekly or monthly
Financial Assistance Offered: Teen Parent Assistance; CCMS; PIC
Cancellation Insurance Available: N/A
Profit/Non-profit: Non-profit–taxpayer

Additional Costs

Books/Bag/Uniform: $50 semi-annually
Lunch Fee: No; USDA Child Food Program
Parents Club Dues: N/A
Annual Fund Drive: To be announced
Discount for Siblings: 10%

Facilities/Services Provided

Computer Lab: Yes
Library: Yes
Snack Procedures: Provided
Before-school Care Program Available: Yes, 6:00 a.m.
After-school Care Program Available: Yes, 6:00 p.m.
Nurse on Staff: Yes
Emergency Procedure Used: Yes
Transportation to and from School: Yes
Counseling and Evaluation Available: Yes

Graduation Information

Testing: N/A
Average SAT Scores: N/A
High School Our Students Usually Attend: N/A
Percentage of Seniors Attending College: N/A

Additional Information

We have very large, spacious classrooms. In addition, there is a huge outdoor fenced playground, a large auditorium, and an all-purpose room for indoor games and progams.

Montessori School of Westchester

290 Westchester Parkway
Grand Prairie, TX 75052
(214) 262-1053

Mapsco: 61Q

Fax: N/A

Office Hours: 8:00 a.m.–4:00 p.m.
School Hours: 6:30 a.m.–6:30 p.m.
School Grades Offered: Preschool and kindergarten
Enrollment: 120
Co-ed: Yes
Boy/Girl Ratio: 1:1
Student/Teacher Ratio: 12:1
Average Class Size: 25
Calendar School Year: Year-round program
Holidays: National holidays observed
Uniform Requirements: No
Founded in: 1989

Philosophy of School

A Montessori environment dedicated to parent-child relationship and growth of total child

Academic Curriculum

Content: Montessori
Grading System Used: Individualized evaluation
Conferences per Year: Two
Tests Administered: N/A
Homework Policy: N/A
Method of Discipline: Redirection/ positive examples

527

Enrichment Curriculum

Extracurricular Activities
Gymnastics, fun tennis

Goals for Students
Academic development and social growth

Faculty/Staff Requirements
Qualifications of Staff: College degree and Montessori certification
Qualifications of Administrator: Montessori certification; eight years' experience

School Information
Brochure Available: Yes
Number of Students in Each Grade: N/A
Parochial: No
Organization Affiliations: Montessori Educational Programs International
Accreditations: MIA; Texas Department of Human Services, MEPI, Internship School
Parental Involvement: Yes
Other Information: Parent education seminars annually

Admittance
Whom to Contact: Cheryl Mitchell
Date to Apply: Open enrollment based upon availability
Testing Procedure per Age/Grade Level:
Fees Involved:
Type of Student Preferred:
Forms Required:
Individual/Group Appointments: Individual
Notification Procedure: Phone call and registration
Waiting List Policy: Spaces limited

Tuition
Approximate Tuition for 1996-97 School Year: $5800 for toddlers (18 months–3 years); $4140 for morning class; $4500 for extended-day program; $5580 for full-day program

Methods of Payment Available: Monthly (based on program selected)
Financial Assistance Offered: No
Cancellation Insurance Available: No
Profit/Non-profit: Profit

Additional Costs

Books/Bag/Uniform: None
Lunch Fee: Hot lunch provided
Parents Club Dues: No
Annual Fund Drive: No
Discount for Siblings: Yes

Facilities/Services Provided

Computer Lab: N/A
Library: N/A
Snack Procedures: Morning and afternoon snacks provided
Before-school Care Program Available: Yes; limited
After-school Care Program Available: Yes; limited
Nurse on Staff: Director and lead teachers are certified in first aid and CPR.
Emergency Procedure Used: Transfer patient to ER facility or to staff trained in CPR and first aid
Transportation to and from School: Yes, to public schools only
Counseling and Evaluation Available: Referrals

Graduation Information

Testing: N/A
Average SAT Scores: N/A
High School Our Students Usually Attend: N/A
Percentage of Seniors Attending College: N/A

Additional Information

Fully equipped classrooms; all Montessori materials are available.

Redeemer Montessori School

120 East Rochelle
Irving, TX 75062
(214) 257-3517

Mapsco: 31B-E

Fax: (214) 255-4173

Office Hours: 8:00 a.m.–4:00 p.m.
School Hours: 7:30 a.m.–6:00 p.m.
School Grades Offered: 2 1/2 years–grade 5
Enrollment: 85
Co-ed: Yes
Boy/Girl Ratio: 1:1 (varies)
Student/Teacher Ratio: 22:2 (3-6 years); 30:3 (elementary)
Average Class Size: 22 (3-6 years); 22-30 (elementary)
Calendar School Year: August–May
Holidays: Thanksgiving break, Christmas (2 weeks), spring break
Uniform Requirements: No
Founded in: 1978

Philosophy of School

Redeemer Montessori School is dedicated to giving children the opportunity to develop to the fullest of their potential so that they experience the joy and success of learning which will enable them to create a framework for a lifetime of cognitive and effective development.

Academic Curriculum

Content: Montessori curriculum; self-paced
Grading System Used: Multi-age grouping (3-6 years); progress (grades 1-5)
Conferences per Year: Two
Tests Administered: Iowa Test of Basic Skills Achievement
Homework Policy: Minimal in elementary; class time emphasized
Method of Discipline: Re-directed to schoolwork; time out

Enrichment Curriculum
Before- and after-school programs (7:30 a.m.-8:30 a.m.; 3:00 p.m.-6:00 p.m.)

Extracurricular Activities
Physical education (twice per week); music (once per week); creative arts (once per week); Spanish (twice per week)

Goals for Students
See Mission Statement.

Faculty/Staff Requirements
Qualifications of Staff: Lead teachers; Montessori certification
Qualifications of Administrator: Montessori certification

School Information
Brochure Available: Packet sent upon request
Number of Students in Each Grade: 40 (ages 3-6); 30 (grades 1-5)
Parochial: No
Organization Affiliations: American Montessori Society
Accreditations:
Parental Involvement: Redeemer School Volunteer Parents (R.S.V.P.)
Other Information: Multi-cultural families and staff

Admittance
Whom to Contact: Donna Hatter, Diana Macnab
Date to Apply: Re-enrollment in March for fall; enroll throughout school year
Testing Procedure for Age/Grade Level: Trial day (ages 3-6); trial week (grades 1-5)
Fees Involved: $175 registration fee; $125 (continuing students)
Type of Student Preferred: N/A
Forms Required: Application, health forms, emergency forms
Individual/Group Appointments: Call school for appointment.
Notification Procedure: Verbal
Waiting List Policy: Ongoing

Tuition
Approximate Tuition for 1996-97 School Year: $3880, elementary; $2820 (half day); $3770 (full day, pre-primary)

Methods of Payment Available: Monthly, yearly
Financial Assistance Offered: Very limited
Cancellation Insurance Available: N/A
Profit/Non-profit: Non-profit

Additional Costs

Books/Bag/Uniform: Supply fees twice a year
Lunch Fee: N/A
Parents Club Dues: N/A
Annual Fund Drive: Fundraising events
Discount for Siblings: 10%

Facilities/Services Provided

Computer Lab: Within classroom
Library: Within classroom
Snack Procedures: Mid-morning for pre-primary; after-school care
Before-school Care Program Available: Yes (7:30 a.m.-8:30 a.m.)
After-school Care Program Available: Yes (3:00 p.m.-6:00 p.m.)
Nurse on Staff: Office staff
Emergency Procedure Used: Notify emergency contact on file
Transportation to and from School: N/A
Counseling and Evaluation Available: Referrals

Graduation Information

Testing: N/A
Average SAT Scores: N/A
High School Our Students Usually Attend: N/A
Percentage of Seniors Attending College: N/A

Additional Information

532

The St. Alcuin Montessori School

6144 Churchill Way
Dallas, TX 75230
(214) 239-1745

Mapsco: 15U

Fax: (214) 934-8727

Office Hours: 7:30 a.m.–6:00 p.m.
School Hours: 8:15 a.m.–3:00 p.m. (middle school–4:00 p.m.)
School Grades Offered: 18 months–14 years (grade 8)
Enrollment: 500
Co-ed: Yes
Boy/Girl Ratio: 1:1
Student/Teacher Ratio: 13:1
Average Class Size: 26
Calendar School Year: Mid-August–end of May
Holidays: Labor Day, Fair Day, Thanksgiving, winter break, spring break
Uniform Requirements: None
Founded in: 1964

Philosophy of School

A Montessori education allows each child to follow his or her own curiosity and supports a natural desire for and enjoyment of learning. Children within a three-year age span are purposefully grouped to foster a sense of community and to serve as models for one another. Each child is allowed to develop to the fullest of his or her own potential, often exceeding the bounds associated with traditional methods of education. The St. Alcuin student has the opportunity to achieve a deep understanding of all academic basics and other subjects in an interrelated manner. He or she develops a love for learning, a self-assurance, and self-motivation which serve as a preparation not only for secondary and higher education, but also for all of life.

Academic Curriculum

Content: Enriched Montessori curriculum–early childhood (18 months) through middle school (8th grade)

Grading System Used: Not applicable except in middle school (narrative)

Conferences per Year: Individual detailed conferences; two per year minimum

Tests Administered: Otis-Lennon–grades 1, 3, 5, 7; Stanford Achievement grades 3–6; ERB–middle school; ERB Writing–middle school

Homework Policy: N/A

Method of Discipline: Positive reinforcement and logical consequences

Enrichment Curriculum

Spanish, computers, choral and instrument programs, cooking, sewing, art, outdoor education (3-4 days in grades 4, 5 and 6; 3-10 days in middle school)

Extracurricular Activities

After-school activities include art, pottery, scouts, gym, ballet, piano, violin, drama, computer, scouting

Goals for Students

To fulfill the child's own potential in becoming fully himself or herself—mature, capable, responsible, and whole

Faculty/Staff Requirements

Qualifications of Staff: College, Association Montessori Internationale certification

Qualifications of Administrator: M.Ed., Association Montessori Internationale certification

School Information

Brochure Available: Yes

Number of Students in Each Grade: N/A

Parochial: No

Organization Affiliations: Association Montessori Internationale (A.M.I.)

Accreditations: A.M.I.

Parental Involvement: Active parents' club

Other Information: Ongoing parent education; community service in middle school

Admittance

Whom to Contact: Admissions Office; Peggy Larson, Registrar
Date to Apply: Ongoing; decisions made in early spring
Testing Procedure per Age/Grade Level: N/A
Fees Involved: $50 application fee
Type of Student Preferred: Curious, self-motivated
Forms Required: Previous school reports
Individual/Group Appointments: Group orientation; individual interview
Notification Procedure: Majority of acceptance letters in April and May; others as space becomes available
Waiting List Policy: Ongoing

Tuition

Approximate Tuition for 1996-97 School Year: $4190 (toddlers)–$8915 (middle school)
Methods of Payment Available: 9 monthly payments at 10% interest
Financial Assistance Offered: Yes
Cancellation Insurance Available: Yes
Profit/Non-profit: Non-profit

Additional Costs

Books/Bag/Uniform: Books–included in tuition; bag and uniform–n/a
Lunch Fee: N/A
Parents Club Dues: $40
Annual Fund Drive: Yes
Discount for Siblings: No

Facilities/Services Provided

Computer Lab: Yes
Library: Yes
Snack Procedures: Parents provide one week per year for preschool
Before-school Care Program Available: Yes; 7:00 a.m. - 6:00 p.m.
After-school Care Program Available: Yes; 7:00 a.m. - 6:00 p.m.
Nurse on Staff: Yes
Emergency Procedure Used: Contact parents
Transportation to and from School: No
Counseling and Evaluation Available: Referral

Graduation Information

Testing: N/A
Average SAT scores: N/A
High School Our Students Usually Attend: Graduates attend both private and

public high schools and experience a positive transition.
Percentage of Seniors Attending College: N/A

Additional Information

Summer camp and enrichment programs are available. St. Alcuin has a new classroom complex and performing arts center.

St. James Episcopal Montessori School

9845 McCree Road
Dallas, TX 75238
(214) 348-1349

Mapsco: 27U

Fax: (214) 348-1368

Office Hours: 8:00 a.m.–4:00 p.m.
School Hours: 8:30 a.m.–3:30 p.m.
School Grades Offered: Preschool (age 2–kindergarten); elementary (1-3)
Enrollment: 60
Co-ed: Yes
Boy/Girl Ratio: 3:2
Student/Teacher Ratio: 8:1; 13:1; 15:1
Average Class Size: PS-K–24; grades 1-3–15
Calendar School Year: R.I.S.D. school calendar
Holidays: Labor Day, Fair Day, Martin Luther King Day, Good Friday, Memorial Day
Uniform Requirements: Age 3–elementary students
Founded in: 1968

Philosophy of School

To offer a high quality Montessori education from an Episcopal perspective. The goal of the school is to develop the mind, body, and spirit of each individual to the fullest capacity. To achieve this goal, a well qualified faculty is dedicated to using the Montessori Method to nurture children and their academic and spiritual abilities.

Academic Curriculum

Content: The essential principles and disciplines included in the Montessori Method
Grading System Used: Individualized observation
Conferences per Year: Two scheduled annually

537

Tests Administered: Stanford Achievement Test (spring)
Homework Policy: Project related and practice drills
Method of Discipline: Rational communication and time out, behavior modification

Enrichment Curriculum

Gardening, computer education, music, physical education

Extracurricular Activities

Musikids

Goals for Students

The development of the mind, body, and spirit of each individual to the fullest capacity is the school's goal.

Faculty/Staff Requirements

Qualifications of Staff: Preschool–American Montessori Society (AMS) certification; elementary–AMS certification and college degree
Qualifications of Administrator: PhD from TWU; LPC, LMFT Certified Teacher

School Information

Brochure Available: Yes
Number of Students in Each Grade: PS–90, elementary–40
Parochial: Yes
Organization Affiliations: American Montessori Society; National Association of Episcopal Schools (NAES); Southwest Association of Episcopal Schools
Accreditations:
Parental Involvement: Yes
Other Information:

Admittance

Whom to Contact: Nancy E. Hood, PhD, Directress
Date to Apply: Ongoing application procedure
Testing Procedure per Age/Grade Level: Kindergarten and elementary students are given the Stanford Achievement in the spring.
Fees Involved: $200 registration fee, $50 supply fee, elementary extended-day and after-school care of students
Type of Student Preferred: Motivated, academically able, elementary students

538

with previous Montessori experience

Forms Required: Registration, health forms, previous school records, medical permission forms

Individual/Group Appointments: Tours accompanied by principal

Notification Procedure: By mail

Waiting List Policy: First priority–St. James students; second–siblings; third–parishoners; fourth–general public

Tuition

Approximate Tuition for 1996-97 School Year: $2363-$4200 annually

Methods of Payment Available: Monthly or annually, or by semester

Financial Assistance Offered: Some scholarships are available.

Cancellation Insurance Available: No

Profit/Non-profit: Non-profit

Additional costs

Books/Bag/Uniform: Books and bag–no; uniform–$45 minimum cost, age 5 and up

Lunch Fee: Lunches catered

Parents Club Dues: None

Annual Fund Drive: Yes

Discount for Siblings: Yes

Facilities/Services Provided

Computer Lab: Each classroom

Library: Yes; 350 + books

Snack Procedures: Sent from home on an rotating scheduled basis

Before-school Care Program Available: Yes; 7:30 a.m. - 8:15 a.m.

After-school Care Program Available: Yes; 3:30 p.m. - 6:00 p.m.; Extended day for morning students 11:30 a.m. - 3:30 p.m.

Nurse on Staff: No

Emergency Procedure Used: DHR standards

Transportation to and from School: No

Counseling and Evaluation Available: No

Graduation Information

Testing: N/A

Average SAT Scores: N/A

High School Our Students Usually Attend: N/A

Percentage of Seniors Attending College: N/A

West Plano Montessori School

3425 Ashington Lane
Plano, TX 75023
(214) 618-8844

Mapsco: 657C

Fax: (214) 867-6929

Office Hours: 7:00 a.m.–6:00 p.m.
School Hours: 7:00 a.m.–6:00 p.m.
School Grades Offered: Preschool–grade 1
Enrollment: 135
Co-ed: Yes
Boy/Girl Ratio: 1:1
Student/Teacher Ratio: Toddler 7:1; primary and elementary 13:1
Average Class Size: Toddlers: 14–16 with 2 teachers; primary and elementary 24–26 with 2 teachers
Calendar School Year: August–May
Holidays: All major holidays observed
Uniform Requirements: None
Founded in: 1982

Philosophy of School

The main purpose in establishing the West Plano Montessori School was to provide a carefully planned, stimulating environment which will help our children to develop within themselves an excellent foundation for creative learning. Each child is guided individually in each subject according to his/her own individual requirements.

Academic Curriculum

Content: Language, math, geography, history, science, practical life-and-sensorial study
Grading System Used: None
Conferences per Year: Two (fall and spring)
Tests Administered: Continued application and review
Homework Policy: Mostly done in school
Method of Discipline: See school policies and guidelines.

540

Enrichment Curriculum
Spanish, music, art, and computer classes

Extracurricular Activities
Ballet, gymnastics, dance, and creative art classes

Goals for Students
In brief, the school's purpose is to help students develop the fundamental habits, attitudes, skills, appreciation, and ideas essential for a lifetime of creative learning.

Faculty/Staff Requirements
Qualifications of Staff: Certified Montessori teachers
Qualifications of Administrator: Bachelor's or master's degree and Montessori certification

School Information
Brochure Available: Yes
Number of Students in Each Grade: Depends on class
Parochial: No
Organization Affiliations: American Montessori Society
Accreditations: American Montessori Society
Parental Involvement: Yes
Other Information: Programs offered: half-day (8:45 a.m.–11:45 a.m.); extended-day (8:45 a.m.–3:00 p.m.); full-day (7:00 a.m.–6:00 p.m.)

Admittance
Whom to Contact: J.P. Khandpur
Date to Apply: Open
Testing Procedure per Age/Grade Level: Any time prior to enrollment
Fees Involved: Registration and supply fee
Type of Student Preferred: Open
Forms Required: Registration, medical, emergency
Individual/Group Appointments: Individual
Notification Procedure: Personal contact
Waiting List Policy: Ongoing

Tuition
Approximate Tuition for 1996-97 School Year: Depends on program selected

Methods of Payment Available: Monthly, by semester, or yearly
Financial Assistance Offered: No
Cancellation Insurance Available: No
Profit/Non-profit: Profit

Additional Costs

Books/Bag/Uniform: None
Lunch Fee: None
Parents Club Dues: None
Annual Fund Drive: None
Discount for Siblings: None

Facilities/Services Provided

Computer Lab: Computer classes offered to all children ages 4 and above.
Library: Excellent selection of books, cassettes and computer software available in the school library.
Snack Procedures: Morning and afternoon snacks provided
Before-school Care Program Available: Yes
After-school Care Program Available: Yes
Nurse on Staff: Staff trained in first aid and CPR
Emergency Procedure Used: Call 911 and notify parents; call parents in non-emergency situations
Transportation to and from School: No
Counseling and Evaluation Available: Yes

Graduation Information

Testing: N/A
Average SAT Scores: N/A
High School Our Students Usually Attend: N/A
Percentage of Seniors Attending College: N/A

Additional Information

Westwood Montessori School

13618 Gamma Road
Dallas, TX 75244
(214) 239-8598

Mapsco: 14K

Fax: (214) 239-1028

Office Hours: 8:30 a.m.–3:30 p.m.
School Hours: 7:15 a.m.–6:00 p.m.
School Grades Offered: Preschool–grade 8
Enrollment: 100
Co-ed: Yes
Boy/Girl Ratio: 1:1
Student/Teacher Ratio: 10:1
Average Class Size: 20
Calendar School Year: 9 months plus summer break
Holidays: Thanksgiving–3 days; winter break–2 weeks;
spring break–1 week
Uniform Requirements: None
Founded in: 1983

Philosophy of School

Westwood is best known for our ability to provide an atmosphere where academics are stressed and each student's uniqueness is cherished. The Westwood environment promotes the development of social skills, emotional growth, physical fitness, and cognitive preparation. High academic standards are achieved in an atmosphere that fosters independent thinking, personal responsibility, freedom of choice, self-esteem, love, and respect.

Academic Curriculum

Content: Academic Curriculum Program (ACP), Great Books, Science by Mail
Grading System Used: ACP and written evaluation
Conferences per Year: Two and upon request
Tests Administered: ERB achievement tests

543

Homework Policy: Assigned as needed
Method of Discipline: No corporal punishment

Enrichment Curriculum
Music, art, foreign language, computer

Extracurricular Activities
Drama, art, imagination class, foreign language, computer, skating, martial arts, crafts, dance, swimming, music

Goals for Students
High academic standards in addition to independent thinking, personal responsibility, good judgment, self-esteem, and respect for others

Faculty/Staff Requirements
Qualifications of Staff: College degree plus Montessori certification
Qualifications of Administrator: College degree plus Montessori certification for all grades; college instructor

School Information
Brochure Available: Yes
Number of Students in Each Grade: Mixed ages in classrooms
Parochial: No
Organization Affiliations: No
Accreditations: Licensed by A.M.I. Teachers of Texas
Parental Involvement: Parents Booster Club
Other Information:

Admittance
Whom to Contact: Heather Lourcey, Assistant Administrator
Date to Apply: Inquiries welcome at any time; individual tours are recommended; elementary applications should be submitted by March 1.
Testing per Age/Grade Level: Applicants take a grade achievement test for elementary placement and have an on-campus interview.
Fees Involved: Application fee–$100
Type of Student Preferred: All students are welcome.
Forms Required: Application, parent essay, prior records
Individual/Group Appointments: Individual appointments with Assistant

Administrator
Notification Procedure: April 1
Waiting List Policy: Ongoing

Tuition

Approximate Tuition for 1996-97 School Year: $2800 (preschool) to $5200 (elementary)
Methods of Payment Available: Annually, by semester, installments
Financial Assistance Offered: Advanced elementary level only
Cancellation Insurance Available: No
Profit/Non-profit: Profit

Additional Costs

Books/Bag/Uniform: Books-supply list each semester
Lunch Fee: No
Parents Club Dues: None
Annual Fund Drive: No
Discount for Siblings: Yes

Facilities/Services Provided

Computer Lab: Yes
Library: Yes
Snack Procedures: School provides snack refreshments for preschool and after-school care students.
Before-school Care Program Available: Yes, 7:15 a.m.-8:45 a.m.
After-school Care Program Available: Yes, 3:15 p.m.-6:00 p.m.
Nurse on Staff: No
Emergency Procedure Used: Yes
Transportation to and from School: No
Counseling and Evaluation Available: Yes

Graduation Information

Testing: ERB and ACP
Average SAT Scores: N/A
High School Our Students Usually Attend: St. Mark's, Cistercian, Hockaday, Ursuline, Pearce, and Skyline
Percentage of Seniors Attending College: N/A

Additional Information

Summer camp and enrichment programs are available. Graduates attend both private and public high schools and experience a positive transition. Many are noted as strong leaders and graduate with honors.

White Rock Montessori School

3204 Skillman
Dallas, TX 75206
(214) 827-3220

Mapsco: 36Q

Fax: (214) 827-3229

Office Hours: 8:30 a.m.–4:30 p.m.
School Hours: Preschool, 8:30 a.m.–11:30 p.m.; K–6th, 8:30
a.m.–3:00 p.m.; middle school, 8:30–3:30 (before- and after-school
care 7:00 a.m.–8:30 a.m. and 3:00 p.m.–6:00 p.m.)
School Grades Offered: Pk–grade 6; (grades 7 and 8 open
in August 1996)
Enrollment: 93
Co-ed: Yes
Boy/Girl Ratio: 43:53
Student/Teacher Ratio: 11:1, preschool; 15:1, lower elementary;
18:1, upper elementary
Average Class Size: 23, preschool; 18, elementary
Calendar School Year: August–May
Holidays: Labor Day, Fair Day, Thanksgiving, winter
break (2 weeks), spring break (1 week), Easter
Uniform Requirements: No
Founded in: 1975

Philosophy of School

The only valid impulse to learning is the self-motivation of the child. The adult prepares
the environment, directs the activity, functions as the authority, and offers the stimulation, but it is the child who must be motivated by the work itself to persist in his/her
given task. Towards this end, the work is individualized and self-paced. Each child is
encouraged to express himself/herself creatively and to develop to his/her own fullest
potential.

Academic Curriculum

Content: Each classroom offers a full complement of sequential Montessori
materials covering development in practical life and sensorial experiences, as

well as math, reading, language, geography, history, biology, science, geometry, and the fine arts. Other carefully selected materials are used as well.

Grading System Used: Parent-teacher conferences used; progress reports given in December and May; cumulative portfolios

Conferences per Year: Upon request; two scheduled by school

Tests Administered: Stanford Achievement and Diagnostic each spring–elementary students only

Homework Policy: Planned individually for each student when deemed beneficial

Method of Discipline: Emphasis on self-discipline and peer mediation; teachers intervene when necessary; collaboration between teachers and parents emphasized

Enrichment Curriculum

The classroom curriculum incorporates Spanish, cultural studies, cooking, music, art, drama, computer, library, physical education, and care of plants and animals; all of these classes are fully integrated into the curriculum and available for the child to choose daily. Professionals supervise weekly music, art, and Spanish classes and daily physical education classes. Field trips are an important part of the elementary curriculum.

Extracurricular Activities

After-school activities include art classes, piano and violin lessons, soccer teams, campfire and Girl Scouts; fifth and sixth grade students have a spring camp out.

Goals for Students

Our goal is for each child to maintain an enthusiasm for learning and an appreciation for his/her own uniqueness as well as that of others. We want our students to maintain the self-discipline and love of independence that will allow them to develop to their fullest potential. Montessori education is a preparation for life.

Faculty/Staff Requirements

Qualifications of Staff: Must have degrees and AMS certification or the equivalent; 25% of the staff have master's degrees

Qualifications of Administrator: B.A., all levels of Texas State Teachers Certification, AMS certification, 24 years professional experience in teaching

School Information

Brochure Available: Yes

Number of Students in Each Grade: Preschool, 24; lower elementary (grades

1–3), 20; upper elementary (grades 4–6), 20
Parochial: No
Organization Affiliations: American Montessori Society (AMS) and North American Montessori Teacher Association
Accreditations: AMS
Parental Involvement: Parents' club, parent volunteers
Other Information:

Admittance

Whom to Contact: Sue Henry
Date to Apply: March (prior to that for waiting list)
Entrance Testing: No
Fees Involved: $150 deposit when a child enrolls ($100 of which is applied to the first tuition payment)
Type of Student Preferred: Children from supportive families who are eager to learn and are self-disciplined
Forms Required: Yes
Individual/Group Appointments: Individual
Testing Procedure per Age/Grade Level: None for admittance; standardized tests administered each spring to the elementary students to assist the staff in evaluating progress and planning each child's individual curriculum
Notification Procedure: By phone, following interview with parents and child
Waiting List Policy: Ongoing

Tuition

Approximate Tuition for 1996-97 School Year: Preschool 1/2 day, $2434; preschool extended day, $3890; lower elementary, $4154; upper elementary, $4296; middle school, $5000
Methods of Payment Available: Monthly, by the semester, or annually
Financial Assistance Offered: Limited
Cancellation Insurance Available: No
Profit/Non-profit: Non-profit

Additional Costs:

Books/Bag/Uniform: Books–included in tuition; no bag or uniform requirements
Lunch Fee: No
Parents Club Dues: Included in tuition
Annual Fund Drive: Yes
Discount for Siblings: No

Facilities/Services Provided

Computer Lab: White Rock Montessori believes in integrating computer use into the day-to-day environment; therefore, computers are located within the classrooms rather than in a lab setting. Each classroom has a computer center with Macintosh computer, printer, and color monitor. IBM computers are available in some classrooms as well. Children are moved towards computer literacy at their own pace and are encouraged to use the computer when appropriate as a tool as they go about their daily work. Older students publish a school newspaper using desktop publishing.

Library: White Rock Montessori School puts great emphasis on its ever-growing library. Books are kept in areas where they are easily accessed by children, parents, and teachers throughout the school, rather than in one central location. For example, a shelf of books about plants might be located in the classroom next to the botany materials. Each classroom has access to a computerized disk which will enable students and teachers to locate all books in the school library. The school maintains a lending library for parents.

Snack Procedures: Provided for preschool children and after-school children

Before-school Care Program Available: Yes, 7:00 a.m.–8:30 a.m.

After-school Care Program Available: Yes, 3:00 p.m.–6:00 p.m.

Nurse on Staff: No

Emergency Procedure Used: First aid administered in office; all staff members are trained in CPR and first aid.

Transportation to and from School: No

Counseling and Evaluation Available: Yes

Graduation Information

Testing: N/A

Average SAT Scores: N/A

High School Our Students Usually Attend: D.I.S.D., R.I.S.D., Lakehill, Greenhill

Percentage of Seniors Attending College: 95

Additional Information

550

WHITE ROCK
MONTESSORI

TWO LOCATIONS

3204 Skillman   **827-3220**

6202 E. Mockingbird Lane   **827-3220**

Ages 3 through grade 8

MIDDLE SCHOOL OPENING
AUGUST 1996

Montessori:
A method of educating the human potential
with emphasis on each child as an indivdual.

Serving the families of Dallas since 1975, White Rock Montessori
welcomes children of any race, creed, color, ethnicity, or national
origin.

White Rock Montessori School

6202 E. Mockingbird Ln. (satellite location)   Mapsco: 36J
Dallas, TX 75214
(214) 827-3220   Fax: (214) 827-3229

Office Hours: 8:30 a.m.–4:30 p.m.
School Hours: Preschool, 8:30 a.m.–11:30 a.m.
K–6th, 8:30 a.m.–3:00 p.m.; lower elementary, 8:30 a.m.– 3:00
p.m. (before- and after-school care: 7:00 a.m.–8:30 a.m. and
3:00 p.m.–6:00 p.m.)
School Grades Offered: PK–grade 6; (grades 7 and 8 open
in August 1996)
Enrollment: 93
Co-ed: Yes
Boy/Girl Ratio: 43:53
Student/Teacher Ratio: 11:1, preschool; 15:1, lower elementary;
18:1 upper elementary
Average Class Size: 23, preschool; 18, elementary
Calendar School Year: August–May
Holidays: Labor Day, Fair Day, Thanksgiving, winter
break (2 weeks), spring break (1 week), Easter
Uniform Requirements: No
Founded in: 1975

Philosophy of School

The only valid impulse to learning is the self-motivation of the child. The adult prepares
the environment, directs the activity, functions as the authority, and offers the stimulation, but it is the child who must be motivated by the work itself to persist in his/her
given task. Towards this end, the work is individualized and self-paced. Each child is
encouraged to express himself/herself creatively and to develop to his/her own fullest
potential.

Academic Curriculum

Content: Each classroom offers a full complement of sequential Montessori

materials covering development in practical life and sensorial experiences, as well as math, reading, language, geography, history, biology, science, geometry, and the fine arts. Other carefully selected materials are used as well.
Grading System Used: Parent-teacher conferences used; progress reports given in December and May; cumulative portfolios
Conferences per Year: Upon request; two scheduled by school
Tests Administered: Stanford Achievement and Diagnostic each spring–elementary students only
Homework Policy: Planned individually for each student when deemed beneficial
Method of Discipline: Emphasis on self-discipline and peer mediation; teachers intervene when necessary; collaboration between teachers and parents emphasized

Enrichment Curriculum

The classroom curriculum incorporates Spanish, cultural studies, cooking, music, art, drama, computer, library, physical education, and care of plants and animals; all of these classes are fully integrated into the curriculum and available for the child to choose daily. Professionals supervise weekly music, art, and Spanish classes and daily physical education classes. Field trips are an important part of the elementary curriculum.

Extracurricular Activities

After-school activities include art classes, piano and violin lessons, soccer teams, campfire and Girl Scouts; fifth and sixth grade students have a spring camp out.

Goals for Students

Our goal is for each child to maintain an enthusiasm for learning and an appreciation for his/her own uniqueness as well as that of others. We want our students to maintain the self-discipline and love of independence that will allow them to develop to their fullest potential. Montessori education is a preparation for life.

Faculty/Staff Requirements

Qualifications of Staff: Must have degrees and AMS certification or the equivalent; 25% of the staff have master's degrees
Qualifications of Administrator: B.A., all levels of Texas State Teachers Certification, AMS certification, 24 years professional experience in teaching

School Information

Brochure Available: Yes

Number of Students in Each Grade: Preschool, 24; lower elementary (grades 1–3), 20; upper elementary (grades 4–6), 20
Parochial: No
Organization Affiliations: American Montessori Society (AMS) and North American Montessori Teacher Association
Accreditations: AMS
Parental Involvement: Parents' club, parent volunteers
Other Information:

Admittance

Whom to Contact: Sue Henry
Date to Apply: March (prior to that for waiting list)
Entrance Testing: No
Fees Involved: $150 deposit when a child enrolls ($100 of which is applied to the first tuition payment)
Type of Student Preferred: Children from supportive families who are eager to learn and are self-disciplined
Forms Required: Yes
Individual/Group Appointments: Individual
Testing Procedure per Age/Grade Level: None for admittance; standardized tests administered each spring to the elementary students to assist the staff in evaluating progress and planning each child's individual curriculum
Notification Procedure: By phone, following interview with parents and child
Waiting List Policy: Ongoing

Tuition

Approximate Tuition for 1996-97 School Year: Preschool 1/2 day, $2434; preschool extended day, $3890; lower elementary, $4154; upper elementary, $4296; middle school $5000
Methods of Payment Available: Monthly, by the semester, or annually
Financial Assistance Offered: Limited
Cancellation Insurance Available: No
Profit/Non-profit: Non-profit

Additional Costs:

Books/Bag/Uniform: Books–included in tuition; no bag or uniform requirements
Lunch Fee: No
Parents Club Dues: Included in tuition
Annual Fund Drive: Yes
Discount for Siblings: No

Facilities/Services Provided

Computer Lab: White Rock Montessori believes in integrating computer use into the day-to-day environment; therefore, computers are located within the classrooms rather than in a lab setting. Each classroom has a computer center with Macintosh computer, printer, and color monitor. IBM computers are available in some classrooms as well. Children are moved towards computer literacy at their own pace and are encouraged to use the computer when appropriate as a tool as they go about their daily work. Older students publish a school newspaper using desktop publishing.

Library: White Rock Montessori School puts great emphasis on its ever-growing library. Books are kept in areas where they are easily accessed by children, parents, and teachers throughout the school, rather than in one central location. For example, a shelf of books about plants might be located in the classroom next to the botany materials. Each classroom has access to a computerized disk which will enable students and teachers to locate all books in the school library. The school maintains a lending library for parents.

Snack Procedures: Provided for preschool children and after-school children

Before-school Care Program Available: Yes, 7:00 a.m.–8:30 a.m.

After-school Care Program Available: Yes, 3:00 p.m.–6:00 p.m.

Nurse on Staff: No

Emergency Procedure Used: First aid administered in office; all staff members are trained in CPR and first aid.

Transportation to and from School: No

Counseling and Evaluation Available: Yes

Graduation Information

Testing: N/A

Average SAT Scores: N/A

High School Our Students Usually Attend: D.I.S.D., R.I.S.D., Lakehill, Greenhill

Percentage of Seniors Attending College: 95

Additional Information

Windsong Montessori School

4331 Allencrest Lane
Dallas, TX 75244
(214) 239-0537

Mapsco: 14Y

Fax: (214) 490-0537

Office Hours: 7:30 a.m.–6:00 p.m.
School Hours: 9:00 a.m.–4:00 p.m.
School Grades Offered: Kindergarten (age 5)–grade 4
Enrollment: 25
Co-ed: Yes
Boy/Girl Ratio: 1:1
Student/Teacher Ratio: 11:1
Calendar School Year: August–May
Average Class Size: 22
Holidays Observed: Labor Day, Thanksgiving, Christmas, spring break
Uniform Requirements: No
Founded in: 1992

Philosophy of School

The Windsong Montessori School offers a unique individualized program. At the Windsong Montessori School, there is an enduring commitment to Dr. Montessori's method of education. The goal of the school is to give students the foundation for developing a strong reasoning ability, an exceptional method for studying effectively, and a deep-rooted love of learning. The depth to which any topic can be understood is limited only by a student's interest and ability. The core curriculum, which includes math, geometry, reading, writing, and spelling, is highly individualized and carefully monitored to ensure each student's maximum individual program.

Academic Curriculum

Content: Montessori math, language (reading, spelling, grammar, composition, literary analysis for older students), cultural subjects (zoology, botany, geometry, geography, geology), portfolio (advanced elementary students)

556

Grading System Used: Teacher progress reports; rating system 1-4
Conferences per Year: Three
Tests Administered: Stanford Achievement; Albanesi Curriculum Placement
Homework Policy: None
Method of Discipline: Peer problem solving; adult mediator; sitting aside

Enrichment Curriculum

Art appreciation, scientific enrichment and martial arts may be introduced throughout the year as enjoyable additions.

Extracurricular Activities

Summer programs may include swimming, drama, art, and field trips.

Goals for Students

High level of academic achievement combined with a lifelong enjoyment of learning.

Faculty/Staff Requirements

Qualifications of Staff: Certified Montessori teachers; Montessori interns
Qualifications of Administrator: Both of the co-directors have Montessori certification; one has regular secondary certification and an M.S. in Special Education.

School Information

Brochure Available: Yes
Number of Students in Each Grade: Multi-age grouping; population fluxuates in mixed grades
Parochial: No
Organization Affiliations: A.M.I.T.O.T.
Accreditations: A.M.I.T.O.T.
Parental Involvement: Field trip support; reader-listeners
Other Information:

Admittance

Whom to Contact: Admission office: Jere Albanesi or Frances Bradshaw
Date to Apply: Admissions open year-round; February, March, April are ideal.
Testing Procedure per Age/Grade Level:
Fees Involved: $150 covers application and testing fees.
Type of Student Preferred: Students who prefer self-paced learning instead of

regimented classes
Forms Required: Application forms and previous school records
Individual/Group Appointments: Testing and evaluation are conducted during class.
Notification Procedure: By conference
Waiting List Policy: N/A

Tuition

Approximate Tuition for 1996-97 School Year: $4900
Methods of Payment Available: Monthly, by semester, or annually
Financial Assistance Offered: 10% discount for additional students of same family enrolled at the same time
Cancellation Insurance Available: N/A
Profit/Non-profit: Profit

Additional Costs

Books/Bag/Uniform: No
Lunch Fee: Voluntary–catered
Parents Club Dues: N/A
Annual Fund Drive: N/A
Discount for Siblings: 10%

Facilities/Services Provided

Computer Lab: Macintosh and IBM
Library:
Snack Procedures: N/A
Before-school Care Program Available: 7:30 a.m.–9:00 a.m.
After-school Care Program Available: 4:00 p.m.–6:00 p.m.
Nurse on Staff: No
Emergency Procedure Used: Apply first aid; call parents or 911
Transportation to and from School: No
Counseling and Evaluation Available: No

Graduation Information

Testing: N/A
Average SAT Scores: N/A
High School Our Students Usually Attend: Private and public schools
Percentage of Seniors Attending College: N/A

Additional Information

The school is an internship site for M.T.I. student teachers.

NAEYC
National Association for the Education of Young Children

1509 16th Street N.W.
Washington, D. C. 20036-1426
(800) 424-2460
Dr. Sue Bredekamp

The National Association for the Education of Young Children (NAEYC), the nation's oldest and largest organization of early childhood educators, is a non-profit, professional organization comprised of educators, parents, pediatricians, students, directors, and other individuals who are concerned with and involved in the development of children ages birth through eight. The National Academy of Early Childhood Programs administers a national, voluntary accreditation system for all types of preschools, kindergartens, child care centers, and school-age child care programs. Accreditation is a three-step process which involves a self-study, validation visit, and a commission decision. The accreditation process improves the quality of programs by evaluating curriculum, administration, staff qualifications and development, physical environment, health and safety, interactions among staff and children, and parental involvement. Accreditation from NAEYC is valid for a three-year period. At the end of the term, programs must re-apply for accreditation. You may request a list of accredited programs by writing NAEYC.

> **Akiba Academy Early Childhood Education (see SACS)**
> **Callier Child Development Preschool**
> **The Children's Workshop**
> **The Creative Preschool Co-op**
> **The Creative School**
> **Early Learning Center at First Christian Church**
> **East Dallas Community School (see Montessori)**
> **Epiphany Day School (pending, see SAES)**
> **First United Methodist Church Day School (Preschool & Kindergarten)**
> **Glen Oaks School**
> **Glenwood Day School**

Highland Park United Methodist Church Child Development Program
Jewish Community Center at Dallas Preschool
Lakewood United Methodist Developmental Learning Center
Lovers Lane United Methodist Church Weekday School
Northaven Co-operative Preschool and Kindergarten
North Dallas Day School
The Parish Day School (see ISAS)
Preston-Royal Preschool
Rainbow Connection of Central Christian Church
Schreiber Methodist Preschool
Temple Emanu-El Preschool
Westminster Presbyterian Preschool & Kindergarten (pending)

Callier Child Development Preschool

1966 Inwood Rd.   Mapsco: 34T
Dallas, TX 75235-7298
(214) 883-3094   Fax: (214) 883-3022

Office Hours: 7:30 a.m.–4:00 p.m.
School Hours: 7:30 a.m.–6:00 p.m.
School Grades Offered: Preschool–kindergarten
Enrollment: 140
Co-ed: Yes
Boy/Girl Ratio: Varies
Student/Teacher Ratio: 7:1
Average Class Size: 16
Calendar School Year: Year round
Holidays: Traditional, one-week spring break
Uniform Requirements: No
Founded in: 1977

Philosophy of School

The U.T. Dallas Callier Child Development Preschool offers a warm, accepting environment for young children. Qualified, degreed teachers provide learning activities and experiences in a stimulating, creative atmosphere designed to encourage curiosity, exploration, and discovery.

Children develop positive attitudes about themselves as they learn daily routines, master new skills, expand interests, and participate in planning and decision-making. A developmental approach allows teachers to program for needs, abilities, interests, and personal learning pace and style. Ongoing assessment is an essential tool in planning.

Believing that the family is the child's primary environment, Callier is committed to supporting and strengthening the child-parent relationship. Parents are always welcome and visitors have standing invitations for lunch and field trips. An active Parents'

Association helps to maintain a close partnership between parents and school.

Activities for ages 2-5 are organized with multi-age grouping through team teaching. Teachers move through the three years of preschool with their classes to facilitate the primary caregiver relationship. The kindergarten teacher does not rotate.

A special part of the preschool curriculum is cooperative programming with the DISD-Dallas Regional Day School for the Deaf programs, also on the Callier campus. Each preschool class includes students who are hearing-impaired. Some students at each level have the opportunity to learn sign language. This colloboration enriches the educational experiences of all students.

Eligibility for classes is determined by age as of September 1. Enrollment for the coming school year's new two-year-old class begins the preceding April; no waiting list for that class is maintained until enrollment opens. In other classes, openings are filled from the waiting list as they occur.

Our program is child-centered, developmentally appropriate, active learning.

Academic Curriculum
Content: Developmental; state-essential elements
Grading System Used: Student-centered assessment
Conferences per Year: Two or as needed
Tests Administered:
Homework Policy: Kindergarten, age-appropriate
Method of Discipline: Positive guidance

Enrichment Curriculum
Bi-monthly field trips

Extracurricular Activities
Dance, swimming

Goals for Students
The Callier Child Development Preschool's developmental philosophy incorporates the following goals:
1. To provide for all aspects of a child's developmental needs including communication and language skills, physical abilities, emotional and social growth, and cognitive development

2. To emphasize learning as a social process that stresses exploration and interaction with adults, other children, and materials
3. To emphasize learning as an active process, using experiences that are concrete, real, and relevant to the lives of young children
4. To foster an environment in which children have an opportunity to communicate, play, and develop friendships with children whose interests, abilities, levels of hearing, and/or methods of communication may be different from their own

Faculty/Staff Requirements

Qualifications of Staff: Degreed teachers
Qualifications of Administrator(s): M.S., early childhood teaching certification; M.A., supervisor certification

School Information

Brochure Available: Yes
Number of Students in Each Grade: 2's–20; 3's–28; 4's–28; 5's–14
Parochial: No
Organization Affiliations: U.T. Dallas; Dallas Public Schools; Dallas Regional Day School for the Deaf
Accreditations: NAEYC (since 1986)
Parental Involvement: High
Other Information:

Admittance

Whom to Contact: Education office
Date to Apply: Two-year-olds–enrollment in April
Testing Procedure for Age/Grade Level: N/A
Fees Involved: $50 enrollment fee
Type of Student Preferred:
Forms Required: Enrollment packet, including immunization records
Individual/Group Appointments: Individual
Notification Procedure: Personal
Waiting List Policy: On-going

Tuition

Approximate Tuition for 1996-97 School Year: $250/month for 2 yr. olds; $400/month for 3 and 4 yr. olds; $410/month for kindergarten
Methods of Payment Available: Monthly billing
Financial Assistance Offered: Limited; in special circumstances
Cancellation Insurance Available: No
Profit/Non-profit: Non-profit

Additional Costs

Books/Bag/Uniform: No; field trip–$10/semester
Lunch Fee: $6.25/week
Parents Club Dues: No
Annual Fund Drive: No
Discount for Siblings: No

Facilities/Services Provided

Computer Lab: Yes, in classrooms
Library: Yes
Snack Procedures: Included in tuition
Before-school Care Program Available: N/A
After-school Care Program Available: N/A
Nurse on Staff: Yes
Emergency Procedure Used: Posted
Transportation to and from School: Only for deaf-education students
Counseling and Evaluation Available: Yes

Graduation Information

Testing: N/A
Average SAT Scores: N/A
High School Our Students Usually Attend: N/A
Percentage of Seniors Attending College: N/A

Additional Information

The Children's Workshop

1409 14th St.
Plano, TX 75074
(214) 424-1932

Mapsco: 659X

Fax:

Office Hours: 8:30 a.m.
School Hours: Varies
School Grades Offered: Preschool (3 years)–grade 5
Enrollment: 155
Co-ed: Yes
Boy/Girl Ratio: Varies by year
Student/Teacher Ratio: 10:1, 9:1
Average Class Size: 18
Calendar School Year: August–May (eight-week summer program)
Holidays: Same as Plano Independent School District
Uniform Requirements: None
Founded in: 1972

Philosophy of School

We build on the strengths of each child. We believe children are born wanting to discover, learn, grow, and be loved and accepted by others. Our school fosters the individual child's strengths while giving help in those areas in which the child has difficulty. Children and teachers alike are learning in an atmosphere that fosters discovery, critical thinking, language development, and respect for the genius in each of us.

Academic Curriculum

Content: Language arts, math, science, social studies and geography, Spanish, music, arts and crafts, computer, field trips
Grading System Used: None–Parents are constantly advised of their children's progress.
Conferences per Year: Two scheduled, but as many as necessary

(Teachers are in close contact with the parents.)
Tests Administered: In-class test for primary students
Homework Policy:
Method of Discipline:

Enrichment Curriculum
Constant attention to child's language development; each child receives individual, undivided attention from his/her teachers.

Extracurricular Activities

Goals for Students
To develop into compassionate, thoughtful individuals; to understand that effort and desire to achieve can overcome obstacles; to keep alive each child's natural curiosity and verve for learning

Faculty/Staff Requirements
Qualifications of Staff: Minimum: bachelor's degree and teaching/parenting experience
Qualifications of Administrator: Teaching certificate; UN, London; 20 years ongoing experience learning, teaching, and administering

School Information
Brochure Available: Yes
Number of Students in Each Grade: N/A
Parochial:
Organization Affiliations: NAEYC, CCAEYC
Accreditations: NAEYC
Parental Involvement: Yes
Other Information:

Admittance
Whom to Contact: Jo Howser, Neva Smith–office (214) 424-1932
Date to Apply: Registration in February each year; we accept children during the year as space is available.
Testing Procedure per Age/Grade Level:
Fees Involved: Registration

Type of Student Preferred:
Forms Required: Necessary medical verification
Individual/Group Appointments: Each parent is required to meet with the director and visit classes.
Notification Procedure: By mail
Waiting List Policy: Varies, according to class

Tuition

Approximate Tuition for 1996-97 School Year: $900–$2925
Methods of Payment Available: Monthly payments
Financial Assistance Offered: N/A
Cancellation Insurance Available: N/A
Profit/Non-profit:

Additional Costs:

Books/Bag/Uniform: N/A
Lunch Fee: Primary children bring lunch; juice provided; picnic under trees
Parents Club Dues: N/A
Annual Fund Drive: N/A
Discount for Siblings: N/A

Facilities/Services Provided

Computer Lab: Computers are available to all age children in subject areas and in composing and editing the school newspaper.
Library: Each of our three buildings has a catalogued library of books and visual aids.
Before-school Care Program Available: No
After-school Care Program Available: No
Nurse on Staff: No, our staff is trained in basic first aid and CPR.
Emergency Procedure Used: Parent contacted immediately
Transportation to and from School: By parents, car pools, help available
Counseling and Evaluation Available: School can recommend professionals with whom we have worked.

Graduation Information

Testing: N/A
Average SAT Scores: N/A
High School Our Students Usually Attend:
Percentage of Seniors Attending College: N/A

Additional Information

Our staff of experienced, caring, creative individuals love learning with the children. Our homelike setting in an historic, tree-shaded area of Plano provides a secure, memorable beginning to a child's school experiences.

Creative Preschool Co-op

1210 West Beltline Road   Mapsco: 16C
Richardson, TX 75080
(214) 234-4791   Fax:

Office Hours: 8:30 a.m.–12:30 p.m.
School Hours: 9:00 a.m.–12:00 p.m.
School Grades Offered: Preschool
Enrollment: 88
Co-ed: Yes
Boy/Girl Ratio: 50:50
Student/Teacher Ratio: 6:1 (2-year-olds); 7:1 (3 & 4-year-olds);
with parent co-oping in class
Average Class Size: 12
Calendar School Year: August–May
Holidays: Same as R.I.S.D.
Uniform Requirements: None
Founded in: 1972

Philosophy of School

The Creative Preschool Co-op seeks to:
- develop in each child high self-esteem and a love of learning
- facilitate positive social development
- foster the child's imagination and creativity
- support parents and help them develop their parenting skills to their highest potential

Academic Curriculum

Content: Music, art, computer orientation, familiarization with letters and numbers
Grading System Used: None
Conferences per Year: Two
Tests Administered: None

570

Homework Policy: None
Method of Discipline: Help children accept and express feelings and work out positive outcomes

Enrichment Curriculum
Music teacher for all classes once or twice per week; familiarization with computer keyboard and mouse; pets in all classrooms

Extracurricular Activities
Extended day until 2:30 p.m. on Tuesdays, Wednesdays, and Thursdays; field trip with dads twice a year; family outings

Goals for Students
To learn through creativity and play in a stimulating and supportive environment with teachers and parents; develop gross motor skills in the muscle room and on the new state-of-the-art playground

Faculty/Staff Requirements
Qualifications of Staff: College degree
Qualifications of Administrator: College degree

School Information
Brochure Available: Yes
Number of Students in Each Grade: 12 (2-year-olds)–14 (4-year-olds)
Parochial: Non-denominational
Organization Affiliations: None
Accreditations: NAEYC
Parental Involvement: Assist teacher in classroom on a rotation schedule; help administer school
Other Information: Parents' Day Out available; parents help each other by babysitting siblings for co-op workers

Admittance
Whom to Contact: Annie Konidaris, Director
Date to Apply: Anytime
Testing Procedure for Age/Grade Level: None
Fees Involved: $60 registration; $65 P.D.O.; $100 2-day class; $120 3-day class; $145 4-day class; supply fees: $7.50 P.D.O.; $15 2-day class; $22.50 3-day class; $30 4-day class

Type of Student Preferred: Open to all preschool students, regardless of race, gender, or disability
Forms Required: Up-to-date vaccination history and medical history signed by doctor; filled out Creative Preschool Co-op enrollment forms
Individual/Group Appointments: Call the school to arrange a visit.
Notification Procedure: Parents notified of acceptance either at time of the visit or by phone
Waiting List Policy: Ongoing

Tuition

Approximate Tuition for 1996-97 School Year: Monthly tuition: $65 (PDO); $100 (2-day class); $120 (3-day class); $145 (4-day class)
Methods of Payment Available: Parents pay by check monthly.
Financial Assistance Offered: None
Cancellation Insurance Available: Registration fee and supply fee non-refundable; prepaid May tuition refundable for students who withdraw before January
Profit/Non-profit: Non-profit

Additional costs:

Books/Bag/Uniform: None
Lunch Fee: Extended-day students bring their own lunch; tuition $25 per month
Parents Club Dues: None
Annual Fund Drive: Fundraising projects ongoing
Discount for Siblings: Registration fee $40; monthly tuition $5 off

Facilities/Services Provided

Computer Lab: Three computers in muscle room
Library: Music book library for children; parenting library for adults
Snack Procedures: The co-op parent provides a nutritious snack and drink for entire class.
Before-school Care Program Available: None
After-school Care Program Available: Extended-day program on Tuesdays, Wednesdays, and Thursdays until 2:30 p.m.
Nurse on Staff: No, but all staff members are trained in CPR and first aid.
Emergency Procedure Used: Fire drill, tornado drill; parents fill out forms specifying medical emergency procedure.
Transportation to and from School: None
Counseling and Evaluation Available: Teacher conferences twice a year; referrals for counseling available on request

Graduation Information

Testing: N/A
Average SAT Scores: N/A
High School Our Students Usually Attend: Public
Percentage of Seniors Attending College: N/A

Additional Information

Parents administer the school.

The Creative School

Walnut Hill United Methodist Church
10066 Marsh Lane
Dallas, TX 75229
(214) 352-0732

Mapsco: 23M

Fax: (214) 357-3753

Office Hours: 8:00 a.m.–3:00 p.m.
School Hours: 9:00 a.m.–2:00 p.m.
School Grades Offered: 18 months–kindergarten
Enrollment: 88
Co-ed: Yes
Boy/Girl Ratio: Varies
Student/Teacher Ratio: Varies according to age
Average Class Size: 12
Calendar School Year: Traditional 9-month calendar
Holidays: Labor Day, Thanksgiving, Christmas, New Year's
Day, Martin Luther King Day, Presidents' Day, Easter, spring
break
Uniform Requirements: None
Founded in: 1956

Philosophy of School

We seek to offer each child a safe, nurturing environment in which to learn and grow.
We strive for each child to develop in the healthiest way–emotionally, socially,
cognitively, and physically.

Academic Curriculum

Content: Active learning units
Grading System Used: None
Conferences per Year: Two
Tests Administered: None
Homework Policy: None
Method of Discipline: Positive guidance

Enrichment Curriculum
Computers in each room; weekly music and motor lab with specialized teachers

Extracurricular Activities

Goals for Students
To develop a love of learning, a respect for self and others, and a positive self-image

Faculty/Staff Requirements
Qualifications of Staff: College degree in a field related to child development or early childhood education, experience with young children
Qualifications of Administrator:

School Information
Brochure Available: Yes
Number of Students in Each Grade: Varies
Parochial: No
Organization Affiliations:
Accreditations: National Association for the Education of Young Children
Parental Involvement: Parent Council and Do-Dads
Other Information: Licensed through the Texas Department of Human Services

Admittance
Whom to Contact: Mary Ellen Douglas, Director; Debbie Blades, Administrative Assistant
Date to Apply: February
Testing Procedure for Age/Grade Level: None
Fees Involved: Annual enrollment fee due at time of enrollment
Type of Student Preferred: All are welcome
Forms Required: Enrollment packet
Individual/Group Appointments: May schedule appointment or drop in
Notification Procedure:
Waiting List Policy: For open enrollment, 1st come, 1st served

Tuition
Approximate Tuition for 1996-97 School Year: Varies according to age
Methods of Payment Available: Monthly, by semester, yearly

Financial Assistance Offered: Scholarships available
Cancellation Insurance Available: N/A
Profit/Non-profit: Non-profit

Additional costs:

Books/Bag/Uniform: None
Lunch Fee: None
Parents Club Dues: None
Annual Fund Drive: Several fundraisers throughout the year
Discount for Siblings: No

Facilities/Services Provided

Computer Lab: Computers in each room
Library: Available to teachers for classrooms
Snack Procedures: Snacks furnished by children
Before-school Care Program Available: No
After-school Care Program Available: Extended care 12:00 p.m.–2:00 p.m. Monday–Friday
Nurse on Staff: No
Emergency Procedure Used: N/A
Transportation to and from School: N/A
Counseling and Evaluation Available: N/A

Graduation Information

Testing: N/A
Average SAT Scores: N/A
High School Our Students Usually Attend: N/A
Percentage of Seniors Attending College: N/A

Additional Information

Early Learning Center at First Christian Church

601 E. Main
Richardson, TX 75081
(214) 235-8233

Mapsco: 17H

Fax: N/A

Office Hours: 8:15 a.m.–12:15 p.m.
School Hours: 8:45 a.m.–11:45 a.m.; optional extended days,
Tuesday and Wednesday until 1:45 p.m.
School Grades Offered: 6 months–5 years
Enrollment: 60-70
Co-ed: Yes
Boy/Girl Ratio: 1:1
Student/Teacher Ratio: Infant 4:1; toddler 6:1; preschool 10:1
Average Class Size: 8
Calendar School Year: September–May
Holidays: Same as R.I.S.D.
Uniform Requirements: None
Founded in: 1974

Philosophy of School

To provide a positive environment that encourages children to feel good about
themselves, others, and their school experience. Through many structured and
unstructured activities, we reinforce developmentally appropriate readiness skills in
physical, social, emotional, and intellectual areas. Stressing "academics" is not our
philosophy–nurturing the whole child is.

Academic Curriculum

Content: Developmentally appropriate; supplemented with Music/Body
Rhythmics
Grading System Used: N/A
Conferences per Year: Two

577

Tests Administered: N/A
Homework Policy: N/A
Method of Discipline: Positive reinforcement; redirection

Enrichment Curriculum

Sand and Water Room; Bible stories; Music/Body Rhythmics; field trips; guest speakers

Extracurricular Activities

Goals for Students

To create a positive environment that allows children to participate in meaningful play that benefits their developmental needs and coincides with their interests and abilities.

Faculty/Staff Requirements

Qualifications of Staff: Varies; some have education degrees. All staff receive 15 hours of training yearly. All are trained in first aid and CPR.
Qualifications of Administrator: B.S. in Elementary Education; M.Ed.; 20 hours of training yearly

School Information

Brochure Available: Yes
Number of Students in Each Grade: N/A
Parochial: N/A
Organization Affiliations: NAEYC, MNKA, DAEYC
Accreditations: NAEYC; licensed by state
Parental Involvement: Volunteers, field trips, conferences, Open House, Father's Night, Preschool Board, Mother's Day Tea, all-school picnic; class parties
Other Information:

Admittance

Whom to Contact: Diana Miller, Director (214) 235-8233
Date to Apply: Spring and fall, but spaces may be available any time
Testing Procedure for Age/Grade Level: N/A
Fees Involved: Registration $75 (MDO), $110 (preschool)
Type of Student Preferred: N/A
Forms Required: Contract, emergency release, physician statement and

various licensing required papers
Individual/Group Appointments:
Notification Procedure: N/A
Waiting List Policy: Some (depends on age)

Tuition
Approximate Tuition for 1996-97 School Year: Ranges from $420–$1440
Methods of Payment Available: Monthly payments
Financial Assistance Offered: Check with office
Cancellation Insurance Available: No
Profit/Non-profit: Non-profit

Additional costs:
Books/Bag/Uniform: N/A
Lunch Fee: N/A
Parents Club Dues: N/A
Annual Fund Drive: N/A
Discount for Siblings: N/A

Facilities/Services Provided
Computer Lab: Computers in the preschool rooms
Library: Reading center in each room; parent-resource area
Snack Procedures: Healthy snacks provided by school
Mondays, Tuesdays, and Wednesdays; provided by parents Thursdays and
Fridays
Before-school Care Program Available: N/A
After-school Care Program Available: Available through HUGS program;
after school until 6:00 p.m.
Nurse on Staff: No; all staff trained in first aid and CPR
Emergency Procedure Used: Parents notified; if necessary, child transported
by EMT
Transportation to and from School: No
Counseling and Evaluation Available: No

Graduation Information
Testing: N/A
Average SAT Scores: N/A
High School Our Students Usually Attend: N/A
Percentage of Seniors Attending College: N/A

First United Methodist Church Day School (Preschool and Kindergarten)

801 W. Ave. B at Glenbrook
Garland, TX 75040
(214) 494-3096 or (214) 272-3471

Mapsco: 19Y

Fax: (214) 272-3473

Office Hours: 8:30 a.m.–2:30 p.m.
School Hours: 9:00 a.m.–12:00 p.m.; extended day 12:00 noon–2:30 p.m.
School Grades Offered: Preschool (ages 3 and 4) and kindergarten (age 5)
Enrollment: 160
Co-ed: Yes
Boy/Girl Ratio: Varies according to enrollment
Student/Teacher Ratio: 10:2–14:2
Average Class Size: 10–14
Calendar School Year: Early September–end of May
Holidays: Same as Garland Independent School District
Uniform Requirements: No
Founded in: 1968

Philosophy of School

To provide learning experiences for children of the church membership and the community in an environment which encourages the child to:

- ask questions
- explore, experiment
- develop a new security and independence in the world outside the home
- make friends and learn to get along with children and adults
- find that he/she is a person to be valued for his/her own unique being–a child of God.

Our school is Christian oriented but not denominationally sectarian. We stress those elements of the faith common to all Christians.

We plan for our enrollment to include a cross-section of races, nationalities, and economic backgrounds.

Under the leadership of quality teachers, the classes include a balance of guided play activities, creative art work, music, outdoor play, conversation, storytime, dramatic play, and group activities. Each child is helped to grow in independence, social development, and to develop his/her own unique talents and abilities.

Academic Curriculum

Content: Developmentally appropriate activities in conjunction with Developmental Learning Materials Curriculum
Grading System Used: No
Conferences per Year: Two (fall and spring)
Tests Adminstered: None
Homework Policy: No
Method of Discipline:

Enrichment Curriculum

Body-rhythmics classes which correlate with units of study; field trips; special children's programs; children's entertainers; authors

Extracurricular Activities

See Enrichment Curriculum.

Goals for Students

1. To provide opportunities for being with other children in a setting conducive to the development of wholesome social relationships
2. To provide appropriate play experiences that contribute to the developmental needs of the child
3. To provide meaningful activities that are based on the child's individual needs, interests, and ability to build important foundations for future skills and pursuits

Faculty/Staff Requirements

Qualifications of Staff: College degree and experience
Qualifications of Administrator: B.S. in Elementary Education; M.Ed. in Early Childhood Education; Certified Director of Christian Education, United

Methodist Church; Diaconal Minister, United Methodist Church; teacher and administrator, 23 years

School Information
Brochure Available: Yes
Number of Students in Each Grade: 3's–85; 4's–154; kindergarten–18
Parochial: No
Organization Affiliations: Association for Childhood Education International, DAEYC, NAEYC, SACUS, Kindergarten Teachers of Texas, Dallas Methodist Nursery Kindergarten Association, Ecumenical Childcare Network
Accreditations: NAEYC, National Academy of Early Childhood Program, Texas Department of Human Services
Parental Involvement: Volunteers; parenting programs; class activities
Other Information:

Admittance
Whom to Contact: Grace Ashley, Director
Date to Apply: Any time
Testing Procedure per Age/Grade Level: N/A
Fees Involved: $70–$95 enrollment fee
Type of Student Preferred: Open
Forms Required: Yes
Individual/Group Appointments: Either, any time
Notification Procedure: Letter sent
Waiting List Policy: When classes fill

Tuition
Approximate Tuition for 1996-97 School Year: Two-day class–$95/month; three-day class–$110/month; five-day class–$155/month
Methods of Payment Available: Monthly
Financial Assistance Offered: No
Cancellation Insurance Available: No
Profit/Non-profit: Non-profit

Additional Costs
Books/Bag/Uniform: N/A
Lunch Fee: No
Parents Club Dues: No
Annual Fund Drive: No
Discount for Siblings: No

Facilities/Services Provided

Computer Lab: No
Library: Yes
Snack Procedures: Yes
Before-school Care Program Available: No
After-school Care Program Available: Tuesdays and Wednesdays until 2:30 p.m.
Nurse on Staff: Staff certified in CPR and first aid
Emergency Procedure Used: Stated in school handbook
Transportation to and from School: No
Counseling and Evaluation Available: No

Graduation Information

Testing: N/A
Average SAT Scores: N/A
High School Our Students Usually Attend: N/A
Percentage of Seniors Attending College: N/A

Additional Information

Glen Oaks School

12105 Plano Road
Dallas, TX 75243
(214) 231-3135

Mapsco: 18W

Fax: (214) 231-3135

Office Hours: 6:30 a.m.–6:15 p.m.
School Hours: 8:30 a.m.–3:00 p.m.
School Grades Offered: Primary grades (K–3); early childhood (18 months–5 years)
Enrollment: 260
Co-ed: Yes
Boy/Girl Ratio: 1:1
Student/Teacher Ratio: Primary grades, 17:1; early childhood, 6:1 to 13:1 (varies depending on age)
Average Class Size: 15
Calendar School Year: Mid-August through May; extended care year round
Holidays: Labor Day, Thanksgiving, winter break, Martin Luther King Day, spring break
Uniform Requirements: None
Founded in: 1979

Philosophy of School

Mission Statement:
The mission of Glen Oaks School is to provide a nurturing environment where children, parents, and staff work together to empower each child to reach his/her fullest potential.

Goals of the School:
For Children: To enable students to develop their full potential for life. (The social, emotional, cognitive, and physical development of each child is viewed as a whole, and each child is given the opportunity to develop at his/her own individual pace.)

For Parents: To be a resource in the areas of child development and appropriate

584

parenting methods. To encourage parents to interact with the staff and their child in the developmental process at Glen Oaks School.

For the Community: To support community efforts to improve the condition for the care and education of children through teacher training workshops, parent seminars, and advocacy efforts.

Academic Curriculum

Content: Developmental

Grading System Used: Varies by age; includes samples of student work, checklists; letter and numerical grades

Conferences per Year: Ongoing

Tests Administered: No standardized testing; performance reviewed every six weeks

Homework Policy: Daily assignments designed for children to complete in class; projects are designed for parents to complete with their children.

Method of Discipline: Glen Oaks School's basic philosophy and policy concerning discipline is that children need guidance rather than punishment. Children are learning to develop their own inner controls, and it is the responsibility of adults to guide them in the process. Limits are set and explained to the children. When children overstep these limits, positive guidance practices are used. These include restating the limits, redirection to another activity, or separation from the current activity. No physical punishment, such as spanking, hitting, or shaking, is used. We believe that loving, firm, consistent discipline is the most effective and appropriate way to guide young children.

Enrichment Curriculum

To achieve the school's goals, the students are given a variety of experiences, such as art, music, language-enrichment activities, cooperative games, field trips, and guest speakers in addition to the traditional academic content areas. The curriculum is designed to provide the child with skills that encourage self-assurance and problem-solving capabilities. Children become actively involved in the learning process by participating in hands-on activities that reflect their daily lives. As the child becomes older and enters the primary grades, more time is spent in teacher-directed activities and learning materials with more abstract symbols are introduced.

The curriculum emphasizes the growth of the whole child. As children grow and develop, the classroom schedule and learning environment become more complex. Activities are organized into age-appropriate units. Unit themes provide the vehicle for introducing language, math, and science concepts. Related classroom activities provide opportunities to share, explore, interact with others, and learn responsibility.

The program is under the direction of well-qualified teachers. The daily schedule and the weekly lesson plans are posted outside each classroom door.

Extracurricular Activities
Swim lessons, foreign language, physical education, dance, field trips, computer classes

Goals for Students
See "Philosophy of School."

Faculty/Staff Requirements
Qualifications of Staff: Primary grades–bachelor's degree; early childhood–child development degree, certificate or experience
Qualifications of Administrator: Same as faculty's requirements plus at least three years experience

School Information
Brochure Available: Yes
Number of Students in Each Grade: Varies
Parochial: No
Organization Affiliations: Association for the Education of Young Children
Accreditations: NAEYC; CCMS four-star status; TDPRS
Parental Involvement: Strongly encouraged; we have a parent-support group that meets monthly. Each class has a potluck dinner to get to know other families, parent-education seminars, class parties, open house, and end-of-the-year celebrations.
Other Information:

Admittance
Whom to Contact: Arlene Graham
Date to Apply: Registration open to the public in February
Testing Procedure for Age/Grade Level: N/A
Fees Involved: School term ($30 to $75) plus refundable deposit
Type of Student Preferred: Families who value the development of the whole child–physically, intellectually, socially, and emotionally
Forms Required: Enrollment, medical, field-trip, swimming, and emergency forms
Individual/Group Appointments: Available upon request; open-door policy
Notification Procedure: Two weeks
Waiting List Policy: Priority given to current families; complete enrollment forms for waiting list (no fees)

Tuition

Approximate Tuition for 1996-97 School Year: $350 a month + $50 for extended care (Tuition covers all school supplies, field trips, and meals.) Participation in fundraising activities and extracurricular activities is voluntary.
Methods of Payment Available: Monthly payments
Financial Assistance Offered: CCMS
Cancellation Insurance Available:
Profit/Non-profit: Profit

Additional costs:

Books/Bag/Uniform: No
Lunch Fee: No
Parents Club Dues: N/A
Annual Fund Drive: Voluntary
Discount for Siblings: N/A

Facilities/Services Provided

Computer Lab: Computers in classrooms
Library: Visit twice per month
Snack Procedures: Morning and afternoon; included in tuition
Before-school Care Program Available: Yes
After-school Care Program Available: Yes, 3:15–6:30
Nurse on Staff: No
Emergency Procedure Used: Contact parent–if not available, contact nearest hospital
Transportation to and from School: No
Counseling and Evaluation Available: Refer

Graduation Information

Testing: N/A
Average SAT Scores: N/A
High School Our Students Usually Attend: N/A
Percentage of Seniors Attending College: N/A

Additional Information

We offer summer camp and extended day care.

Glenwood Day School

2446 Apollo
Garland, TX 75044
(214) 530-4460

Mapsco: 19A

Fax: N/A

Office Hours: 7:30 a.m.–5:30 p.m.
School Hours: 6:30 a.m.–6:15 p.m.
School Grades Offered: Pre-K (18 months)–kindergarten; before-and after-school programs
Enrollment: 180
Co-ed: Yes
Boy/Girl Ratio:
Student/Teacher Ratio: Varies (NAEYC accreditation ratios); kindergarten–15:1
Average Class Size: 12–24
Calendar School Year: August-May; open year round
Holidays: Standard
Uniform Requirements: None
Founded in: 1993

Philosophy of School

The mission of Glenwood Day School is to provide a nurturing environment where children, parents, and staff work together to empower each child to reach his/her fullest potential.

Academic Curriculum

Content: Theme-based units taken from Texas Essential Elements
Grading System Used: Progress reports based on developmental levels
Conferences per Year: One
Tests Administered: None
Homework Policy: Weekly for kindergarten
Method of Discipline: Redirection, time out, parent involvement

Enrichment Curriculum
Monthly field trips, classroom computers

Extracurricular Activities
Ages 3-5 years–gymnastics, dance, Computers by High Tech Kids

Goals for Students
To develop the full potential for life that is in each child; the social, emotional, cognitive, and physical development of each child is viewed as a whole, and each child is given the opportunity to develop at his/her own individual pace.

Faculty/Staff Requirements
Qualifications of Staff: (Kindergarten) bachelor's degree in education
Qualifications of Administrator: Bachelor's degree in elementary education; master's degree in early childhood development

School Information
Brochure Available: Yes
Number of Students in Each Grade: (Kindergarten) 15
Parochial: No
Organization Affiliations: National Association for the Education of Young Children (NAEYC)
Accreditations: NAEYC; four-star vendor of Child Care Management Services (CCMS)
Parental Involvement: Parent committees
Other Information:

Admittance
Whom to Contact: Christine Hartley
Date to Apply: Year-round
Testing Procedure for Age/Grade Level: Classroom assignments by age (5 years old by September 1)
Fees Involved: Supply fee $75; enrollment deposit $182.50
Type of Student Preferred:
Forms Required: Enrollment forms from Glenwood, shot records
Individual/Group Appointments: Individual with principal
Notification Procedure: Parents are called.
Waiting List Policy: Ongoing

589

Tuition

Approximate Tuition for 1996-97 School Year: $200–$410 per month
Methods of Payment Available: Weekly, monthly
Financial Assistance Offered: No
Cancellation Insurance Available: None
Profit/Non-profit: Profit

Additional Costs

Books/Bag/Uniform: None
Lunch Fee: None
Parents Club Dues: None
Annual Fund Drive: None
Discount for Siblings: None

Facilities/Services Provided

Computer Lab: Classroom computers
Library: Monthly visits
Snack Procedures: Morning and afternoon snacks in classroom with teachers
Before-school Care Program Available: Yes, 6:30 a.m.–7:30 a.m.
After-school Care Program Available: Yes, 3:00 p.m.–6:15 p.m.
Nurse on Staff: No
Emergency Procedure Used: CPR/first aid certified; children released only to authorized adults
Transportation to and from School: No
Counseling and Evaluation Available:

Graduation Information

Testing: N/A
Average SAT Scores: N/A
High School Our Students Usually Attend: N/A
Percentage of Seniors Attending College: N/A

Additional Information

Highland Park United Methodist Church Child Development Program

3300 Mockingbird Lane
Dallas, TX 75205
(214) 521-2600

Mapsco: 35K

Fax: (214) 520-6451

Office Hours: 7:30 a.m.–6:00 p.m.
School Hours: 7:30 a.m.–6:00 p.m.
School Grades Offered: Infants–kindergarten
Enrollment: 170
Co-ed: Yes
Boy/Girl Ratio: N/A
Student/Teacher Ratio: Age appropriate
Average Class Size: 10
Calendar School Year: Preschool: September–May; full-day program–year round
Holidays: 12 holidays observed
Uniform Requirements: None
Founded in: 1973

Philosophy of School

To acknowledge and encourage the emotional, social, physical, spiritual, intellectual, and creative development of each individual child. We emphasize the value of each child and foster self-esteem, self-discipline, and intrinsic motivation.

Academic Curriculum

Content: Developmental
Grading System Used: N/A
Conferences per Year: Two
Tests Administered: None
Homework Policy: None
Method of Discipline: Positive

Enrichment Curriculum
Music, movement, chapel, computers in classrooms for four- and five-year-olds

Extracurricular Activities

Goals for Students
Our goal is that each child will:
1. Develop an ability to communicate effectively with teachers and classmates, to hear and imitate sounds used to form words, and to understand and follow simple instructions.
2. Develop a growing concept of the relationship of numbers, time, space, and form.
3. Have opportunities for observing and understanding the basic phenomena of weather and seasonal change.
4. Be introduced to the growth cycle of plants and animals.
5. Develop an awareness of music, an appreciation of sound and rhythm, and an ability to participate in some form of musical appreciation.
6. Learn more about self and others through informal role play.
7. Have opportunities for using art and craft materials to develop an increasing appreciation of form, color, and texture.
8. Understand that God has something to say to each person in every situation that will ever be encountered.
9. Learn how to understand what God says to each person through knowledge of the Bible, especially in relation to Jesus Christ, and through the work of the Holy Spirit in self and in others.
10. Become aware that each person is worthy of God's love and the love of other human beings.
11. Grow in assuming personal responsibility for self and others.
12. Develop understandings, attitudes, and skills appropriate for the child's particular age.
13. Experience the loving care of adults whose own lives exemplify commitment to the Christian community.
14. Develop a healthy body and promote wellness through practice of good hygiene.
15. Enhance physical development through opportunities to exercise both gross and fine motor skills.

Faculty/Staff Requirements
Qualifications of Staff: College degree in early childhood or child development
Qualifications of Administrator: Master's degree

School Information
Brochure Available: Yes
Number of Students in Each Grade: Varies
Parochial: Yes
Organization Affiliations: United Methodist Church
Accreditations: National Academy of Early Childhood Programs
Parental Involvement: Yes
Other Information:

Admittance
Whom to Contact: Martha Beddoe
Date to Apply: February
Testing Procedure per Age/Grade Level: N/A
Fees Involved: Registration; deposit
Type of Student Preferred:
Forms Required: Enrollment; medical
Individual/Group Appointments:
Notification Procedure: By letter
Waiting List Policy: Apply each year; every student must register each year.

Tuition
Approximate Tuition for 1996-97 School Year: Varied by program
Methods of Payment Available: Monthly or by semester
Financial Assistance Offered: No
Cancellation Insurance Available: No
Profit/Non-profit: Non-profit

Additional Costs
Books/Bag/Uniform: No
Lunch Fee: No
Parents Club Dues: No
Annual Fund Drive: Yes
Discount for Siblings: No

Facilities/Services Provided
Computer Lab: N/A
Library: N/A
Snack Procedures: Morning and afternoon snacks provided
Before-school Care Program Available: No
After-school Care Program Available: After kindergarten

Nurse on Staff: No
Emergency Procedure Used: 80% of teachers trained in first aid and CPR
Transportation to and from School: No
Counseling and Evaluation Available: No

Graduation Information

Testing: N/A
Average SAT Scores: N/A
High School Our Students Usually Attend: N/A
Percentage of Seniors Attending College: N/A

Additional Information

.

Jewish Community Center of Dallas Preschool

7900 Northaven
Dallas, TX 75230
(214) 739-0225

Mapsco: 26A

Fax: (214) 368-4709

Office Hours: 7:30 a.m.–6:00 p.m.
School Hours: 7:30 a.m.–6:00 p.m.
School Grades Offered: 16 months–kindergarten
Enrollment: 243
Co-ed: Yes
Boy/Girl Ratio:
Student/Teacher Ratio: Toddler, 10:2; 2-year-olds, 12:2;
3-year-olds, 16:2; 4-year-olds, 17:2; kindergarten, 22:2
Average Class Size:
Calendar School Year: August–May
Holidays: All Jewish holidays and national holidays
Uniform Requirements: No
Founded in:

Philosophy of School

Children are encouraged to express themselves creatively through music, art, dance, and language. The curriculum helps children to be enthusiastic learners who become independent, self-confident, and inquisitive. Children are helped to feel good about themselves, who they are, and what they can do.

Academic Curriculum

Content: Age-appropriate curriculum
Grading System Used: N/A
Conferences per Year: Two
Tests Administered: N/A

Homework Policy: N/A
Method of Discipline: Redirection

Enrichment Curriculum
Enrichment classes including gymnastics, cooking, computers, woodworking, dance

Extracurricular Activities
N/A

Goals for Students
Children learn individually, in small groups, and with the entire class. Our goal is that each child maximize his/her potential.

Faculty/Staff Requirements
Qualifications of Staff: Degree in elementary education, early childhood; many years of experience
Qualifications of Administrator: M.A. in Child Development; 20+ years of experience

School Information
Brochure Available: Yes
Number of Students in Each Grade: Differs according to age
Parochial:
Organization Affiliations: N/A
Accreditations: National Association for the Education of Young Children
Parental Involvement: Parent-Teacher Organization; Board of Education
Other Information: North Branch location available in Plano

Admittance
Whom to Contact: Marcia Mauch
Date to Apply: February
Testing Procedure per Age/Grade:
Fees Involved: Registration $150–$200; enrollment available first to current students
Type of Student Preferred: N/A
Forms Required: Registration form, membership in JCC
Individual/Group Appointments: Call to schedule visit
Notification Procedure: Parent called
Waiting List Policy: Ongoing

Tuition

Approximate Tuition for 1996-97 School Year: $2750 + JCC membership; additional charge for afternoon classes/child care

Methods of Payment Available: Monthly payments

Financial Assistance Offered: Scholarship

Cancellation Insurance Available:

Profit/Non-profit: Non-profit

Additional costs

Books/Bag/Uniform: N/A

Lunch Fee: N/A

Parents Club Dues: (Membership in Jewish Community Center)

Annual Fund Drive: N/A

Discount for Siblings: No

Facilities/Services Provided

Computer Lab: Computers in kindergarten

Library: Yes

Snack Procedures: Snacks provided twice daily

Before-school Care Program Available: Yes; 7:30–8:30 a.m.

After-school Care Program Available: Yes; 11:45/1:45–6:00 p.m.

Nurse on Staff: No

Emergency Procedure Used:

Transportation to and from School: Parents responsible for transportation

Counseling and Evaluation Available: Inclusion/special needs coordinator on staff; social worker available

Graduation Information

Testing: N/A

Average SAT Scores: N/A

High School Our Students Usually Attend: N/A

Percentage of Seniors Attending College: N/A

Additional Information

Camp program offered in summer

Lakewood United Methodist Developmental Learning Center

2443 Abrams Rd. (at Lakeshore)
Dallas, TX 75214
(214) 824-1352

Mapsco: 36Y

Fax: (214) 823-9213

Office Hours: 9:00 a.m.–6:00 p.m.
School Hours: 7:30 a.m.–6:00 p.m.
School Grades Offered: 6 weeks old–pre-k
Enrollment: 45
Co-ed: Yes
Boy/Girl Ratio: Varies
Student/Teacher Ratio: 3:1–infants; 8:1–pre-kindergarten
Average Class Size: 6–8
Calendar School Year: Year round
Holidays: Traditional holidays
Uniform Requirements: None
Founded in: 1985

Philosophy of School

We are a developmentally centered school within a church setting. Good teachers present many different experiences to encourage the physical, cognitive, emotional, and social growth of our children. The rooms of the older children are organized into centers to allow for choice and creativity in play and for teacher-directed activities.

Academic Curriculum

Content: N/A
Grading System Used: N/A
Conferences per Year: N/A
Tests Administered: N/A

598

Homework Policy: N/A
Method of Discipline: N/A

Enrichment Curriculum
Music class for three- and four-year-olds

Extracurricular Activities

Goals for Students
To develop to their fullest potential as they progress from infant to preschooler so they will be prepared to go into kindergarten

Faculty/Staff Requirements
Qualifications of Staff: Experience or degree
Qualifications of Administrator: Master of Science in Child Development

School Information
Brochure Available: Yes
Number of Students in Each Grade: 6–14
Parochial: No
Organization Affiliations: MNKA (Methodist Nursery-Kindergarten Association)
Accreditations: NAEYC (National Academy)
Parental Involvement: Room-parents committee (organize fund-raisers and parties)
Other Information:

Admittance
Whom to Contact: Judy Granger, Director
Date to Apply: Rolling admissions
Testing Procedure for Age/Grade Level: N/A
Fees Involved: $100 enrollment fee
Type of Student Preferred: All comers!
Forms Required: Health, emergency release, general information
Individual/Group Appointments: N/A
Notification Procedure: N/A
Waiting List Policy: Ongoing

Tuition

Approximate Tuition for 1996-97 School Year: $600/month for infants to $440/month for pre-kindergarten
Methods of Payment Available: Weekly, bi-monthly, monthly
Financial Assistance Offered: No
Cancellation Insurance Available: No
Profit/Non-profit: Non-profit

Additional Costs

Books/Bag/Uniform: N/A
Lunch Fee: N/A
Parents Club Dues: N/A
Annual Fund Drive: N/A
Discount for Siblings: 10% off fee for older child

Facilities/Services Provided

Computer Lab: No
Library: No
Snack Procedures: Catered mornings and afternoons
Before-school Care Program Available: N/A
After-school Care Program Available: N/A
Nurse on Staff: No
Emergency Procedure Used: Yes; close to Baylor Hospital
Transportation to and from School: N/A
Counseling and Evaluation Available: N/A

Graduation Information

Testing: N/A
Average SAT Scores: N/A
High School Our Students Usually Attend: N/A
Percentage of Seniors Attending College: N/A

Additional Information

Lovers Lane United Methodist Church-Weekday School

9200 Inwood Road
Dallas, TX 75220
(214) 691-4721

Mapsco: 24R

Fax: (214) 692-0803

Office Hours: 8:30 a.m.–2:00 p.m.
School Hours: 9:00 a.m.–2:00 p.m.
School Grades Offered: 6 months–kindergarten
Enrollment: 300
Co-ed: Yes
Boy/Girl Ratio: No
Student/Teacher Ratio: Depends on age of the child
Average Class Size: Depends on age of the child
Calendar School Year: Labor Day–Memorial Day
Holidays: Fair Day, Thanksgiving, Christmas, spring break, Easter, conference days
Uniform Requirements: No
Founded in: 1960

Philosophy of School

Our program offers developmentally appropriate activities for each child. These activities encourage growth in the whole child by focusing on social skills, physical skills, and academics. We want each child to have a positive self-concept and to know he or she is unique.

Academic Curriculum

Content: DLM; Alpha Time; developmentally appropriate; hands-on
Grading System Used: No grades given
Conferences per Year: Two scheduled; more if needed
Tests Administered: No

Homework Policy: None
Method of Discipline: Redirection; time-out

Enrichment Curriculum
Tumbling, music, cooking

Extracurricular Activities
None

Goals for Students
To be happy and to learn in a fun, exciting environment

Faculty/Staff Requirements
Qualifications of Staff: Preschool–college degree
Qualifications of Administrator: College degree

School Information
Brochure Available: Yes
Number of Students in Each Grade: MDO–175; preschool–150; kindergarten–14
Parochial: No
Organization Affiliations: NAEYC, DAEYC, MNKA
Accreditations: NAEYC
Parental Involvement: Yes
Other Information:

Admittance
Whom to Contact: Weekday office–8:30 a.m.-2:00 p.m.
Date to Apply: Main registration in February; ongoing when we have openings
Testing Procedure for Age/Grade Level: N/A
Fees Involved: $10 application fee (church members exempted)
Type of Student Preferred: No particular type preferred
Forms Required: Health card; application card; signed notarized form for medical emergencies
Individual/Group Appointments: Any time
Notification Procedure: Verbal or written
Waiting List Policy: Applicants must re-apply every year.

Tuition

Approximate Tuition for 1996-97 School Year: Kindergarten $1575; preschool $105-$160 per month; MDO $60 per month

Methods of Payment Available: Kindergarten–yearly or monthly; preschool and MDO–monthly

Financial Assistance Offered: Some scholarships are available.

Cancellation Insurance Available: No

Profit/Non-profit: Non-profit (church-affiliated)

Additional costs:

Books/Bag/Uniform: None

Lunch Fee: None

Parents Club Dues: None

Annual Fund Drive: None

Discount for Siblings: No

Facilities/Services Provided

Computer Lab: Computers in kindergarten

Library: Church library

Snack Procedures: Parents and school provide snacks.

Before-school Care Program Available: Yes

After-school Care Program Available: Yes

Nurse on Staff: No

Emergency Procedure Used: Depends on emergency

Transportation to and from School: No

Counseling and Evaluation Available: We refer to several area therapists.

Graduation Information

Testing: No

Average SAT Scores: N/A

High School Our Students Usually Attend: N/A

Percentage of Seniors Attending College: N/A

Additional Information

Northaven Co-operative Preschool & Kindergarten

11211 Preston Rd. (Preston at Northaven)   Mapsco: 25K
Dallas, TX 75230
(214) 691-7666   Fax:

Office Hours: 9:00 a.m.–3:00 p.m. approximately
School Hours: 9:00 a.m.–12:15 p.m., preschool; 9:00 a.m.–2:00 p.m., second-semester kindergarten; Tuesday and Thursday, extended day until 2:15 p.m.
School Grades Offered: 20 months (toddlers)–kindergarten
Enrollment: 126
Co-ed: Yes
Boy/Girl Ratio: Balanced
Student/Teacher Ratio: 4:1–9:1
Average Class Size: 8–18 (depending on age)
Calendar School Year: September–May
Holidays: Two-week winter break; one-week spring break
Uniform Requirements: No
Founded in: 1969

Philosophy of School

Informal, experience-based program with developmental philosophy and parental involvement

Academic Curriculum

Content: Developmentally appropriate exposure to all skills areas
Grading System Used: Informal assessments; no grades
Conferences per Year: Formal conferences scheduled mid-year; others as requested
Tests Administered: None

604

Homework Policy: None
Method of Discipline: Redirection, reflecting feelings; positive encouragement of self-discipline and respect for others

Enrichment Curriculum
Enrichment is integrated into ongoing classroom and field trip experiences.

Extracurricular Activities

Goals for Students
To nurture positive self-esteem as physical, social, emotional, and cognitive growth is fostered

Faculty/Staff Requirements
Qualifications of Staff: Most have advanced degrees, experience, and education in child development and/or early childhood education.
Qualifications of Administrator: Director has been at Co-op 22 years, has B.A. in Psychology, M.S. in Child Development, and Ph.D. in Early Childhood Education.

School Information
Brochure Available: Yes
Number of Students in Each Grade: Approximately 15·
Parochial: No
Organization Affiliations:
Accreditations: NAEYC-accredited program; licensed by the state
Parental Involvement: Parents' board and committees operate school; parents help in classrooms.

Admittance
Whom to Contact: Kathy Delsanter
Date to Apply: Mid-February and as vacancies occur; class observation required
Testing Procedure per Age/Grade Level: N/A
Fees Involved: $50 toddlers; $100 preschoolers; $150 kindergarteners
Type of Student Preferred: 20 months through kindergarten
Forms Required: Enrollment, health, medical emergency
Individual/Group Appointments: Individual

Notification Procedure: Mid-February
Waiting List Policy: Maintained throughout year; must be renewed annually

Tuition

Approximate Tuition for 1996-97 School Year: Toddlers, $585; two- and three-year-olds, $990; three- and four-year-olds, $1170; four- and five-year-olds, $1395; kindergarten students, $2250
Methods of Payment Available: By check for one or more months
Financial Assistance Offered: Yes
Cancellation Insurance Available: No
Profit/Non-profit: Non-profit

Additional Costs

Books/Bag/Uniform: None
Lunch Fee: $6 per Extended Day for tuition
Parents Club Dues: None
Annual Fund Drive: None
Discount for Siblings: No

Facilities/Services Provided

Computer Lab:
Library:
Snack Procedures: Provided by one parent per class each day
Before-school Care Program Available: No
After-school Care Program Available: Tuesdays and Thursdays until 2:15 p.m. for children ages three and older
Nurse on Staff: No
Emergency Procedure Used: Posted
Transportation to and from School: No
Counseling and Evaluation Available: Teacher conferences

Graduation Information

Testing: N/A
Average SAT Scores: N/A
High School Our Students Usually Attend: N/A
Percentage of Seniors Attending College: N/A

Additional Information

Northaven Co-op is a parent-cooperative school with much parental involvement and participation in the classroom and in the administrative, ongoing functioning of the school.

Toddlers attend one morning per week; two- and three-year-olds attend two mornings per week; three- and four-year-olds attend three mornings per week; four- and five-year-olds attend four mornings per week; kindergarten students attend five mornings per week first semester and until 2:00 p.m. second semester.

Summer programs are offered to the community in June and July for toddlers through seven-year-olds.

North Dallas Day School

9619 Greenville Avenue   Mapsco: 26H
Dallas, TX 75243
(214) 341-4366   Fax:

Office Hours: 6:45 a.m.–6:00 p.m.
School Hours: 8:30 a.m.–3:00 p.m.
School Grades Offered: Six-week-olds–grade 2
Enrollment: 150
Co-ed: Yes
Boy/Girl Ratio: 1:1
Student/Teacher Ratio: 6:1 to 15:1
Average Class Size: 12
Calendar School Year: North Dallas Day School is open
from 6:45 a.m. to 6:00 p.m. Monday through Friday year
round. School terms coincide with the Richardson I.S.D.
calendar. Special camp programs are offered each summer.
Holidays: Labor Day, Thanksgiving, Christmas, New
Year's Day, Memorial Day, Independence Day
Uniform Requirements: No
Founded in: 1977

Philosophy of School

North Dallas Day School is dedicated to providing an educational, recreational, and
extended-day program for children from age one through the second grade of
elementary school. In 1987, North Dallas Day School was accredited by the National
Academy of Early Childhood Programs. The high quality child-development program
includes planned learning activities, specially trained teachers who have college
degrees, a healthy and safe environment, and superior interactions among adults and
children. We believe that for each child to achieve his/her potential, we must preserve
and build a sense of self-worth, self-confidence, and responsibility.

Academic Curriculum

Content: NAEYC Guidelines
Grading System Used: A–D for elementary students; skills checklist for preschool students
Conferences per Year: In January or at the request of parent or teacher
Tests Administered: Standardized achievement tests administered in May (pre-K through elementary)
Homework Policy: At teacher's discretion
Method of Discipline: Age-appropriate consequences and rewards

Enrichment Curriculum

See "Extracurricular Activities" below.

Extracurricular Activities

Various extracurricular activities taught on campus by professionals from the community. Activities include ballet and tap, gymnastics, computer, piano, swimming, creative drama, visual art, cooking, soccer, and karate.

Goals for Students

North Dallas Day School's basic goal is to foster the intellectual, physical, social, and emotional growth and development of each individual child. We want the children to be successful in their learning, to be curious, to learn self-control, to express their ideas freely, to cooperate with others, and to learn to make their own decisions.

Faculty/Staff Requirements

Qualifications of Staff: Degrees in teaching area; continuing education hours
Qualifications of Administrator: Degrees in education; years of teaching experience

School Information

Brochure Available: Yes
Number of Students in Each Grade: 10-20
Parochial: No
Organization Affiliations:
Accreditations: NAEYC
Parental Involvement: Active parent volunteers group
Other Information:

Admittance

Whom to Contact: Director or Assistant Director
Date to Apply: Any time
Testing Procedure per Age/Grade Level: None
Fees Involved: Included in registration fee
Type of Student Preferred: Open; non-discriminatory admissions
Forms Required: Previous school and health records
Individual/Group Appointments: Individual
Notification Procedure: Personal contact
Waiting List Policy:

Tuition

Approximate Tuition for 1996-97 School Year: $420-$500 per month; the tuition schedule includes many groups of students, from $420 per month for three-year-olds through elementary to $500 per month for six-week-olds. Please check with the school for your category and for part-time rates.
Methods of Payment Available: Monthly
Financial Assistance Offered: No
Cancellation Insurance Available: N/A
Profit/Non-profit: Profit

Additional Costs

Books/Bag/Uniform:
Lunch Fee: $35 per month for kindergarten and elementary students; lunch included for preschool students at no additional cost
Parents Club Dues: N/A
Annual Fund Drive: N/A
Discount for Siblings: 5% when three children in one family are enrolled

Facilities/Services Provided

Computer Lab: In kindergarten–grade 2
Library: Yes
Snack Procedures: Provided by school twice a day
Before-school Care Program Available: Yes, from 6:45 a.m. for nearby Richardson schools
After-school Care Program Available: Yes, until 6:00 p.m.
Nurse on Staff: Staff trained in CPR and first aid
Emergency Procedure Used: Parents notified
Transportation to and from School: Only for Kids' Club's after-school program
Counseling and Evaluation Available: Yes

Graduation Information

Testing: N/A
Average SAT Scores: N/A
High School Our Students Usually Attend: N/A
Percentage of Seniors Attending College: N/A

Additional Information

Please call for further information.

Preston-Royal Preschool

5600 Royal Lane
Dallas, TX 75229
(214) 987-3446

Mapsco: 25E

Fax: (214) 369-8939

Office Hours: 8:30 a.m.–2:00 p.m.
School Hours: 8:00 a.m.–2:00 p.m.
School Grades Offered: Age 2 to pre-kindergarten
Enrollment: 80
Co-ed: Yes
Boy/Girl Ratio: 1:1
Student/Teacher Ratio: 8:1
Average Class Size: 8
Calendar School Year: September-July
Holidays: Thanksgiving, Christmas-New Year's Day, Martin Luther King Day, Presidents' Day, spring break, Good Friday, Memorial Day, Independence Day
Uniform Requirements: None
Founded in: 1958

Philosophy of School

Preston-Royal Preschool encourages the natural development of children through developmentally appropriate activities. Children learn best through experiential learning and hands-on activities. Each child is encouraged to enjoy his/her environment and the people, animals, and objects within it. All children are treated with affection and respect.

Academic Curriculum

Content: Hands-on, experiential learning
Grading System Used: None
Conferences per Year: Two
Tests Administered: None

Homework Policy: None
Method of Discipline: Respect and cooperation on part of teachers and children

Enrichment Curriculum
Art, science, social studies, pre-math and pre-reading skills, music and body movement, literature, cooking, field trips

Extracurricular Activities
Family dinners, Parent's Club, Parent/Child Work Day

Goals for Students
We want our students to think school is fun and learning is exciting. We encourage socialization, experimentation, and discovery.

Faculty/Staff Requirements
Qualifications of Staff: Qualifications vary from college and teaching experience to master's degree in early childhood education
Qualifications of Administrator: Master's degree in early childhood education, 20 years' experience

School Information
Brochure Available: Yes
Number of Students in Each Grade: 7-10 in each class
Parochial: No
Organization Affiliations: Program of Central Congregational Church
Accreditations: National Academy of Early Childhood Programs
Parental Involvement: Encouraged, as substitute teachers and field trip assistants
Other Information:

Admittance
Whom to Contact: Director Carol Stewart
Date to Apply: In February for pre-enrollment; openings at any time
Testing Procedure for Age/Grade Level: None
Fees Involved: $60 enrollment
Type of Student Preferred: Ages two–pre-kindergarten
Forms Required: Enrollment, health
Individual/Group Appointments: Call to arrange informal visits and conferences

Notification Procedure: Phone or mail; when opening is available
Waiting List Policy: Renewed annually

Tuition

Approximate Tuition for 1996-97 School Year: $90/month–$310/month
Methods of Payment Available: Monthly or by special arrangement
Financial Assistance Offered: Yes, 50% of tuition
Cancellation Insurance Available: None
Profit/Non-profit: Non-profit

Additional Costs

Books/Bag/Uniform: Bag, activity fee–$10-$20
Lunch Fee: None
Parents Club Dues: $15/year
Annual Fund Drive: None
Discount for Siblings: 10%

Facilities/Services Provided

Computer Lab: No
Library: Yes, for in-school use
Snack Procedures: Snack provided every day
Before-school Care Program Available: Yes, 8:00–8:50 a.m. Classes begin at 8:50.
After-school Care Program Available: No
Nurse on Staff: No
Emergency Procedure Used: First aid, CPR; call parents
Transportation to and from School: Provided by parents
Counseling and Evaluation Available: Referral to other agencies

Graduation Information

Testing: None
Average SAT Scores: N/A
High School Our Students Usually Attend: N/A
Percentage of Seniors Attending College: N/A

Additional Information

Preston-Royal Preschool serves children ages five and under.

Rainbow Connection of Central Christian Church

1651 E. Campbell Rd.
Richardson, TX 75082
(214) 644-0283

Mapsco: 8T

Fax: (214) 231-7093

Office Hours: 8:15 a.m.–3:45 p.m.
School Hours: 8:45 a.m.–3:30 p.m.
School Grades Offered: Preschool and kindergarten
Enrollment: 120
Co-ed: Yes
Boy/Girl Ratio: 1:1
Student/Teacher Ratio: 7:1 (two-year-olds); 10:1 (three-year-olds); 12:1 (four-year-olds)
Average Class Size: 7 (two-year-olds); 10 (three-year-olds); 12 (four-year-olds)
Calendar School Year: September-May
Holidays: Thanksgiving, Christmas, spring break
Uniform Requirements: No
Founded in: 1980

Philosophy of School

Our program provides an experience-based learning environment firmly grounded in principles of child development. This approach includes a concern for the whole child for balanced physical, social, emotional, intellectual, and spiritual growth.

Academic Curriculum

Content: Weekly unit themes
Grading System Used: Portfolio
Conferences per Year: One formal
Tests Administered: N/A

Homework Policy: N/A
Method of Discipline: Positive redirection

Enrichment Curriculum

Activities and experiences are designed to help the child express himself/herself creatively and intellectually through imaginative play, music, art, movement, books, blocks, water, sand, and games.

Extracurricular Activities

Parent activities, such as Thanksgiving Feast, Father-Child Activity, Mother's Day Tea

Goals for Students

Enhancing optimal development for the whole child

Faculty/Staff Requirements

Qualifications of Staff: College degree; many have graduate degrees.
Qualifications of Administrator: B.S. in Education

School Information

Brochure Available: Yes
Number of Students in Each Grade: 7-12
Parochial: Christian
Organization Affiliations: Central Christian Church
Accreditations: NAEYC accreditation
Parental Involvement: Yes
Other Information:

Admittance

Whom to Contact: Naomi Hurst
Date to Apply: February 1
Testing Procedure for Age/Grade Level: N/A
Fees Involved: Enrollment fee $55
Type of Student Preferred:
Forms Required: Yes
Individual/Group Appointments: Yes
Notification Procedure: N/A
Waiting List Policy: Re-apply annually but school keeps ongoing waiting list

Tuition

Approximate Tuition for 1996-97 School Year: Two days per week–$950; three days per week–$1275; five days per week–$1800 (half days)

Methods of Payment Available: Monthly

Financial Assistance Offered: Minimum scholarship assistance

Cancellation Insurance Available: N/A

Profit/Non-profit: Non-profit

Additional Costs

Books/Bag/Uniform: N/A

Lunch Fee: N/A

Parents Club Dues: None

Annual Fund Drive: 2 fund raisers annually

Discount for Siblings: Yes

Facilities/Services Provided

Computer Lab: N/A

Library: Yes

Snack Procedures: Yes

Before-school Care Program Available: No

After-school Care Program Available: Extended day

Nurse on Staff: No

Emergency Procedure Used: Outlined in handbook

Transportation to and from School: No

Counseling and Evaluation Available: Yes

Graduation Information

Testing: N/A

Average SAT Scores: N/A

High School Our Students Usually Attend: N/A

Percentage of Seniors Attending College: N/A

Additional Information

Schreiber Methodist Preschool

4525 Rickover Drive
Dallas, TX 75244
(214) 387-8191

Mapsco: 14U

Fax:

Office Hours: 8:30 a.m.–12:30 p.m. Monday; 8:30 a.m.–2:30 p.m. Tuesday–Friday
School Hours: 9:00 a.m.–12:00 p.m. Monday; 9:00 a.m.–2:20 p.m. Tuesday–Friday
School Grades Offered: MDO–pre-kindergarten
Enrollment: 250
Co-ed: Yes
Boy/Girl Ratio: 1:1
Student/Teacher Ratio: Depends on age of the children
Average Class Size: Varies from 4 to 14
Calendar School Year: Labor Day to Memorial Day
Holidays: Same as D.I.S.D.
Uniform Requirements: None
Founded in: 1975

Philosophy of School

The Schreiber Methodist Preschool program is designed to provide a happy, caring Christian environment with opportunities for a variety of experiences which will meet the emotional, intellectual, social, and physical needs of each child.

Our goals for each child are that he/she will grow in the following ways:

1. Have a positive self-image
2. Make progress toward better social adjustment
3. Learn to work in and take responsibility in a group situation
4. Develop manipulative skills and acceptable work habits
5. Develop understandings, attitudes, and skills appropriate for his/her age
6. Learn to listen to and follow directions
7. Increase his ability to think for himself/herself and communicate verbally

618

8. Be able to express himself/herself freely through music and art activities
9. Learn to observe, understand, and appreciate the world around him/her
10. Grow in appreciation of God's love

Academic Curriculum

Content: Unit-based and skill development
Grading System Used: None
Conferences per Year: Two
Tests Administered: Metropolitan given to four-year-olds in April
Homework Policy: None
Method of Discipline: Time out used in the most severe situations

Enrichment Curriculum

Music and Body Rhythms

Extracurricular Activities

None

Goals for Students

See Philosophy of School.

Faculty/Staff Requirements

Qualifications of staff: Minimum: high school graduate and training in early childhood education
Qualifications of Administrator: Minimum: elementary education degree, training in early childhood education, experience as school director

School Information

Brochure Available: Yes
Number of Students in Each Grade: Nursery–8; young 1's–20; toddlers–20; 2's–36; 2 1/2's–24; 3's–60; 4's–62; pre-K's–14
Parochial: No
Organization Affiliations: DAEYC, NAEYC, TAEYC, and MNKA
Accreditations: NAEYC
Parental Involvement: Parties, field trips, parent's club

Admittance

Whom to Contact: Marilyn Hodge, Director
Date to Apply: February; ongoing if openings remain
Testing Procedure per Age/Grade Level: Only students entering pre-kindergarten are tested.
Fees Involved: None
Type of Student Preferred: Any
Forms Required: Enrollment, medical
Individual/Group Appointments: May visit any time
Notification Procedure: By phone
Waiting List Policy: Annual

Tuition

Approximate Tuition for 1996-97 School Year: P.D.O. is $60/month to $155/month for pre-kindergarten
Methods of Payment Available: Check or cash
Financial Assistance Offered: As needed
Cancellation Insurance Available: No
Profit/Non-profit: Non-profit

Additional Costs

Books/Bag/Uniform: None
Lunch Fee: None
Parents Club Dues: None
Annual Fund Drive: Yes
Discount for Siblings: No

Facilities/Services Provided

Computer Lab: No
Library: No
Snack Procedures: Provided by school
Before-school Care Program Available: Yes; 7:30 a.m.–9:00 a.m.
After-school Care Program Available: No
Nurse on Staff: No–all staff members are certified in first aid and CPR.
Emergency Procedure Used: Parents called; call 911 if necessary
Transportation to and from School: Provided by parents
Counseling and Evaluation Available: By referral

Graduation Information

Testing: N/A
Average SAT Scores: N/A

High School Our Students Usually Attend: N/A
Percentage of Seniors Attending College: N/A

Additional Information

Temple Emanu-El Preschool

8500 Hillcrest
Dallas, TX 75225-4288
(214) 368-3613

Mapsco: 25V

Fax: (214) 706-0025

Office Hours: 9:00 a.m.–5:00 p.m.
School Hours: 8:00 a.m.–6:00 p.m. Monday–Thursday
8:00 a.m.–5:30 p.m. Friday
School Grades Offered: 18 months–kindergarten; Parents'
Day Out (PDO)–6-18 months
Enrollment: 160
Co-ed: Yes
Boy/Girl Ratio:
Student/Teacher Ratio: PDO, 4:1; 18 months, 4:1; 2
years, 6:1; 3 years, 8:1; 4 years, 8:1
Average Class Size: 12–16
Calendar School Year: September–May
Holidays: Jewish holidays, legal holidays, day before
Thanksgiving
Uniform Requirements: No
Founded in: 1980

Philosophy of School

Developmental philosophy with programs designed to meet the child's emotional,
cognitive, social and physical needs. The developmental program is based on the
assumptions that 1) growth is a sequential and orderly process, and 2) children do
indeed pass through stages of development that occur in a predictable sequence in this
process.

Academic Curriculum

Content: Developmental preschool
Grading System Used: Parent-teacher conference forms
Conferences per Year: Two conferences per year

622

Tests Administered: N/A
Homework Policy: N/A
Method of Discipline: N/A

Enrichment Curriculum
Capers for Kids, music, physical education, chapel

Extracurricular Activities
Cook-a-Book, pottery, computer, Imagine That

Goals for Students
To provide a developmental program with a strong academic emphasis in a nurturing environment for children ages 18 months–6 years

Faculty/Staff Requirements
Qualifications of Staff: All teachers have college degrees.
Qualifications of Administrator: M.S. in Early Childhood Education

School Information
Brochure Available: Yes
Number of Students in Each Grade: PDO, 10; toddlers, 30; two-year-olds, 45; three-year-olds, 48; pre-k, 40; k, 20
Parochial: No
Organization Affiliations: Temple Emanu-El
Accreditations: Texas Department of Human Resources; NAEYC
Parental Involvement: Active parents' association
Other Information:

Admittance
Whom to Contact: Jane Kadosh
Date to Apply: January, prior to fall enrollment
Testing Procedure per Age/Grade Level: None
Fees Involved: $150 registration fee
Type of Student Preferred:
Forms Required: Application
Individual/Group Appointments: Visiting days in January
Notification Procedure:
Waiting List Policy: Enrollment based on availability

Tuition

Approximate Tuition for 1996-97 School Year: $1710–$7200
Methods of Payment available: Monthly, by semester, or annually
Financial Assistance Offered: Yes
Cancellation Insurance Available: No
Profit/Non-profit: Non-profit

Additional Costs

Books/Bag/Uniform: No; supply fee–$35/year
Lunch Fee: Parents provide child's lunch.
Parents Club Dues: No
Annual Fund Drive: N/A
Discount for Siblings: No

Facilities/Services Provided

Computer Lab: N/A
Library: Children's library
Snack Procedures: Parents provide morning snacks; school provides afternoon snacks.
Before-school Care Program Available: Yes; 8:00 a.m.
After-school Care Program Available: Yes; 6:00 p.m.
Nurse on Staff: No
Emergency Procedure Used: Call 911; notify parents; notify other emergency contacts
Transportation to and from School: No; parents make arrangements.
Counseling and Evaluation Available: By referral

Graduation Information

Testing: N/A
Average SAT scores: N/A
High School Our Students Usually Attend: N/A
Percentage of Seniors Attending College: N/A

Additional Information

WESTMINSTER PRESBYTERIAN PRESCHOOL & KINDERGARTEN

Celebrating 30 years of excellence in Early Childhood Education. Westminster offers imaginative programs for young children ranging from Mother's Day Out through Kindergarten. Each program is designed to develop the "whole child" through a journey of discovery and creative learning.

The failure free environment at Westminster develops a lasting foundation for the child's interest in learning. Our interactive, hands-on curriculum provides a balance of developmental, educational and spiritual growth through activities the children find both fun and challenging.

Please come by to visit us and find out what we can do to help you chart out the future for your children...

8200 Devonshire Drive • Dallas, Texas 75209
(214) 350-6155

Westminster Presbyterian Preschool and Kindergarten

8200 Devonshire Drive
Dallas, TX 75209
(214) 350-6155

Mapsco: 35A

Fax:

Office Hours: 8:30 a.m.–12:30 p.m.
School Hours: 9:00 a.m.–12:00 p.m.
School Grades Offered: (Mother's Day Out) 12 months–kindergarten (extended)
Enrollment: 195
Co-ed: Yes
Boy/Girl Ratio: Varies by age
Student/Teacher Ratio: Ranges from 12:3-16:2
Average Class Size: 10-16
Calendar school year: September–May
Holidays: Standard holidays observed
Uniform Requirements: No
Founded in: 1969

Philosophy of School

Westminster provides a learning environment where all areas of development–social, emotional, physical, and cognitive–are nurtured for our children. The children meet with success daily in a stimulating, challenging, and inviting setting. Through age-appropriate, hands-on learning activities, our children experience a successful school environment.

Academic Curriculum

Content: Developmental early childhood and kindergarten curriculum
Grading System Used: N/A
Conferences per Year: Two–fall and spring
Tests Administered: No testing administered

626

Homework Policy: N/A
Method of Discipline: Positive guidance that facilitates self-discipline

Enrichment Curriculum

Music, art, computer, language experiences, motor skills, Capers for Kids, library, literature

Extracurricular Activities

In addition to the enrichment listed above, chapel is offered weekly for optional participation for ages 4 and kindergarten.

Goals for Students

1. The environment is nurturing, warm, and inviting for children to discover and create learning.
2. The environment is failure-free to enable children to explore their full potential.
3. We encourage children to work, develop, and grow at their own rate, in their own style, for their personal best.

Faculty/Staff Requirements

Qualifications of Staff: Professional, experienced staff; college degrees
Qualifications of Administrator: B.S., M.S. in Child Development; adjunct college faculty, educational workshop training

School Information

Brochure Available: Not currently available, but we welcome scheduled visits.
Number of Students in Each Grade: Varies from 10-16
Parochial: No
Organization Affiliations: NAEYC, MNKA
Accreditations: Currently seeking National Academy of Early Childhood Programs; NAEYC
Parental Involvement: Opportunities available, encouraged, and appreciated

Admittance

Whom to Contact: Cristine L. Watson, M.S.
Date to Apply: Ongoing process; average two-year wait
Testing Procedure per Age/Grade Level: N/A
Fees Involved: Non-refundable registration fee due at time of enrollment
Type of Student Preferred: Open enrollment
Forms Required: Yes

Individual/Group Appointments: Individual
Notification Procedure: As available spaces occur or after February registration
Waiting List Policy: Ongoing; updated annually

Tuition

Approximate Tuition for 1996-97 School Year: Varies from $70-$350 per month
Methods of Payment Available: Monthly tuition payments
Financial Assistance Offered: Scholarships available
Cancellation Insurance Available: No
Profit/Non-profit: Non-profit

Additional Costs

Books/Bag/Uniform: No
Lunch Fee: No
Parents Club Dues: Varies
Annual Fund Drive: No
Discount for Siblings: No

Facilities/Services Provided

Computer Lab: No, but systems are available in many classrooms
Library: Yes
Snack Procedures: Provided by school
After-school Care Program Available: No
Before-school Care Program Available: No
Nurse on Staff: Not currently
Emergency Procedure Used: Contact parents; call 911
Transportation to and from School: No, Parents' Club assists in establishing carpools
Counseling and Evaluation Available: Referrals available

Graduation Information

Testing: N/A
Average SAT Scores: N/A
High School Our Students Usually Attend: N/A
Percentage of Seniors Attending College: N/A

TDPRS
Texas Department of Protective and Regulatory Services

Minimum standards for regulating child care facilities are developed and monitored by the Texas Department of Protective and Regulatory Services.

Bent Tree Child Development Center
Beth Torah Preschool
Cambridge Square Private School of DeSoto
The Children's Center of First Community Church
Christ Our Savior Lutheran School (see LSA)
Christian Childhood Development Center
The Cornerstone School
Dallas North Montessori School (see Montessori)
The daVinci School
DeSoto Private School
Discovery School at Canyon Creek
East Dallas Developmental Center
Fair Oaks Day School
The Harrington School Private Early Childhood Academic Center
Hearthstone Kindergarten
The Hillcrest Academy
The Lakewood Presbyterian School
The Little Red Schoolhouse
Maryview Academy and Private School
Meadowbrook Private School (see Montessori)
Northbrook School
NorthPark Presbyterian Day School
Palisades Day School
The Peanut Gallery
Primrose School of Chase Oaks
Prince of Peace Christian School (see LSA)

Providence Christian School of Texas
St. Barnabas Pathways Preschool
Trinity Episcopal Preschool
Williamson School

Bent Tree Child Development Center

17275 Addison Rd.
Addison, TX 75248
(214) 931-0868

Mapsco: 4U

Fax: (214) 931-2118

Office Hours: 7:00 a.m.–6:30 p.m.
School Hours: 7:00 a.m.–6:30 p.m.
School Grades Offered: 18 months–kindergarten; after-school program
Enrollment: 160
Co-ed: Yes
Boy/Girl Ratio: Appropriate
Student/Teacher Ratio: Toddler I–6:1; toddler II–7:1; primer preschool–8:1; young preschool–11:1; older preschool–12:1; pre-kindergarden–14:1; kindergarten–15:1
Average Class Size: Depends on age level
Calendar School Year: Year round
Holidays: Closed major holidays
Uniform Requirements: No
Founded in: 1991

Philosophy of School

Each child's individual interest and abilities are fostered through careful development, planning, and evaluation. Flexibility in programming and a balance of activities are provided for optimal interaction between the child and the environment. These factors contribute to the child's development of a positive self-concept and a feeling of worth and his/her advancement in physical, cognitive, language, and social skills.

Academic Curriculum

Content: Developmental Pre-Academic
Grading System Used: N/A

Conferences per Year: One; more scheduled as needed
Tests Administered: Early Childhood Developmental Assessment
Homework Policy: N/A
Method of Discipline: Praise and re-direction

Enrichment Curriculum
Multi-sensory hands-on learning in all major preschool areas

Extracurricular Activities
Fine arts program, kindermusik, computers in classrooms, ballet/dance

Goals for Students
For each child to develop a positive self concept and feeling of worth as well as advancement in physical, cognitive, language, and social skills

Faculty/Staff Requirements
Qualifications of Staff: Child development/early childhood degree
Qualifications of Administrator: Experience with early childhood program (teacher and administrator); degree in childhood development/early childhood

School Information
Brochure Available: Yes
Number of Students in Each Grade: Class size dependent on age level
Parochial: Non-denominational
Organization Affiliations:
Accreditations: TDPRS
Parental Involvement: Yes, it's a major focus.
Other Information:

Admittance
Whom to Contact: Marlyn Conrow
Date to Apply: Fall classes begin in late August. Availability is limited in some classes throughout the year.
Testing Procedure for Age/Grade Level: N/A
Fees Involved: $35 evaluation fee; $100 registration fee
Type of Student Preferred: Readiness for hands-on multi-sensory program
Forms Required: Past medical immunization records, general family information

Individual/Group Appointments: Drop-in welcome; appointments preferred
Notification Procedure: As appropriate
Waiting List Policy: Ongoing

Tuition

Approximate Tuition for 1996-97 School Year: According to age group
Methods of Payment Available: Cash or check
Financial Assistance Offered: N/A
Cancellation Insurance Available: N/A
Profit/Non-profit: Profit

Additional Costs

Books/Bag/Uniform: N/A
Lunch Fee: N/A
Parents Club Dues: N/A
Annual Fund Drive: N/A
Discount for Siblings: No

Facilities/Services Provided

Computer Lab: Included in preschool classrooms at no additional fee
Library: Reading Book Center in all classrooms
Snack Procedures: Provided in mid-morning and afternoon
Before-school Care Program Available: Yes
After-school Care Program Available: Yes
Nurse on Staff: Mildly-ill Room available when child is not feeling well
Emergency Procedure Used: Notify parents; contact nearest medical facility
Transportation to and from School: Parents provide transportation
(exception: transportation from area elementaries to after-school program)
Counseling and Evaluation Available:

Graduation Information

Testing: N/A
Average SAT Scores: N/A
High School Our Students Usually Attend: Public
Percentage of Seniors Attending College: N/A

Additional Information

Beth Torah Preschool

720 Lookout Drive
Richardson, TX 75080-2136
(214) 234-1549

Mapsco: 7K

Fax: (214) 783-1463

Office Hours: 8:30 a.m.–4:30 p.m.
School Hours: 9:00 a.m.–1:00 p.m.; kindergarten
9:00 a.m.–2:00 p.m.
School Grades Offered: 18 months–kindergarten; Mommy
& Me program
Enrollment: 100
Co-ed: Yes
Boy/Girl Ratio: 50:50
Student/Teacher Ratio: 6:1
Average Class Size: 12
Calendar School Year: Late August through May
Holidays: National and Jewish holidays
Uniform Requirements: No
Founded in: 1985

Philosophy of School

To provide a conservative Jewish atmosphere where children can develop a positive
self-image and a love of learning

Academic Curriculum

Content: Early childhood curriculum with emphasis on developing self-esteem
and language skills
Grading System Used: N/A
Conferences per Year: Individual conferences held twice; more scheduled if
necessary
Tests Administered: N/A
Homework Policy: N/A
Method of Discipline:

Enrichment Curriculum
Creative movement, music, art, computers, Shabbat mini-service, activities for Jewish holidays, field trips

Extracurricular Activities
After-school enrichment: creative movement, science, storytime, cooking, computers, arts and crafts

Goals for Students
To encourage self-confidence and large and small motor development; to develop social and language skills

Faculty/Staff Requirements
Qualifications of Staff: College degrees
Qualifications of Administrator: Degree–early childhood development

School Information
Brochure Available: Yes
Number of Students in Each Grade: 12
Parochial: Yes, United Synagogue affiliation
Organization Affiliations: Conservative Judaism
Accreditations: Texas Department of Human Services
Parental Involvement: Yes (many opportunities to volunteer)
School Grades Offered: 18 months–kindergarten
Other Information:

Admittance
Whom to Contact: Esther Cohen
Date to Apply: Rolling admissions (if space permits)
Testing Procedure per Age/Grade Level: N/A
Fees Involved: Yes
Type of Student Preferred: N/A
Forms Required: Yes
Individual/Group Appointments: Individual
Notification Procedure: N/A
Waiting List Policy: Yes, depending on age group

Tuition

Approximate Tuition for 1996-97 School Year: $3500 for five-day program; other options available

Methods of Payment Available: Flexible; individual arrangements can be made.

Financial Assistance Offered: Limited basis

Cancellation Insurance Available: No

Profit/Non-profit: Non-profit

Additional Costs

Books/Bag/Uniform: No

Lunch Fee: Child provides lunch. The school provides a hot lunch four times per year.

Parents Club Dues: No

Annual Fund Drive: Yes

Discount for Siblings: Yes

Facilities/Services Provided

Computer Lab: 4 years and k have computer lab /weekly instruction

Library: Children check out books weekly; parents read aloud during library time.

Snack Procedures: School provides

Before–school Care Program Available: Arrangements made upon request

After–school Care Program Available: Yes, 1-2 p.m.

Nurse on Staff: No

Emergency Procedure Used: Yes

Transportation to and from School: N/A

Counseling and Evaluation Available: Yes

Graduation Information

Testing: N/A

Average SAT Scores: N/A

High School Our Students Usually Attend: N/A

Percentage of Seniors Attending College: N/A

Additional Information

Cambridge Square Private School of DeSoto

1121 East Pleasant Run Road
DeSoto, TX 75115
(214) 224-5596

Mapsco: 74W

Fax:

Office Hours: 6:30 a.m.–6:00 p.m.
School Hours: 8:00 a.m.–3:30 p.m
School Grades Offered: Three-year-olds through grade 8
Enrollment: 250
Co-ed: Yes
Boy/Girl Ratio: 1:1
Student/Teacher Ratio: 12:1
Average Class Size: 12
Calendar School Year: Mid-August–May
Holidays: National holidays observed
Uniform Requirements: No
Founded in: 1981

Philosophy of School

To encourange and guide each child to develop his/her greatest potential in a secure, loving, and stimulating environment

Academic Curriculum

Content: Language arts (reading, phonics); English (grammar, literature, writing, spelling, handwriting, vocabulary); mathematics (basic math through algebra); natural science (life, earth, physics); social science (history, civics, sociology, law); French; art; music; physical education; health; library
Grading System Used: Six weeks reports; A (93–100); B (82–92); C (70–81); failing (below 70)
Conferences per Year: Scheduled and by request; arranged through school office

Tests Administered: Stanford Achievement Test in March
Homework Policy: As required by subject and grade level for students to enrich their classroom learning
Method of Discipline: Appropriate for the offense; developed in conjunction with the student's parents

Enrichment Curriculum
Computer, Science Fair, electives offered grades 2–8, art, music history/appreciation, drama, field trips

Extracurricular Activities
Odyssey-of-the-Mind competition, National Spelling Bee, Invention Competition, National Geography Bee, Newscurrents Competition, various literary competitions, regional and state art contests, Junior Achievement

Goals for Students
To extend creativity and expression to their fullest potential and develop a love of learning and self-motivation

Faculty/Staff Requirements
Qualifications of Staff: Bachelor's degree required in major teaching field
Qualifications of Administrator: Master's degree

School Information
Brochure Available: Yes
Number of Students in Each Grade: Varies
Parochial: No
Organization Affiliations: Junior Achievement, OM
Accreditations: Texas Department of Human Services
Parental Involvement: Yes
Other Information:

Admittance
Whom to Contact: Mary Lowrey
Date to Apply: March through July as space allows
Testing Procedure per Age/Grade Level: N/A
Fees Involved: Yes
Type of Student Preferred: Eager student waiting to be challenged

Forms Required: Yes
Individual/Group Appointments: Individual
Notification Procedure: Within two weeks of receiving application and transcripts
Waiting List Policy: Ongoing

Tuition

Approximate Tuition for 1996-97 School Year: $3000
Methods of Payment Available: Monthly, by semester, or yearly
Financial Assistance Offered: No
Cancellation Insurance Available: No
Profit/Non-profit: Profit

Additional Costs

Books/Bag/Uniforms: Books (approximately $125)
Lunch Fee: No
Parents Club Dues: No
Annual Fund Drive: No
Discount for Siblings: Yes

Facilities/Services Provided

Computer Lab: Networked, IBM units with CD ROM and laser printer; Apple computers in classrooms.
Library:
Snack Procedures: Provided by school
Before-school Care Program Available: Yes; 6:30 a.m. - 8:00 a.m.
After-school Care Program Available: Yes; 3:30 p.m. - 6:00 p.m.
Nurse on Staff: Yes
Emergency Procedure Used: As appropriate; hospital less than one mile away
Transportation to and from School: No
Counseling and Evaluation Available: Yes

Graduation Information

Testing: Stanford Achievement Test
Average SAT Scores: Class scores within top 10% nationally on Stanford Achievement Test
High School Our Students Usually Attend: 50%–neighborhood public high schools; 50 %–private and parochial high schools in the metroplex
Percentage of Seniors Attending College: N/A

Additional Information

Cambridge Square Private School of DeSoto maintains small class sizes so each child may maximize his/her talents and potential. Our curriculum, textbooks, and supplemental materials are minimum one year above public-school level. We combine traditional teaching styles with innovative methods so students can use different senses as they experience and participate. We use "hands-on" manipulatives to illustrate concepts and encourage students to explore ideas on their own. As an example, to explore basic engineering and math, students use large put-together models to experiment and calculate reactions. Students work on group projects several times during the year to learn the teamwork skills of working together while they share ideas and responsibilities.

We group students according to their ability. Our school is departmentalized so teachers teach their area of specialization and students relate to more than one teacher. Gifted students have special schedules that challenge them in their special areas yet let them relate to their peers in elective classes. Kindergarten is a full-day program that stresses phonics, reading, handwriting, and math. Beginning in second grade, students read six classic novels each year in their English classes. They learn to appreciate and understand literature and its elements, write creatively and analytically, and participate in group activities.

Offered to students in second grade and above, electives provide enrichment in various subjects–study skills, etiquette, origami, morals and values, geography, home economics, logic and reasoning skills, CPR/first aid, creative writing, life skills, and tutorial classes in reading, English, and math. To learn about twenty-first century technology, students use a computer network to develop skills in typing, word processing, basic flow charting, and programming.

Several cross-curriculum units of study are developed each year so students can explore a particular time period from several inter-disciplinatry viewpoints. As an example, during the ancient civilization unit, students learn about astrology and constellations named from the gods in their science classes while they read about the same gods as they study mythology in their English classes. In their history classes, students learn aspects of our government and its organization is derived from that period. In their math classes, they recreate buildings and cities to scale; in P.E. classes they recreate the olympic games.

The Children's Center of First Community Church

6355 East Mockingbird Lane
Dallas, TX 75214
(214) 823-2119

Mapsco: 36J

Fax:

Office Hours: 8:30 a.m.–1:30 p.m.
School Hours: 9:00 a.m.–12:00 p.m.
School Grades Offered: Preschool–kindergarten
Enrollment: 140
Co-ed: Yes
Boy/Girl Ratio:
Student/Teacher Ratio: 8:1 (3-year-olds); 12-15:1 (4-year-olds);
16:1 (kindergarten)
Average Class Size: 3-year-olds, 8; 4-year-olds, 12–15; K, 16
Calendar School Year: September–May
Holidays: Labor Day, Fair Day, Thanksgiving, Christmas, Easter,
spring break
Uniform Requirements: No
Founded in: 1952

Philosophy of School

To provide a school of excellence for little children; to create a happy, loving
environment where children can learn to make decisions, explore God's world, and be
motivated to the joy of learning

Academic Curriculum

Content: Core of curriculum: "Attitude Program," creative art, readiness
Grading System Used: N/A
Conferences per Year: As needed; conferences scheduled in February for all
parents
Tests Administered: Metropolitan (kindergarten students)

Homework Policy: None
Method of Discipline: Behavior modification and our own "Attitude Program"

Enrichment Curriculum

"Attitude Program" (developed by our school)–the core of our curriculum; motor-skill development program (Body Rhythmics) with a special teacher; music–traditional children's songs, Orff instruments, rhythm band

Extracurricular Activities

None

Goals for Students

To make every child feel unique and special; to be prepared for first grade and for life; to learn to make decisions

Faculty/Staff Requirements

Qualifications of Staff: Gentle spirit, energetic, and dedicated to school's goals; most are certified; some have master's degrees.
Qualifications of Administrator: Present director was on teaching staff for 14 years, has all-level certification, and has served as the school's director for 24 years.

School Information

Brochure Available: No
Number of Students in Each Grade: 8-16 based on developmental level
Parochial: No
Organization Affiliations: Sponsored by First Community Church as a service to the community
Accreditations: TDPRS
Parental Involvement: Much; encouraged
Other Information: We have a computer lab with a full-time computer teacher. Parents volunteer to assist with the program.

Admittance

Whom to Contact: School office
Date to Apply: Ongoing waiting list
Testing Procedure for Age/Grade Level: No testing
Fees Involved: $100 enrollment fee at time of enrollment
Type of Student Preferred:

Forms Required: Immunization records
Individual/Group Appointments: Individual
Notification Procedure: School calls students on the waiting list and schedules appointments for them to visit the school. (Most enroll at that time.)
Waiting List Policy: Ongoing waiting list

Tuition

Approximate Tuition for 1996-97 School Year: $1545 (ages 2 1/2-3, two-day program), $1645 (ages 3-3 1/2, three-day program), $1930 (ages 3 1/2-5, five-day program), $2140 (kindergarten)
Methods of Payment Available: Annual contract with option to pay monthly
Financial Assistance Offered: No
Cancellation Insurance Available: No
Profit/Non-profit: Non-profit

Additional Costs

Books/Bag/Uniform: None
Lunch Fee: None
Parents Club Dues: None
Annual Fund Drive: Sponsored by parents
Discount for Siblings: No, but they receive priority for enrollment

Facilities/Services Provided

Computer Lab: Yes–four computers, special teacher
Library: Maintained in classrooms to be age-appropriate
Snack Procedures: Students bring snacks for a week. Parents choose the week at the beginning of school.
Before-school Care Program Available: No
After-school Care Program Available: Church has Parents' Day Out on Wednesdays 9:00 a.m.-3:00 p.m.; accommodates students from the Children's Center
Nurse on Staff: No; staff trained in first aid and CPR
Emergency Procedure Used: Fire drills for evacuation training; disaster drills
Transportation to and from School: Car pools
Counseling and Evaluation Available: No professional counselor on staff

Graduation Information

Testing: N/A
Average SAT Scores: N/A
High School Our Students Usually Attend: N/A
Percentage of Seniors Attending College: N/A

Christian Childhood Development Center

9015 Plano Road
Dallas, TX 75238
(214) 349-4489

Mapsco:

Fax: 349-0888

Office Hours: 8:00 a.m.–4:00 p.m.
School Hours: 9:00 a.m.–2:30 p.m.
School Grades Offered: Crib (5 months old by Sept. 1)–4 years
Enrollment: 265
Co-ed: Yes
Boy/Girl Ratio: N/A
Student/Teacher Ratio: Infants–4:1; 4 year olds–8:1
Average Class Size: 14
Calendar School Year: Mid-August–mid-May
Holidays: Same as R.I.S.D.
Uniform Requirements: None
Founded in: 1974

Philosophy of School

The Christian Childhood Development Center provides an atmosphere of Christian love and caring and a guidance program that considers the developmental needs of each child.

Academic Curriculum

Content: Developmentally appropriate
Grading System Used: N/A
Conferences per Year: One
Tests Administered: None
Homework Policy: N/A
Method of Discipline: Positive guidance

Enrichment Curriculum
Music daily

Extracurricular Activities
N/A

Goals for Students

Faculty/Staff Requirements
Qualifications of Staff: Lead teachers have degrees
Qualifications of Administrator: Master's degree in early childhood education

School Information
Brochure Available: N/A
Number of Students in Each Grade: N/A
Parochial: N/A
Organization Affiliations: N/A
Accreditations: N/A
Parental Involvement: N/A
Other Information: N/A

Admittance
Whom to Contact: Marilyn Hyde or Sally Fifer
Date to Apply: Early February
Testing Procedure for Age/Grade Level: None
Fees Involved: None to apply
Type of Student Preferred: No preference
Forms Required: N/A
Individual/Group Appointments: In January
Notification Procedure: Letter–early March
Waiting List Policy: Re-apply annually

Tuition
Approximate Tuition for 1996-97 School Year: $1000
Methods of Payment Available: Cash or check
Financial Assistance Offered: None
Cancellation Insurance Available: None
Profit/Non-profit: Non-profit

Additional Costs

Books/Bag/Uniform: N/A
Lunch Fee: Parent provides
Parents Club Dues: N/A
Annual Fund Drive: N/A
Discount for Siblings: N/A

Facilities/Services Provided

Computer Lab: N/A
Library: N/A
Snack Procedures: C.C.D.C. provides morning snack.
Before-school Care Program Available: No
After-school Care Program Available: No
Nurse on Staff: No
Emergency Procedure Used: Contact parents
Transportation to and from School: No
Counseling and Evaluation Available: No

Graduation Information

Testing: None
Average SAT Scores: N/A
High School Our Students Usually Attend: N/A
Percentage of Seniors Attending College: N/A

Additional Information

The Cornerstone School

12302 Park Central Drive
Dallas, TX 75251
(214) 387-8567

Mapsco: 16W

Fax:

Office Hours: 8:00 a.m.–6:00 p.m.
School Hours: Preschool, 8:30 a.m.–11:30 a.m.; kindergarten,
8:30 a.m.–3:00 p.m.; elementary, 8:30 a.m.–3:30 p.m.
(extended day available for all ages)
School Grades Offered: Preschool–grade 6
Enrollment: 235
Co-ed: Yes
Boy/Girl Ratio: Approximately 1:1
Student/Teacher Ratio: 8–14:1
Average Class Size: 12–14
Calendar School Year: Mid-August to end of May
Holidays: Regular school vacations, but the
facility is open for child care all but eight days per calendar
year.
Uniform Requirements: None
Founded in: 1976

Philosophy of School

Children are naturally curious and will seek to explore and learn about their
environment.

Each child is unique, and individual differences must be respected and encouraged.
Instruction should be given individually and based on the child's level, learning style,
and interests.

Children learn best in an accepting, non-threatening environment.

The school must be concerned with the development of the whole child. Thus, besides
being concerned with the child's intellectual growth, the school must help foster the

child's creativity, as well as emotional, social, and physical growth.

Children learn best through actual experiences and active involvement.

Academic Curriculum

Content: Developmental preschool; traditional elementary curriculum
Grading System Used: Preschool and kindergarten–written evaluations and skill lists; elementary–letter grades
Conferences per Year: Two
Tests Administered: In May, achievement testing (Metropolitan Readiness Tests and Stanford Achievement Tests); in July, placement testing
Homework Policy: Determined by the individual teachers
Method of Discipline: Time-out for preschool; positive reinforcement for elementary

Enrichment Curriculum

Music, Spanish, physical education, computer, art

Extracurricular Activities

Drama, computer, piano, cooking, soccer, ballet, jazz, tennis, gymnastics, Kung Fu, manners class, swimming lessons daily in summer as part of summer camp

Goals for Students

The primary goal of the program is to develop in the child a positive attitude toward himself/herself and toward learning. We want children to succeed in their learning, to learn to make their own decisions, to be curious and involved, to learn self-control, to learn how to get along, to express their feelings and ideas freely and constructively, and to cooperate.

With respect to the child's intellectual development, we are concerned with encouraging his or her problem-solving ability. Reading, writing, mathematics, science, and social studies are important parts of the program and are always based on the level and interest of the particular child. The emphasis is on the child's exploring, experimenting, discovering, and seeking to understand. Kindergarten and elementary students learn to understand and use workbooks and other materials to reinforce these learning procedures.

Faculty/Staff Requirements

Qualifications of Staff: B.S. or M.S. degrees; previous teaching experience;

continuing education credit
Qualifications of Administrator: M.Ed. and doctoral work; 26 years' experience; professional seminars and organizations; corporate consultant

School Information

Brochure Available: Yes
Number of Students in Each Grade: Preschool–75; kindergarten–60; elementary–100
Parochial: No
Organization Affiliations: NAEYC
Accreditations: Licensed by Texas Department of Human Services
Parental Involvement: Voluntary parents' association
Other Information: Parents are welcome to participate at school in any way they choose.

Admittance

Whom to Contact: Mimi Goldman
Date to Apply: Beginning in January
Testing Procedure per Age/Grade Level: Appointments for placement tests are scheduled in late July.
Fees Involved: Included in registration fees
Type of Student Preferred: Open admissions policy
Forms Required: Yes–packet distributed during enrollment
Individual/Group Appointments: Individual
Notification Procedure: Immediately upon applying; all accepted on space availability
Waiting List Policy: Ongoing

Tuition

Approximate Tuition for 1996-97 School Year: Ranges from $900 to $4400
Methods of Payment Available: Monthly, by semester, or annually (discount for semester or annual payment)
Financial Assistance Offered: No
Cancellation Insurance Available: No
Profit/Non-profit: Profit

Additional Costs

Books/Bag/Uniform: Books included in registration fee; supply fee $250 (elementary); no bag or uniform requirements
Lunch Fee: $35 per month

Parents Club Dues: None
Annual Fund Drive: None
Discount for Siblings: None

Facilities/Services Provided

Computer Lab: Computers in classrooms; listening center in elementary building
Library: Yes
Snack Procedures: Provided by school
Before-school Care Program Available: Yes (begins at 6:50 a.m.)
After-school Care Program Available: Yes (until 6:00 p.m.)
Nurse on Staff: No; staff trained in first aid and CPR
Emergency Procedure Used: Contact parent; go to Medical City Hospital with signed parental permission form
Transportation to and from School: Assist with setting up car pools
Counseling and Evaluation Available: Yes

Graduation Information

Testing: N/A
Average SAT scores: N/A
High School Our Students Usually Attend: N/A
Percentage of Seniors Attending College: N/A

Additional Information

The Cornerstone School provides full summer-camp programs with on-site swimming available. In addition, we have holiday care and after-school care programs for children from selected area schools.

The da Vinci School

5442 La Sierra Drive
Dallas, TX 75231
(214) 373-9504

Mapsco: 26K

Fax: None

Office Hours: 8:00 a.m.–5:30 p.m.
School Hours: 8:45 a.m.–2:15 p.m.
School Grades Offered: 18 months–kindergarten and primer
Enrollment: 90
Co-ed: Yes
Boy/Girl Ratio: 50:50
Student/Teacher Ratio: (Range) 5:1–14:1
Average Class Size: (Range) 5–14
Calendar School Year: Sept.–May (Camp: June, July, and August)
Holidays: Thanksgiving, two-week winter break, Martin Luther King Day, spring break, two-week break in late May, one-week break with Independence Day holiday, two-week break in late August
Uniform Requirements: No
Founded in: 1987

Philosophy of School

"One of Dallas' best-kept secrets," the da Vinci School recognizes that children begin learning the moment they are born. Professionals everywhere agree that the early years of life are an especially sensitive time for establishing basic skills and for fostering joy, ability, and interest in learning. The da Vinci School provides its students with a unique environment and experiences that advance equally intellectual, physical, emotional, psychological, social, artistic (creative), and practical life growth.

Academic Curriculum

Content: Strong science and social studies orientation with high content level;

651

hands-on experiences; solid academic foundations in reading, writing, math, and thinking skills interwoven in weekly science themes. Teachers adjust their teaching styles and methods to match their students' needs, and they incorporate developmental checklist items into the curriculum.

Grading System Used: No grades; teachers maintain developmental checklist/ profiles on each student and incorporate them into the curriculum. These are the basis for parent conferences and insure thorough progress in all developmental areas.

Conferences per Year: Two (or as needed)

Tests Administered: At all levels, teachers assess each individual's level of understanding and present the information in a new format when needed; standardized tests are given to students beginning in kindergarten.

Homework Policy: N/A

Method of Discipline: Redirect and re-focus; talk with child about what to do; may use time out

Enrichment Curriculum

All classes have daily time in the gymnasium. Field trips and special visitors enhance academic units and themes.

Extracurricular Activities

Computer instruction available after school

Goals for Students

For each child to
- develop and maintain a love of learning and regard learning as fun
- gain a solid developmental and academic foundation in reading, writing, math, and science
- acquire a broad-based set of learning experiences that introduce the child to the world
- build self-esteem, confidence, and interactive skills in a positive social environment

Faculty/Staff Requirements

Qualifications of Staff: K and above must have degrees and experience; preschool–degree required, but experience and other qualifications are considered; a psychologist screens the staff for positive and supportive attitudes toward children and learning; staff must be versatile and creative in their teaching.

Qualifications of Administrator: Degree in psychology; 20+ years experience in early childhood development and education, gifted education from birth to sixth grade, and parent/baby education

School Information

Brochure Available: Yes
Number of Students in Each Grade: Kindergarten/primer–14; 4's–9; 3's–8; 2 1/2's–7; 2's–6; toddlers–5
Parochial: No
Organization Affiliations: None
Accreditations: Have not sought accreditation; licensed by Texas Department of Human Services
Parental Involvement: Active, involved parents with high priority on welfare of their child and his/her education; Parents' Association; parents and children benefit greatly from our parent education classes, which are available as soon as the child is born.
Other Information:

Admittance

Whom to Contact: Mary Ann Engel-Greene
Date to Apply: March through school year; we accept students on space-available basis any time during the school year.
Testing Procedure per Age/Grade Level: N/A
Fees Involved: $200 registration fee
Type of Student Preferred: Broad social, cultural, ethnic, and religious diversity encouraged
Forms Required: Registration, immunization, enrollment application/information tuition contract
Individual/Group Appointments: Call to schedule observation of classes and discussion with director; appointments available days, evenings, or weekends if necessary to accommodate both parents
Notification Procedure: N/A
Waiting List Policy: Re-apply annually; students are placed if space is available mid-year.

Tuition

Approximate Tuition for 1996-97 School Year: $140–$330/month (preschool); $395/month (K and primer)
Methods of Payment Available: Yearly tuition can be paid monthly; summer camp paid weekly; we are willing to work with families to meet individual needs.
Financial Assistance Offered: N/A
Cancellation Insurance Available: N/A
Profit/Non-profit: Non-profit

Additional Costs

Books/Bag/Uniform: K and primer–$70/year; fees for consumables range from $110—$245/year depending on number of days enrolled
Lunch Fee: N/A
Parents Club Dues: $10 (part of consumables fee)
Annual Fund Drive: N/A
Discount for Siblings: Inquire at school

Facilities/Services Provided

Computer Lab: Computer class is a regular part of kindergarten and primer curriculum; optional for 3 and 4 year olds
Library: Teachers select books from library for clasroom use.
Snack Procedures: Daily morning snack provided–wholesome foods, no sugar, 100% fruit juice; snacks often complement unit or theme in curriculum
Before-school Care Program Available: Yes–8:00 a.m.
After-school Care Program Available: Limited–until 3:00 p.m.
Nurse on Staff: No
Emergency Procedure Used: Contact parent or indicated alternate person, hospital if necessary; all staff required to have CPR and first-aid training
Transportation to and from School: None provided; parents can arrange car pools.
Counseling and Evaluation Available: Recommendations can be made.

Graduation Information

Testing: N/A
Average SAT Scores: N/A
High School Our Students Usually Attend: N/A
Percentage of Seniors Attending College: N/A

Additional Information

Founded under the corporate name "Texas Foundation for Educational Advancement," the da Vinci School operates as a non-profit, tax-exempt organization.

The da Vinci School has developed a reputation as one of Dallas' best-kept secrets. Our program is unique in several ways. We provide education for parents beginning when the baby is born to insure a sense of parental confidence and know-how, to foster a solid bond between parent and child, and to provide optimal enrichment for the baby. Children coming through our program are emotionally happy and healthy, have a close relationship with their parent(s), and are ready, eager learners. Some of these children continue with us into The da Vinci School's toddler, preschooler, and k programs. Children who go into public or private schools from "da Vinci" are superbly prepared and do very well indeed.

654

The da Vinci School creates a comfortable environment for its young students. Staff members are warm and happy people, the atmosphere is calm, and the classes are small so as not to overwhelm a small child. Parents often comment on how their children love coming to The da Vinci School.

To quote a former student who was asked to compare his previous private school with The da Vinci School: "Well, I like _____ school OK, but at da Vinci, I learn about the world." R.A., age 5.

DeSoto Private School

301 E. Beltline Rd.
De Soto, TX 75115
(214) 223-6450

Mapsco: 84F

Fax: (214) 230-0629

Office Hours: 6:30 a.m.–6:00 p.m.
School Hours: 8:00 a.m.–3:30 p.m.; extended day-care until 6:00 p.m.
School Grades Offered: Preschool (age 3) through grade 6
Enrollment: 600
Co-ed: Yes
Boy/Girl Ratio: 1:1
Student/Teacher Ratio: 12:1
Average Class Size: 8 (3K)–21 (primary)
Calendar School Year: August–May
Holidays: Labor Day, Thanksgiving, Christmas, New Year's Day, Memorial Day
Uniform Requirements: Yes
Founded in: 1972

Philosophy of School

To meet the individual needs and differences of each student
(DeSoto Private School is concerned with the development of the whole child.)

Academic Curriculum

Content: Mathematics, phonics, reading, whole language, art, computer, social sciences, creative writing, music, spelling, health, P.E., library
Grading System Used: Nine-week grading period, 5K; six-week grading periods, first through sixth grades
Conferences per Year: Yes, by request
Tests Administered: California Achievement Tests (C.A.T.)
Homework Policy: Expected consistency
Method of Discipline: Self-discipline; teacher/headmaster

Enrichment Curriculum
Cooperative learning, science fair, foreign language, life skills, literary appreciation, drama, computer, music, library skills

Extracurricular Activities
Dance studio, skating

Goals for Students
Optimum development of each individual's abilities

Faculty/Staff Requirements
Qualifications of Staff: College degree required for teachers of K5–grade 6
Qualifications of Administrator: College degree

School Information
Brochure Available: Yes
Number of Students in Each Grade: Varies
Parochial: No
Organization Affiliations: TACCA, NAEYC
Accreditations: Texas Department of Human Services
Parental Involvement: Yes
Other Information: DeSoto Private School has evolved into an excellent preparatory school. Many of our former students attend Greenhill, St. Mark's, Hockaday, Cistercian, and other well-known preparatory schools. We offer multisensory math and language curricula for all grade levels. Our strong areas include phonics and whole language, math, and science. Our fees represent a very cost-effective program for all levels of income. We have had the same administrative management for 23 years.

Admittance
Whom to Contact: Kenneth or Carolyn Larson
Date to Apply: March (before the school year begins in August)
Testing Procedure for Age/Grade Level: Testing in March
Fees Involved: Yes
Type of Student Preferred: Dedicated, ambitious, self-disciplined
Forms Required: Enrollment forms, medical report
Individual/Group Appointments: Individual
Notification Procedure: By letter
Waiting List Policy: Reapply

Tuition

Approximate Tuition for 1996-97 School Year: $3100
Methods of Payment Available: Monthly
Financial Assistance Offered: No
Cancellation Insurance Available: No
Profit/Non-profit: Profit

Additional Costs

Books/Bag/Uniform: Books, bag, school supplies
Lunch Fee: Yes
Parents Club Dues: N/A
Annual Fund Drive: Carnival
Discount for Siblings: Yes

Facilities/Services Provided

Computer Lab: With library
Library: Multi-media center with computers
Snack Procedures: None
Before-school Care Program Available: Yes, 6:30 a.m.–8:00 a.m.
After-school Care Program Available: Yes, 3:30 p.m.–6:00 p.m.
Nurse on Staff: Staff is trained in first aid and CPR.
Emergency Procedure Used: Call for minor emergencies; call 911 for major emergencies.
Transportation to and from School: No
Counseling and Evaluation Available: Yes

Graduation Information

Testing: N/A
Average SAT Scores: N/A
High School Our Students Usually Attend: N/A
Percentage of Seniors Attending College: N/A

Additional Information

Discovery School at Canyon Creek

400 W. Campbell Rd.
Richardson, TX 75080
(214) 669-9454

Mapsco: 7U

Fax: (214) 238-8214

Office Hours: 8:00 a.m.–4:00 p.m.
School Hours: K–3 (8:35 a.m.–2:30 p.m.);
ages 3–4 (9:30 a.m.–12:30 p.m.)
School Grades Offered: Three-year-olds–grade 3 (One
grade per year will be added until grade 6 is added.)
Enrollment: 170
Co-ed: Yes
Boy/Girl Ratio: 1:1
Student/Teacher Ratio: Younger–10:1; older–12:1; elementary–
14:1
Average Class Size: 10
Calendar School Year: Preschool: Sept.–May;
K–3: Aug.–May
Holidays: Same as Richardson Independent School
District
Uniform Requirements: Kindergarten–elementary
Founded in: 1987

Philosophy of School

To provide every child an opportunity to grow in all areas–mentally, spiritually,
emotionally, socially, and physically

Academic Curriculum

Content: Computer, music, Spanish, physical education, Houghton-Mifflin's
reading program, Everyday Math's math program
Grading System Used: Preschool–K: conferences; elementary–report cards
Conferences per Year: One or two

Tests Administered: Metropolitan Reading Readiness
Homework Policy: Kindergarten–occasionally; elementary–spelling, math
Method of Discipline: Good behavior is recognized and encouraged. If necessary, brief, supervised separation from the group is enforced or the parents are notified.

Enrichment Curriculum
Computer, music, Spanish, sports camp; extended day for enrichment

Extracurricular Activities
Extended day, sports camp, Bible camp, Eagle Club, ice skating, roller skating, bowling, bicycles

Goals for Students
Each student will develop necessary skills to become a lifelong learner–basic skills in communication, computation, and research–and know how to use them to solve complex problems. Our goal is to help each child reach his/her unique potential as a whole person.

Faculty/Staff Requirements
Qualifications of Staff: College degrees
Qualifications of Administrator: College degree and state certification

School Information
Brochure Available: Yes
Number of Students in Each Grade: (Number in each age group–not in each class) 3's–40; 4's and 5's–66; kindergarten–38; grade 1–14; grade 2–14; (10–14 children per class)
Parochial: Presbyterian Church
Organization Affiliations: Presbyterian Church
Accreditations: Texas Department of Human Services
Parental Involvement: Family activities, Parents' Club, Fall Carnival, Dads' Derby, Dads' Breakfast, Science Night, Center Days, "brown bag" lunches, silent auction, graduation
Other Information:

Admittance
Whom to Contact: Marna Brown, Director; Tonny Tabor, Administrator

Date to Apply: February
Entrance Testing: No
Fees Involved: Yes
Type of Student Preferred: Any boy or girl (We are not equipped to handle children with special needs.)
Forms Required: Yes
Individual/Group Appointments: Yes
Testing Procedure per Age/Grade Level:
Notification Procedure: Telephone call or letter
Waiting List Policy: Reapply annually

Tuition

Approximate Tuition for 1996-97 School Year: $1125–$3650
Methods of Payment Available: Monthly or yearly
Financial Assistance Offered: Scholarship based on individual need
Cancellation Insurance Available: No
Profit/Non-profit: Non-profit

Additional Costs

Books/Bag/Uniform: Books–none; bag–$5 to $7; uniforms–kindergarten and elementary (J.C. Penney and Lands End)
Lunch Fee: N/A
Parents Club Dues: None
Annual Fund Drive: Silent auction
Discount for Siblings: 10%

Facilities/Services Provided

Computer Lab: Yes
Library: Yes
Snack Procedures: Provided for kindergarten and elementary students
Before-school Care Program Available: Early arrival at 8:30 a.m.
After-school Care Program Available: Until 4:30 p.m.
Nurse on Staff: No
Emergency Procedure Used: Immediate first aid; parents notified; taken to hospital across the street
Transportation to and from School: No
Counseling and Evaluation Available: No counselors; evaluation by teacher; in-depth evaluation done by Dr. Imogene Jones

Graduation Information

Testing: N/A

Average SAT Scores: N/A
High School Our Students Usually Attend: N/A
Percentage of Seniors Attending College: N/A

Additonal Information

East Dallas Developmental Center

1926 Skillman
Dallas, TX 75206
(214) 821-7766

Mapsco: 37Q

Fax:

Office Hours: 7:30 a.m.–6:00 p.m.
School Hours: 7:30 a.m.–6:00 p.m.
School Grades Offered: Infant–preschool
Enrollment: 70 children
Co-ed: Yes
Boy/Girl Ratio:
Student/Teacher Ratio: Infants–4:1; toddlers–6:1;
2's–7:1; 3's–8:1; 4's–10:1; 5's–12:1
Average Class Size: Same as above
Calendar School Year: Year round
Holidays: Major holidays
Uniform Requirements: None
Founded in: 1980

Philosophy of School
See school brochure.

Academic Curriculum
Content:
Grading System Used: N/A
Conferences per Year: Yes
Tests Administered: N/A
Homework Policy: N/A
Method of Discipline: Time out and redirection

Enrichment Curriculum

Visits are made to retirement center for inner-generational program.

Extracurricular Activities

Dance and gymnastics classes are provided one per week.

Goals for Students

Goals are set for each class at age appropriate levels.

Faculty/Staff Requirements

Qualifications of Staff: College degrees (child development, education, psychology)

Qualifications of Administrator: College degree in early childhood development

School Information

Brochure Available: Yes

Number of Students in Each Grade:

Parochial: No

Organization Affiliations: DAEYC and NAEYC

Accreditations: State certified

Parental Involvement: Yes

Admittance

Whom to Contact: Linda Laws, Director

Date to Apply: Year round

Testing Procedure per Age/Grade Level: None

Fees Involved: Deposit (1/2 month's tuition); annual entrance fee ($100)

Type of Student Preferred: We do not discriminate.

Forms Required: Enrollment forms and immunization records

Individual/Group Appointments: Individual

Notification Procedure:

Waiting List Policy: Ongoing

Tuition

Approximate Tuition for 1996-97 School Year: Call for information.

Methods of Payment Available: Monthly

Financial Assistance Offered: None

Cancellation Insurance Available: None
Profit/Non-profit: Non-profit

Additional Costs

Books/Bag/Uniform: None
Lunch Fee: Hot lunch provided
Parents Club Dues: None
Annual Fund Drive: Fundraising done year round
Discount for Siblings: None

Facilities/Services Provided

Computer Lab: Yes
Library: Pre-kindergarten class makes weekly trips to the library.
Snack Procedures: Morning and afternoon snacks daily
Before-school Care Program Available: No
After-school Care Program Available: No
Nurse on Staff: No
Emergency Procedure Used: Yes
Transportation to and from School: No
Counseling and Evaluation Available: Yes

Graduation Information

Testing: N/A
Average SAT scores: N/A
High School Our Students Usually Attend: N/A
Percentage of Seniors Attending College: N/A

Additional Information

Fair Oaks Day School

7825 Fair Oaks Avenue
Dallas, TX 75231
(214) 340-1121

Mapsco: 26R

Fax: N/A

Office Hours: 7:00 a.m.–6:30 p.m.
School Hours: 7:00 a.m.–6:30 p.m.
School Grades Offered: Preschool–kindergarten
Enrollment: 138
Co-ed: Yes
Boy/Girl Ratio: N/A
Student/Teacher Ratio: 9:1
Average Class Size: 18
Calendar School Year: Year-round
Holidays: Labor Day, Thanksgiving, Christmas, New Year's Day, Memorial Day, Independence Day
Uniform Requirements: None
Founded in: 1987

Philosophy of School

Fair Oaks Day School provides a warm, nurturing environment for children to play, learn, and grow in a healthy, safe atmosphere.

Academic Curriculum

Content: DLM Springboards–in kindergarten
Grading System Used: N/A
Conferences per Year: 2
Tests Administered: Metropolitan Readiness Test in kindergarten
Homework Policy: N/A
Method of Discipline: N/A

Enrichment Curriculum
N/A

Extracurricular Activities
Computer, art, dance, gymnastics

Goals for Students

Faculty/Staff Requirements
Qualifications of Staff: Must meet minimum staff standards for day-care school
Qualifications of Administrator: College degree; must meet minimum staff standards for day-care school

School Information
Brochure Available: Yes
Number of Students in Each Grade: N/A
Parochial: No
Organization Affiliations: N/A
Accreditations: N/A
Parental Involvement: Yes, field trips, parent lunches, open house
Other Information:

Admittance
Whom to Contact: Greg Stone, Frances Bresert
Date to Apply: Open enrollment
Testing Procedure for Age/Grade Level: N/A
Fees Involved: Registration
Type of Student Preferred: N/A
Forms Required: Yes
Individual/Group Appointments: Any time between 7:00 a.m. and 6:30 p.m.
Notification Procedure:
Waiting List Policy: Ongoing

Tuition
Approximate Tuition for 1996-97 School Year: Call the school for rates.
Methods of Payment Available: Cash or check

Financial Assistance Offered: N/A
Cancellation Insurance Available: N/A
Profit/Non-profit: Profit

Additional Costs

Books/Bag/Uniform: N/A
Lunch Fee: N/A
Parents Club Dues: N/A
Annual Fund Drive: N/A
Discount for Siblings: None

Facilities/Services Provided

Computer Lab: N/A
Library: N/A
Snack Procedures: Snacks and hot lunch provided daily
Before-school Care Program Available: Yes
After-school Care Program Available: Yes
Nurse on Staff: N/A
Emergency Procedure Used: N/A
Transportation to and from School: Yes
Counseling and Evaluation Available: N/A

Graduation Information

Testing: Metropolitan Readiness Test for kindergarten students
Average SAT Scores: N/A
High School Our Students Usually Attend: N/A
Percentage of Seniors Attending College: N/A

Additional Information

The Harrington School Private Early Childhood Academic Center

2638 Valley View Lane
Farmers Branch, TX 75234
(214) 484-4215

Mapsco: 13V

Fax: N/A

Office Hours: 7:30 a.m.–6:00 p.m.
School Hours: 7:30 a.m.–6:00 p.m.
School Grades Offered: Preschool–kindergarten (3-6 years old)
Enrollment: 40
Co-ed: Yes
Boy/Girl Ratio: Varies
Student/Teacher Ratio: 12:1
Average Class Size: 12
Calendar School Year: Open all year
Holidays: Standard
Uniform Requirements: No
Founded in: 1987

Philosophy of School

THE HARRINGTON SCHOOL, INC., was founded in 1987 to provide a quality private-school education for exemplary children. Our program has been designed around the concept of meeting each child's individual needs in a structured, educational environment.

Children from 3-6 years have unique needs. We recognize that these children have short attention spans and are still very active. The rooms are designed with learning centers so children can move freely. One-on-one math and reading experiences are alternated with group activities.

THE HARRINGTON SCHOOL is concerned with the development of the whole child. We strive to encourage growth in intellectual, social, and physical abilities. By keeping our classes small, we are able to make each child feel special. The group is like a family, and every child contributes and asks questions. Our students see learning as an active, pleasant experience. There is a spirit of cooperation rather than competition in all aspects of school life.

Academic Curriculum

Content: Reading and math experiences are taught one-on-one by the teacher while the other children are in learning centers. Every child has an individual lesson plan for these academic areas. Concrete, meaning "hands-on," materials are used to introduce each new concept. Educational research has proven this method is ideal.

Grading System Used: Preschool and prekindergarten–student evaluation sent home in November, February, and May; kindergarten–report card sent home every six weeks with numerical grades

Conferences per Year: N/A

Tests Administered: N/A

Homework Policy: N/A

Method of Discipline: N/A

Enrichment Curriculum

Music, physical education, Spanish, computer, drama–fall musical and spring musical (on stage in auditorium)

Extracurricular Activities

Goals for Students

Faculty/Staff Requirements

Qualifications of Staff: Elementary education degrees; Texas teaching certificates; areas of specialization include early childhood education, reading specialist, special education, and exceptional early childhood; certificates posted on front bulletin board; all staff members are trained and certified in first aid and CPR; college interns and aides are employed to help as needed.

Qualifications of Administrator: B.S. in Elementary Education, Early Childhood Endorsement, Reading Specialist Endorsement, Special Education Endorsement, Exceptional/Gifted Endorsement

School Information

Brochure Available: Yes
Number of Students in Each Grade: 12
Parochial: No
Organization Affiliations: Farmers Branch Chamber of Commerce, Farmers Branch Rotary Club
Accreditations: Texas Department of Human Services, Texas Education Agency
Parental Involvement: Volunteer Program
Other Information: Open year round

Admittance

Whom to Contact: Robin Harrington
Date to Apply: Open enrollment
Testing Procedure per Age/Grade Level: N/A
Fees Involved: None
Type of Student Preferred: N/A
Forms Required: Standard Enrollment Form
Individual/Group Appointments: Individual
Notification Procedure: At time of testing
Waiting List Policy: In some grades

Tuition

Approximate Tuition for 1996-97 School Year: $3978
Methods of Payment Available: $77 per week (due each Monday)
Financial Assistance Offered: No
Cancellation Insurance Available: N/A
Profit/Non-profit: Profit

Additional Costs

Books/Bag/Uniform: Preschool–no fee; prekindergarten–$44; kindergarten–$114; supply fee–$10 (September, January, June)
Lunch Fee: Sack lunch or $2 per day for restaurant-catered meal
Parents Club Dues: No
Annual Fund Drive: No
Discount for Siblings: No

Facilities/Services Provided

Computer Lab: Kindergarten class
Library: On site

Snack Procedures: 10:00 a.m. and 2:30 p.m. (provided by school)
Before-school Care Program Available: N/A
After-school Care Program Available: N/A
Nurse on Staff: No
Emergency Procedure Used: Call 911, parents, doctor, hospital
Transportation to and from School: No
Counseling and Evaluation Available: Yes

Graduation Information

Testing: N/A
Average SAT Scores: N/A
High School Our Students Usually Attend: N/A
Percentage of Seniors Attending College: N/A

Additional Information

Hearthstone Kindergarten

10303 Webbs Chapel Rd.
Dallas, TX 75229
(214) 324-9020

Mapsco: 23L

Fax: None

Office Hours:
School Hours: 8:45 a.m.–12:45 p.m.
School Grades Offered: Kindergarten
Enrollment: 18
Co-ed: Yes
Boy/Girl Ratio: 1:1
Student/Teacher Ratio: 18:3
Average Class Size: 18
Calendar School Year: Same as D.I.S.D.
Holidays: Same as D.I.S.D.
Uniform Requirements: None
Founded in: 1983

Philosophy of School

Hearthstone Kindergarten is a Waldorf school, part of the largest non-sectarian educational movement in the world. The curriculum is non-academic and developmental. Young children are highly creative and imaginative. At Hearthstone, the teachers help the children give form to their creative impulses through carefully planned activities, inviting materials, and teacher example. The school offers a warm homelike environment, including a beautiful garden, natural toys and materials, and ample time to play with other children.

Academic Curriculum

Content: Each child's creative abilities are nurtured and developed through activities which include water color painting, beeswax modeling, finger knitting, gardening, baking, storytelling, singing, crafts, and seasonal activities.
Grading System Used: None
Conferences per Year: 2

673

Tests Administered: None
Homework Policy: None
Method of Discipline: Redirection, giving children time and space to settle down

Enrichment Curriculum
Enrichment is built into our curriculum.

Extracurricular Activities
Celebration of seasonal festivals and traditional holidays

Goals for Students
Capacities for wonder, gratitude, and responsibility are nurtured along with the skills that allow each child to express herself/himself creatively.

Faculty/Staff Requirements
Qualifications of Staff: Waldorf-kindergarten training
Qualifications of Administrator: Extensive experience in administration and Waldorf education

School Information
Brochure Available: Yes
Number of Students in Each Grade: 18
Parochial: No
Organization Affiliations: Waldorf Kindergarten Association
Accreditations: N/A
Parental Involvement: We have a very active parents' group.
Other Information: Licensed by Texas Department of Human Services

Admittance
Whom to Contact: Christy Williams
Date to Apply: Ongoing
Testing Procedure for Age/Grade Level: None
Fees Involved: $100 annual supply fee
Type of Student Preferred: Students with negligible exposure to television and other electronic media
Forms Required: Enrollment, health
Individual/Group Appointments: Pre-enrollment interview

Notification Procedure: We maintain close contact with applicants during the application process.
Waiting List Policy: Ongoing

Tuition

Approximate Tuition for 1996-97 School Year: $1620
Methods of Payment Available: Tuition due on the first of every month
Financial Assistance Offered: Board of Directors accepts applications for financial assistance.
Cancellation Insurance Available: N/A
Profit/Non-profit: Non-profit

Additional costs:

Books/Bag/Uniform: N/A
Lunch Fee: Children bring lunch and a small snack.
Parents Club Dues: None
Annual Fund Drive: Parents participate in organizing Christmas Bazaar.
Discount for Siblings: Yes

Facilities/Services Provided

Computer Lab: No
Library: No
Snack Procedures: Children bring a piece of fruit daily to contribute to class fruit salad.
Before-school Care Program Available: Can be arranged
After-school Care Program Available: Can be arranged
Nurse on Staff: No
Emergency Procedure Used: Follow Texas Department of Human Services' Guidelines
Transportation to and from School: Parents
Counseling and Evaluation Available: No

Graduation Information

Testing: N/A
Average SAT Scores: N/A
High School Our Students Usually Attend: N/A
Percentage of Seniors Attending College: N/A

The Hillcrest Academy

5923 Royal Lane
Dallas, Texas 75230
(214) 490-1161

Mapsco: 15R

Fax: (214) 490-1072

Office Hours: 8:00 a.m.–4:00 p.m. (Mon.–Fri.)
School Hours: 8:30 a.m.–3:30 p.m.
School Grades Offered: Preschool; full-day kindergarten;
grades 1–8
Enrollment: 160
Co-ed: Yes
Boy/Girl Ratio: 60:40
Student/Teacher Ratio: 12:1
Average Class Size: 12–15
Calendar School Year: End of August-end of May
Holidays: Labor Day, state fair holiday, Thanksgiving, winter
break (two weeks), New Year's Day, Martin Luther King Day,
Memorial Day
Uniform Requirements: Yes, K–grade 8
Founded in: 1976

Philosophy of School

Hillcrest Academy is an independent, non-sectarian, coeducational, non-profit institution. It offers children the opportunity to achieve the highest academic excellence based on consistent, competitive standards. Hillcrest Academy creates an environment that nurtures personal integrity, self-esteem, and individual artistic and imaginative expression. Students learn to assume responsibility for their actions and to respect other people and the educational process.

Academic Curriculum

Content: Reading, language arts, mathematics, science, social studies/history, Spanish, French, physical education, health, music, computer
Grading System Used: Letter and number grades, depending on the grade level

Conferences per Year: Two
Tests Administered: Stanford Achievement Test used for standardized testing
Homework Policy: Varies by age/grade level
Method of Discipline:

Enrichment Curriculum
Spanish, French, computer, speech, art, music, physical education

Extracurricular Activities
Ballet, computer, pottery, gymnastics, martial arts, private music lessons, optional sports program

Goals for Students
To foster intellectual, academic, and artistic excellence for each of our students in a warm and nurturing environment

Faculty/Staff Requirements
Qualifications of Staff: Degree from accredited college; certification
Qualifications of Administrator: B.A. in Education; teacher certification

School Information
Brochure Available: Yes
Number of Students in Each Grade: 12–30
Parochial: Non-denominational
Organization Affiliations: No religious affiliations, NAEYC, DAEYC, Texas Department of Protective and Regulatory Services
Accreditations: See "Organization Affiliations"
Parental Involvement: Yes, Parents' Association
Other Information:

Admittance
Whom to Contact: Director of Admissions
Date to Apply: Year-round depending on space availability
Testing Procedure per Age/Grade Level: Preschool evaluation is completed by preschool lead teachers; testing is completed on a one-to-one basis by a licensed diagnostician
Fees Involved: Application fee–$50; preschool evalution fee–$50; diagnostic testing fee–$200

677

Type of Student Preferred: Average to above-average ability
Forms Required: Yes
Individual/Group Appointments: Individual interview and individual testing
Notification Procedure: Letter of acceptance sent to parents
Waiting List Policy: Yes

Tuition

Approximate Tuition for 1996-97 School Year: $3810–$6610 (deposit required upon acceptance to school)
Methods of Payment Available: Full tuition due before school begins or 1/2 before school begins and 1/2 in January
Financial Assistance Offered: Not at this time
Cancellation Insurance Available: Not at this time
Profit/Non-profit: Non-profit

Additional costs

Books/Bag/Uniform: Uniform–approximately $75–$100
Lunch Fee: Catered at $2.80/day or bring lunch from home
Parents Club Dues: $20 annually
Annual Fund Drive: $300 per child
Discount for Siblings: Not at this time

Facilities/Services Provided

Computer Lab: Yes; IBM DOS oriented computer lab set up to run Windows; CD ROM available for student use
Library: Yes; a small school library containing fiction, non-fiction, and resource materials for student use; small parent library also available
Snack Procedures:
Before-school Care Program Available: Yes; 7:30 a.m.–8:15 a.m.
After-school Care Program Available: Yes; after school until 6:00 p.m.
Nurse on Staff: No, faculty trained in CPR and first aid
Emergency Procedure Used: Parents and guardians notified as listed on Health Form
Transportation to and from School: Families arrange their own car pools.
Counseling and Evaluation Available:

Graduation Information

Testing: Stanford Achievement Test: kindergarten–grade 8; administered in April
Average SAT Scores: N/A

High School Our Students Usually Attend: Most students stay within the private sector of education.
Percentage of Seniors Attending College: 98

Additional Information

Lakewood Presbyterian School

7020 Gaston Avenue
Dallas, TX 75214
(214) 321-2864

Mapsco: 37W

Fax: N/A

Office Hours: 8:00 a.m.–12:00 noon (Tuesday–Friday)
School Hours: 8:00 a.m.–12:00 noon (Tuesday–Friday)
School Grades Offered: 7–12
Enrollment: 75
Co-ed: Yes
Boy/Girl Ratio: 50:50
Student/Teacher Ratio: 6:1
Average Class Size: 10
Calendar School Year: September–May
Holidays: Thanksgiving, Christmas, Easter
Uniform Requirements: None
Founded in: 1990

Philosophy of School

Parents and church carry out covenantal responsibilities to bring up children in the nurture and admonition of the Lord. Intellectual training takes place within the context of faithfulness to God and His Word.

Academic Curriculum

Content: Bible, literature, history, Latin, math, sciences
Grading System Used: A, B, C, D, F
Conferences per Year: As needed
Tests Administered: PSAT
Homework Policy: Do it.
Method of Discipline: Verbal; suspension

Enrichment Curriculum

None beyond core courses

Extracurricular Activities
Basketball, drama, choir; initiated by parents, approved by school; at student's expense

Goals for Students
To become young adults who love God with all their hearts, minds, souls, and strength; to possess and grow in wisdom; to be disciples of Christ, observing what He commanded; to exercise a godly dominion over creation; to take every thought captive to Christ; to love their neighbor as themselves

Faculty/Staff Requirements
Qualifications of Staff: Christian character, love of teaching, competency in subject area
Qualifications of Administrator: B.A., Th.M.

School Information
Brochure Available: Yes
Number of Students in Each Grade: 14
Parochial: Lakewood Presbyterian Church, P.C.A.
Organization Affiliations: Presbyterian Church in America
Accreditations: None sought
Parental Involvement: Extensive, if desired
Other Information:

Admittance
Whom to Contact: Arnie Robertstad
Date to Apply: Spring and summer
Testing Procedure per Age/Grade Level: N/A
Fees Involved: Various
Type of Student Preferred: Responsible and willing
Forms Required: Application
Individual/Group Appointments: Yes
Notification Procedure: Phone call or letter
Waiting List Policy: Ongoing

Tuition
Approximate Tuition for 1996-97 School Year: $1350
Methods of Payment Available: Monthly for nine months
Financial Assistance Offered: No

Cancellation Insurance Available: May cancel with loss of first month's tuition
Profit/Non-profit: Non-profit

Additional Costs

Books/Bag/Uniform: Books–$100-$250; bag–n/a; uniform–n/a
Lunch Fee: No
Parents Club Dues: No
Annual Fund Drive: No
Discount for Siblings: $20 per month

Facilities/Services Provided

Computer Lab: N/A
Library: A small library is maintained
Snack Procedures: None
After-school Care Program Available: No
Before-school Care Program Available: No
Nurse on Staff: No
Emergency Procedure Used: Call 911
Transportation to and from School: No
Counseling and Evaluation Available: Counseling

Graduation Information

Testing: PSAT
Average SAT scores: 1160
High School Our Students Usually Attend: N/A
Percentage of Seniors Attending College: 100

Additional Information

The Little Red Schoolhouse

412 S. Bryan—Belt Line
Mesquite, TX 75149
(214) 285-3962

Mapsco: 49A-V

Fax:

Office Hours: 8:20 a.m.–4:00 p.m.
School Hours: 8:20 a.m.–12:00 noon (morning session),
12:30 p.m.–3:20 p.m. (afternoon session)
School Grades Offered: Pre-kindergarten (3- and 4-year-
olds); kindergarten; grade 1
Enrollment: 200
Co-ed: Yes
Boy/Girl Ratio: Varies
Student/Teacher Ratio: 3-year-olds–15:1; 4-year-olds–
20:1; kindergarten–22:1; grade 1–22:1 (two aides
available)
Average Class Size: Varies with age of children
Calendar School Year: September—May
Holidays: Thanksgiving, Christmas, Easter, spring break
Uniform Requirements: No
Founded in: 1960

Philosophy of School

The Little Red Schoolhouse was established in 1960. Our primary objective was to
develop a creative learning center with a highly enriched curriculum. It is our
philosophy that every child's self-esteem is a priceless treasure to be cherished and
nurtured through positive reinforcement in a unique informative environment.

Academic Curriculum

Content: Curriculum on all levels phonetically based
Grading System Used: Grade 1–letter grades; kindergarten and pre-k–check
marks (excellent, good, needs improvement)
Conferences per Year: One required before school begins; usually several
throughout the school year

Tests Administered: C.A.T. 5 Readiness/C.A.T. 5 Achievement
Homework Policy: Homework required only in grade 1
Method of Discipline: One-on-one discussion; time out; parent-teacher-child conference
Other Information:

Enrichment Curriculum
Science/social studies unit activities, holiday studies and special projects

Extracurricular Activities
Fiesta after Spanish study; field trips

Goals for Students
To succeed to the optimum of their abilities in the most exciting learning setting possible

Faculty/Staff Requirements
Qualifications of Staff: Bachelor's degree
Qualifications of Administrator: Master's degree

School Information
Brochure Available: Yes
Number of Students in Each Grade: Pre-K, 75; K, 75; 1st, 50
Parochial: No
Organization Affiliations: Local chamber of commerce
Accreditations: TDPRS
Parental Involvement: Open-door policy; parents very involved in academic projects and special activities
Other Information:

Admittance
Whom to Contact: Marilyn Chappell (Office Manager)
Date to Apply: October 15 for upcoming year
Testing Procedure per Age/Grade Level: Pre-kindergarten–no testing ; kindergarten–C.A.T. Readiness Test; grade 1–C.A.T. Achievement Test; (age and grade determine testing)
Fees Involved: Registration fee/supply fee (each semester); insurance
Type of Student Preferred: No selective student preference

Forms Required: Information sheet; immunization records
Individual/Group Appointments: Available on request; not required after registration
Notification Procedure: By telephone and mail
Waiting List Policy: Re-apply each year

Tuition

Approximate Tuition for 1996-97 School Year: Grade 1-$1600; kindergarten (5)-$1400; kindergarten (4)-$1300;
Methods of Payment Available: 10 monthly payments (August through May) or total payment in advance
Financial Assistance Offered: None
Cancellation Insurance Available: None
Profit/Non-profit: Profit

Additional Costs

Books/Bag/Uniform: Supply fee-$90 (grade 1); $90 per semester (kindergarten and pre-K); activity fee-$35 (grade 1), $25 (kindergarten and pre-K)
Lunch Fee: None
Parents Club Dues: None
Annual Fund Drive: None
Discount for Siblings: None

Facilities/Services Provided

Computer Labs: None
Library: Use local libraries and branches
Snack Procedures: Parents provide for their own children.
Before-school Care Program Available: No
After-school Care Program Available: No
Nurse on Staff: Medical technician
Emergency Procedure Used: Call 911, fire station, and numbers provided by parent
Transportation to and from School: Parents provide own transportation; parents car pool
Counseling and Evaluation Available: Referrals-not on staff

Graduation Information

Testing: N/A
Average SAT Scores: N/A
High School Our Students Usually Attend: N/A
Percentage of Seniors Attending College: N/A

Maryview Academy and Private School

115 W. Wintergreen
DeSoto, TX 75115
(214) 709-7991

Mapsco: 84F

Fax: (214) 709-8098

Office Hours: 8:00 a.m.–3:30 p.m.
School Hours: 8:00 a.m.–3:00 p.m.
School Grades Offered: 2 years–grade 5
Enrollment: 303
Co-ed: Yes
Boy/Girl Ratio: 1:1
Student/Teacher Ratio: 13:1
Average Class Size: 20-25
Calendar School Year: August–May
Holidays: Traditional
Uniform Requirements: No
Founded in: 1988

Philosophy of School

Maryview promotes interactive learning and encourages the child's construction of knowledge. We want to help students grow socially, emotionally, physically, and cognitively. We want to encourage their positive feelings and attitudes toward learning as they acquire knowledge and skills. We believe learning is meaningful and relevant to children's lives.

Academic Curriculum

Content: Varies with each grade level
Grading System Used: Preschool–observational checklist; kindergarten–E, S, N; grades 1-5– numerical grades
Conferences per Year: As needed; at least two per year
Tests Administered: SOI, Iowa Test of Basic Skills

686

Homework Policy: 15-20 minutes per night
Method of Discipline: Assertive discipline

Enrichment Curriculum
Art, music, Spanish, field trips

Extracurricular Activities
Summer camp, field trips

Goals for Students
To be well-adjusted socially and develop a love for learning

Faculty/Staff Requirements
Qualifications of Staff: 2-, 3-, and 4-year-olds–CDA; K-grade 5–bachelor's degree
Qualifications of Administrator: Master's degree (minimum)

School Information
Brochure Available: Yes
Number of Students in Each Grade: Varies
Parochial: No
Organization Affiliations: NAEYC, TLCCA, NCCA
Accreditations: NCCA, TDPRS
Parental Involvement: Meetings four times per year; two fundraisers
Other Information:

Admittance
Whom to Contact: Dr. Dan Lake
Date to Apply: March 1
Testing Procedure per Age/Grade Level: K and above–SOI
Fees Involved: $125
Type of Student Preferred: Average and above-average
Forms Required: Registration card, enrollment forms
Individual/Group Appointments: Individual for school visits
Notification Procedure: Letter or phone call
Waiting List Policy: Ongoing

Tuition

Approximate Tuition for 1996-97 School Year: $3300
Methods of Payment Available: Check, Visa, MasterCard, monthly
Financial Assistance Offered: No
Cancellation Insurance Available: No
Profit/Non-profit: Profit

Additional Costs

Books/Bag/Uniform: Books–$100 per year
Lunch Fee: No
Parents Club Dues: $5 per year
Annual Fund Drive: No; two fundraisers
Discount for Siblings: Yes

Facilities/Services Provided

Computer: Macs in every classroom
Library: Use Desoto Public Library
Snack Procedures: Morning snacks provided
Before-school Care Program Available: Yes, 6:30–7:45 a.m.
After-school Care Program Available: Yes, 3:00–6:00 p.m.
Nurse on Staff: No
Emergency Procedure Used: 911 used in an emergency
Transportation to and from School: No
Counseling and Evaluation Available: Referrals made

Graduation Information

Testing: N/A
Average SAT Scores: N/A
High School Our Students Usually Attend: N/A
Percentage of Seniors Attending College: N/A

Northbrook School

5608 Northaven Rd.   Mapsco: 25E
Dallas, TX 75230
(214) 369-8330   Fax:

Office Hours: 6:45 a.m.–6:00 p.m.
School Hours: Preschool 8:30 a.m.–11:30 a.m.;
kindergarten 8:30 a.m.–3:00 p.m.; elementary 8:30 a.m.–
3:30 p.m.
School Grades Offered: Preschool (2 years)–grade 4
Enrollment: 94
Co-ed: Yes
Boy/Girl Ratio: 1:1
Student/Teacher Ratio: 12:1
Average Class Size: 12
Calendar School Year: Mid-August–May; summer camp
available
Holidays: National holidays
Uniform Requirements: No
Founded in: 1992

Philosophy of School

Each child is unique, and individual differences must be respected and encouraged.
Instruction is based on the child's level and learning style. The school is concerned with
the development of the whole child. Thus, besides being concerned with the child's
intellectual growth, the school helps to foster the child's creativity, as well as
emotional, social, and physical growth.

Academic Curriculum

Content: Developmental preschool; traditional elementary curriculum; our
curriculum prepares students for success in public or private college-preparatory
programs.
Grading System Used: Preschool and kindergarten–written evaluations and
skill lists; elementary–letter grades
Conferences per Year: Two

689

Tests Administered: Placement tests (July); achievement tests (May)
Homework Policy:
Method of Discipline: Age-appropriate consequences and rewards

Enrichment Curriculum
Spanish, art, drama, computer, music, piano, cooking, soccer, ballet, gymnastics–once per week; swimming lessons–daily in summer as part of a full summer-camp program

Extracurricular Activities
See "Enrichment Curriculum."

Goals for Students
The primary goal of the program is to develop in the children a positive attitude toward themselves and toward learning. We want the children to meet with success in their learning, to learn to make their own decisions, to be curious and involved, to learn self-control, and to learn how to get along and to express their feelings and ideas freely and constructively, and to cooperate with their teachers and peers.

With respect to the child's intellectual development, we are concerned with encouraging his or her problem-solving ability. Reading, writing, mathematics, science, and social studies are important parts of the program and are always based on the level and interest of the particular child. The emphasis is on the child's exploring, experimenting, discovering, and seeking to understand. Kindergarten and elementary students learn to understand and use workbooks and other materials to reinforce these learning procedures.

Faculty/Staff Requirements
Qualifications of Staff: B.S. or M.S. degrees, previous teaching experience, continuing education
Qualifications of Administrator: Same as staff qualifications but with administrative experience; participation in professional seminars, organizations; director credentials

School Information
Brochure Available: Yes
Number of Students in Each Grade: 30 preschool; 25 kindergarten; 30 elementary
Parochial: No
Organization Affiliations: NAEYC
Accreditations: Licensed by state of Texas

Parental Involvement: Yes
Other Information:

Admittance
Whom to Contact: Director
Date to Apply: Spring
Testing Procedure per Age/Grade Level: In summer for placement only
Fees Involved: Included in registration fees
Type of Student Preferred: Open-admissions policy
Forms Required: Health and school records
Individual/Group Appointments: Individual
Notification Procedure: Depends on space availability
Waiting List Policy:

Tuition
Approximate Tuition for 1996-97 School Year: $1080–$3735 (includes registration and supply fees)
Methods of Payment Available: Bi-monthly, monthly, by semester, or annually; (pre-payment discounts available)
Financial Assistance Offered: No
Cancellation Insurance Available: No
Profit/Non-profit: Profit

Additional Costs
Books/Bag/Uniform: N/A
Lunch Fee: $35 per month
Parents Club Dues: Voluntary
Annual Fund Drive: No
Discount for Siblings: 5% if three or more in one family are enrolled

Facilities/Services Provided
Computer Lab:
Library:
Snack Procedures: Provided by school twice a day
Before-school Care Program Available: Yes, from 6:50 a.m.
After-school Care Program Available: Yes, until 6:00 p.m.
Nurse on Staff: No; staff trained in first aid and CPR
Emergency Procedure Used: Contact parent; go to closest hospital with signed parental release
Transportation to and from School: After-school transportation is available

from selected area schools to our facility for after-school care.
Counseling and Evaluation Available: Yes

Graduation Information

Testing: N/A
Average SAT Scores: N/A
High School Our Students Usually Attend: N/A
Percentage of Seniors Attending College: N/A

Additional Information

Full summer-camp programs are available. In addition, we have holiday care and after-school care programs for children from selected area schools.

NorthPark Presbyterian Day School

P.O. Box 820726–D. 75382–0726   Mapsco: 26F
9555 N. Central Expressway
Dallas, TX   75231
(214) 361-8024   Fax: (214) 368-1957

Office Hours: 9:00 a.m.–3:00 p.m.
School Hours: 9:00 a.m.–12:00 p.m. (M,T); 9:00 a.m.–2:00 p.m. (W, Th, F)
School Grades Offered: One year–kindergarten
Enrollment: 165
Co-ed: Yes
Boy/Girl Ratio: 1:1
Student/Teacher Ratio: Varies: 1 year–4:1; 2 years–6-8:1; three years–8-10:1; 4 years–12:1; kindergarten–15:1
Average Class Size: 6-12 (varies according to age)
Calendar School Year: September-May
Holidays: R.I.S.D. major holidays
Uniform Requirements: None
Founded in: 1964

Philosophy of School

NorthPark Presbyterian Day School strives to provide young children opportunities to grow and develop physically, mentally, socially, and spiritually and to develop their senses of self-worth and identity within the context of the Christian faith. We do not discriminate on the basis of race or color for hiring or enrollment.

Academic Curriculum

Content: Age appropriate, developmental
Grading System Used: No grades; objective observation
Conferences per Year: Preschool–at mid-year; kindergarten–fall and spring

693

Tests Administered: None; informal evaluation
Homework Policy: N/A
Method of Discipline: Positive discipline techniques

Enrichment Curriculum

Music and Movement offered Monday–Friday for all students ages two and older; conversational French offered on Wednesdays for four- and five-year-olds; creative drama offered weekly for children three and older

Extracurricular Activities

Occasional field trips for pre-K and K classes

Goals for Students

Develop solid base of social–emotional security to maximize academic and emotional potential

Faculty/Staff Requirements

Qualifications of Staff: Most have degrees; others have more than three years' experience, several master's degrees, two RN staff members
Qualifications of Administrator: M.Ed. in Elementary and Early Childhood; 20 years teaching experience; Director since 1987

School Information

Brochure Available: Yes
Number of Students in Each Grade: N/A
Parochial: Presbyterian (USA)
Organization Affiliations: NAEYC, DAEYC, MNKA
Accreditations: No
Parental Involvement: Ongoing volunteer activities (optional participation)
Other Information: Fall open house, Christmas program, Spring Program for Mothers, Father's Night

Admittance

Whom to Contact: Director Charlotte Echols
Date to Apply: January-February
Testing Procedure for Age/Grade Level: None
Fees Involved: Registration fee–non-refundable if placement is available; based on number of days per week
Type of Student Preferred: Non-discrimination policy

Forms Required: Health, emergency
Individual/Group Appointments: Individual with Director or with teachers
Notification Procedure: By mid-March
Waiting List Policy: Ongoing (no fee required to be on waiting list)

Tuition

Approximate Tuition for 1996-97 School Year: One day (9:00 a.m.-2:00 p.m.) $65; two days $85; three days $110; five days $150, kindergarten $200
Methods of Payment Available: Monthly, by semester, annually
Financial Assistance Offered: No
Cancellation Insurance Available: No
Profit/Non-profit: Non-profit

Additional Costs

Books/Bag/Uniform: School bag–$5 (optional); school pictures–$9 (optional)
Lunch Fee: Lunch Bunch (12:00 p.m.-2:00 p.m.); Wednesday, Thursday, and Friday–students bring their lunches; $25 per month
Parents Club Dues: No
Annual Fund Drive: No
Discount for Siblings: No

Facilities/Services Provided

Computer Lab: No
Library: No
Snack Procedures: Provided by parents and school
Before-school Care Program Available: No
After-school Care Program Available: No
Nurse on Staff: No
Emergency Procedure Used: Notarized Emergency Release required
Transportation to and from School: No
Counseling and Evaluation Available: Yes, when recommended or requested; a pastoral counseling satellite center for children, adolescents, adults, and families

Graduation Information

Testing: N/A
Average SAT Scores: N/A
High School Our Students Usually Attend: N/A
Percentage of Seniors Attending College: N/A

Palisades Day School

505 Alma Rd.   Mapsco: 7D
Plano, TX 75075
(214) 423-5557   Fax: N/A

Office Hours: 7:30 a.m.–5:30 p.m.
School Hours: 6:45 a.m.–6:00 p.m.
School Grades Offered: Pre-k, kindergarten, grades 1-4
Enrollment: 200
Co-ed: Yes
Boy/Girl Ratio: N/A
Student/Teacher Ratio: Depends on age
Average Class Size: Depends on age (elementary–15)
Calendar School Year: August–May
Holidays: Labor Day, Thanksgiving, Christmas, spring break,
Memorial Day
Uniform Requirements: No
Founded in: 1971

Philosophy of School

We believe in the uniqueness of each child, and our policy is to take children from
wherever they are academically, socially, emotionally, and physically to the maximum
they are able to gain and have them enjoy it.

Academic Curriculum

Content: Traditional
Grading System Used: Letter grades
Conferences per Year: As many as needed
Tests Administered: Stanford Achievement Test in May for grades 1-4
Homework Policy: Usually none
Method of Discipline: Redirection

Enrichment Curriculum
The school brings in many programs.

Extracurricular Activities
Gymnastics and dance available

Goals for Students
To be the best they can be, feel good about themselves, and develop confidence in their abilities

Faculty/Staff Requirements
Qualifications of Staff: College degree, experience
Qualifications of Administrator: Degree in education, 30 years' experience

School Information
Brochure Available: Yes
Number of Students in Each Grade: K-4–approximately 15
Parochial: No
Organization Affiliations: None
Accreditations: None
Parental Involvement: As much as they want to participate
Other Information:

Admittance
Whom to Contact: Pat Campbell
Date to Apply: April and May
Testing Procedure for Age/Grade Level: N/A
Fees Involved: $110 registration fee
Type of Student Preferred: Bright students who want traditional–but individualized–program
Forms Required: Health
Individual/Group Appointments:
Notification Procedure:
Waiting List Policy: Ongoing

Tuition
Approximate Tuition for 1996-97 School Year: $3800
Methods of Payment Available: Monthly, quarterly

Financial Assistance Offered: No
Cancellation Insurance Available:
Profit/Non-profit: Profit

Additional Costs

Books/Bag/Uniform: N/A
Lunch Fee: N/A
Parents Club Dues: N/A
Annual Fund Drive: N/A
Discount for Siblings: Yes

Facilities/Services Provided

Computer Lab: In classroom
Library: In classroom
Snack Procedures: Two or three snacks daily
Before-school Care Program Available: Included in tuition
After-school Care Program Available: Included in tuition
Nurse on Staff: No
Emergency Procedure Used:
Transportation to and from School: No
Counseling and Evaluation Available: Yes

Graduation Information

Testing: N/A
Average SAT Scores: N/A
High School Our Students Usually Attend: N/A
Percentage of Seniors Attending College: N/A

Additional Information

The Peanut Gallery

2151 Rosemeade   Mapsco: 654X
Carrollton, TX 75007
(214) 492-2448   Fax:

Office Hours: 6:30 a.m.–6:30 p.m.
School Hours: 6:30 a.m.–6:30 p.m.
School Grades Offered: 6 weeks–12 years
Enrollment: 1200
Co-ed: Yes
Boy/Girl Ratio: Varies
Student/Teacher Ratio: Varies
Average Class Size:
Calendar School Year: Year round
Holidays: Labor Day, Thanksgiving, Christmas, Memorial Day, Independence Day
Uniform Requirements: None
Founded in: 1981

Philosophy of School

Infant, toddler, and preschool education; full day care program; after-school and summer full-day program for school age

Academic Curriculum

Content: Developmentally theme-based
Grading System Used: None
Conferences per Year: As needed
Tests Administered: No
Homework Policy: No
Method of Discipline: Redirection

Enrichment Curriculum
Gymnastics

Extracurricular Activities
Field trips, puppet shows, computers

Goals for Students
To develop at their own rate physically, mentally, and socially while being stimulated and challenged

Faculty/Staff Requirements
Qualifications of Staff: Varies
Qualifications of Administrator: Experience in childcare

School Information
Brochure Available: Yes
Number of Students in Each Grade: Varies
Parochial: No
Organization Affiliations: No
Accreditations: No
Parental Involvement: No
Other Information: No

Admittance
Whom to Contact: Director
Date to Apply: Any time
Testing Procedure for Age/Grade Level: N/A
Fees Involved: Varies
Type of Student Preferred:
Forms Required: Immunization
Individual/Group Appointments: N/A
Notification Procedure: N/A
Waiting List Policy: Ongoing

Tuition
Approximate Tuition for 1996-97 School Year: Varies by age level. Please call specified locations.
Methods of Payment Available: Weekly

Financial Assistance Offered: No
Cancellation Insurance Available: No
Profit/Non-profit: Profit

Additional costs:
Books/Bag/Uniform: None
Lunch Fee: None
Parents Club Dues: None
Annual Fund Drive: None
Discount for Siblings: Three or more children

Facilities/Services Provided
Computer Lab: N/A
Library: N/A
Snack Procedures: Two daily
Before-school Care Program Available: Yes
After-school Care Program Available: Yes
Nurse on Staff:
Emergency Procedure Used: Call 911
Transportation to and from School: Yes
Counseling and Evaluation Available: No

Graduation Information
Testing: N/A
Average SAT Scores: N/A
High School Our Students Usually Attend: N/A
Percentage of Seniors Attending College: N/A

Additional Information
The Peanut Gallery has these locations:

The Peanut Gallery-Rosemeade
Director: Monica Perkins
2151 Rosemeade
Carrollton, TX 75007
(214) 492-2448

The Peanut Gallery-Branch Hollow
Director: Tracy Mitnick
1855 Branch Hollow
Carrollton, TX 75007
(214) 394-0613

The Peanut Gallery-Corner
Director: Connie Crill
8061 Walnut Hill Lane
Dallas, TX 75231
(214) 696-2882

The Peanut Gallery-Noel Road
Director: Janet Puddicombe
13255 Noel Road
Dallas, TX 75240
(214) 702-9063

701

The Peanut Gallery-Colony
Director: Christie Adams
5740 N. Colony
Carrollton, TX 75056
(214) 625-9867

The Peanut Gallery-Greenville
Director: Tish Detrick
2100 N. Greenville Ave., Suite 200
Dallas, TX 75082
(214) 907-9891

Primrose School at Chase Oaks

6525 Chase Oaks Blvd.
Plano, TX 75023
(214) 517-1173

Mapsco: 559W

Fax: (214) 517-1173

Office Hours: 6:30 a.m.–6:30 p.m.
School Hours: 6:30 a.m.–6:30 p.m.
School Grades Offered: Infants–4-year-olds (preschool)
Enrollment: 135
Co-ed: Yes
Boy/Girl Ratio: 1:1
Student/Teacher Ratio: Lower than Texas state requirements
Average Class Size: 15-20
Calendar School Year: Traditional calendar plus summer camp
Holidays: Labor Day, Thanksgiving, Christmas Day, New Year's Day, Memorial Day, Independence Day
Uniform Requirements: None
Founded in: July 1996

Philosophy of School

Primrose School's mission is to provide families with a safe, secure environment and quality educational child-care programs. Our goal is to offer social, emotional, physical, and intellectual early childhood development that instills in each child the joy of learning and positive self-esteem.

Academic Curriculum

Content: To prepare children for kindergarten
Grading System Used: N/A
Conferences per Year: Two
Tests Administered: N/A
Homework Policy: N/A

Method of Discipline: Positive reinforcement; redirection; conflict resolution; logical, natural consequences

Enrichment Curriculum
Adopt-a-Grandparent Program, Ecology and Pollution, Nature and Gardening, Children Around the World, Computers, Spanish

Extracurricular Activities
Spring Fling to raise funds for Ronald McDonald House

Goals for Students
To appreciate the diversity of the world in which they live and introduce students to the joys of exploration and self-discovery

Faculty/Staff Requirements
Qualifications of Staff: All staff members receive Primrose School's comprehensive training.
Qualifications of Administrator: Licensed by state of Texas

School Information
Brochure Available: Yes
Number of Students in Each Grade: 15-20
Parochial: No
Organization Affiliations: Texas Licensed Child Care Association
Accreditations: Primrose Franchising Corporation's annual review, TDPRS minimum standards
Parental Involvement: Requested and encouraged
Other Information:

Admittance
Whom to Contact: Rochelle Strandstra, owner
Date to Apply: Year-round enrollment
Testing Procedure for Age/Grade Level: N/A
Fees Involved: Registration fee $60-$80
Type of Student Preferred: Open enrollment
Forms Required: Application for enrollment
Individual/Group Appointments: Individual
Notification Procedure: As openings occur
Waiting List Policy: First come, first served

Tuition

Approximate Tuition for 1996-97 School Year: Call for schedule; varies by age group

Methods of Payment Available: Weekly or monthly

Financial Assistance Offered: N/A

Cancellation Insurance Available: N/A

Profit/Non-profit: Profit

Additional Costs

Books/Bag/Uniform: N/A

Lunch Fee: Lunch provided to full-time students

Parents Club Dues: N/A

Annual Fund Drive: N/A

Discount for Siblings: N/A (discount for monthly tuition payments)

Facilities/Services Provided

Computer Lab: Yes

Library: No

Snack Procedures: Morning and afternoon

Before-school Care Program Available: Yes

After-school Care Program Available: Yes

Nurse on Staff: No

Emergency Procedure Used: Detailed in student handbook

Transportation to and from School: Yes

Counseling and Evaluation Available: No

Graduation Information

Testing: N/A

Average SAT Scores: N/A

High School Our Students Usually Attend: N/A

Percentage of Seniors Attending College: N/A

Additional Information

Providence Christian School of Texas

8787 Greenville
Dallas, TX 7243
(214) 340-7768

Mapsco: 26L

Fax: (214) 340-7768

Mailing address: P. O. Box 25068
Dallas, TX 75225
(214) 340-7768

Office Hours: 7:30 a.m.–4:30 p.m.
School Hours: 8:10 a.m.–2:30 p.m.
School Grades Offered: Grades 1–8 and Enrichment
Preschool
Enrollment: 290
Co-ed: Yes
Boy/Girl Ratio: 48:52
Student/Teacher Ratio: 12:1
Average Class Size: 12
Calendar School Year: August (last week)–May
Holidays: Thanksgiving (one week); Christmas (two
weeks); spring break (one week)
Uniform Requirements: Yes
Founded in: 1989

Philosophy of School

Providence Christian School of Texas offers its students an education that is both
classical and Christian. The school offers a rich humanities/arts/social studies
curriculum that integrates the study of literature and the arts with the study of history
and geography. The mathematics-and-science program enables students to master the
content and skills necessary to participate knowledgeably in the scientific and

technological discussions of the modern world. Students are encouraged to develop a world view that integrates Christian faith with all areas of learning.

Academic Curriculum
Content: Classical and Christian
Grading System Used: Letter grades given in grades 4-8
Conferences per Year: Three
Tests Administered: CTP III (Educational Records Bureau)
Homework Policy: All students have daily homework.
Method of Discipline: Various procedures used (from missing playtime to detentions to suspensions)

Enrichment Curriculum
Art, nature studies, art history, music, math, limited phonics

Extracurricular Activities
Sculpture, needlework, sewing, manners classes, golf, tennis (varies each year)

Goals for Students
The mission of Providence Christian School of Texas is to provide academically able students with a challenging educational experience designed to help them know, love, and practice that which is true, good, and excellent, and to prepare them to live purposefully and intelligently in the service of God and man.

Faculty/Staff Requirements
Qualifications of Staff: Bachelor's degree (minimum)
Qualifications of Administrator: Bachelor's degree (minimum)

School Information
Brochure Available: Yes
Number of Students in Each Grade: 1st–39, 2nd–42, 3rd–42, 4th–38, 5th–34, 6th–20, 7th-8th–14
Parochial: Non-denominational
Organization Affiliations: TANS
Accreditations: N/A
Parental Involvement: Parents' Council Organization
Other Information: N/A

Admittance

Whom to Contact: Eileen Morse, Director of Admissions

Date to Apply: December to February (applications accepted thereafter if there are openings)

Testing Procedure per Age/Grade Level: Testing dates scheduled in January and February and as needed thereafter until classes are full

Fees Involved: $50 application fee

Type of Student Preferred: N/A

Forms Required: Birth certificate, medical form, parental authorization

Individual/Group Appointments: N/A

Notification Procedure: Letter sent on March 1

Waiting List Policy: Ongoing

Tuition

Approximate Tuition for 1996-97 School Year: Grades 1-3, $3900; 4-6, $4300; 7-8, $4700

Methods of Payment Available: Tuition due in full by first day of class

Financial Assistance Offered: Yes

Cancellation Insurance Available: N/A

Profit/Non-Profit: Non-profit

Additional Costs

Books/Bag/Uniform: Uniform

Lunch Fee: N/A

Parents Club Dues: N/A

Annual Fund Drive: Reading Rally, gift wrap sale

Discount for Siblings: 20% for third child

Facilities/Services Provided

Computer Lab: Yes

Library: Yes

Snack Procedures: N/A

Before-school Care Program Available: No

After-school Care Program Available: No

Nurse on Staff: No

Emergency Procedure Used: Parents contacted immediately

Transportation to and from School: Provided by parents

Counseling and Evaluation Available: Yes

Graduation Information

Testing: N/A
Average SAT Scores: N/A
High School Our Students Usually Attend: N/A
Percentage of Seniors Attending College: N/A

St. Barnabas Pathways Preschool

1220 W. Beltline Rd.   Mapsco: 16B
Richardson, TX 75080
(214) 690-4107   Fax: 235-2016

Office Hours: 8:30 a.m.–2:30 p.m.
School Hours: 9:00 a.m.–1:00 p.m.
School Grades Offered: Ages 3 and 4
Enrollment: 51
Co-ed: Yes
Boy/Girl Ratio: 1:1
Student/Teacher Ratio: 15:1
Average Class Size: 12
Calendar School Year: Mid-August–May
Holidays: Same as R.I.S.D.
Uniform Requirements: No
Founded in: 1996

Philosophy of School

The St. Barnabas Pathways School provides a challenging and developmentally appropriate experience for young children within a nurturing, safe, and Christian environment.

Academic Curriculum

Content: Integrated thematic units including all subject areas (i.e., science, social studies, reading readiness, math, computer, large and fine motor skills)
Grading System Used: Conferences, developmental skills checklist
Conferences per Year: Two; additional as needed
Tests Administered: N/A
Homework Policy: N/A
Method of Discipline: Postiive behavior management

710

Enrichment Curriculum
Computers, music

Extracurricular Activities
N/A

Goals for Students
That our students develop to their individual highest potential cognitively, emotionally, physically, socially, and spiritually

Faculty/Staff Requirements
Qualifications of Staff: Bachelor's degree (minimum)
Qualifications of Administrator: B.S. in Elementary Education; graduate work in behavior management; 12 years' teaching experience (2-year-olds–grade 5)

School Information
Brochure Available: Yes
Number of Students in Each Grade: 3's–13; 4's–15
Parochial: No
Organization Affiliations:
Accreditations: Meet NAEYC guidelines; meet DHS standards
Parental Involvement: Welcomed; voluntary
Other Information: St. Barnabas is a Christian school that opened in 1996 with classes for 3- and 4-year-olds. We will expand to include classes for children as the community need arises.

Admittance
Whom to Contact: Cheryl Clarkson
Date to Apply: Fall enrollment begins in January.
Testing Procedure for Age/Grade Level: Developmental screening as needed
Fees Involved: Registration/Program, $150; supplies, $50 (both annual)
Type of Student Preferred: Any Christian boy or girl
Forms Required: Yes
Individual/Group Appointments: Both
Notification Procedure: Completed registration forms
Waiting List Policy: Ongoing

Tuition

Approximate Tuition for 1996-97 School Year: $130 per month
Methods of Payment Available: Monthly payments
Financial Assistance Offered: No
Cancellation Insurance Available: No
Profit/Non-profit: Non-profit

Additional Costs

Books/Bag/Uniform: No
Lunch Fee: No
Parents Club Dues: To be set by vote of the parents
Annual Fund Drive: Yes
Discount for Siblings: Yes

Facilities/Services Provided

Computer Lab: Classroom computers
Library: Classroom library
Snack Procedures: Provided by school
Before-school Care Program Available: No
After-school Care Program Available: No
Nurse on Staff: No; all staff members are trained in CPR and first aid.
Emergency Procedure Used: Contact parents first; emergency contact person on file
Transportation to and from School: No
Counseling and Evaluation Available: No

Graduation Information

Testing: N/A
Average SAT Scores: N/A
High School Our Students Usually Attend: N/A
Percentage of Seniors Attending College: N/A

Additional Information

St. Barnabas is a non-profit church-sponsored school striving to educate all Christian chldren.

Trinity Episcopal Preschool

3401 Bellaire Drive South
Fort Worth, TX 76109
(817) 926-0750

Mapsco: Fort Worth

Fax:

Office Hours: 9:00 a.m.–noon
School Hours: 9:00 a.m.–2:00 p.m.
School Grades Offered: Preschool (ages 2, 3, 4, 5)
Enrollment: 45
Co-ed: Yes
Boy/Girl Ratio: Balanced
Student/Teacher Ratio: 6:1
Average Class Size: 15
Calendar School Year: September–May
Holidays: Christian, traditional
Uniform Requirements: None
Founded in: 1952

Philosophy of School

Trinity Episcopal Preschool is committed to helping each child realize his or her full potential. The program is designed to enrich each child's life in the present with joyful, meaningful, and purposeful experiences. Trinity Episcopal Preschool is a combination of traditional preschool methods and Maria Montessori's philosophy of individual liberty preparation of the environment and observation.

Care for individual needs enables each child to feel confident and good about self and others and allows exploration of the wonders of the world with excitement and delight.

As a Christian school, we are committed to structuring a loving and happy environment in which each child has the responsibility, the freedom, and the encouragement to become what God created him or her to be.

Academic Curriculum

Content: Traditional and Montessori

Grading System Used: N/A
Conferences per Year: Two (January and May)
Tests Administered: Skills checklist (age appropriate)
Homework Policy: N/A
Method of Discipline: Positive communication

Enrichment Curriculum

Extrracurricular Activities
Summer two-week program

Goals for Students
To provide many opportunities for social adjustments. Your child will experience this
through learning to play and work with other children, sharing toys and equipment, and
taking turns and learning the rights of others.
To focus on the immediate environment around your child. This will be done through
activities that interest the child: counting, drawing, listening to stories, and make
believe.
To give opportunities for your child to express himself freely. This will be done through
the use of art materials, blocks, dramatic play, books, games, etc.
To allow your child to use his/her whole body and develop a good attitude toward it.
This goal is strengthened through the use of gross motor equipment and through music
and listening activities.

Faculty/Staff Requirements
Qualifications of Staff: College degree or Montessori certificate
Qualifications of Administrator: College degree and 2-3 years of experience

School Information
Brochure Available: Yes
Number of Students in Each Grade: Two-year-olds–12; three-year-olds–15;
four-year-olds and five-year-olds–18
Parochial: Episcopal
Organization Affiliations: Southern Association of Episcopal Schools; Fort
Worth Association of Education of Young Children
Accreditations: Licensed by state of Texas (TDPRS)
Parental Involvement: Yes
Other Information:

Admittance

Whom to Contact: Dainty Kostohryz

Date to Apply: Enrollment begins in late February.

Testing Procedure per Age/Grade Level: N/A

Fees Involved: $55 enrollment fee

Type of Student Preferred: We admit children of any race, color, or ethnic origin.

Forms Required: Physician's immunization records, emergency form

Individual/Group Appointments: Individual tours by appointment

Notification Procedure: N/A

Waiting List Policy: Ongoing

Tuition

Approximate Tuition for 1996-97 School Year: Two-year-olds–$80; three-year-olds–$105; four-year-olds and five-year-olds–$160

Methods of Payment Available: Monthly or yearly

Financial Assistance Offered: Aid available based on need

Cancellation Insurance Available: No

Profit/Non-profit: Non-profit

Additional Costs

Books/Bag/Uniform: N/A

Lunch Fee: Children bring sack lunches from home.

Parents Club Dues: No

Annual Fund Drive: No

Discount for Siblings: No

Facilities/Services Provided

Computer Lab: Yes

Library: Yes

Snack Procedures: For extended-day students

Before-school Care Program Available: No

After-school Care Program Available: No

Nurse on Staff: No

Emergency Procedure Used: Staff trained in CPR and first aid

Transportation to and from School: No

Counseling and Evaluation Available: By appointment with priest

Graduation Information

Testing: N/A

Average SAT Scores: N/A
High School Our Students Usually Attend: N/A
Percentage of Seniors Attending College: N/A

Additional Information

Williamson School

1825 W. Clarendon
Dallas, TX 75208
(214) 946-3846

Mapsco: 54J

Fax: (214) 617-9566

Office Hours: 8:00 a.m.–5:00 p.m.
School Hours: 7:00 a.m.–6:30 p.m.
School Grades Offered: 18 months–grade 2
Enrollment: 110
Co-ed: Yes
Boy/Girl Ratio: Varies
Student/Teacher Ratio: Varies with age group
Average Class Size: Varies with age group
Calendar School Year: Mid-August–May
Holidays:
Uniform Requirements: No
Founded in: 1924

Philosophy of School
To instill in each individual child a feeling of self-acceptance and a love of learning so that he/she may reach the highest level of potential

Academic Curriculum
Content: Variety of curriculum materials available for each grade level
Grading System Used: Report cards sent every six weeks in graded classes
Conferences per Year: Two required
Tests Administered: ITBS
Homework Policy: Varies with age group
Method of Discipline: Clear and explicit instructions and expectations; time out and withdrawal of privileges for deliberate disobedience

Enrichment Curriculum
N/A

Extracurricular Activities
Dance lessons, gymnastic lessons, karate lessons, keyboard lessons

Goals for Students
For each child to feel good about himself/herself and to strive to reach his/her potential

Faculty/Staff Requirements
Qualifications of Staff: All have training and/or experience.
Qualifications of Administrator: Master's degree in education

School Information
Brochure Available: Yes
Number of Students in Each Grade: Varies by grade
Parochial: No
Organization Affiliations: NAEYC
Accreditations: Texas Department of Human Services
Parental Involvement: Family-School Association
Other Information:

Admittance
Whom to Contact: Katrina Mayo
Date to Apply: After March 1
Testing Procedure per Age/Grade Level: Achievement scores
Fees Involved: None
Type of Student Preferred: Open to all children
Forms Required: Enrollment application
Individual/Group Appointments: Individual
Notification Procedure: Within one week of application
Waiting List Policy: Ongoing

Tuition
Approximate Tuition for 1996-97 School Year: $2000-$3000
Methods of Payment Available: Cash or check; weekly or monthly payments
Financial Assistance Offered: No

Cancellation Insurance Available: No
Profit/Non-profit: Profit

Additional Costs

Books/Bag/Uniform: Books–$70-$200; bag–not required; uniform–not required
Lunch Fee: Included in tuition for students 18 months old-kindergarten; optional for students in grades 1–2 ($10 per week)
Parents Club Dues: $10 per year
Annual Fund Drive: Fundraising activities determined by parents' group
Discount for Siblings: Yes

Facilities/Services Provided

Computer Lab: N/A
Library: N/A
Snack Procedures: Twice daily for children in 18-month program through the kindergarten classes; afternoon only for children in grades 1–2
Before-school Care Program Available: Yes, 7:00–8:00 a.m.
After-school Care Program Available: Yes, 12:00–6:30 p.m.; 3:00–6:30 p.m.
Nurse on Staff: No
Emergency Procedure Used: Stated in Policy Bulletin
Transportation to and from School: Pick up only from local public schools
Counseling and Evaluation Available: No

Graduation Information

Testing: N/A
Average SAT Scores: N/A
High School Our Students Usually Attend: N/A
Percentage of Seniors Attending College: N/A

Additional Information

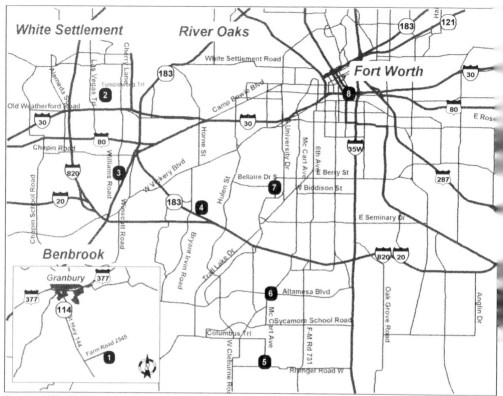

1	Happy Hill Farm Academy\Home	3 Redeemer Lutheran School	6 Trinity Valley School
2	All Saints Episcopal School	4 Fort Worth Country Day	7 Trinity Episcopal School
		5 Sycamore School	8 St. Paul Lutheran School

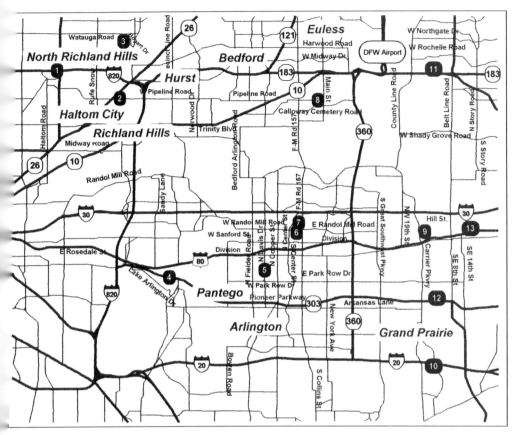

1	Glenview Christian School
2	St. John The Apostle Catholic School
3	Fort Worth Christian School
4	Oakridge School
5	St. Alban's Episcopal School
6	Texas Christian Academy
7	Country Day School of Arlington
8	TreeTops School International
9	St. Andrew's Episcopal School
10	Montessori School of Westchester
11	Holy Family of Nazareth School
12	Evangel Temple Christian School
13	Immaculate Conception School

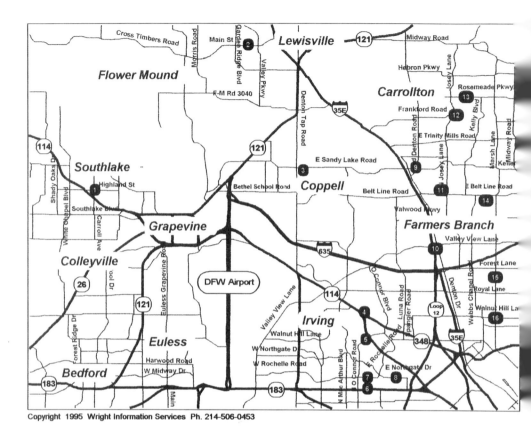

Copyright 1995 Wright Information Services Ph. 214-506-0453

1 Highland Meadow Montessori	6 St. Therese Academy	12 Prince of Peace Christian School
2 Montessori Episcopal School	7 Redeemer Montessori School	13 Peanut Gallery
3 Christ Our Savior Lutheran School	8 Highlands School	14 Harrington School
4 Cistercian Preparatory	9 A Child's Garden Montessori	15 Holy Cross Lutheran School
5 Montessori School of Las Colinas	10 Lexington Academy	16 Creative School at Walnut Hill U.M.C.
	11 Carrollton Christian Academy	

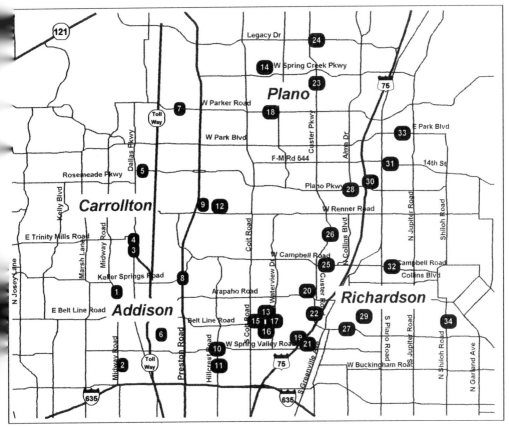

1	Greenhill School	12 Solomon Schecter Academy	25 Discovery School at Canyon Creek
2	Westwood Montessori School	13 Richardson Adventist School	26 Beth Torah Preschool & Kindergarten
3	Trinity Christian Academy	14 West Plano Montessori	27 Early Learning Center at First Christian Church
4	Bent Tree Child Development Center	15 Creative Preschool Co-op	28 Palisades Day School
5	Prince of Peace Catholic School	16 St. Barnabas Presbyterian Preschool	29 Alexander School
6	Walden Preparatory School	17 Highland Academy	30 Keystone Academy
7	Coughs & Cuddles for Mildly ill Children	18 Bethany Christian School	31 Children's Workshop
8	Fairhill School	19 St. Paul the Apostle School	32 Rainbow Connection of Central Christian Church
9	Montessori School of North Dallas	20 Dallas North Montessori School	33 Faith Lutheran School
10	Parish Day School of the Episcopal Church	21 Dallas Learning Center	34 Glenwood Day School
11	Hillcrest Academy	22 Epiphany Day School	
		23 Glen Lakes Academy	
		24 Primrose School of Chase Oaks	

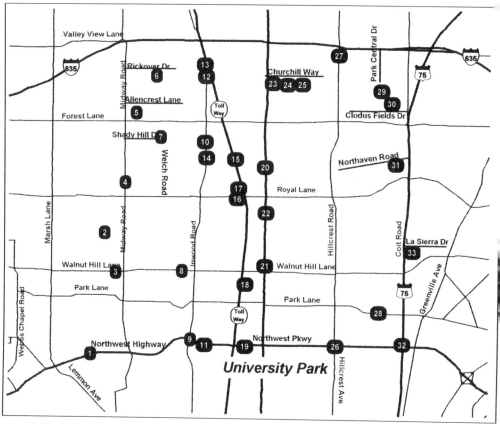

1 Lakemont Academy	12 Jesuit College Preparatory School	24 St. Alcuin Montessori School
2 Episcopal School of Dallas	13 St. Rita Catholic School	25 Akiba Academy
3 St. Monica Catholic School	14 Grace Academy of Dallas	26 Temple Emanu-El Preschool
4 Good Shepherd Episcopal School	15 Northbrook School	27 Academic Achievement Associates
5 Windsong Montessori School	16 Preston Royal Preschool	28 Our Redeemer Lutheran School
6 Schreiber Methodist Preschool	17 Winston School	29 Cornerstone School
7 Hockaday School	18 Yavneh Academy	30 Bridgeway School
8 Ursuline Academy of Dallas	19 St. Michael's Campus (ESD)	31 Jewish Community Center of Dallas Preschool
9 Lovers Lane UMC Weekday School	20 Northaven Co-operative Preschool	32 Northpark Presbyterian Day School
10 Lamplighter School	21 Preston Hollow Weekday School	33 DaVinci School
11 Meadowbrook Private School	22 St. Mark's School of Texas	
	23 Dallas International School	

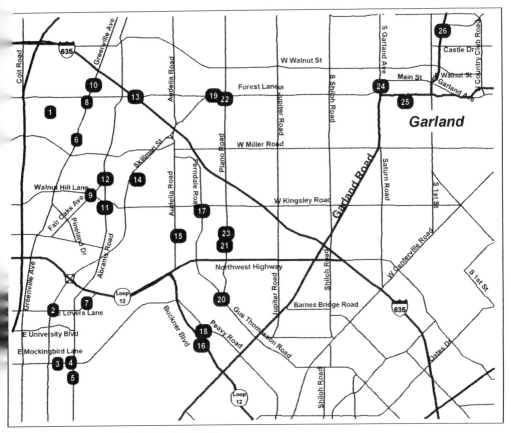

Copyright 1995 Wright Information Services Ph. 214-506-0453

1 Lutheran High School of Dallas	9 Fair Oaks Day School	19 Autistic Treatment Center
2 Zion Lutheran School	10 Bending Oaks High School	20 Eastlake Christian School
3 White Rock Montessori School (Satellite)	11 Montessori Children's House & School	21 Christian Childhood Development Center
4 Children's Center of First Community Church	12 Scofield Christian School	22 Glen Oaks School
5 St. Thomas Aquinas School	13 Southwest Academy	23 Highlander School
6 Providence Christian School of Texas	14 White Rock North School	24 Good Shepherd Catholic School
7 Oak Hill Academy	15 St. James Episcopal Montessori School	25 First United Methodist Church Day School
8 North Dallas Day School	16 Dallas Academy	26 Garland Christian Academy
	17 St. Patrick School	
	18 St. John's Episcopal School	

725

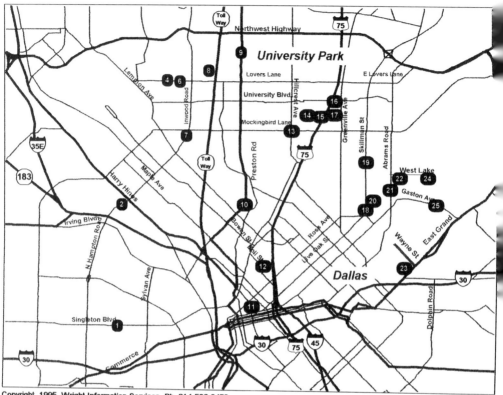

1	St. Mary of Carmel School	9	Christ The King School	18	East Dallas Developmental Center
2	Callier Child Development Preschool	10	Holy Trinity Catholic School	19	White Rock Montessori School
3	Vanguard Preparatory School	11	First Baptist Academy	20	Branch Schools
4	Carlisle School	12	Notre Dame of Dallas School	21	Lakewood United Methodist Developmental Learning Center
5	June Shelton School and Evaluation Center	13	Highland Park United Methodist Church CDP	22	Lakehill Preparatory
6	Shelton School and Evaluation Center	14	Study Skills Course (SMU)	23	East Dallas Community School
7	Montessori School of Park Cities	15	Summer Accelerated Language Training (SMU)	24	Hearthstone Kindergarten
8	Westminster Preschool & Kindergarten	16	Highland Park Presbyterian Day School	25	Lakewood Presbyterian School
		17	Hillier School of Highland Park Presbyterian Church		

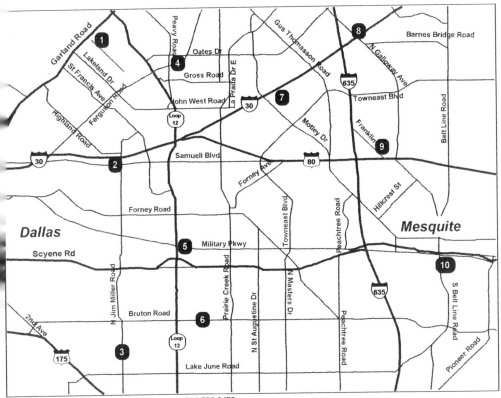

Copyright 1995 Wright Information Services Ph. 214-506-0453

1 St. Bernard of Clairvaux	5 St. Philip the Apostle Catholic School	8 Dallas Christian School
2 Dallas Montessori Academy	6 Metropolitan Christian School	9 Meadowview School
3 Montessori School of Pleasant Grove	7 Youth Crossing Academy	10 Little Red Schoolhouse
4 Bishop Lynch High School		

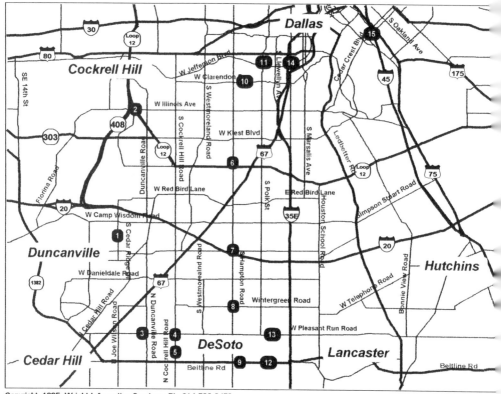

1 ChristWay Academy	7 Arbor Acre Preparatory School	13 Cambridge Square Private School
2 Gospel Lighthouse Christian Academy	8 Maryview Academy	14 J. Erik Jonsson Community School
3 Trinity Christian School	9 DeSoto Private School	15 St. Philip's School and Community Center
4 Canterbury Episcopal School	10 Williamson School	
5 Cross of Christ Lutheran School	11 Tyler Street Christian Academy	
6 St. Elizabeth of Hungary Catholic School	12 Helen-Hardrick Christian School	

728

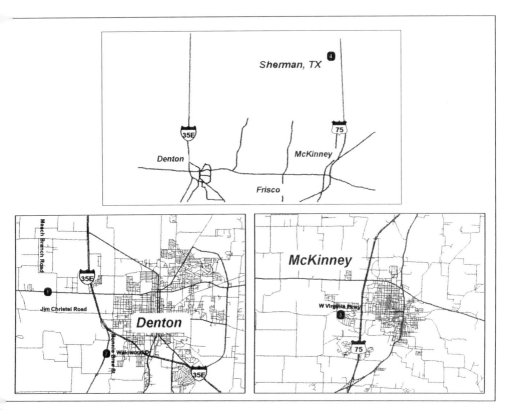

1	Selwyn School	3	Good Shepherd Montessori School	4	St. Mary's Catholic School
2	Liberty Christian School				

729

A Guide To Dallas Learning Specialists
&
A Guide To Dallas Private Schools

ORDER FORM

Quantity	Price	Tax	Shipping	Total
_____ Learning Specialists	$15.95	$1.32	$1.73	$19.00
_____ Private Schools	$24.95	$2.05	$3.00	$30.00
_____ Combination Set	$34.95	$2.88	$4.17	$42.00

(COMBINATION SET=$7 SAVINGS! BEST VALUE!)

Quantity	Price	Tax	Shipping	Total
_____ X $	_____ + $	_____ + $	_____ = $	_____

Name _____

Address _____

_____

City _____ State _____ Zip _____

Phone (_____) _____

Please make checks payable to :

Private In Print
5232 Forest Lane
Suite 120
Dallas, Texas 75244
(214) 739-4501

We will ship your books within 2 days of receipt of your order.
We Appreciate Your Business!